From Spinning Tops to Laptops:

A Memoir

To Subashnie,

With love & best-wishes,

Petrick.

From Spinning Tops to Laptops:

A Memoir

PATRICK N O'FARRELL

Published by Patrick N O'Farrell

A CIP catalogue record for this book is available from the British Library.

ISBN 978-1-5262-0949-8

Book layout and cover design by Clare Brayshaw
Photo 118877903 © Nikolay Antonov | Dreamstime.com
Photo 14895930 / Spinning Top © Ajijchan | Dreamstime.com

Prepared and printed by:

York Publishing Services Ltd
64 Hallfield Road
Layerthorpe
York YO31 7ZQ

Tel: 01904 431213

Website: www.yps-publishing.co.uk

Contents

Preface

Since my life has not been especially noteworthy, I have set this memoir against the background of political, social and cultural change that has occurred since my birth in 1941. Having been born and reared in Dublin and subsequently lived in Northern Ireland, Wales and Scotland, I have been a witness to and participated in major processes of social change.

I was born against the background of World War 2 (The Emergency in Ireland); my teenage years coincided with the relative poverty of the 1950s, followed by my university education in the early sixties, the onset of the Troubles in Northern Ireland, the three-day week, the rise of feminism, the changing role of universities and the relative decline of the UK both economically and politically during the 1980s.

These events flicker into life from time to time throughout this memoir. There have been many departures and arrivals, deaths, births, farewells and nostalgia that underlie my memories. Most people described here are still alive and may disagree with my portrayals of them. Although I have no desire whatever to hurt anyone's feelings, my obligation has not been to flatter people but to be faithful to my memories and experiences. The memory makes its own choices, its own decisions about what is important, fun, interesting, moving, or even painful to recall. Inevitably there will lapses as memory is always partial and incomplete. Since memory itself is an act of construction, the past is always illuminated by the present. The child that I was is still part of me and also quite separate from me; the past is a partial script for the present. Everything is true as I remember it, but it may not be everybody's truth. I am entirely responsible for what I have recalled and observed and I apologise in advance to anyone who is offended.

I suggest that what matters in life includes the values and material circumstances of our parents, the place and country where one grew up, one's social class and – important in Ireland – one's religious background. They were part of what influenced my expectations and fantasies, along with the possibilities that I had inherited. Writing about myself has not been easy. As an academic, I am more familiar with researching and writing research papers, books and monographs which are, by definition, dry and dull. I have to depend upon two not wholly reliable contributors to this narrative: my memory and my sense of who I am. Both are inevitably somewhat selective. I have tried to be as accurate as possible in describing my experiences growing up in Ireland, my school, university education and social life, how I made friends, and the constraints imposed on Irish society by an ultra- conservative state. I have made many choices, some of which I regret, and I have neglected to make others, a few of which I also regret. This is the story of growing up in a middle – class household in Dublin during the Emergency of the 1940s, the stagnant 1950s when old Irish beliefs, customs and habits seemed forever frozen in time until the slow emergence of change during the 1960s.

CHAPTER 1

The Emergency

Unlike most people in Ireland, I have a mixed Catholic and Protestant heritage, of which I have always been proud. O'Farrell is the 35th most common name in Ireland and is derived from the Gaelic, O'Fearghail, meaning 'man of valour.' The historical stronghold of the O'Farrells was County Longford. However, County Longford was planted by English and Scottish settlers in 1620 and much of the land owned by the O'Farrells was confiscated and granted to these new owners. The wholesale appropriation of the land was completed during the Cromwellian invasion of the 1650s and dispossession of the O'Farrells was complete. My paternal grandfather, William J O'Farrell, was born in 1863 and was raised a Catholic; my other three grandparents were Presbyterians. William O'Farrell trained for the Catholic priesthood, but then declared himself an atheist, an act that must have required considerable moral courage in the Ireland of the 1890s. He went on to marry Jeannie McCleery who came from a radically different blood line from his: she was of Scottish Presbyterian descent – dating from the Ulster Plantation – and lived in Balieborough, County Cavan. Jeannie McCleery and William O'Farrell married in the First Balieborough Presbyterian church in April 1898 when Jeannie was only 19 years of age and William was 35. William O'Farrell was a cartographer and surveyor who made the six – inch Ordnance survey maps of County Donegal. This resulted in long periods away from home in Dublin, frequently staying in digs in Glencolumbkille, west Donegal. William O'Farrell and Jeannie McCleery had three sons, the eldest of whom, also William, was a despatch rider at Gallipoli in the First World War. Their second son, Tom, contracted tuberculosis while undergoing training for the First World War at Blandford Forum barracks. He never fully recovered and died at the age of 42. My father, Neil O'Farrell, was born more than a decade after his brothers on 16th December 1911.

My paternal great- grandfather, Thomas O'Farrell, was also a cartographer and surveyor. He was transferred from Ireland to Scotland in 1850 in order to make the first Ordnance survey maps of the Shiant Islands in the Minches between the Scottish mainland and the Outer Hebrides. He also produced the original Ordnance Survey maps of sections of Harris and Lewis and the Flannan Isles, 20 miles west of Lewis in the Atlantic. Thomas O'Farrell landed on the Shiant Islands on 17 October 1851 and author Adam Nicholson concludes from examining his notebook that Thomas O'Farrell was 'measuring, estimating, a little fearful (of the currents), unable to dissociate his description of the place from his apprehension over it.'[1] To the west of the Shiants is a chain of steeply banked rocks called the Galtachan or Galtas and as Thomas O'Farrell observed them in 1851 the tide is run savage between them 'as at all times especially at Spring tides there is a rapid current about them the tide flows exceedingly strong, flowing the same as a large River.'[2] Mapping the Shiant Islands in late October 1851- when they were then uninhabited – must have been a most challenging assignment.

My mother, Georgina Anne Flynn, was born in Dublin on 12 February 1910. Her Scottish mother, Elizabeth Gordon, had been born in Stornoway on the Isle of Lewis in 1876 where her father was an employee of the Goathill estate. Subsequently, Elizabeth Gordon's father was appointed factor of an estate near Tinahealy in County Wicklow. Elizabeth Gordon's husband, James Flynn, was born in Glenmalure, County Wicklow to Edward Flynn, a constable in the Royal Irish Constabulary, and his wife, Sarah Jane(nee Miley). Elizabeth Gordon and James Flynn married in 1899. James subsequently became manager of Findlater's shop in Rathmines. My mother's only sibling, Edward (Ted) Flynn, captained Palmerston Rugby Club 1st XV from 1937-1939 and was also capped for Leinster; he was an accomplished goal kicker.

My parents met at Leinster Tennis Club in Rathgar and married in Rathgar Presbyterian Church in 1940 when my mother was 30 and my father 28. My mother, like so many middle-class women of her generation, simply accepted that permanently ceasing paid employment after marriage was not to be questioned. It remained a distinguishing mark of a man's social position in the Ireland of the 1950s if his wife was at home. This was underpinned by the practice of the civil service and other public sector organisations of requiring women to resign on marriage. Furthermore, on the radio, in films and in women's magazines and newspapers, femininity was almost always associated with the home and the nurturing of children. The male assumption of superiority in the workplace was a deeply entrenched cultural norm that was strongly endorsed by the Catholic Church. Irish women, therefore, did not have their own narratives but were confined by a conservative culture of traditional femininity. The extent to which this deprived the Irish economy and society of ideas, innovation and expertise cannot be underestimated.

We do not choose our parents or our birthplace. I have never been back to see the nursing home at 28, Terenure Road East, Dublin where my late twin sister, Sheila, and I were born on 18 April 1941, the same year as Bob Dylan, Joan Baez, Alex Ferguson and President Michael D Higgins. This was the year that the USA joined World War 2 after the Japanese attack on Pearl Harbour; Nazi Germany launched Operation Barbarossa and invaded the Soviet Union; Royal Navy warships sank the German battleship, Bismarck; and the Enigma Code was broken at Bletchley Park. Orson Welles released his masterpiece, *Citizen Kane,* in 1941 and James Joyce died in Zurich.

For the first two years of my life we lived in a flat at the top of my maternal grandmother's Victorian house on Rathgar Avenue. In 1943, when my mother was pregnant with my younger sister, Judy, we moved to rent a house on Albert Road, one mile from Dalkey. My first clear recollection dates from 1945 when as a child of four I discovered that our Scotty dog, Jean, would growl menacingly when I inched towards her wearing my clogs. I also remember trying to push our side-wheel Pennsylvania 14 inch lawn mower; I don't recall how far I could push it at five years of age, but I could not possibly have mown the complete lawn. Although early recollections are somewhat patchy, my memory of this is real in the sense that I can transport myself back to the large back garden of the inter-war bungalow on Albert Road. Old memories shape you, whether they are true, a photograph or simply an event related by an adult. My parents rented the bungalow until 1947 when I was six years of age. My brother Brian was born in March 1947 at the end of one of the severest winters on record. Albert Road was flooded on the day my mother arrived home with him from the nursing home. We peeped into the Moses – basket to see the new arrival. Brian was a contented and placid infant. I loved the smell of talcum powder after my mother had bathed him. I have tried to resurrect my siblings – two of whom are sadly deceased – from the shadows of our common history and into the (fading) light of my memory.

My mother was a very popular person. Enid Chaloner, the 93 year old daughter of my mother's cousin, recently told me that 'she loved my mother who was gentle, charming, always smiling and had an aura about her.' She was methodical, with a rigid daily routine. After each meal, she would light a Churchman's cigarette while reading the *Irish Times* and, as soon as she had smoked it, she would embark upon the chores. Her work involved an unrelenting routine of washing, ironing, cooking, scrubbing, shopping and dressmaking, all of which she performed without complaint, usually while whistling a tune slightly off-key. After the war, it was necessary to adopt a mend-and-make-do approach, so my mother was constantly stitching and repairing, tearing up old items and remaking them. I loved to watch her repair, darn, sew and knit. When shirt collars became frayed, she simply turned them and the shirt was wearable again. Then there was the weekly darning. She had a sewing basket full of wools of many colours and the essential darning mushroom. This was shoved into the torn sock and held behind the hole. She would quickly use the darning needle to take in all the ragged edges and stitches; and then she commenced the difficult task of drawing the thread to and fro across the hole. Darning seems to be a lost art as incomes have risen and socks are relatively cheap. She knitted Aran sweaters for us at night by the fire, knit one purl one; the needles click-clacked at speed as she sat there, patient and persistent, without ever looking at her hands. Twine was never thrown away, but was rolled up ready to be re-used. Jam-jars were washed and stored for future use; and similarly, lemonade bottles were returned to the shop to retrieve the deposit. Corks were kept for reuse and back copies of the *Irish Times* were used to line drawers and to act as firelighters.

My father was intelligent, but somewhat lazy and selfish. He frequently had different (superior) food to the rest of the family, something that I resolved never to do. He was extrovert and amusing company, a humorous person given to exhibitionism, who always enjoyed being the centre of attention. He dominated most conversations insisting on having the final word, something that I found irksome at times. Facts in which he had faith were granted undue weight, even if I knew a contrary fact. In the evenings he read the *Irish Times* by the fire and listened to the radio, or sometimes made leather wallets and bags, at which he was very competent. He never became part of the local community or established close friendships with any of the neighbours. There were friends with whom he went shooting in winter and fishing in summer. Nobody really knows the interior of their parents' marriage, but no matter how irritating my father could be, my mother knew that he loved her.

I wanted to have a father who supported me and was always on my side. He did not express any warmth or affection towards me on a personal level. He never praised me for either academic performance or sporting achievements. Even if I recorded a success, he either ignored or diminished it; he always wanted the limelight and sought to keep me in the shade. I hoped for an intimacy which was not available from most middle-class Protestant parents at the time. After I graduated from Trinity College, he never tried to understand why I wished to be an academic rather than to have what he regarded as a 'proper' job and make lots of money. My existence at home was frequently pervaded by a chilly and unspoken disapproval. My father's commitment was to himself, then to my mother, and then my twin sister, Sheila, younger brother, Brian, sister, Judy, and only after that, to me. I did not resent it at the time, although it taught me to be independent, but it became more obvious in adulthood. During the seven years that I worked at two universities in Northern Ireland, he never once visited me, although Belfast is only 100 miles from Dublin. This may have made me somewhat anxious to please and I reached adulthood harbouring a certain fear of rejection. Also, we had strong political differences: he voted Fianna Fail in Ireland and was a strident Tory in the British context, whereas I have always voted Labour. I was just not the type of son he would have wished me to be and, sadly, we were never close.

* * *

Ireland remained neutral throughout the Second World War and declared a State of Emergency in September 1939 ('The Emergency') which gave sweeping powers to the government during the duration of the war, including internment, censorship of the press and government control of the economy. The policy of neutrality during the war was controversial, although it was supported in the Dail. The Taoiseach, De Valera's reasoning was blinkered since his anti-British hostility led him to see a worldwide conflagration only in the narrowest parochial terms. The period since independence in 1921 had been characterised by an isolationism encouraged by official ideology and protected by censorship. Irish neutrality was most under threat in the summer of 1940 – the period of the Battle of Britain – when the Germans were closest to invading. The war effectively cut off Ireland from the European continent. The state had to achieve an unprecedented degree of self-sufficiency and it was Sean Lemass's role, as Minister of Supplies, to ensure this.

Some Irish people viewed neutrality as shameful indifference in the struggle against fascism. The great Irish poet, Louis MacNeice, who had been on vacation in Ireland when war broke out, was not comfortable with Irish neutrality. He was clear about his identity as he wrote in the 1941 edition of *Penguin New Writing*: 'I never really thought of myself as British; if there is one country I feel at home in, it is Eire.' While his friends Auden and Isherwood had controversially relocated to the USA for the duration of the war, MacNeice chose to remain in London, writing propaganda for the BBC and serving as a fire-watcher during the Blitz. In 1943, he attacked his native country in his poem *Neutrality* in which he sees Ireland as wedged between the darkness of the continent at war in the east and the turbulent Atlantic to the west.

There is a revisionist argument that Irish neutrality was in reality one of friendly neutrality on the Allied side. De Valera certainly favoured the Allies' cause and gave much surreptitious help to the British. The evidence for this is derived from a letter written by Viscount Cranborne, British Secretary of State for Dominion Affairs, on 21 February 1945 to the British War Cabinet regarding British–Irish cooperation during 1939-1945.[3] The examples of collaboration included, *inter alia*: consent for British aircraft based on Lough Erne to fly over the 'Donegal Corridor' and Irish territorial waters to reach the north Atlantic; immediate transmission to the UK of reports of submarine activity; an agreement for Britain to use Lough Foyle for naval and air purposes; communicating meteorological reports to Britain; the use by British ships and aircraft of two wireless direction–finding stations on Malin Head; supplying Britain with details of German crashed aircraft and crew; interning all German fighting personnel reaching Ireland, while conversely allowing Allied servicemen to depart freely; an agreement to intern or return any German prisoners who escaped over the border into the South, while no obstacles were placed in the way of people from the South wishing to fight with UK forces. Ireland also permitted Britain to establish a radar station in the South for use against submarine activity. From December 1940 onwards the Dublin government accepted over 2,000 British women and children evacuated from London due to the Blitz. Communications with Britain remained quite open during the war: some 245,000 Irish people moved to Britain to work during the war. The Irish intelligence service and its British counterpart maintained contacts. A total of 52,147 British servicemen were recruited from Northern Ireland. Despite the neutrality of the South, it is estimated that 78,826 men from the South served in the British armed forces,[4] of whom 4,800 were members of the Irish armed services who are estimated to have deserted or left legally to join British forces.[5] Soldiers from the South won a total of 780 decorations, including 7 Victoria crosses. Furthermore, English newspapers still circulated and Irish papers relied heavily on English reports for their coverage of external events; while the BBC dominated radio listening.[6] After the war, the Irish government ignored the contribution its citizens had made in defeating fascism and it was not until 1995 that it formally sponsored a memorial to those who served in the struggle against Nazi Germany.

The major incidents of the war in Ireland occurred during the week of my birth. The 'Belfast Blitz' commenced on Easter Tuesday, 15 April 1941, when wave after wave of two hundred bombers of the *Luftwaffe* attacked military and manufacturing targets. They dropped 200 tons of high explosives, 80 landmines and 800 firebombs on the city. More than 1,000 people were killed, 1,500 injured and 56,000 homes (more than half the city's housing stock) were damaged leaving 100,000 people homeless. Apart from those on London, this was the greatest loss of life in any night raid during the Blitz. At 4.30am Basil Brooke, Prime Minister of Northern Ireland, asked de Valera for help and de Valera responded by sending 13 fire tenders from the South across the Irish border to assist. Volunteers were sought at each station and, in every instance, all the men stepped forward. Following the air raid, almost a quarter of a million people fled from Belfast and on 18th April (my birthdate) hundreds of refugees were transported by train to Dublin from the areas of Northern Ireland that suffered most from the blitzkrieg. On the night of 30 May 1941, Dublin was also the target of a Luftwaffe raid: 38 people were killed and 2,500 were made homeless in the North Strand and Circular Road area.

De Valera opposed conscription in Northern Ireland at a meeting of the Dail on 26 May 1941 arguing that ' There could be no more grievous attack on any fundamental human right than to force an individual to fight in the forces of another country to which he objected to belong.'[7] Conversely, on 28 May 1941, the Prime Minister of Northern Ireland, John Andrews, asserted that 'conscription is the only fair method of recruitment of the forces of the Crown.'[8] It is argued that de Valera had no option other than a policy of non-belligerence since Ireland's army was tiny, there was no navy and her air force was only a token one; it would have been impossible to defend the extensive coastline from invasion.[9] There is, however, no way that Ireland's position during the war could be recognised as an honourable one in the face of the cruel Nazi tyranny. Worse was to follow as the Irish government was indifferent to Jewish victims of the Holocaust both during and after the war, despite de Valera having knowledge of the crimes committed against the Jews as early as 1943.[10] After the war ended, Jewish groups had difficulty obtaining refugee status for Jewish children, while at the same time a plan to bring over 400 Catholic children from the Rhineland encountered no difficulties. The Department of Justice explained in 1948 that: 'It has always been the policy of the Minister of Justice to restrict the admission of Jewish aliens, for the reason that any substantial increase in our Jewish population might give rise to an anti-Semitic problem.'[11] Hence, Ireland created bureaucratic difficulties about admitting Jews and only let 150 children enter in 1948 after de Valera overruled the Department of Justice. The State, to its shame, had failed the Jews. Furthermore, de Valera caused widespread fury, especially in the USA, when he visited the German embassy in Dublin on 2 May 1945 to express his condolences on the death of Hitler at a time when he was fully aware of the mass murders of the Holocaust.

Industrial output fell by one-fifth during the war, private motoring was banned from 30 April 1942, rationing commenced in May 1942, and inflation rose dramatically by 70 per cent between 1942 and 1946. The coupon from the ration book became as reliable and as vital as currency. The state pre-empted the usual laws of supply and demand as the government fixed the prices of all rationed commodities. Bread was rationed from 1942 onwards following tea, sugar and fuel, which had already been subject to rationing. Many other products were rationed, including butter, flour, cloth, cigarettes, tobacco and shoes. It cannot have been easy for my mother to feed us all, given that by June 1943 and the birth of my sister, Judy, she had three children under three years of age. I can vividly remember eating the dark coarse brown bread that Irish mills were forced to produce when wheat imports were terminated. White bread was then replaced by a 90 per cent wheat extraction loaf; it did, however, contain potent laxative powers. The maximum weekly tea ration was reduced to just one ounce in February 1943, a major sacrifice in a country where tea consumption *per capita* was the second highest in the world. There were no bananas until Findlater's imported 1,950,000 in April 1946 and sold them at 6d to 8d each. The butter allowance in 1946 was 4 ounces per person. Petrol was also rationed: the official allowance for ordinary people with cars was eight gallons a month up to 10hp; and twelve gallons a month for cars of

10-16hp. Trains began to use turf instead of coal, which lengthened journey times. For those addicted to tobacco it was especially difficult and men were known to smoke turf and dried leaves in their pipes. The tea ration was reduced to half an ounce a week in 1945 and a form of tea made from dried dandelion leaves was on sale, as well as ersatz coffee, made from rhubarb. The people of Ireland were more fortunate than the population of Britain since meat was not rationed.

From March 1942 the gas supply to domestic customers was cut off every day between 8.30a.m. and 11.30a.m.; from 1.30p.m. to 5.00p.m. and between 10.30p.m. and 7.00a.m. the next morning. However, even this draconian policy did not defeat the ingenuity of the Dublin housewife, who soon discovered – by the simple process of trial and error – that even when the gas was switched off at the mains, enough was left trickling through the pipes to enable anyone to boil a kettle or heat up a can of baked beans. The residual gas left in the pipes when the supply was officially turned off was known as 'the glimmer' and it gave rise to a new job description – the Glimmerman – a state employed inspector whose job it was to prowl around the area during periods when the gas was turned off and to catch housewives in the act of using the glimmer. Many people would leave the glimmer on and use it to boil water or cook a stew. If children saw a strange man wandering about, the glimmer would be turned off and – if he was the Glimmerman – it was hoped that the top of the cooker would be cold before he reached the house. If not, the gas was cut off for several weeks.[12] My law-abiding mother never used the gas outside the hours prescribed by the government.

Although the war ended in 1945, it was to be another six years before rationing ceased in Ireland on 17 December 1951. However, 500 tons of raisins arrived in Dublin in November 1945 in time for Christmas; oranges were on sale for the first time since before the war at 2d and 3d each; petrol was available for private motoring; and queues formed to purchase the first fully fashioned silk stockings since before the war.[13] Growing up during and after the war seems like a misfortune, but as children at the time, we were not aware of that. We did not miss what we never possessed. Relative poverty, rations, few sweets, and no imported fruit and vegetables were the reality for everyone. Tuberculosis, however, was ravaging the country during the 1940s, especially the poor crammed together in inadequate housing. In 1948, at the age of 32, Dr. Noel Browne – who suffered from tuberculosis himself – became a controversial but dynamic and innovative Minister of

Health. He immediately introduced mass free screening for TB patients and launched a major construction programme to build new hospitals and sanitoria. Dr. Browne's initiative, along with the introduction of streptomycin and BCG, dramatically reduced the incidence of tuberculosis in Ireland. Without Browne's ruthless commitment and compassion, many more people would have died; it was one of the few great Irish political achievements of the twentieth century.

We moved to live in Dalkey six months after my brother, Brian, was born in March 1947. Flann O'Brien memorably described Dalkey as a 'little town…huddled, quiet, pretending to be asleep…a humble settlement which must, the traveller feels, be next door to some place of the first importance and distinction. And it is – a vestibule of a heavenly conspection.'[14] As a boy, George Bernard Shaw moved to live in Dalkey in 1866 and he recalled towards the end of his long life that 'I owe more than I can express to the natural beauty of that enchanting situation commanding the two great bays between Howth and Bray Head' with 'its canopied skies such as I have never seen elsewhere in the world.' His playground was Killiney Hill where he learnt to 'love nature when I was a half-grown nobody; I am a product of Dalkey's outlook' he declared, its beauty evoked a happiness that 'takes you out, far out, of this time and this world.'[15] Were these literary giants alive today, they would no doubt be surprised to know that Dalkey has become, arguably, the most desirable place to live in Ireland.

My parents purchased a new semi-detached four-bedroom house in 1947 located in a cul-de-sac (Hyde Park) some 600 metres from the main shopping street of Dalkey. The house boasted built-in-cupboards, coal fires, electric points in all rooms, a bathroom with a separate lavatory, an outdoor lavatory and, above all – the ultimate in 1947 modernity – a (small) built-in-fridge in the kitchen, a rarity in suburban Dublin in 1947. Soon after we moved we acquired a single tub, top-loading washing machine with a wringer on top. I remember entering the house for the first time and smelling dust, cement and fresh paint. We had become part of the aspiring bourgeois property-owning society which Cyril Connolly, whose grandfather owned Clontarf Castle, railed against: 'Slums may well be breeding grounds of crime, but middle-class suburbs are incubators of apathy and delirium.'[16] The house was heated by coal fires, usually lit in one room only. There were three reception rooms, although eventually the drawing room and dining room were amalgamated. There was a sideboard stacked with silver and Waterford cut glass decanters;

and my parents displayed paintings of Irish landscapes by Paul Henry and Humbert Craig.

My mother was a very keen and able gardener. She created a lovely front garden with flower beds bordered by granite stones, trees, beautiful shrubs and a pyracantha creeper on the front of the house. In October 2019, I returned to Dalkey for a visit and I strolled up Hyde Park to the house that was our home. Gone are the flower and rose beds that my mother tended with such care; gone are all the trees and shrubs that she pruned so neatly; gone also is the lawn that she laid and mowed so carefully; and the pyracantha creeper has also been removed. All have been obliterated to be replaced by tarmacadam in order to create a parking area for several large cars. As I stood there I thought of my mother – now dead 47 years – and how she would be so shocked to see how the beautiful front garden she so lovingly created has been destroyed.

Until we moved to the new house, my mother always had the assistance of a live-in maid. However, in 1947 the maid took my twin sister, Sheila and me to her house in Glasthule where we both contracted impetigo, which prompted my parents to release her and to continue parenting with only a day-time maid. On October 1, 1947, we received the first coal rations since 1941, although it turned out to be low grade slack. When painters, plumbers or coalmen came to the house my parents treated them as different from us. The coalmen wore their caps reversed under which their faces were streaked with coal dust. The coal was delivered in reusable jute sacks, each containing a hundredweight of coal. The coalmen were only permitted to use the outside loo and, furthermore, my mother served them tea in cups that were reserved solely for the use of tradesmen so that no workman would sully the family's china cups.

Initially we were surrounded by fields and woods where the country roads smelt of May blossom, the song of the male corncrake was heard and larks soared skywards emitting torrents of song in early summer. There was scant light pollution, little traffic noise, few aircraft, just clear starlight, frost on the pavements and the toll of the Angelus bell. There were few new houses in 1947. Soon, however, the green spaces began to disappear as more housing estates swamped the fringes of Dublin during the early fifties. Everywhere we looked we could see new ribbons of development as the fields near our home were rapidly covered with concrete roads, cosy plots, houses and bungalows stretching south to Dundela Park, Avondale Road, Watson's nurseries,

Ballybrack and beyond. The call of the corncrake could no longer be heard. An old way of life was changing forever, although we did not realise it at the time. This was the type of suburban growth – blurring the distinction between town and country – that was excoriated in an article by Ian Nairn in the *Architectural Review* of June 1955 on which he bestowed the name Subtopia. Subtopia was defined by Nairn as 'Making an ideal of suburbia. Visually speaking, the universalization and idealization of our town fringes.' But 'what is not to be borne', he argued, was that its ethos should 'drift like a gaseous pink marshmallow over the social scene, over the mind of man, over the land surface, over the philosophy, ideals and objectives of the human race.'[17] There is no doubt that Dublin's suburban sprawl led to a subtopian phenomenon that sucked the character and diversity out of places, tending towards the creation of a uniform sterile pattern. When I revisit Hyde Park now, some 73 years after we moved in and 57 years after leaving, I know only one person on the cul-de-sac. The streets where I played and skated are redolent with memories. Dalkey shaped my childhood and is in my heart and soul. I feel a deep passion for belonging when I visit, but although I will never be a stranger to Dalkey, it has become a stranger to me. I am no longer truly at home anywhere.

I did not receive any formal education until September, 1947 when – at the age of six years and five months – I was enrolled with my twin sister, Sheila, and younger sister, Judy (aged four) at Miss Savage's kindergarten school on Albert Road, Glenageary. I learnt to write letters in chalk on screaming slates; the slate was thick and shiny which made writing even more difficult. We were instructed in how to use a needle and wool to make patterns on lace curtain material; and how to cut things out with a blunt scissors. I displayed scant aptitude for needlework and wondered whether I would ever be competent at anything. My only accomplishment of note at Miss Savage's was learning how to knit. I knitted a dishcloth which I brought home to my mother; and my knitting developed to the stage that when I went to St Andrew's College in 1949 I knitted a school scarf that I wore for some years. This was my apotheosis and final flourish as a knitter. I was also awarded a prize at the kindergarten for what test I know not, but I remember it only because another pupil, Patricia, who later blossomed into a good tennis player, burst into tears as she clearly thought an injustice had been done. I had been totally unaware until then that there was a competitive dimension to life, even at a kindergarten in the 1940s.

Our first family holiday was in 1948 to a house in Kilcoole, a tiny village near the sea three miles south of Greystones, a place where J P Donleavy wrote *The Ginger Man*. Kilcoole is now a booming commuter town for Dublin, but then it seemed, like Llareggub in *Under Milk Wood*, to be always sleeping. I was seven and my brother, Brian, was then 18 months old which is why we holidayed close to home. At Kilcoole I learned for the first time that to travel hopefully is better than to arrive. The sea nearby seemed like a good prospect, but the reality was a disappointment in the form of an unattractive wind-swept shingle beach parallel with the Dublin to Rosslare railway line where we placed pennies on the track to be flattened by the trains. I played cricket in the garden with a tree as the wicket when I could persuade my parents to play with me. In Kilcoole our cocker spaniel dog was seriously injured after he fell into a cess pit. We had a Riley car with running boards on the outside and trafficators boasting little amber arms that flicked out if the vehicle was turning left or right. The Riley looked beautiful and smelled evocatively of leather seats and wood panelling, but it was unreliable. It spluttered to a halt on a hill near Greystones and my father jumped out of the vehicle to shove the starting handle through the hole in the front bumper and into the crankshaft of the engine. He turned it once, twice without success, and then the engine spluttered into life at the third attempt. Later in the holiday the engine of the Riley overheated on a hill, as cars built in the 1940s lacked an electric fan and the coolant could not perform its task on steep hills in summer. My father was competent mechanically – in a way that I have never been – and I was always confident that he could restart the car, which he usually did.

One of the highlights of the holiday was a day trip to Bray, which was a pale imitation of an English resort, but whose attractions included a run-down harbour, a windswept (unheated) open-air swimming pool, a crumbling Victorian promenade, chip shops and a funfair. This consisted of dodgems, shooting stalls with rifles, chairoplanes and slot machines. There was a unique aroma of hot dogs and onions, candyfloss (which I hated), perfume and diesel oil from the dodgems. It was tacky and had none of the glamour of Scarborough or Margate that I saw later on British Pathe news at the cinema. Sitting on Bray's shingle beach before swimming, I could see Dalkey Island and the beach at White Rock near Dalkey, which was far superior, not something I mentioned to my parents. I wondered how many people away on holiday can stand on a beach and almost see the roof of their own home! Music drifted over the shingle from the funfair – Doris Day singing 'It's Magic' and Perry Como crooning 'Because.' This music carried with it hints of a wonderful life beyond Bray and its decaying promenade. On the way back to the car, my parents stopped at a sweet shop on Quinsboro Road – opposite to the Royal cinema – where we were allowed to choose a treat. Glancing across the road, there was a life-size poster outside the cinema of Rita Hayworth wearing an off-the-shoulder black satin dress for the role of the femme fatale in the *film noir, Gilda*. I had never seen anyone so glamorous before. In 2019, on a visit back to Dublin, I took the train to Bray for the first time in 55 years and walked along the promenade where my parents had courted in the 1930s. I thought of them strolling along there at a time when I did not exist. Now they have not existed for 47 years; the picture of Rita Hayworth is no longer outside the cinema (now closed); and the voices of Doris Day and Perry Como are silent.

During the winter of 1948-49 my father, with the help of a carpenter, Joe Pearce, built a caravan in our front garden and in the summer of 1949 we towed it to its holiday location on McDaniel's farm at Jack's Hole on Brittas Bay, some six miles south of Wicklow and 30 miles from Dalkey. We travelled down most weekends of that summer and we would urge my father to push the Commer station wagon up to the dazzling speed of 50 miles per hour on straight sections of the road. A speed limit of 50mph was not introduced until 1961. After leaving Wicklow town, the car struggled over the crest of a hill and we children strained to be the first to call out – 'I see the sea.' The caravan site was perched on top of a cliff some 80 feet above a crescent-shaped sandy beach. There were only four caravans in the large field, and the beach was frequently deserted. We idled away the summer holidays and many weekends at the caravan. I slept in the back of the station wagon and, as an eight year old, I loved the sense of freedom of those nights sleeping on my own outside the security of the caravan, although I was slightly scared when I was woken at 6.00a.m. by cows nuzzling the side of the vehicle and scratching themselves on the posts around the caravan. My parents frequently left us alone in the evening and walked to the Rockfield Hotel to drink in the bar at a time when I was nine years of age, a justifiable risk in 1950 that would be unthinkable today. The four caravans in the field have long since gone and been replaced by two beach resorts with dozens of holiday homes, tennis courts and a par-three golf course. However, the field and the site of our caravan overlooking the beach are there etched in my memory with, above all, a feeling of timelessness and of endless summer days.

The beach at Brittas Bay was the world for me: its infinity, the rhythm of the tide, transience and persistence, the place where I learned to swim in clear sea water off pristine sands. Swimming at Brittas is graphically imagined by Derek Mahon in his poem – *A Swim in Co. Wicklow*:

> Spindrift, crustacean patience
> And a gust of ozone,
> You come back once more
> To this dazzling shore,
> Its warm uterine rinse,
> Heart- racing heave and groan.

I measured our passing summers by memories of the sea. Below the high-water mark at Brittas Bay, in the inter-tidal zone, the rocks were covered in barnacles, mussels, anemones, limpets and bladderwrack. With arctic terns screeching overhead and oystercatchers and dunlin wheeling in close-packed harmony, the rock pools were a source of wonder, especially the scuttling hermit crabs. Brittle starfish appeared in the shallows and crabs spawned among the rocks. I loved to pick up a shell, place it to my ear and listen to the sound of the sea. The sea was forever changing: wild and rough; flat as a millpond; shiny silver; metal grey; shafts of sun creating pools of light. Dogs and children ran free; time had stopped, but not the sea. These were the long lazy days of summer when the sand was hot to touch, when I could gaze down ten feet into the water and see shoals of small fish; days that seemed to a small boy to last forever. There is something restorative about watching the waves break and flow up a beach propelled by the pulse of a rising tide. I do not think that my soul can do without it so that even now I live 200 yards from it. It's just there forever changing, moving in and out, obeying the lunar rhythms.

* * *

There were queues for English-made nylons in May 1948, selling for 12/6 a pair in the Dublin shops; these were the first nylons ever seen in Ireland, apart from a few pairs given to Irish girls by American GIs stationed in Belfast in return for the pleasure of their company.[18] The British Prime Minister, Clement Attlee, who was on holiday in Ireland in July 1948, signed a new four year Anglo-Irish Trade Agreement giving Irish agricultural and industrial products free access to the British market, while still protecting some new indigenous industries by tariffs.[19] The first post-war motor car to be available in Ireland was the Austin A40, which also appeared in 1948, but the Morris Minor proved to be more popular when it went on sale in April 1949 for £397.

Memories of the late 1940s were of an overwhelming grimy drabness: decaying buildings, dimly lit narrow streets along which occasional cars or lorries passed, manoeuvring around numerous horse-drawn carts and cyclists. There was, however, little vandalism or graffiti; and the phone boxes were all fully glazed and contained the relevant directory. Trams ran on rails down the middle of the street the nine miles from Dalkey to Nelson's Pillar on O'Connell Street. I remember as a seven-year-old boy being fascinated by the trams at the tramyard terminus in Dalkey, which is still visible today. The driver hauled over the bogey ready for the return journey back to Nelson's Pillar, while the conductor walked down the aisle reversing the seats and then wound back the indicator on the front. There were still some trams operating on the Dalkey route with an open balcony at each end of the top deck. I would jump up on the slatted platform and run up the stairs so that my mother would not opt to travel on the lower deck. To sit in the open balcony squeezed into the corner and be exposed to the wind on my face as the tram swayed and clanged down Bulloch Hill, while the overhead trolley spat flames against the wires, was thrilling. On a tight bend, the tram's wheels moaned on the tracks, while above us the trolley hummed in harmony. Travelling by tram was basic but romantic and so much more of an event than the smooth new double-decker Leyland buses that replaced them after 9 July 1949.

Cars and lorries were almost all British-made, noisy, notoriously unreliable and prone to rust. We always owned a car, which my father drove to work at Guinness's brewery every day after petrol rationing was ended. Safety was a concern in the 1940s since there were no speed limits on country roads and no cars were fitted with seat belts. The appearance of people on the street in the late 1940s would shock anyone under the age of 60: pale faces, gaunt features (obesity was almost non-existent), drab, unstylish clothing and beggars swathed in black shawls. Most people looked (and were) very poor. Unemployed men stood around on street corners smoking, chewing tobacco and spitting into the gutter. Half-smoked cigarettes littered the pavements and some of these were picked–up and smoked. Like anyone born during World War 2, I can be transported back to the 1940s by the noise of a tram, the buzz of wasps around a family picnic, the sound of a corncrake, the noise of a horse and cart, by the great Frank Sinatra crooning 'All or Nothing at All' or by the glorious voice of John McCormack singing 'I hear You Calling Me.' Shawl- clad women with a baby in their arms often knocked on the door and promised that we would go straight to heaven if we helped them, not realising that as Protestants we did not believe in purgatory!

Ireland in 1949. Poverty endemic; the highest rates of infant and maternal mortality in Europe; no supermarkets, no frozen food, no motorways, no lager, no microwaves, no dishwashers, no formica, no cassette tapes, no CDs, no mobile phones, no laptops, no iPads, no seat belts, no duvets, no leisure wear, no trainers, no contraceptives, no divorce, no abortion, homosexuality illegal, capital punishment legal, no laundrettes, no automatic washing machines, no TV.[20] Shops on every corner, pubs on every street, numerous cinemas, telephone boxes, Catholic shrines at cross-roads, steam trains, trams, grass running tracks, wooden tennis racquets, Taylor-Keith lemonade, woodbine smoke in the air, coke boilers, coal fires, ice inside bedroom windows, grimy streets, elbow patches on jackets, home-knitted cardigans and sweaters, rumpled clothes, chilblains, petrol-pump attendants, the toll of the Angelus bell, lino on bedroom floors, cars breaking down, riding a carousel, frothy candyfloss. No avocados, no asparagus, no blueberries, no couscous, no olive oil, no mango fruit, no olives, no pineapples, no teabags. Suburban semis, starting handles, Ford Anglias, Austin Sevens, Morris Minors, BSA motorbikes, bakelite wirelesses, milk of magnesia, Vick rub, Enos, germolene, cloth caps, food rationing, shop home delivery services, heavy leather rugby balls, and a pint meaning only Guinness.

From late November there was an air of anticipation as the festival of Christmas approached. Weeks before the celebration my mother gathered the ingredients for the Christmas pudding, including currants, raisins, flour, beaten eggs, spices, margarine, whiskey and Guinness. They were all mixed up in a bowl, covered with a layer of greaseproof paper and secured with string; she then placed the bowl in a saucepan and boiled it for an interminable length of time. Next, she made the Christmas cake, laden with fruit and alcohol, covered with thick layers of marzipan and icing with Santa in his sleigh on top. The decorations were taken down from the attic. The paper chains, tinsel and the glass balls for the Christmas tree were unpacked and the tree decorated by my mother assisted by all of us. The tree was never garlanded with electric lights, yet somehow it was magical: the glittering balls, the paper chains, the tinsel, the home-made decorations and the carol singers in the street created imperishable memories.

Prior to Christmas we would visit Henry Street in Dublin which was garishly decorated and came alive with brilliantly coloured strings of lamps swaying from one side to the other. There were giant flashing Santa Clauses, cheap tree decorations and crowds of people haggling with the hawkers. Ireland was still an extremely poor country, but the humour and joyousness of Dubliners was so infectious at Christmas. After visiting Henry Street, we walked down O'Connell Street, past Trinity College and into the refined world of Grafton Street, which boasted Ireland's two premier department stores, Brown Thomas and Switzer's. Santa was present in both of these stores, but I have no recollection of ever being ushered into the presence of the mythical figure. What I do vividly remember was the beautiful window display in Switzer's shop with a complex Hornby Dublo railway layout and two trains gliding through tunnels and emerging into a snowy landscape; I could not draw myself away from this magical scene every Christmas. I longed passionately to own an electric train set and importunately hinted at my desire for it; but no electric train set ever arrived. It was impossible as my parents were having to pay school fees at a time when the Irish economy was depressed and thousands were emigrating. I did manage, however, to build up a collection of Dinky replica Grand Prix racing cars, including Maseratis, Ferraris and Alfa Romeos. These were beautifully made to scale in metal, with rubber tyres. I used to race them on a track constructed on the carpet with wool used to make rugs. I nudged the cars around the track accompanied by my imaginary running commentary. I cherished the Dinkies and always stored them in red and yellow cardboard boxes. I was also given my first bicycle in 1949, a second-hand model sporting new mudguards purchased from Coombes' shop in Dalkey.

Poverty in 1940s Ireland was of a different kind than today: many households lacked sufficient food; a winter overcoat and strong shoes were luxuries; houses were inadequately heated and there were insufficient blankets on cold winter nights. Poverty today is qualitatively different: worries about paying for a large wedding, the lack of a second car or a TV set. Hence, Christmas presents in the Ireland of the late 1940s were meagre by contemporary expectations. Frugality was a necessity not a choice in post-war Ireland and yet somehow the magic of Christmas was apparent. Few sensations in life could compare with the thrill of waking early on Christmas morning and feeling the stocking crammed with toys and treats. Money was short, expectations were low and toys were in scarce supply, but were appreciated accordingly: maybe either a Dinky toy or a board game, a jigsaw puzzle, colouring pencils or a bag of marbles and an orange would nestle in the stocking. One year I received a wooden multi-coloured spinning top which I enjoyed activating by using a small whip. Later I was given a Meccano set and spent many frustrating hours studying the manual and trying to manipulate tiny screws and vital parts, but I never became accomplished at building the more complex structures such as cranes and bridges. Frequently I received an annual – either the *Dandy*, *Beano* or *Eagle* (from 1950). These contained a collection of strip cartoons, stories, games and puzzles that commanded my attention over the Christmas holiday. Then the smell of the turkey and vegetables cooking; the table laid with a special cloth and crackers; the turkey on a huge platter with stuffing, sprouts and roast potatoes. The highlight after the turkey was watching my father soaking the pudding with a large measure of Jameson's whiskey and then setting fire to it. The taste of the pudding infused with whiskey was unique and quite unforgettable; the smiles and laughter and the excitement when, for once, we could drink as much as we liked from a lemonade siphon. The Christmas holiday was also the peak period for playing board games with my siblings, principally Monopoly, Ludo, snakes and ladders, draughts, tiddly winks, and, my favourite, Cluedo. Card games never held much appeal for me. I derived more enjoyment from games where one needed to pit one's wits against another person, like noughts and crosses, draughts and chess.

Our parents would take us to a pantomime at the Gaiety theatre starring Jimmy O'Dea and Maureen Potter, Ireland's premier comedienne. To an eight-year-old the theatre was magical: the hum of expectation; the sound of the orchestra warming up; the glass chandeliers that blazed like stars until they dimmed and the curtain lifted to reveal the dazzling set behind; the entrance of the dame, played by O'Dea, and the Principal Boy with long slender legs and lovely face. I enjoyed the flamboyant cross-dressing characters, the puns, silly jokes and play on words, the colourful costumes, and the audience participation, when you were encouraged to shout as loud as possible. It was an entirely different world. I loved the way the actors came up to the edge of the stage to talk to us as if they had known us all our life. I recall one panto where Mickser Reid, a dwarf in those politically incorrect days, was fired from a cannon and many children, including my younger sister, were so frightened that they had to be taken into the foyer to recover.

Ireland was a profoundly conservative country in 1949, a land of orderly queuing at shops and cinemas, of men walking on the outside of the pavement, of seats on buses given up to the elderly and infirm, of men in suits sitting on the beach, of schoolboys wearing caps, of gardeners removing caps and praying at the sound of the Angelus, of heavily censored books (frequently by Irish authors), of censored films, of marriage often being a lifetime sentence, of men spitting out tobacco in the street, and of widespread poverty. A country of hierarchical social assumptions in which authority (usually clerical) was respected; of the unquestioned assumption that the teachings of the Catholic Church dominated many aspects of people's lives, including those of the Protestant community.

CHAPTER 2

Will Anything Ever Happen?

Ireland in the 1950s. Electric bread vans, caravan holidays, home deliveries, coffee bars, cycle clips, Sturmey -Archer three speed gears, cyclists with a child on the crossbar, wing indicators, bespoke tailors, head scarves, crests on blazers, school caps, gabardine macs, short corduroy trousers with a belt in the shape of a snake, Norton and AJS motorbikes, saluting AA patrolmen. Meccano, Dinky toys, Hornby Dublo electric train sets, popcorn, tapioca, semolina, HB ice cream, spangles, aniseed balls and toffee bars. Silvikrin, balsa-wood planes, Monopoly, Cluedo, Ludo, Subbuteo, cap guns, water pistols, potato guns, beetle drives, scout camps. Sailing both from Dun Laoghaire and Bulloch harbours, swimming at the White Rock and the Forty Foot, nightwatchmen huddling in huts by a brazier at road repair sites, young women on clicking stiletto heels, sea fishing. Although Ireland was poor throughout the 1950s, some important innovations diffused into the more prosperous parts of Dun Laoghaire and Dalkey including: the Jowett Jupiter, Aston Martin DB2, the Bic crystal ballpoint pen, Kenwood chef, and Oral–B toothpaste in 1950; the Jaguar C–Type, Ford Consul and Ford Zephyr in 1951; the Austin-Healey in 1952; the Ford Popular, Babycham and the washer–spin dryer in 1953; the transistor radio and Jaguar XK140 in 1954; Shreddies, Dove toiletries, Bird's Eye Fish Fingers and the Mercedes-Benz 190SL in 1955; Hillman Minx, Diorissimo and Play-Doh in 1956; Ready Brek, the hula hoop and Spandex in 1958; and the Mini, Ford Anglia, Surf and Xerox914 in 1959.

Our family was middle class but not rich, although we were certainly not poor as my father was a manager at Guinness's brewery. Hence, we were close enough to prosperity to know what it looked like, especially as my father's shooting and fishing companions included directors of Guinness's and a doctor. We owned a modern house (with a built-in fridge), had food to eat, a coal fire, the radio to listen to, the *Irish Times* every day, comics to read and the *Observer, Sunday Times* and *Sunday Independent* at the weekend. Given that from 1947 onwards we were a family of four children, thrift was a necessity; nothing was thrown away if it could be of any use. The screw drivers, spanners and adjustable wrench in my toolbox today were purchased and used by my father in the 1940s and have rarely been employed since! Being raised in the post-war era it would never occur to me to purchase a new one if the old one was not broken or lost. If a bicycle tyre was punctured, we simply patched it with a kit from Coombes' bicycle shop in Dalkey. Trousers were mended, sweaters had patches knitted into them and shoes were repaired. A form of coal dust called slack was scattered on top of the blazing fire and it would ultimately acquire a red glow that lasted for hours. We were given pocket money for which we had to perform a rotation of domestic tasks, including hoovering, dusting, cleaning out the fire, clearing the table and drying the dishes. There was little money to spend on delights such as chewing gum (which I never liked), bubble gum (which I couldn't blow into bubbles), children's sugary cigarettes, bulls' eyes or toffee bars. We learned to be satisfied with our lot as Ireland in the 1950s was a poor country with a stagnant economy blighted by mass emigration. By 1961, 45 per cent of those born in Ireland between 1931 and 1961 and 40 per cent of those born between 1926 and 1941 had emigrated.[1]

There were many so-called educational toys in the 1950s, few of which survive today: magnets, the plastic drinking bird, the diving man, Meccano, metal puzzles, balsa wood, and plasticine. I displayed no aptitude for building constructions from Meccano or solving metal puzzles. Solid balsa-wood kits are no longer available as the only skill now required to make a model aircraft is a light touch with the plastic parts and a steady hand with the glue. In the 1950s one matched up a block of balsa against a rudimentary diagram and shaped it using a razor blade, with which I sliced my finger as readily as it carved the balsa. If the result was recognisable as an aeroplane, you were an expert. If my finger was still recognisable as a finger, I was lucky. The ultimate challenge for the new plane was a test flight: once airborne all of my planes invariably dive-bombed kamikaze-like into the lawn.

Dalkey was a safe environment for children to grow up and we had the freedom to play out all day. It was an unashamedly unregulated and unsupervised world in which the concept of 'health and safety' did not exist. We sped down the streets on roller skates with metal wheels that made a loud gritty noise, one of the few childhood pastimes at which I was competent. We climbed trees, lit fires, built dens and played cowboys and Indians in Jo Pinkster's garden armed with a Colt 45 and a roll of caps or a potato-gun. We listened to Slim Whitman singing 'Rose Marie' on Pinkster's walnut radiogram, heard the toll of the Angelus bell as it rang across the gardens twice a day to call people – including the gardeners – to prayer. We dug bait (ragworm) in Bulloch harbour and fished for pollack, mackerel and conger eels off the granite rocks at the Forty Foot. We wore short trousers until we were around 12 so our knees were chapped and sore in winter. We walked over Dalkey Hill, much of which had been quarried and transported on the Atmospheric railway to construct the piers at Dun Laoghaire harbour, leaving sheer granite cliffs with a ruined castle perched on the edge. We collected frog spawn from ponds, picked blackberries and played with yo–yos. We careered downhill on bogeys made from wood and pram wheels; attached playing cards to bikes to simulate a motor-cycle and rode bikes sitting on the back carrier. I learned to play cricket by myself with accompanying running commentary; and we bashed conkers in the school yard. In summer we would alternate between swimming at the Forty Foot and the White Rock. To reach White Rock we would cycle through Dalkey, down past Colliemore harbour to Sorrento Point where the magnificent vista of Killiney Bay opens to the south with the railway line hugging the edge of the cliffs, and where Bray Head and the two quartzite Sugar Loaf mountains tumble into the sea. There were no trainers, denim jeans or track suits in those days. I wore short corduroy trousers, a hand–knitted sweater and a corduroy zipped jerkin. We got dirty, fell from trees, regularly ripped our trousers, grazed our knees and cut ourselves. My mother always had a bottle of iodine in the house to disinfect cuts and grazes and the sting from the iodine dabbed on a cut was usually more painful than the original fall. If I caught a cold, my mother rubbed Vick onto my chest at night and I had to swallow Veno's cough mixture.

We swam regularly at the famous Forty Foot bathing place, which was then exclusively reserved for gentlemen, many of whom swam in the nude. The Women's Liberation Movement invaded this male sanctuary in August 1974, plunged into the water and the Forty Foot has been open to women and children ever since. The sea at the Forty Foot never seemed really cold when I was growing up, although the daily water temperature reading seldom exceed 15 degrees Celsius. The Forty Foot is located below the Martello tower at Sandycove. This Martello tower is immortalised in the first scene of Joyce's masterpiece *Ulysses* when Buck Mulligan stands shaving on the top looking out across Dublin Bay and refers to 'the snotgreen sea. The scrotumtightening sea.' Although I had not read Joyce as a ten- year- old, there is no doubt that swimming at the famous Forty Foot was a 'scrotumtightening' experience. I plucked up the courage to dive in off the diving board some nine feet above the Irish sea swell and I can still feel the fear and excitement of these dives down, down into the depths of the chilly water; then kicking out with my legs up towards the light above, lungs bursting, agonisingly slow; and then gasping at the surface to draw the air in. This was a different environment from the school swimming pool at St Andrew's College, wild and potentially dangerous, with the screech of seagulls and oystercatchers overhead, the sea swell crashing into the cliff and the sense of latent power as each wave sucked back off the rocks. We would swim to a raft some 60 yards offshore, although in a rough sea it seemed like halfway to Anglesey, drag ourselves aboard for a breather and then swim back. There were pools in which to go searching for crabs. At the Forty Foot there were rocks to climb from which we could see the mailboat setting out for Holyhead carrying emigrants, who stood on deck as Dun Laoghaire grew tiny in their wake. Most of the emigrants never returned. If the wind was from the east, it blew in the smell of the sea; and on a foggy day Howth Head across the bay loomed like a liner out of the mist. We knew that we were in a special place. There was a haze out to sea and tar bubbles on the road on days when the sun shone; and you could see a shimmer as if the road was rising up to greet you.

Nobody ever came to harm in this place of unlocked doors, gorse and wooded hills; we had never heard of paedophiles and had no cause to worry about them. We felt safe. If my mother asked me where I was going to on my bike in the morning, I would reply 'to meet Dave Thomas and John Keery'. We then roamed free till lunchtime without our parents having any idea where we had been. One of our favourite playgrounds was Killiney Hill with its panoramic views, and its steep wooded slopes dropping down to White Rock beach. I frequently return to this hill in my dreams when it is always a summer day. We passed hedgerows covered with flowering currants and damson shrubs white with blossom. Reaching the obelisk on Killiney Hill, we watched the cloud shadows moving across Dalkey island and south towards Bray Head and Sugar Loaf mountain. It's a wonder that those of us growing up in this place in the 1950s actually managed to survive. We cycled everywhere without helmets, never ever wore a life-jacket when sailing, dived off rocks into the Irish sea, jumped off walls, climbed trees, lit fires, shot each other with potato guns and catapults, skimmed pebbles across the water, roller- skated at maximum speed, and climbed in the Wicklow mountains with no adult supervision. What is most remarkable is that Dave and John remain good friends to this day. John Keery and I lost touch from around 1970 till 2010, but have been in regular contact again since 2014. John is an intelligent conversationalist, a loyal Liberal Democrat councillor who has served the Glastonbury community for more than 40 years, a totally reliable and interesting friend of great integrity. Dave Thomas and I have been in close touch since we met some 70 years ago and what is so striking about him is that he has not changed fundamentally in all that time: thoughtful, compassionate, a conscientious doctor, a complete absence of ego, politically aware, self-effacing, generous and great fun.

Lying in bed at night I often heard the plangent, haunting sound of the foghorn on the East pier at Dun Laoghaire, a lonely, melancholic noise echoing across the vastness of the Irish Sea, responding to the dull thud of the Kish light seven miles to the east. Occasionally, if the wind was north-west, I would hear the moan of the Bailey lighthouse on Howth Head, some 11 miles distant. The initial low note of the foghorn was followed by an even lower one designed to penetrate banks of fog offshore. This was evocatively captured by Derek Mahon in *Beyond Howth Head*:

> And here I look close; for look, across
> Dark waves where bell- buoys dimly toss
> The Baily winks beyond Howth Head
> And sleep calls from the silent bed;
> While the moon drags her kindred stones
> Among the rocks and the strict bones
> Of the drowned, and I put out the light
> On shadows of the encroaching night.

The moan of the Kish light and clamour of a gale brings to mind the joy of sounds: the patter of heavy rain against the canvas while tucked up in a sleeping bag inside a tent; the plaintive call of a curlew across an estuary at dusk; leaves rustling in the breeze – each species of tree responding to the breeze with a unique sound which one learned to identify; the crackle of flames around a campfire; the swish and suck of the sea as it retreats from a rocky headland; and the distant rumble of thunder as it moves away. The sound that ran through my head most of all was that of the seawater breaking over the granite boulders at Bulloch harbour. I could hear it lying in bed and could tell the direction of the wind. A view of the sea refreshed my soul. It was my first language, my first awareness of the natural power of seawater. We were lucky as children today are constrained, not permitted to wander off to roam freely, to explore, to be courageous by climbing high trees or diving unsupervised into the sea.

Corporal punishment was not a social issue at the time. It was normal in 1950s Ireland for parents to smack their children in order to instil obedience; it was frequent and regarded as an acceptable way of correcting behaviour. The concept of the child as a potentially vulnerable and creative individual that needed encouragement and care was not widely held at the time. The daughter of my mother's cousin, Edith Chaloner, who is now 93 years of age, informed me in 2021 that when she visited our house in the 1950s she observed that my father was a 'severe disciplinarian' and some of the punishment administered with whatever was near to hand – such as a belt – was harsh. Obedience was demanded by fear. What disturbed me was that the physical punishment was more often visited upon me than my two sisters and I can vividly recall being beaten with the poker on numerous occasions. No forgiveness was ever forthcoming for the physical cruelty involved. Threats were made not just to smack but to thrash me and, some years later, my mother, whom I came to love and respect deeply, admitted that she had sought to break my spirit. I don't know whether the beatings at home affected my character, but I have always been anxious to please and have feared rejection by anyone. I resolved at the time that when I became a parent I would never beat any of my children, one resolution that I did manage to keep. The rewards from not smacking are inevitably slower to manifest themselves but eventually they become apparent in the following generation.

Even as a teenager, we were expected to obey parental discipline without question. What was missing was physical intimacy. We slept in our own beds. There was no snuggling into the parental bed, or curling up on a lap, even when one was ill. I craved to be hugged, but my father never did so. My mother did not tell us that she loved us; I knew by her actions that she did, but I wanted to feel it. She displayed a formality that could not be altered and a distance that allowed no one to pass beyond a point of familiarity that only she determined. None of us ever knew what she really thought of us.

There was no universal emotional framework in the household so that we each had bilateral relationships with her. She battled on and never shared her fears despite having no close friends or relations who could help if required. She was calm, measured, dignified, hard-working and very charming – loved by all who knew her – but was always somewhat remote and distant, never showing her emotions; I cannot recall being touched by her since I was a baby. I have had a respect for authority ever since. I worry every time I open an income tax payment demand, or car tax renewal form, or a council tax notice. This extended to school where I tried to please the teachers; I was seldom in trouble and never caned in my ten years at St Andrew's, not because I was inherently good, but out of an excessive regard for authority figures.

I lived in the house in Hyde Park for 16 years until I graduated from university. It was a good house for a child to grow up in. Everything was always tidy, clean and neat. Dishes were not left in the sink unwashed; and floors were never dirty or furniture undusted. The fire in the breakfast room was lit in autumn and winter, although the rest of the house was cold. There were always flowers picked from the garden on the hall table. The breakfast-room table was covered with a clean tablecloth for every meal. Most middle-class mothers in the 1950s had a strict routine with the same meals every day of the week. On Sunday we ate a joint of meat, covered in gravy, to be followed on Monday by cottage pie using the left-overs from Sunday's joint. Tuesday was usually a stew, or chops with mashed potatoes; Wednesday was roast ham and potatoes and Thursday, Irish stew, made of mutton with carrots, onions and potatoes layered on top of each other; Friday was always fish and on Saturday my father had a steak and the rest of us usually mince or sausages and chips. Occasionally my mother would make a traditional Irish dish – colcannon – a mashed potato recipe made from potatoes, cabbage, scallions and milk, with butter melted in the centre of the spuds. Vegetables tended to be basic and seasonal; asparagus, artichokes and sweet potatoes were never available at the greengrocers in Dalkey during the 1950s. Olive oil was sold at the chemist, but my mother only used it to drip into my ear to remove wax, and never poured it over a salad. Salads, eaten only in summer, were composed entirely of lettuce, tomatoes and cucumber – all grown by my mother. Potatoes were not regarded as a vegetable but as the core of most meals around which were arranged the other components, including perhaps cabbage, ham, sausages or a chop.

Fruit was always seasonal, fresh and usually Irish-grown. My mother did cook some tasty puddings, including bread–and-butter pudding, apple pie, or steamed rhubarb pie. Rice pudding was less popular, especially as it was frequently served at school meals, where tapioca and semolina were universally hated. In the absence of imported fruit, tinned peaches in cans soaked in a sweet syrup and covered in Carnation milk were popular in the 1950s. However, bread and jam or fried bread were staples, with cocoa and cream crackers before bed. Part of the soundscape every morning was the noise of the horse-drawn cart of the HB milkman, followed by the rattle of the bottles in the metal crate and the distinctive sound of the bottles being placed on the doorstep. The milkman and the horse and cart proceeded up the road, stopping and starting, making deliveries on both sides of the road, while the horse munched from a nosebag. When the horses were replaced by an electric van in 1959, the delivery service took longer as the horse knew precisely at which houses it needed to stop. The milk always had cream floating on the top; and before it was opened we shook it to dilute the cream. The street also echoed to the clippety-clopping sound of the rag-and-bone man. Pedlars also called regularly with a suitcase of wares, including thread, needles, and ribbons; and tinkers knocked at the door seeking to repair pots and pans.

Although we were by not poor, my parents insisted on not wasting food, on eating everything on the plate, and on being grateful. Some of the food was memorable, notably my mother's fruit cakes, parkin biscuits and scones. My mother's menus were restricted by the very limited range of food in the shops. There was no olive oil or balsamic vinegar, but I recall pouring masses of Heinz Salad Cream on almost everything, and tomato ketchup on chips. We each had our own place around the table and we were required to ask politely if we wished to leave. If one of us placed our elbows on the table, or held a knife the wrong way – the handle vulgarly pointing upwards between forefinger and thumb rather than neatly tucked under – a ticking off followed. If a visitor did it, the appropriate social inference was drawn.

The most desirable, if not exotic, fruit I ate were cherries. I cannot remember when I first spotted them in Findlater's store, probably the early 1950s. I am not sure whether they were grown locally or were imported from Kent, but it was high summer and they were not available for long. It was possible to purchase a pound of them in a paper bag and I loved to bite into them gently until the fruit released a squirt of juice. Above all, it's the sharpness of the taste that I remember, and if my parents were out of sight, seeing how far I could spit out the stone. Rationing, post-war austerity and the limited range of goods in the shops cultivated a feeling of equality and even if – as in the case of our family – we had a bit more money than most, there was a limit to what we could spend it on. My father dressed in hand-made jackets and suits – made by a tailor in Bray – and we always had a one month holiday every summer, usually in Donegal. The growth in consumerism did not happen in Ireland until the late sixties and was not widespread throughout the population.

My mother's principal hobby was gardening, at which she excelled. The front garden was a splendid sight in spring and summer when her trees, shrubs, flowers and creepers – all of which she had planted – were in bloom. She grew roses, nerines, lavender, lilacs, pansies, wallflowers, irises, and many other flowers. In the back garden a trellis for the sweet peas was constructed in the form of a rustic wooden archway spanning the path and leading into the vegetable garden. Here she grew tomatoes in a greenhouse, potatoes, parsnips, lettuce, onions, beetroot, sprouts and carrots. Nothing reminds me of her more than the fragrance of sweet peas released into the air on a summer evening. The world of coffee mornings, flower-arranging classes, indoor bowling or having people round for drinks was never one in which Mum participated. I rarely ever heard her chat on the telephone, which seemed only to be used for brief communications such as ordering supplies from the chemist or butcher.

Heating, to the extent that it existed, was confined to the breakfast-room, except at weekends when a fire would be lit in the sitting room. The breakfast-room fire also helped to heat the water by closing a metal flap which diverted the flames to a water heater at the back of the fire. Even with that, baths were only once weekly. In the evenings my parents sat by the fire, my father reading the *Irish Times* or doing some leatherwork, accompanied by the BBC Light Programme, while my mother knitted or darned. Later my mother would close the draught control and shovel on slack to dampen down the fire in order to make it easier to light the following morning, a process that often involved placing a double-spread of the *Irish Times* across the entire fireplace opening to create a draught from beneath the grate. Making toast in an era before toasters, involved skewering a slice of bread or barmbrack with a brass toasting fork and holding it as close as possible to the fire, hoping it would turn brown before one had to pull one's hand away. Although the downstairs rooms and my parents' bedroom were all carpeted, the floors of the other three bedrooms were covered with lino. I frequently woke to find ice inside my bedroom window on winter mornings with slivers of cold creeping under the door. Having not had the benefit of a hot water bottle, getting out of bed was an uncomfortable experience. I dreaded the thought of sliding my leg out from under the bedcovers to stand on the cold lino floor. I engaged in a complex set of manoeuvres to dress, taking care not to let my feet hit the lino until absolutely necessary. Many women walking around Dalkey in winter had legs that were mottled pink and red caused by the habit of pulling up their skirts and roasting their shins by the fire.

Reading comics was an important weekly ritual to escape the prevailing dullness of early 1950s Ireland. The comics read by most Irish children in the 1950s were British. A new comic for boys, *Eagle*, took flight in 1950 (costing 3d). It was 20 pages, with eight in full colour, and was an immediate hit with boys, achieving sales of over 800,000 in the first year, rising to a peak of two million in the mid-fifties. The person responsible for this success was an Anglican vicar, Marcus Morris, aided by his assistant Chad Varah (the future founder of Samaritans). *Eagle* was targeted at the middle classes with its wholesome adventure stories and bites of knowledge. Morris, its first editor, had a moral message to communicate to the child in the form of appropriate values and attitudes, with a heavy emphasis on British patriotism. There were illustrated biographies of famous imperial heroes like Nelson, Baden-Powell and Montgomery and a comic strip of the life of Christ; and there was always a cutaway of a warship, aircraft, or racing car in the centre spread of the comic. The major feature of the *Eagle* was the square-jawed 'Dan Dare Pilot of the Future' and his sidekick Digby. Dare was written and drawn by a brilliant illustrator – Frank Hampson – who modelled Dare on the stereotype English flying ace. Hampson created a metropolis, Mekonta, on Venus and provided Dare with an extraordinary enemy whom he confronted each week – the Mekon – an evil creature with an elongated green head, a large brain and no body. A sister comic, *Girl*, was launched in 1951 and was read by my two sisters; it featured youthful exuberance in boarding schools, practical jokes, and equestrian adventures. Although popular in Ireland, *Eagle* presented an image of Britain as a conservative, Christian and patriotic country characterised by decency and bravery and also as morally and intellectually superior to other countries in this pre-Suez era. Comics such as *Eagle* and *Girl* portrayed a way of life that was based on private schools, an inherent racial superiority and acceptance of, if not support for, British imperialism and the heroism of the British Armed Forces. There was simply no equivalent Irish comic available in 1950.

Meanwhile, D C Thompson in Dundee had published popular comics since before the war, including the *Beano* and the *Dandy* at tuppence each. I liked the *Beano* best with its cast of characters, including Roger the Dodger, Minnie the Minx, the Bash Street Kids, and Dennis the Menace. My favourite was Dennis the Menace with the unruly hair and his questioning of authority, getting into trouble, usually humiliated by his adult adversaries, but sometimes triumphing over the severe parent, teacher or bully. In these comics people were stereotyped with Welshmen referred to as 'Taffy' and Scots as 'Jock,' while Englishness was associated with leadership and being normal. The *Beano* and the *Dandy* have survived largely unchanged with most of the characters getting into some form of mischief every week. The British (English) jingoism displayed by the imported comics we read in the 1950s passed unnoticed by us as ten-year-olds when we rushed to purchase them every Thursday or Friday. Irish boys and girls, however, did miss out when the comics contained a free gift, such as a balsa-wood aircraft or cardboard dolls with cut-out frocks since such offers 'did not apply in Eire.'

Shopping in the 1950s was not yet a leisure activity, but a near-daily drudge as perishable foods needed to be purchased regularly in small quantities. I do not recall any shops in Dalkey in the 1950s where ready-made food could be purchased. A shopping trip to the main street of Dalkey might involve calling into the grocer, greengrocer, butcher, pork butcher, fishmonger, newsagent and chemist. Several times a week Mum asked me to cycle over to Dalkey for 'the messages.' Many of the shops were dark and gloomy and, if an item was out of stock, it might be several weeks before it was procured. There were no supermarkets, charity shops or fast- food restaurants. Produce was fresh and local, whilst buying anything out of season was unusual. Grapes and bananas were a rarity and, if available, they would only be so for a brief period. It was an era when orders were delivered by boys riding a messenger bike with a cavernous wicker basket in front, a service supplied by numerous shops including the butcher (Dunne's), pork butcher's (Hick's), chemist (Maxwell's) and grocer's (Findlater's). Johnson Mooney and O'Brien's electric-powered bread van would glide up Hyde Park every day to provide door-to-door bread deliveries; this service was later driven to extinction by supermarkets.

The anchor store of Dalkey in the fifties, although nobody would use such a descriptor at the time, was Findlater's grocery shop with its splendid clock (which survives to this day). Most items were sold loose in Findlater's; the surfeit of plastic packaging that bedevils the present-day shopping experience – and causes so much pollution of the seas – simply did not exist. Nothing had logged up thousands of air miles to reach Dalkey so almost all the items on sale had been produced locally in Ireland. As I entered Findlater's, the air was sweetened both by a whiff of tea – loose in a wooden chest – a wheel of cheese wrapped in muslin, a side of bacon sliced to order into rashers, and freshly baked bread. The internal layout included a series of counters: one served fruit and vegetables; another sold tea and coffee, cakes and biscuits, butter and cheese, and so on. I walked around the shop with the list: a tin of Lyle's Golden Syrup, HP Sauce, salad dressing, a half-pound of butter, cheese, half a dozen eggs, Bird's Custard Powder, a packet of Rinso, a bar of Sunlight, custard creams, rashers and so on.

When I asked for a pound of butter, the shop assistant, who was wearing a white apron, sliced a chunk off a large mound of butter on a marble slab, judged its weight by eye, placed it on a sheet of greaseproof paper and then patted it into a rectangular shape using two wooden butter paddles with ridged surfaces. Tea, sugar and flour were all dispensed from open sacks with a silvery scoop, weighed on brass scales and the contents poured into brown paper bags. They were then bounced gently on the counter to settle before being placed on the scales. Rashers were sliced off a side of bacon, which was set at the required thickness. The shelves were stocked with jars of pickle and jams and boxes of biscuits and cereals. The Jacob's biscuit tins were enticing as they had a see-through glass top. My favourites were the springy marshmallow-and-jam biscuits with fluffy coconut pieces sprinkled on top. Cheese was sliced with a wire. The choice of cheese was very limited since food production was almost entirely for the domestic market. I remember Calvita cheese from Mitchelstown Coop and the small cheese triangles from Dairylea, designed so that you had to stick your fingers into the corner of the foil wrapper to extract the cheese. Hygiene was not the highest of priorities. Following an order of rashers, the bacon slicer would seldom be wiped before serving the next customer.

The method of payment in Findlater's was the time-consuming pre-1914 Lamson cash railway system, an ingenious network of wires running overhead, like an aerial train set, which was hypnotic for a ten-year-old boy. The shop assistant wrote an invoice, took the money and placed both in a cylinder, pulled a lever and the cash was whisked away above my head zooming along the wires to the central cash station high above the floor. An employee opened them, checked the order and the money, put the change and receipt back in the cylinder and then sent it flying back down the wire to the station (there were two for each counter). One wonders why Findlater's did not trust individual shop assistants to handle the money. Shopping was a slow and painstaking process; Findlater's were late in turning to self-service and were one of many Protestant-owned businesses that dwindled during the 20th century. The individual service provided by the company's shops and the large number of staff employed could not compete on price with the new self-service supermarkets, which had started to sprout on Irish high streets from 1959. Nowhere was immune to the onward march of the supermarkets and new patterns of consumer behaviour. All of Findlater's shops closed by 1969, and the once-renowned business survives to this day only as a wine and spirit merchants.

After leaving Findlater's on my shopping trip, I often popped into Gemma's newsagents next door to purchase ice cream and sweets. The shop was owned by Mr.Gemma – I never knew his real name – a kind, grey-haired man who treated everyone alike even if you were only spending a penny on a toffee bar. The standard (small) sized twopenny ice cream consisted of a thin portion of ice cream cut from a block and sandwiched between two wafers; a fourpenny one was much more enjoyable, while the sixpenny version was too large since I found it impossible to lick it all the way around fast enough before it melted and dripped onto the pavement. This was my first lesson in the concept of optimality. Gemma's was also stocked with a range of delicious confectionery: penny toffee bars, packs of sweet cigarettes with red tips on them, Rowntree's fruit gums and fruit pastilles, Cleeve's toffee, black-and-white bull's eyes, lollipops, bars of Urney's chocolate and dolly mixtures. Behind the counter, the shelves along the wall were packed with huge jars of sweets that you purchased by weight, normally two ounces at a time. There were dozens of different types of sweets: pear drops, everlasting gobstoppers, aniseed balls, jelly babies, liquorice, marshmallows and many more. All of these were eaten without any concern for our teeth. Gemma's kept the gobstoppers in a large glass jar and I was allowed to dip my (dirty) fingers inside to choose the colour I preferred. Shops had assistants who measured out, weighed and bagged the sweets. My favourite sweet was sherbet, a sweet fizzing powder that came in the form of a sherbet dab. This was a paper packet of sherbet with a mini-lollipop sticking out of the corner. Once the lollipop was licked, it was dabbed back in the sherbet and when the dab was sucked it fizzed and dissolved on the tongue.

A visit to Dunne's butchers was very different. I stood on a carpet of thick sawdust and contemplated the large bloody carcasses hooked onto chains hanging down from the ceiling. The butcher always threw a piece of spare meat (free) into my mother's order to feed our cocker spaniel, Widgie, as there were no special dog foods available in the early 1950s. Smaller shopkeepers added the money up in their heads or on the back of a paper bag, summing totals like 18/11, 10/6 and 3/7, often with the complexity of halfpennies and farthings thrown in. Some of today's shop assistants panic if they try to add £2-36 and £4-65 together using a calculating machine. Dalkey was humming with activity during the day, but everything (except the pubs) closed after five o'clock, or one o'clock on Saturday and the Wednesday half-day. The shutters went up and everyone went home. Cafes and restaurants were extremely scarce and also closed at five o'clock. I cannot recall ever being in a restaurant before I was a teenager in the mid-fifties. Shops and supermarkets did not sell alcohol in the 1950s and there were no wine shops or off-licences. However, we always had alcohol at home since my father brought home bottles of Guinness Export stout and Harp lager.

Every month I cycled to Fitzgerald's barber's shop on Railway Road, Dalkey for a haircut. Mr Fitzgerald was a stocky man with a bright red face, who emitted a constant flow of conversation both with the client in the chair and those who were waiting. Hairdressers were segregated by gender in the 1950s so Fitzgerald's barber's was a select male enclave. There was an untidy collection of well-thumbed film magazines, in which one would see glamorous photos of Marilyn Monroe or Grace Kelly, several comics – The Beano and the Dandy – a daily newspaper and the Racing Post. Each customer took a painfully long time; it was not that Mr Fitzgerald was slow at the cutting, rather it was because he became involved – in classic Irish style- in several different conversations simultaneously. Your acceptance into the elite membership of this male fraternity was based on your knowledge of horses and dogs. There were long pauses between cutting the hair or shaving a customer while Fitzgerald discussed the Racing Post tips for the day's race meetings at Leopardstown, the Curragh, or Kempton Park. National politics, football and rugby would occasionally be debated, but the focus would swiftly be switched back to racing odds and the finer skills of the leading Irish jockeys. Even if a schoolboy requested an Elvis Presley haircut, Fitzgerald would not deviate from his standard 'short back and sides.' When I strolled down Castle Street in Dalkey in October 2019, I noticed an Italian Organic hairdresser, as different from Fitzgerald's in the 1950s as it is possible to imagine. I poked my head inside: the walls were lined with glass jars of clays and oils; the salon was lit by scented candles and packed with fresh flowers, herbs and spices; soft music was playing; and the proprietors were using organic deodorants, cleansing and beauty products. There was also a table of spices, flowers, fruit and herbs, chosen for each client to suit their individual needs. There were no copies of the *Racing Post*.

Ma Reilly's paper shop exemplified the vast difference between the Dalkey of the fifties and that of today. Picture a tiny woman wearing boots, a torn cardigan and hairnet, with filthy hands in which you could germinate seeds. Ma Reilly never returned unsold papers so, gradually, they filled the shop. The papers rose in huge towers up to the ceiling so there was no longer a counter or a shop, only a space at the front where Ma Reilly stood while her customers queued outside in front of the window, which was filled with rusty toys and dead insects. As Hugh Leonard recorded, by squinting through the dirty glass in the early morning you would see Ma Reilly's head appear as she climbed a ladder and went sliding down the bales of papers into the only space; in the evenings she stepped into the street, locked the door and took the door knob with her.[2] When I walk down the main street of Dalkey today I experience difficulty in recognising that my childhood had been here somewhere amongst the new wine bars, numerous exclusive restaurants, Italian hairdressers and boutiques; the only shop fronts I recognise are Hick's pork butchers and Maxwell's the chemist. Only those of us who remember practising writing using a steel–nibbed pen and inkwell, travelling on the Dalkey tram or hearing Mantovani's strings playing his 1951 hit 'Charmaine' would think there was anything unusual about Dalkey's main street today.

* * *

My mother despatched me to Dun Laoghaire by bike for messages twice a month. I loved going to Dun Laoghaire. It is an elegant town of Regency and Victorian terraces and squares which developed after Ireland's first railway from Dublin to Kingstown (Dun Laoghaire) was opened in 1834, establishing the town as a key suburb of Dublin. By the 1950s, this splendid architectural heritage displayed a faded grandeur, although it remained a town of genteel respectability. Dun Laoghaire is dominated by its magnificent granite harbour, constructed as a consequence of a maritime tragedy in November 1807 when during a fierce storm as two vessels were driven onto the rocks west of Dun Laoghaire with the loss of almost 400 lives. Having secured access to a plentiful supply of granite on Dalkey Hill with which to construct the harbour, John Rennie, the great Scottish engineer, was commissioned to design it. Originally it was intended to build only one pier (the East Pier, 3,500 feet long) but Rennie insisted that this would result in sand drifting behind it and that a second pier (the West Pier at 4,950 feet) would prevent this from occurring. A railway was constructed linking the Dalkey quarries to Dun Laoghaire harbour and up to 300 horse-drawn wagons of granite were transported the two miles from the quarries to the harbour each day. The route survives as a cycleway and footpath between Dun Laoghaire and Dalkey, known as The Metals. A monument on the Dun Laoghaire seafront commemorates both 'the first stone of the eastern pier laid by his Excellency Earl Whitworth, Lord Lieutenant of Ireland on 31 May 1817,' and the visit of George IV in 1821. Thackeray – on seeing the monument – commented that: 'on my arrival in Kingstown I was confronted by a hideous erection comprising a crown atop four fat balls. Apparently it's dedicated to George IV. And seems eminently appropriate to that monarch.' On departure from the new harbour, George IV designated it as the 'Royal Harbour of King George IV' and he also renamed Dunleary as 'Kingstown.' This name survived for a century until it was changed to Dun Laoghaire in 1922.

After Irish independence a somewhat neglectful, if not scornful, attitude was adopted towards the buildings and monuments of the Regency and Victorian periods. There was also a view amongst some narrow-minded politicians that no special effort should be made to preserve the architecture of the British colonial era. The speculators moved in to buy properties for new office development in Dublin and councillors and planners largely ignored the representations of the Irish Georgian Society. The most notorious example dates from 1964 when 16 Georgian houses on Fitzwilliam Street – part of the world's longest continuous row of Georgian houses – were demolished to create an office block for the Electricity Supply Board. Dun Laoghaire boasted a lovely wrought- iron fountain erected on the seafront to commemorate the visit of Queen Victoria in 1900. It was badly vandalised in

1981 but was beautifully restored in 2001. Similarly, the People's Park, which was constructed on the site of an old quarry and opened in 1890, features splendid examples of Victorian architecture with a Pavilion, Gate Lodge, two fountains, wrought-iron railings and a bandstand boasting the original gaslight standards. The park has been tastefully restored.

When I shopped for my mother in Dun Laoghaire, I cycled past the entrance gate of the People's Park and westwards to the main shops which were located on George Street – a narrow, straight thoroughfare built by the British apparently to link up their Martello towers' defence system. Dun Laoghaire afforded opportunities to explore a wider range of shops than in Dalkey, of which Woolworth's was a favoured destination. Woolworth's had wooden parquet-floored aisles and mahogany counters with glass dividers where you could purchase both discounted biscuits and broken Fry's chocolate creams. The branch in Dun Laoghaire opened in 1920 and traded until 1984 when it was replaced by a Marks and Spencer's food store. McCullough's drapery shop was boring for a young boy, but I do recall woollen sweaters, nylon blouses and a meagre selection of depressing clothing. Soft Irish tweeds, and hand-knitted sweaters had yet to appear on Irish shopping streets. My favourite shop in Dun Laoghaire was Grace's toy shop where I regularly scanned the window in the hope of adding to my burgeoning collection of Dinky model Formula 1 racing cars with exotic names such as Maserati, Ferrari, Mercedes Benz, and Alfa Romeo. Having spotted a favoured Dinky racing car and entered the shop, Mr Grace placed my chosen purchase in its yellow box on the glass-topped counter, I paid him and cycled home in a state of pure joy. Years later, sadly without consultation, my mother threw out my collection of Dinky racing cars all in the original boxes; she was not to know that they now fetch hundreds of pounds at auction. Edward Lee's furniture store has now been replaced by a Dunne's Stores and a McDonald's; while on the opposite side of George Street, the Dun Laoghaire Shopping Centre, built in 1977, is an aesthetically unappealing development, especially when compared with the fine Victorian and red brick buildings that were demolished in order to construct it. Occasionally we visited Fuller's tea shop on Marine Road where the spiral staircase led to a seating area with a view of the sea. There were white tablecloths on the tables with napkins and white china, while the menu was encased in a leatherette cover. We were served by waitresses in white hats and aprons carrying silver-plated teapots, buttered scones, eclairs, apple tarts, sponge cakes. If it was a birthday, Mum might buy us a knickerbocker glory, a tall glass full of raspberry jelly, strawberries, tinned peach, meringue and ice creams – all eaten with a long spoon. Other people were eating a high tea of fried eggs, rashers, chips, tea and bread in the middle of the afternoon. Later, in 1959, my mother took me to Montague Burton's shop on the corner of Upper George Street and Mulgrave Street in order to buy me a jacket before I commenced my degree course at Trinity College Dublin. There were mosaic tiles with the company's logo in the doorway, and inside there were parquet–floors smelling of polish. Numerous dapper salesmen with tape measures slung around their necks glided up to customers seeking to help. Burton's in Dun Laoghaire has long gone as their business model failed to keep abreast of changing patterns of retailing.

We often walked from home to the East Pier of Dun Laoghaire harbour where Bernard Shaw, Oscar Wilde, James Joyce, Samuel Beckett and Bram Stoker had all strolled and, like countless others, subsequently emigrated from. As the aroma from the sea drifted on the air, we ambled by the handsome Victorian bandstand, returning past the swimming baths on the seafront to Teddy's café for an ice cream. Something of the previous elegance may still be seen in the large, handsome slightly decayed old terraces facing the sea. The post boxes still have the royal initials 'VR' or 'GR' faintly visible under thick layers of green paint. Popping into Murray's record shop was a regular delight after we obtained a portable record player in 1954 with three speeds 78rpm, 45 rpm and 33rpm. The record player had a device for stacking up the records so that they let themselves down one by one, to produce a stream of continuous music. It was in Murray's shop that I purchased my first record, a 45EP of operatic arias sung by the incomparable Jussi Bjorling. Pop record singles were still '78s' and cost six-and-sixpence (approximately 32 pence today). Invariably I left my bike unchained outside any shop or the dentist or at Bulloch harbour and never worried that it might be stolen.

From the age of eight onwards, my two sisters and I were permitted to take the number 8 bus to Ballsbridge where we changed to the number 18 and travelled to Rathgar Avenue to visit our grandmother. Alternatively, we caught the train from Glenageary station to Sandymount before completing the journey on the 18 bus. There was a machine at the station where I could print my name onto a metal strip using an alphabet pointer and a handle to print the letters. The train was my initiation into the concept of social class as the carriages were separated into First and Third Class compartments; the First Class passengers had more comfortable seating, but both were heated by steam radiators. The concept of a Second Class seems to have bypassed CIE. The CIE trains in the early 1950s consisted of closed compartments with two upholstered bench seats facing each other with a door on either side and photos of attractive holiday destinations such as Killarney, Bundoran and Tramore on the walls. We each attempted to be the first to call out the names of stations – Sandycove, Dun Laoghaire, Seapoint, Blackrock, Booterstown, Sydney Parade, and Sandymount where we alighted and changed to the number 18 bus.

My Scottish maternal grandmother lived in a large detached Victorian villa in Rathgar. The drawing- room was furnished and decorated in the Victorian style with heavy curtains, curio cabinets and numerous photographs, while the dining room sideboard contained trifle glasses with pink stems, cake knives, EPNS salad spoons, a cheese slice, biscuit tins and magazines. Granny Flynn had been born Elizabeth Gordon in Stornoway on the island of Lewis before her father was appointed to manage an estate in County Wicklow. Her husband was deceased by the 1950s. We always enjoyed visiting her as she was less of a disciplinarian than our parents and always had different varieties of sweets available in large quantities, which she obtained from her son, Ted, a stalwart of Palmerston rugby club, who worked for Williams and Woods, confectionary manufacturers and wholesalers. These sweet treasures included Rolos, Kit Kat, Smarties, Aero bars or Fry's cream chocolate. Furthermore, she gave us film magazines, of which our parents disapproved, and allowed us to roam freely in her large garden to collect apples and plums. The house was later sold, demolished and replaced by 14 properties.

We grew up unwittingly practising a green lifestyle in the 1950s. We never drank from plastic bottles; and lemonade bottles were returned to the shop to be reused and to claim the threepence deposit. Bullseye sweets were decanted from a jar and wrapped in a cone of paper. Sugar was sold loose; butter and cheese were cut from a slab and wrapped in greaseproof paper. Milk was delivered in bottles and recycled back on the doorstep when empty. I remember the horse-drawn flat carts of the rag-and-bone man, who was elderly with a dirty flat cap and even looked like a bundle of rags. He would let out a loud cry which I could not understand and did not seem to mean anything. However, when I was roller-skating, he allowed me to hang on to the back of his cart and be towed until he reached the end of the road. Pig swill – the slops of food and drink comprising vegetable peelings and uneaten food – was also collected in malodorous barrels balanced on a cart by the 'pig man.' When any cart appeared on the road, my mother would dash out of the house with a shovel to pick up the manure deposited by numerous horses in order to fertilise her roses; this was a job that I studiously avoided, if possible. One task that nobody carried out in the 1950s was to scoop up faeces left by their dogs, including our cocker spaniels. We regularly trampled on dog turds on the pavement and brought them back home. We walked to church, took a bus home from school, and only had a bath once per week. Thrift was a way of life. Given that there was only a two year age gap between Sheila and Judy, my mother frequently altered Sheila's clothes for her sister: sleeves, hems, waistband and buttons were moved before a garment was ultimately discarded. My mother and I always cycled to Dalkey and Dun Laoghaire for 'the messages.' It is not easy to envisage people today adopting these practices by choice in order to reduce their carbon footprint.

* * *

Popular music in the early 1950s was still dominated by ballroom dance numbers, big-band swing and romantic crooners. The concept of a hit parade, which had existed in the USA since the 1930s, did not reach the UK until the early 1950s and Ireland even later. The first British number 1 on 14 November 1952 was 'Here in my Heart' sung by Italian–American crooner, Al Martino. The remainder of the top five were Jo Stafford, Nat King Cole, Bing Crosby and Guy Mitchell. Nat King Cole was not only a beautiful crooner, but also a superb jazz pianist. Throughout 1952-53 the chart was totally dominated by crooners singing ballads. Of these Sinatra and Nat King Cole were supreme, closely followed by Dean Martin, Tony Bennett and Perry Como. America also boasted incomparable female vocalists, including Ella Fitzgerald, Sarah Vaughan and Dinah Washington. They sang ballads, often backed by lavish string orchestras such as that of Nelson Riddle. British popular music was but a pale imitation of the American scene. Dance bands such as the Ted Heath Orchestra were modelled on the Glenn Miller and Tommy Dorsey bands and most singers copied Sinatra (unsuccessfully). The British crooners David Whitfield, Dickie Valentine, Ronnie Hilton and Frankie Vaughan could not emulate the vocal technique, musicality and relaxed delivery of their American rivals, at least not until Matt Monro – the former bus driver with the smooth baritone voice – became Britain's greatest crooner.

The radio was the background of family life in the fifties, something that we all shared. The wireless in its wooden case with glowing valves was, together with the coal fire, the central focus of the living room in the 1950s as the RTE television service was not launched until December 1961. The valve sets took some time to warm up before the sound flooded the room; it was exciting to jump between the light and medium wave and to hear foreign languages penetrate the background interference. The BBC sound waves crossed the Irish Sea and permeated our homes with imperfect reception. It was a period of radio dominance and, living in Dalkey, it was possible to listen to all three BBC radio stations. The Home Service was middlebrow, offering a diet of news, plays and lectures; the Light Programme – rebranded as Radio 2 in 1967 – supplied a diet of light music, comedy and soap operas; and the Third Programme was fundamentally elitist, specialising in classical music and lectures. Of the three networks, the Light Programme attracted about two-thirds of listeners, whereas the Third Programme accounted for only one per cent of the radio audience in 1946.[3]

The BBC in the 1950s was a highly paternalistic organisation with a strict moral code. In 1951, for example, it ordained that news bulletins on national radio were henceforth to be read only by men, and, moreover, men with 'consistent pronunciation,' in other words devoid of a regional accent. The official explanation for the gender discrimination was that 'a large number of people do not like the news of momentous or serious events to be read by the female voice.' Radio Three was launched as the Third Programme in 1946 and has been instrumental in sustaining a crop of outstanding symphony orchestras and the classical record industry. It is now my favourite radio station, but my taste in radio in 1950 was no more refined than *Dick Barton Special Agent* on the Light Programme. This was a serial with a tense climax at the end of each 15 minute episode followed by the unforgettable signature tune, 'The Devil's Gallop.' The programme also reflected the British class system: Dick was somewhat urbane and well spoken, while his two sidekicks, Jock and Snowy, were Scottish and Cockney, with appropriate matching accents. Later, when I attended film shows on Saturday nights in the St Andrew's College assembly hall, Dick Barton featured each week and was often more exciting than the main feature. I was also an avid listener to the BBC schools' broadcasts which aired on the Home Service on weekdays between 2.00pm and 3.00pm and for which I regularly ordered the booklets that accompanied the programmes.

BBC radio offered a wide range of quality programmes in the 1950s, of which *The Goon Show* was peerless. It was launched originally as *Crazy People* on 21st May, 1951; the BBC commissioned a second series in 1952 and *The Goon Show* was born. The show regularly commanded almost two million listeners and ran until 1960. The Goons – Spike Milligan, Harry Secombe, Peter Sellers and Michael Bentine (who left in 1953) – met during the war and fashioned an anarchic and surreal style of humour. They mercilessly ridiculed the British establishment, the officer class and the Commonwealth with brilliant parodies complete with funny voices and accents. Spike Milligan, a comic genius and son of an Irish father serving in the British Indian army, was the major writer of the show's zany scripts. There was no formula to what Spike wrote: each episode exploded from the radio and went anywhere. Milligan, with his extraordinary imagination, had to write an episode of the *Goons* every week; and he is now recognised as the godfather of alternative comedy. Celebrating the 40th anniversary of the first *Goon Show,* David Gelly declared that: 'There is a case for claiming that the fifties actually began in May 1951 with the opening of the Festival of Britain and the start of the *Goon Show*...which set about reducing to rubble the redundant edifice of British Imperial smugness.'[4] The argument that the fifties began in Ireland in May 1951 is more difficult to sustain; I prefer to date it from 1956 with the impacts both of the film *Rock around the Clock* and Elvis Presley's releases 'Heartbreak Hotel' and 'Hound Dog.'

My passion for the Goons was not embraced, however, by my two sisters and parents, who thought it was silly. I was captivated from the start and the Goons became an addiction that involved attempting to master the nonsense songs, silly voices and catchphrases such as Bluebottle's 'You rotten swine, you deaded me;' Spike's simpleton character Eccles 'Hello der, I'm the famous Eccles;' the aristocratic cad Hercules Grytpype-Thynne' 'You silly twisted boy you;' Major Dennis Bloodnok 'Damn those curried eggs;' and the heroic idiot Ned Seagoon's 'Needle–nardle–noo' used to punctuate his lines. Milligan regularly debunked sacrosanct British institutions such as the Army, the Church and the Foreign Office with 'jibes embedded in the madness' in Philip Norman's apt words 'like hooks in blubber.'[5] The Goons were still in vogue during my undergraduate days at Trinity College Dublin (the last series was 1959-60) when we sat around in tweed jackets and corduroy trousers quaffing our staple diet of Guinness and enjoyed reproducing their voices, names and catchphrases. I was not talented at mimicry, but was able to memorise the catchphrases at the time. The Goons had a greater influence than any other radio programme on later generations of comedy writers and performers, such as *Beyond the Fringe* and *Monty Python's Flying Circus*.

A new comedy show, *Hancock's Half Hour*, made its debut on the BBC Light Programme in 1954 starring Tony Hancock, Sid James and Kenneth Williams. This was to become a cult programme mirroring many of the prevailing aspirations and frustrations, above all sexual and social. Hancock's character was a middle-aged bachelor frustrated by the gap between his aspirations and grim reality; there were no jokes and Ray Galton and Alan Simpson (the scriptwriters) relied on caricature, realistic story lines and situation humour. Hancock reached his apotheosis on TV with the 'Blood Donor' episode transmitted in June 1961 in which Hancock, with his usual mixture of bravado and absurdity, decided that it was a matter of 'becoming a blood donor or join the Young Conservatives.'[6] When he is told that he must donate a pint he responds 'but a pint, that's nearly an armful.' Hancock subsequently broke with scriptwriters Galton and Simpson and spiralled downwards into alcoholism and an early death. There were other BBC comedy programmes such as *The Navy Lark* and *Educating Archie* (at 1.45pm on Sundays), but neither of these shows appealed to me. Conversely, *Beyond our Ken* and its successor *Round the Horne,* featured for the first time a camp pair – Julian and Sandy – played by Kenneth Williams and Hugh Paddick – engaging in incessant innuendo. It built an audience of 15 million people for its brand of parody and satire starring the sophisticated Kenneth Horne and the versatile Kenneth Williams.

* * *

My parents were not religious: my mother seldom ever went to a church service and my father never did. They did insist, however, that certain Protestant Sabbath traditions be maintained, notably by not hanging out washing or lighting a bonfire on a Sunday and not allowing us to play out on the road. They also prevented me from playing sport. The ban they imposed regarding Sunday sport was somewhat selective: it was not permissible to attend a rugby or football match or to play rugby or cricket; but it was acceptable to play golf or participate in yacht racing in Dun Laoghaire. Meanwhile, Catholics – once they had attended Mass – were free to play any sport and to attend the cinema or dances on a Sunday night, activities that were totally eschewed by the

Protestant community. However, we children were required to attend Sunday School at St Patrick's church, Dalkey every Sunday morning. It was then that I realised that being a Protestant was different from being a Catholic. St Patrick's was low church Anglican so that anything such as incense or genuflecting to the alter was regarded with deep suspicion. I was moved, however, by the beauty of the liturgy. Sunday school, held in the parochial hall, was not a transformational experience from a religious perspective. A total of around 60 children were split up into groups of eight, each with its own circle of chairs, stratified by both age and gender. Sadly, girls of the same age were in a different group. Through this process, we learned the discipline of sitting still for an hour while a noble adult volunteer told us boring stories, and we were also expected to have completed a piece of homework from the previous Sunday, usually memorising passages of prayers or psalms. We were taught about good, emanating from God, and evil, the work of the Devil. We were told Bible stories, sang hymns – such as 'All Things Bright and Beautiful'- and learned how to pray. On one occasion I recall asking the teacher 'How can you prove that the Bible story is true?' He mumbled about the accuracy of the scriptures and centuries of Christian scholarship. I was not convinced. Apart from the opportunity to take home a picture with coloured biblical illustrations on them to stick in a book, Sunday School was totally uneventful. However, I did imbibe two principles at Sunday School: to always tell the truth; and to be honest in all my dealings.

Sunday School was complemented by Children's Service every Sunday afternoon when we walked back to the church again. Eventually the Children's Service morphed into confirmation classes leading on to the ceremony when I was 15. I remember nothing of the weekly confirmation classes in terms of what Rev. Des Murray discussed. I admired the conviction of his belief without completely accepting it. Doubts had set in concerning the virgin birth, the resurrection and miracles. God had not called me. The attraction of confirmation classes was also the prospect of meeting and hopefully engaging with the girls who also attended; it was not only the confirmation that I wanted at 15 but also a girlfriend. There was an attractive girl, Heather, who wore a bobble hat and I resolved regularly to approach her after church, but I wilted every time because of shyness and fear of rejection. Hence, I continued only daydreaming that I would walk along Dun Laoghaire pier with her hand-in-hand. At 15, I longed for a girlfriend, but achieved absolutely nothing. Real girlfriends did not materialise on a regular basis until I was 17.

After confirmation, I was qualified to attend Communion services at 8.00am on Sunday mornings. Having received Communion, I tried to feel different and to achieve a better understanding of God, but it proved to be an illusion. However, I picked up the hymns, psalms, the Magnificat, the *Nunc Dimittis* and the Creed, chanting the words derived from the 1662 version of the Book of Common Prayer from memory: 'Lord, now lettest thou thy servant depart in peace according to thy word; For mine eyes have seen thy salvation.' I have always enjoyed the Anglican liturgy and the quality of choral church music, especially from the Renaissance period. For a while I accepted it to be true, but there was a growing uneasy feeling of serious doubt within me about the truth of the Bible story. I still enjoy visiting churches and, even though I do not believe the dogma, there is an air of peace and a sense of tranquil spirituality that cannot be experienced elsewhere.

Having attended Sunday school at St Patrick's church, Dalkey, we returned home to the smell of roast beef, gravy and potatoes and two veg wafting from the kitchen to be followed usually by rhubarb crumble and custard. The meal was accompanied by two-way *Family Favourites* on the BBC Light Programme, in conjunction with the British Forces Broadcasting Service in Germany. Introduced by its theme tune – 'With a Song in my Heart'- it was broadcast from noon till 1.15pm and featured the avuncular Cliff Michelmore and the warm tones of Jean Metcalfe. She presented the London end of the show while Michelmore provided the Hamburg link. They did not meet face-to-face for six months, but after meeting they were quickly married, which Michelmore described as a case of 'love at first hearing.' The attraction for me was that it was one of the few BBC programmes in the 1950s that was devoted solely to playing records and occasionally a quality classical recording would be played, such as Kathleen Ferrier singing 'What is Life to me without thee' from Gluck's *Orfeo*. Her voice was mellow and thrilling, even though the range was limited, all made more poignant by her early death.

Following *Family Favourites* at 1.15pm was a favourite programme of my father's, the ghastly but popular *Billy Cotton Band Show* with Cotton's characteristic introduction, 'Wakey Waakkeey' followed by popular music, frequent banter with his resident vocalist, Alan Breeze, singing (and frequently mangling) the hits of the day. Alma Cogan and Lita Rosa became famous by appearing on this programme. Cogan's hits included excruciating songs such as 'Twenty Tiny Fingers' and 'Never Do a Tango with an Eskimo.' Rosa became the first British woman to have a number-one hit in April 1953 with the novelty ballad 'How much is that Doggy in the Window?' Later my parents also listened to *Sing Something Simple* with the Cliff Adams Singers accompanied by Jack Emblow on accordion, which was broadcast on Sunday nights and survived until 2001 when it became the longest-running continuous music programme in the world. *Your Hundred Best Tunes*, another favourite of my parents, was presented by Alan Keith for 43 years; the programme playlist stuck rigidly (and repetitively) to a limited light classical diet, mirrored nowadays by Classic FM. Since the BBC restricted the airtime devoted to records, I turned to Radio Luxembourg, which was the principal way to access rock 'n' roll music – made all the more exciting by listening to it in bed, although the sound tended to fade in and out against a crackling background. I relished the freedom to choose my preferences and to listen for as long as I wished.

Radio Eireannn had the impossible task of trying to satisfy all tastes on a single channel with limited resources and broadcasting hours. This resulted in a conservative broadcasting policy and most Irish listeners along the east coast and border counties also had the option of listening to BBC radio programmes. Radio Eireann opened each weekday morning at 8.00am with news and weather, followed by closedown at 10.00am after just two hours on air. All the morning and lunchtime programmes were sponsored and ran for 15 minutes, interspersed with news bulletins at 9.00am and 1.30pm. There was a twice- weekly soap opera – '*The Kennedy's of Castlerosse*' (sponsored by Fry Cadbury's chocolate) – broadcast at lunchtime on Radio Eireann. Other programmes were sponsored by Donnelly's 'skinless sausages – never burst or break in the pan;' the Imco Dry cleaners with their jingle 'a cleaning and a pressing and a dying for you;' and Walton's Irish music shop sponsored 15 minutes of 'songs our fathers loved' with the jingle 'if you sing a song, sing an Irish song.' Programmes were sober and middlebrow; pop music was marginalised and, instead of playing the original recording, they frequently substituted an (inferior) cover by an Irish showband. More controversially, the Angelus bell was broadcast twice daily at 12 noon and 6.00pm, having been instigated at the behest Dr John Charles McQuaid, Archbishop of Dublin, on 15 August 1950, the Feast of the Assumption. Despite the numerous abuse cases exposed within the Catholic Church and its institutions, the Angelus is still broadcast on Telefis Eireann at 6.00pm, although it infringes the separation of church and state. It is not difficult to imagine what a DUP voter in Northern Ireland thinks of this practice, in effect a state-sponsored advertisement for the Catholic Church. It's a notable anachronism since Ireland has become a proud secular state.

Amidst all the commercial hype on Radio Eireann, I did hear one Irish singer of sublime artistry: John McCormack. His recordings of Irish ballads, which he sang at the end of his classical recitals, were played regularly on Radio Eireann, but it was to be some years later that I discovered that McCormack was a truly great operatic tenor of the *bel canto* school. He made some of the seminal recordings of all time, most notably 'Il mio tesero' from Mozart's *Don Giovanni*, 'O Sleep, why dost thou leave me' from Handel's *Semele*, and 'Come Beloved' from Handel's *Atalanta*. These recordings, made around 100 years ago, are characterised by effortless long unfaltering lines, perfect diction and phrasing, precision, astonishing breath control and a ringing top register that is beyond compare, more musical than Caruso and Pavarotti.

* * *

The 1950s was a period when being a Protestant in Ireland was often regarded by some other Protestants and many Catholics as being synonymous with being English. My parents were essentially political Protestants who identified both with Ireland and Britain; indeed their British orientation – they had been born in Dublin a decade before Irish independence – was occasionally a source of disagreement with me as I was an Irish nationalist who felt no sense of Britishness, in contrast to my younger brother, Brian, who later served as an officer in the Irish Guards in the 1970s. It was also quite common for Protestants to be classified as Anglo-Irish. This is sloppy thinking as we were almost as different from the true Anglo-Irish aristocracy as we were from Catholics, sharing social class with one and religious denomination with the other. When Brendan Behan defined the Anglo-Irish as a 'Protestant with a horse,' it is clear that he recognised correctly that most Protestants like us were middle-class without horses.[7] Unlike the Anglo-Irish, we had no English relatives, did not go to school in England, had different accents, and did not pursue the fox on horseback, although my father was keen on shooting and fishing. My father did bring home two right-wing British magazines – *The Illustrated London News* and *The Sphere* – to read every week; and my mother read English magazines like *Woman's Own*, partly because there was no Irish equivalent. Like many Protestants, the establishment of the Irish Free State in 1922 left them politically and psychologically unprepared for life in the new state. Protestants went from comprising one-quarter of the population of the island to only 7.4 percent of the population of the Free State in 1926. Moreover, almost 192 houses of the gentry were burned down between December 1921 and March 1923, although Terence Brown argues that many of the houses were burned by republicans who considered, probably accurately, that their occupants were supporters of the Treaty party.[8] Protestants continued to constitute most of the upper and upper-middle classes, who no longer exercised any political power.

In order to reach the shops in Dalkey, it was necessary to walk through a council estate – St Begnet's Villas – where the author and playwright, Hugh Leonard, had been raised. The people who lived in the council houses, who cycled to work on bicycles and spoke with a stronger accent, were perceived by my parents as being 'common' and from a different social class. This accounted for the proliferation of tattoos, fake leopard-skin coats, dyed blonde hair and bull terriers roaming the streets. My parents expected us to behave differently than the children in the council houses, who 'screamed, were grubby and played rough games.' My impression was different: the children in the council scheme were energetic and the girls displayed well-practised expertise at hopscotch. Skipping was performed only by girls in time to a skipping rhyme with two ropes tied to a gate flying around in opposite directions. The turner persuaded the rope, with perfect timing, to slap the pavement in time to the skipping rhyme being chanted by the skippers. The skilled skippers could do a trick in one turn of the rope, such as jumping extra high with both feet together, kicking one foot out, or crossing and uncrossing feet and legs. Sometimes two girls would enter the whirling ropes simultaneously and would then pass out from the rope at the end opposite to where they entered. The next two girls would then repeat the action, and so on. These were skills that had never penetrated the social class barrier to the middle class and I was much impressed. Many could also juggle three balls in the air or against a wall while singing a rhyme. Conflict, if it arose, was not between social classes but internalised to each of them. In short, the concept of respectability, the conformity to accepted standards, trumped that of social class. The fact that the children of the council scheme were 100 percent Catholic was simply irrelevant to me. Most, if not all, of these children left school at 14 and it's likely that many 'mute inglorious Miltons here may rest.'

The Irish are not as obsessed with social class as the British, but the notion that Ireland does not have a class system is a myth. There was still a subtle social hierarchy. Class in Ireland was not simply a matter of money, although it was important, but also a range of other factors: birth, education, occupation, income, accent, friendships, cultural attitudes and values. Sport, for which Irish people exhibit a deep passion, was also important. Sports such as golf, tennis, rugby, cricket, hockey, football and sailing are as class-stratified as in Britain. It was widely acknowledged that there were subtle class differences between the memberships of the three yacht clubs in Dun Laoghaire. The Royal St George was the most exclusive in the 19th century with its members drawn from the aristocracy in Victorian Ireland. In the 1950s both the Royal St George and the Royal Irish had a significant proportion of Protestant members and upper-middle class Catholics who spoke with Protestant-like accents. I crewed for two members of the George, on Tom Sheppard's cruiser, '*Foresight*,' and also with Dave Thomas in his Firefly.

Dun Laoghaire holds a crucial place in the history of yacht racing. The Water Wag is the oldest one-design dinghy in the world, having been devised in 1886 and formalised as a one-design class in Ireland in 1887. This was the first time in yachting history that all the boats in a race were identical and that the winners would be the crew with the most skill. This concept of 'one-design' has become the norm worldwide and has been adopted for all Olympic sailing events.[9] The Water Wags are open–decked, 13-feet-long, clinker-built dinghies with a sloop rig and are constructed from larch or silver spruce. The class that gave 'fair' competition to the world of yacht racing is still raced in Dun Laoghaire to this day where the fleet, which numbers 40 boats, is thriving.

In the early fifties on the cul-de-sac where we lived (Hyde Park, Dalkey) one-third of the thirty households were occupied by Protestants, which was high even for a Dalkey private housing estate. There was no overt sectarianism. I played fairly often with my Catholic neighbours, John Doyle and John King, both of whom were far superior at carpentry and boat building than I was! Social contact with them became much less frequent from the age of twelve as I became more embedded into the networks formed by school, St Patrick's Church of Ireland church, the Sea Scouts, the tennis club and sailing. These organisations helped provide the building blocks of my formation. Maybe we would have been friends for life if it was not for the religious difference that culture imposed upon us. There was always polite conversation, neighbourliness and a degree of friendship with the Catholic families on Hyde Park, but the social lives of the two denominations were largely separate. A degree of segregation, accepted by most people without any sectarian hostility, became a normal social convention. This resulted in a somewhat inbred social network among Protestants, which was primarily a result of the Catholic Church's rigorous implementation of the *Ne Temere* decree. However, one latent bond that the two denominations shared was respectability. I am certain that our Catholic neighbours felt more socially comfortable interacting with the Protestants on Hyde Park than with their co-religionists in the council scheme in Dalkey.

* * *

The Ireland of the 1950s in which I grew up was dominated by de Valera and the ethos and rules of the Catholic Church. Politicians of all political parties, including Labour, were very deferential to the Catholic hierarchy and yielded to its authority in a wide range of health, educational, social and moral issues. The country manifested many characteristics of a theocratic state: the Catholic Church managed the state's primary schools and owned and staffed most secondary schools; it also controlled most hospitals and a wide network of mother and baby homes, industrial schools and other institutions. The Catholic Church intervened in the infamous case of the Mother and Child Scheme in 1951 and tarnished its reputation for years. The Mother and Child Scheme, introduced by Dr. Noel Browne, sought to provide a free health service for pregnant mothers and postnatal care for mothers and babies. The Irish Medical Council opposed scheme, but the Catholic Archbishop of Dublin, John Charles McQuaid, led the opposition against Browne's Bill. The Catholic Church insisted that its teachings on social matters should not be ignored and that the married couple must be counselled by the Church, which was rigidly opposed to any state or socialised medicine, although it did not question the establishment of the NHS in Northern Ireland. McQuaid told the government on 5 April 1951 that Browne's scheme was 'opposed to Catholic social teaching.'[10] At cabinet the next day the coalition government – led by John Costello – caved in instantly, withdrew the scheme and Browne was forced to resign, having lost the support of all his colleagues. As Fallon has argued, 'what was really reprehensible, not to say downright contemptible, was the behaviour of some of the Inter-party politicians involved, who virtually kow-towed to the bishops' 'whims.'[11] The *Irish Times* editorial of 12 April was contemptuous: 'The Roman Catholic Church would seem to be the effective government of this country....It seems that the merits of a theocratic Twenty-six Counties outweigh those of a normally democratic Thirty–two. Has the Government made its choice?'[12] The government paid for its pusillanimity in failing to support Browne in his battle with the Catholic hierarchy by losing office. Many Irish politicians saw themselves as Catholics first and legislators second; it is clear that the Catholic Church and the State were in close harmony, or as Sean O'Faolain wrote, 'The Dail proposes and Maynooth disposes.'

Priests and nuns were held in huge respect by the vast majority of people. A teacher who did not abide by the conservative Catholic line could be dismissed by the local parish priest. Even in the 1960s young 'fallen women' – prostitutes and unmarried mothers – were categorised as deeply sinful and, to avoid bringing shame on their families, they were despatched to Magdalen laundries run by Irish Catholic nuns. The inmates of these institutions often included orphans, disabled and abused girls, none of whom had been put on trial or committed a crime. A culture of fear was mirrored by the sometimes violent enforcement of a regime of heavy physical labour – ironing 100 shirts a day at the age of 15 – with no access to the outside world. Most cruelly of all, their babies were taken away from them when they were barely out of the womb to enable the religious order to sell them for adoption and thereby maintain the viability of the institution. The state colluded with Church agencies to send abroad, without the mother's consent, some of the children born to single mothers, a process regulated by Archbishop McQuaid in cooperation with the Department of External Affairs, which issued passports for the children. The mothers were hidden away for years in humiliating physical and psychological circumstances, or were sent away to Britain, which raises concerns about Irish society's responsibilities. Up to 30,000 young women are estimated to have been sent to such laundries (the last one did not close till 1996) for the alleged crime of being an unmarried mother, in some cases having suffered rape. Their sentences to these Church-run institutions were sometimes indefinite; many had nowhere to go due to abandonment and some stayed all their lives, ending in an unmarked grave. The Church had effectively deprived them of their human rights and incarcerated them beyond the reach of the law. The mothers did not receive an apology from the Irish government until 1996, but were still not permitted access to the files of such adoptions.

In parallel with the Magdalen laundries, the state established a second type of institution dedicated to the punishment and control of 'fallen women': mother and baby homes. The priority was to avoid mixing 'redeemable' sinners – sent to mother and baby homes – and 'unreformable' sinners – those with more than one illegitimate pregnancy – who were incarcerated in the Magdalen laundries.[13] A similar culture of fear, abuse, and high infant mortality rates characterised many mother and baby homes where babies would be given up for adoption, either legally or illegally. One of the most notorious institutions was the Bon Secours Mother and Baby Home which operated in Tuam, County Galway between 1925 and 1961. Unwed pregnant women were sent there to give birth. A local historian, Catherine Corless, estimated that almost 800 children had died there and were buried within a structure 'built within a large sewage tank.' Death rates were extraordinarily high: 34 per cent of children died in the Home in 1943 alone, almost all aged between 32 months and three years of age. The system was above the law since for approved clients documents could be faked to show the adoptive mother as the birth mother.

The Report of the Commission to Inquire into Child Abuse, published in 2009, revealed that thousands of children suffered widespread starvation, systematic physical and sexual abuse between the 1930s and 1970s in residential institutions funded by the state but run by Catholic religious orders. Other children were required to work long hours as cheap labour in industrial schools, orphanages, and reformatories run by orders of priests, while legal adoption was resisted on the grounds that it would threaten the religious welfare of children. The network of 52 industrial schools incarcerated almost 50,000 children. Both sexual and extreme physical abuse were endemic in the industrial schools – especially those run by the Christian Brothers. The culture of fear and child slavery within the largest industrial schools – Artane, Letterfrack and Daingean – was sustained by a climate of terror and violence. Ferriter concluded that 'there is no doubt that McQuaid and other bishops failed to protect children from paedophiles;'[14] and it is certain that the government, the police, the clergy and the religious all knew of the physical and sexual abuse but conspired to deny and hide it.[15] The Department of Education was severely criticised for its submissive attitude to religious orders and also for its failure to conduct thorough inspections. Some 102 priests from the Catholic Archdiocese of Dublin were accused of sexual abuse between 1940 and 2006; and by 2006 approximately 350 victims had been identified, with an additional 40 yet to be traced.[16] During the 1950s and 1960s I would frequently cycle past an orphanage or industrial school without having any awareness of the hardship and abuse being visited upon children within them.

The Report of the Commission of Investigation, Catholic Archdiocese of Dublin – chaired by Justice Yvonne Murphy – was published in 2009. It discovered that four successive archbishops of the Dublin archdiocese, including John Charles McQuaid, did not report their knowledge of child sex abuse to the police over a period of three decades. Senior members of the Irish police regarded the actions of priests as being beyond their remit, and some police reported complaints to the archdiocese instead of investigating them. It is inconceivable that the extent of the cruelty inflicted upon unmarried mothers and children was not known to the state authorities, although it was not publicly discussed until the 1990s. It appears that the state abandoned attempts to make these (state) institutions more accountable after the religious orders refused to cooperate. Indeed, Bertie Ahern, Taoiseach, ensured in 2002 that the religious orders who had run the industrial schools would be indemnified from the cost of claims by their victims. By 2015, the state had paid out 1.5 billion euros to settle claims and the religious orders a mere 192 million euros, i.e. the orders paid out a paltry 11 percent of the total.[17] There were also a number of Protestant-run orphanages where physical abuse of children occurred.[18] Ferriter has argued that 'Church and State frequently colluded to protect the lie that Ireland was a beacon of Catholic and sexual purity in an otherwise pagan world.'[19] This also led to a neglect of sex education, even when I was at school in the 1950s. Sean O'Faolain was 20 years old before he learned how childbirth happened, later arguing that pious elders 'sent us naked to the wolf of life…as if they believed that if nobody mentioned sex organs we would not notice that we had them.'[20]

Most of the conservative restrictions under which we lived as teenagers in the 1950s dated from the 1920s and 1930s. Legislation for film censorship was introduced in 1923 and for book censorship in 1929. Divorce was prohibited in 1925 and the importation and sale of contraceptives was outlawed in 1935. Both homosexuality and abortion were illegal. The Garda Siochana were consecrated to the Sacred Heart of Jesus in 1923 and then to the Blessed Virgin in 1930, while even as late as 1951 de Valera attended a ceremony in Dublin at which 'Our Lady, Queen of the Most Holy Rosary' was named as the patroness of the Irish army. This reflected a partitionist mindset that gave no thought to the impact on Protestant communities North and South and simply solidified the border more deeply. This very close church-state relationship reflected not just the power of the bishops but also unquestioning support among politicians and the public for what was effectively a theocracy. Culturally the clergy, as Fallon has argued, were mostly philistines who regarded modern thought, literature and art as predominantly pagan and subversive; and there was 'an overriding conformity and mediocrity.'[21] Most Protestants in the Republic did not speak out against the widespread integration of Catholic teaching into legislation.

* * *

I won a prize at the end of my first year at St Andrew's in 1950 and was presented with *Black Beauty* by Anna Sewell. It was the first novel that I read and it featured affection, loss and cruelty. Prior to 1950 I had read *Just William* stories and Robert Louis Stevenson. My favourite reading as a small boy of 12 was Conan Doyle's Sherlock Holmes stories. Most of the mysteries started in the large living room of the flat which Holmes shared with Dr Watson in Baker Street. The stories were just the correct length so that solving the crime never needed to be padded out by wandering down irrelevant cul-de-sacs. Conan Doyle's plots were also highly original; and my interest in Sherlock Holmes was greatly enhanced by a lengthy series of stories broadcast on the BBC Home Service and starring Carleton Hobbs as the great detective and Norman Shelley as Dr Watson. When I was off school with a heavy cold, my mother would rub Vick Vapour rub on my throat and chest and I would snuggle down in bed and listen spellbound to Carleton Hobbs's acidulated voice and avuncular style as he played Sherlock Holmes and unravelled the complexities of the latest case.

Books were the key to making sense of the world beyond Dalkey, as well as a means of transcending its realities. I frequented the Carnegie library in Dun Laoghaire – opened in 1912 – where the distinctive odour of stacked books was the background to literary discovery. Since then, I have used countless university libraries and the British Library, but I still have the smell of the Dun Laoghaire Carnegie in my memory bank; and the image of the wooden boxes stuffed with library cards and date stamps at the check-out desk. I read my way through R L Stevenson's *Treasure Island* and *Kidnapped*. I then enjoyed books such as *Tom Sawyer, Huckleberry Finn, The Count of Monte Cristo* and

The Man in the Iron Mask. When I was about 13 I moved on to reading *The Thirty Nine Steps* by John Buchan and classics, including *Wuthering Heights, Jane Eyre, Oliver Twist* and *A Christmas Carol.* I also enjoyed the adventure thrillers of Hammond Innes. I tended, as a teenager, to devour the books of a single author before moving on to literary pastures new. After Hammond Innes, the work of John Steinbeck captured my imagination in the late fifties and I was finally on the road to literary enlightenment, especially after reading *Of Mice and Men, Cannery Row* and his masterpiece, *The Grapes of Wrath.* The book was controversial in the USA where it was banned for two years because of Steinbeck's radical views, the negative portrayal of capitalism, and sympathy for the lot of agricultural workers. It made a deep impression on me as a sixteen- year- old.

Being raised in Ireland one was constantly aware that people from all social backgrounds had a passion for words, a love of language for its own sake – whether expressed in novels, poems, conversations in pubs, or on buses; and the realisation that this small island has produced a constant stream of world- class literature and still does. Flann O'Brien was a pseudonym for Brian O'Nolan, a civil servant, who by 1937 was the Private Secretary to the Minister of Local Government. O'Brien became one of the most talented figures in 20th century literature, including books such as *The Third Policeman, The Dalkey Archive* and *At- Swim- Two-Birds,* all masterpieces of comic invention, making the eccentric seem normal and the commonplace hilarious. I read the *Irish Times* from the age of 11 during the halcyon years of Myles na gCopaleen's column – 'Cruiskeen Lawn' ('A Full Jug'). Myles na gCopaleen was another pseudonym for Brian O'Nolan and his column, which was always printed on the leader page, was essentially humorous, but its obsession was language itself. This series of comic vignettes and satirical comments in the tradition of Swift were full of bravura displays of linguistic inventiveness and a manic imagination which no other writer could equal. The columns were written initially in Irish, but soon moved to English with smatterings of German, French or Latin. The targets of his satire included the Dublin literary elite, Irish language revivalists, the Irish government, and the 'Plain People of Ireland.' The column was also devoted to magnificently laborious literary puns, fanciful literary anecdotes, erudite study of clichés, scornful dissection of high-flown literary phraseology, and a general atmosphere of shameless irony.

There was also the recognition that the great Irish writers of the period frequently had their books banned by the censor; indeed it was almost a rite of passage, although it deprived many authors of a large share of their income. Almost every leading Irish fiction writer, except for James Joyce, had books banned between 1929 and the mid-1960s under the Censorship of Publications Act, 1929. The list included Sean O'Casey, Frank O'Connor, Sean O'Faolain, Liam O'Flaherty, Samuel Beckett, Benedict Kiely, Austin Clarke, Kate O'Brien, Bernard Shaw, Maura Laverty, Edna O'Brien (whose first five novels were banned), Brendan Behan, Brian Moore and John McGahern. Brendan Behan quipped that they were the 'best banned in the land,' as he joined the list in 1958 following the publication of *Borstal Boy*. They were marginalised in their country's cultural life and in many cases were also denied a living in Ireland.

A new Censorship of Publications Board in the post-war period continued banning almost wholesale many serious authors. The record for books banned in any one year was established at 1,034 in 1954, indicating that the reformed Board was dedicated to insulating the country from the rest of the world rather than, as Terence Brown argued, attempting 'to protect readers from the grosser forms of pornography.'[22] All that was necessary to have a book banned was to send a copy to the Censorship Board with the offending passages marked, rather than reviewing the merit of the book as a whole. In 1954 the percentage of books banned peaked at 85 percent. An insight into the practices of the censors is given in the notebooks of C.J. O'Reilly, a teacher in a teacher-training college, who examined 481 books in 1955.[23] To O'Reilly a ban was justified for descriptions or references to nudity, 'passionate scenes,' sexual intercourse, masturbation, homosexuality, lesbianism, adultery and infidelity.[24] Furthermore, O'Reilly also prohibited books deemed to misrepresent the Catholic Church or that contained criticism of the clergy, which he regarded as blasphemous.[25] Even after O'Reilly's departure from the Board, the books banned in 1956 included *Molloy* by Samuel Beckett, *The Quiet American* by Graham Greene, and *Picture Post* because it published 'suggestive' pictures of Anita Ekberg. Violence was of much less concern to the censors than love scenes or stories about film stars.

Sean O'Faolain, who had his 1936 book, *Bird Alone*, banned by the censors in 1940, founded a periodical – the *Bell* – and he immediately mounted a vigorous campaign against the Censorship Board. O'Faolain argued that the fact that so many Irish writers had books banned demonstrated how remote the censors were from understanding native taste and standards.[26] O'Faolain launched frequent attacks on the new elite arguing, *inter alia*, that the Gaelic revival had become mere jobbery, the language enthusiasts 'vivisectionists' who had actually 'done irreparable harm to the language; and the vision of the heroic virtue of the west was mere escapism.'[27] As O'Faolain wrote in 1943: 'The romantic illusion, fostered by the Celtic twilight, that the West of Ireland, with its red petticoats and bawneen, is for some reason more Irish then Guinness' Brewery or Dwyers' Sunbeam-Wolsey factory, has no longer any basis whatever.'[28] O'Faolain asserted that Ireland was not a cultural unity but a synthesis, a mosaic, a hybrid society that had developed following the English conquest; and that the 'sum total of our local story is that long before 1900 we had become part and parcel of the general world-process – with a distinct English pigmentation.'[29] O'Faolain was courageously expressing these inclusive views in 1943, years before revisionism percolated into Irish historical discourse. Frank O'Connor, the celebrated short story writer, also raged against anti-intellectualism and clerical obscurantism in 1962: 'We have a Censorship Board but no publishers. We have a great literature published by Englishmen and Americans, and thanks to our censors, ninety per cent of it is out of print and unobtainable, so that we have brought up a generation which knows nothing of its own country or of its own literature.'[30]

When I was 16 in 1957, it was possible to read Joyce's *Dubliners* and *The Portrait of an Artist as a Young Man*. No other book I had read up to then had the impact upon me of the short stories in *Dubliners*. The Dublin of 1960, when I was a student at Trinity College, was still recognisable as the city that Joyce had described, as yet unaffected both by prosperity and the planners' failure to protect its Georgian architecture. The middle–class characters in *Dubliners* were recognisable in the conversations we heard in the pubs and streets around Trinity. The short stories centre on Joyce's idea of an epiphany: a moment when a character experiences a life-changing illumination, and the notion of paralysis where Joyce felt Irish nationalism hindered cultural development. The collection is chronological, beginning with stories of youth and progressing with age culminating with *The Dead*, regarded by many critics as the greatest short story in the English language. My mother owned a copy of *Ulysses* and at 15 I tried to read snatches from it, including Molly Bloom's soliloquy; it was clearly a work of genius but most of it was incomprehensible at that age.

* * *

On 27 January 1951, I attended my first rugby international at Lansdowne Road, accompanied by our close family friend, Tom Sheppard (a colleague of my father's at Guinness's brewery). I was nine years of age and from our vantage point in the open stand I was struck by the absence of colour and by the homogenous appearance of the crowd: boys were dressed like their fathers and grandfathers in jackets, gabardine coats and caps. This was the 'waste not want not' generation and how this philosophy resonated within me; I still use a garden spade that I purchased in 1969. To my boyhood delight, Ireland defeated France 9-8 and secured the Five Nations championship with the remnants of the team that won the Grand Slam in 1948. The inspiration and star of the side was the great Jack Kyle at fly half and this match sparked a lifetime passion for Irish rugby that still resonates deeply within me.

I joined the non-denominational 17th Dublin 2nd Blackrock Scout troop in 1952, which had been part of the Scout Association of Ireland since its foundation in 1908. There was also a separate Catholic Boy Scouts of Ireland, founded in 1927, because the Catholic Church sought a specific Catholic ethos for its youth. They were not united into one organisation – Scouting Ireland – until 2004. I was 11 and used to travel the four miles from Dalkey by bicycle every Friday night, pedalling along the seafront in Dun Laoghaire to Blackrock via Seapoint. Cycling to Blackrock on a cold and windy winter's night frequently involved riding directly into a westerly gale. To cope with this, I cycled in the slipstream of a Johnson Mooney and O'Brien electric bread van, a somewhat dangerous option that would not be acceptable today. I went on a fortnight's Scout camp to Westward Ho in Devon in the summer of 1952; it was my first trip outside Ireland. We travelled by rail to Rosslare, by boat to Fishguard and thence to Swansea by train. From Swansea we embarked on a paddle steamer of the White Funnel Line bound for Ilfracombe. Initially I was excited by the splashing of the paddles, but there was a gale thundering up the Bristol Channel from the western approaches blowing against an ebbing tide (the Bristol Channel has the second largest tidal range in the world after the Bay of Fundy) and consequently the sea was very turbulent. Most of us were seasick and somewhat scared. England was such a contrast with Ireland. The rolling pastures of the Devonshire countryside were similar, but there was one key difference in that all the hedgerows were cut back and neatly trimmed, whereas in Ireland the hedges were inevitably overgrown and the fields were rampant with dock, thistles and bracken. What nobody realised at the time was that the Irish rural landscape was more sustainable than the manicured

English one. The other feature of Westward Ho was the noise of screaming jet fighters overhead all day, especially de Havilland Vampires and Gloster Meteors; it was the first time I had ever seen a jet aircraft. The following summer, in 1953, we were taken to London for a week by our Scoutmaster. We visited the British museum, Madame Tussauds, the Tower of London and other attractions. We stayed in Bayswater and it was impossible to avoid the signs in the windows of boarding houses proclaiming 'No Blacks, No Irish and No dogs.' Nevertheless, it was an exhilarating educational experience to visit a great world metropolis.

My father and I shared an enthusiasm for motor sport and in the 1950s we would follow it on BBC radio. The sport appealed to me in part because it involves speed, times and memorising gaps between competitors after each lap. During the Isle of Man TT week, I would listen to Murray Walker's commentaries. This was a golden era on the Isle of Man with great riders, including Geoff Duke, Bob McIntyre (first man to lap the island at over 100mph in 1957) and Reg Armstrong from Dublin, winner of the 500cc race in 1952. Murray Walker went on to commentate on Formula 1 Grand Prix races for many years. Walker's commentaries, as Clive James commented, 'sounded as if his trousers were on fire' and he simply could not control his enthusiasm and unalloyed joy. This led to comical blunders – called 'Murrayisms' – such as 'he's obviously gone in for a wheel change. I say obviously because I can't see it;' or 'the lead car is unique, except for the one behind which is identical;' or 'and now excuse me while I interrupt myself.' These mistakes and many others simply made him even more endearing to his fans.

We started going to see the Enniskerry hill climb events and motor racing in the Phoenix Park. My first experience of a major event was watching the Leinster Trophy race, which had been the pinnacle of motor racing in Ireland since it was first run in 1934. For many years it was the highlight of the motor-racing calendar across Britain and Ireland mainly due to restrictions which prevented racing on public roads in Britain. The Leinster Trophy came to the 8.4 mile Wicklow circuit of country roads in July 1950. Although I was only nine, my father agreed to take me and we stood on a slope overlooking an S-bend, the Beehive, and waited for the first cars with the largest handicaps to pass through; these were the somewhat mundane 1250cc MGs and 'homemade' specials. The driver on scratch was one Anthony Powys-Lybbe driving a 1938 2.9 litre monoposto Alfa Romeo and I have never forgotten the thrilling sound of the guttural roar from the engine and the smell of the high-octane fuel when he accelerated out of the S-bend below us on the first lap. He won the racing-car class and recorded the fastest average speed of 75.62 mph. The aristocratic Powys-Lybbe was the personification of the English gentleman amateur racing driver who achieved modest success. He frequently came to Ireland to race and he would leave his van at the Liverpool docks and drive the single seater 2.9 litre Alfa Romeo Grand Prix racing car from the Dublin docks to the race meeting, to which the Gardai never raised an objection. This, of course, left Powys–Lybbe without road transport after dark!

The ultimate highlight of my motor- racing experience was travelling with my father and two colleagues from Guinness's to see the Tourist Trophy race at Dundrod, County Antrim on 18 September 1955. My father spent the day in the company of his colleagues and I was left to watch the race on my own. This was the fifth round of the World Sports Car Championship and it attracted works cars from all the leading makes, including three Mercedes Benz 300SLRs, driven by the greatest driver of all time – Juan Manuel Fangio – Stirling Moss and von Trips; a D-Type Jaguar driven by the dashing Mike Hawthorn, two Ferrari 857 Monzas, and works machines from Aston-Martin and Porsche. The race was 84 laps of the 7.42-mile circuit, a distance of 623 miles. A total of 49 cars participated in the Le Mans type start and it seemed a large field for a race circuit made up of narrow country roads with steep banks; it was classic racing in close proximity to lamp posts, kerbs, stone gate-posts, and spectators. The danger was enhanced by the fact that drivers in 1955 competed without seat belts and also lacked fireproof suits and asbestos underwear. It was a fragile balance between safety and catastrophic danger, exacerbated by the fact that the disparity in speed between the D-Type Jaguar and Mercedes Benz, on the one hand, and slower sports cars on the other – often driven by less experienced drivers – was too great. In the first two laps some nine cars were eliminated due to accidents, and tragically three drivers were killed during the race. Fortunately, we were unaware of these tragedies until hours later when we arrived back in Dublin. The race itself was thrilling: Mike Hawthorn led until two laps from the finish when his Jaguar's engine seized, which let Stirling Moss through to win, with Fangio second. The Tourist Trophy race was never held at Dundrod again, although it still hosts motor- cycle racing.

* * *

We spent our summer holidays and numerous weekends at Brittas Bay, near Wicklow, in 1949, 1950 and 1951. In 1952, we holidayed in Donegal for the first time by renting a Victorian cottage, 'Rockmount,' at Portsalon on Lough Swilly. The cottage had no electric light and the water was drawn from a well. Travelling to Portsalon was a major 189-mile journey on bumpy, narrow roads in the unreliable cars of 1950s vintage. My father made me responsible for navigation using a map supplied by the AA, with accompanying comments about the passing landscape. The route to Portsalon involved crossing the border into Northern Ireland at Aughnacloy and thence driving across Tyrone via Omagh and Strabane into Donegal. The customs posts on the southern side of the border were flimsy structures made of wood and corrugated steel, painted green. Smuggling was a problem with a concentration on cigarettes, butter, flour, tea and cattle in the 1950s. The main attraction of cutting through County Tyrone was the opportunity to shop in Strabane as biscuits and sweets were not just cheaper, but better. There were pick 'n' mix stalls in the shops and sweets that were not available in the Republic, most notably Spangles.

The staples of the holiday diet included Kellogg's corn flakes or rice crispies at breakfast, sandwiches, accompanied by wasps for lunch, fish or rashers, eggs and potatoes for dinner, with a mug of cocoa and a cream-cracker biscuit at night. Cakes were rare and and figrolls were my favourite biscuits, although my mother made lovely parkin. Shopping for sweets was a particular pleasure on holidays: aniseed bars and toffee bars were a penny; and a Kit Kat, Rolos, or a bar of Cadbury's milk chocolate were cherished. Also, on holidays, my parents would purchase Fox's glacier mints, a clear boiled sweet with the famous Peppy the polar bear icon. Ice cream in the form of a tuppenny slider, as a wafer was called in Ulster, was a special treat.

Portsalon was different to anything I had seen before: the magnificent long sandy beach of Ballymastocker Bay on the western shore of the glacial fjord of Lough Swilly; the first intoxicating smell of the sea; treeless rocky headlands thrusting into the Atlantic; large cumulus clouds rushing in off the Atlantic interspersed with shafts of sunlight; the rocks and pools to be explored; the excitement of running down to the beach in the morning to be the first to leave footprints in the sand; swallows darting overhead; the dunes where we could play imaginary games; the small fields of meagre pasture; hawthorn spilling over brambles and fuchsia growing wild in the hedges; tiny thatched cottages with stone floors, no electricity and water drawn fresh from a well; the smell of fresh manure on the road; waterproof sweaters made of unwashed greasy wool; walking to the shop to collect milk in an aluminium can and returning past slumbering dogs twitching their tails; accompanying my father on fishing trips to the surrounding lakes; a place where everything was simple, where you could feel rich with the silence broken only by the distant sound of the surf or the pitter- patter of rainfall; steam rising off the road when the sun came out again; and picnics accompanied by the unique sound of the primus stove as my mother pumped it up to make tea. The smell of the turf fires permeated the community; it was so evocative that when I smell it now almost 70 years later it immediately stimulates memories of Portsalon in the early 1950s. I especially enjoyed watching a local farmer cutting a field of long grass with a scythe. His fingers were stained with nicotine and he mowed the grass with long strong swoops of the scythe. I can still hear the tick of the sheaves as the blade cut through them. The grass was turned by pitchfork, gathered-in to create small piles lying loosely to allow the breeze to dry it when it was then stacked into haycocks.

The following summer, in 1953, we returned to a cottage in the dunes on Ballymastocker Bay under Knockalla mountain from where we could hear the surf roaring on the nearby golden strand. I would watch the sun setting slowly across the Fanad peninsula; and by the next morning gusts of summer rain would ride in on a warm zephyr from the Atlantic. Photographs of these holidays in my album suggest (erroneously) that the sun was always shining, but this was because in the early 1950s nobody took pictures with a Box Brownie when the sun was not shining. One notable feature of our holidays was that we were required (not invited) to swim three times per day in the Atlantic, whatever the weather; I can still recall the sting of the rain on my sunburnt back as I ran down the beach to plunge into the sea. On a chilly August day with a north-west wind cutting in off the Atlantic my first inclination was to turn back when my feet touched the water's edge; then there was the moment that I dived in when waist-deep; and finally having swum around in deeper and even colder water, the sea near the beach, in contrast, felt almost warm. My mother was an especially keen swimmer who employed a stroke – the trudgen – that appears to have disappeared from the swimmers' repertoire. The weather in Donegal was very changeable and frequently the sky reached down to touch the sea and the rain, cloud and mist were indistinguishable. Sometimes a westerly gale blew in from the Atlantic and flying sand on Ballymastocker Bay stung my face, penetrated my eyes and clung to my clothes. When it was impossible to go outside, we would play a board game such as Ludo, snakes and ladders, Monopoly, or my favourite, Cluedo. The day following heavy rain we would go to a river and fish with worms in the flood water. It rained frequently in Donegal, but having a month-long holiday gave a different perspective: if you had only a week and it rained every day, it spoiled the holiday; as we were there for a month we waited for sunny spells and they eventually came.

Our summer holiday was a full month's duration to enable my father to spend as much time as possible fishing for sea trout on Mulroy Bay, using a silver devon spinner and, above all, lake and river fly-fishing for brown trout. Hence, 1952 was the first time I ate brown trout, which my father caught in Kinny Loch and sea trout which he caught in Mulroy Bay; ever since I have preferred trout to salmon. Sometimes we children were permitted to fish in the sea off the rocks mainly for pollack or mackerel. My father frequently needed me to row him around the lakes, especially in the evenings while he cast flies to lure trout. He was an accomplished fly fisherman. When he opened his plastic fly box he would identify the flies to use on a cloudy day, or in dark river water on a sunny day, or in a brown swollen river. I so longed to learn to fish for trout as I could see that it was infinitely more skilful and rewarding than sea-fishing. However, when I asked him to teach me to fly-fish, he would never commit to doing it, or to even allow me to try it out on the many trips that I made in order to row him on the loughs. This was a disappointment to me as it revealed a basic attitude that his needs were always paramount.

We spent a holiday in Ballylickey near Bantry in 1954; the house was basic but interesting. It was a wet summer in 1954 and we were close to the Coomhola river where we fished with worms in the flood water with my father and his friend, Benny Aylward. I saw trout in the shallows observing my worms approaching, all facing the same way upstream, they drifted from side to side in a pool of sunshine after the rain. In the evenings my father drove west beyond Glengarriff to fish in Lough Avaul. Together with our mother, we walked down the road two miles to Glengarriff for ice creams. On another occasion, I was rowing our lightweight boat on Lake Bofina near Bantry when bad weather raced in off the Atlantic, accompanied by rain and fierce squalls. Water started to crash in over the side, which was decidedly scary, but with a real struggle I rowed ashore before being blown on to the stones at the end of the lake.

We returned to Donegal in 1955 to stay at Fintra, near Killybegs. Given that there was limited space in the car, my sisters – Sheila and Judy – journeyed with me by rail to Killybegs. This was an interesting trip as it involved travelling north on the main line from Dublin to Belfast, changing trains at Portadown and then onwards to Strabane. We changed again at Strabane to a narrow-gauge three-foot railway line running to Killybegs in south Donegal. This was operated by diesel railcars that meandered slowly through the green pastoral landscape stopping occasionally. It was a unique travel experience and, although the Donegal narrow- gauge system was the largest in the British Isles, it had all closed down by the end of December 1959. The weather during the 1955 summer holiday at Fintra was warm and sunny so that when we emerged from our three (compulsory) swims each day we immediately stopped shivering. Fishing off the rocks, we caught pollack and also wrasse, which to us were inedible, although the owners of the local shop gave us a gobstopper for every wrasse we gave them. We noticed that there was the wreckage of a large aircraft visible on the beach. During World War 2 (The Emergency), there were 44 plane crashes and landings in County Donegal. One such aircraft – a Boeing B-17 Flying Fortress – landed in the sea at Fintra on 20 February 1944. It had run into severe electrical storms and was struck by lightning. It approached the beach at 120 miles per hour and landed on the sea. All ten crew members survived.

Whenever I listened to Blackpool Night on the BBC Light Programme during the early fifties it prompted a sense of longing to experience a type of holiday that simply did not exist anywhere in Ireland. The thought of listening to Reg Dixon playing the mighty Wurlitzer at the Tower ballroom, of laughing at top comedians like Al Read, of hearing singers like Ronnie Hilton, or listening to the Ted Heath Band at the Empress Ballroom was something that seemed so close yet unattainable. My perception of Blackpool as glamorous and exciting at the age of 11 was derived entirely from listening to the radio. After experiencing several family holidays in Donegal, my desire to holiday in Blackpool simply evaporated and I have never visited this quintessential British seaside resort.

CHAPTER 3

Schooldays

The educational system of the Irish Republic is unusual among the countries of the European Union in that private institutions receive public funding. The 1950s was a period when the Irish state did not fully finance secondary education so it was necessary for families to pay fees in order for their children to attend secondary schools. As a consequence, drop out levels from primary to secondary were high: 421,000 attended primary schools in 1959, but there were only 73,500 pupils in the secondary system suggesting that approximately 80 per cent terminated their education at fourteen, the legal school leaving age.[1] The government implemented a specific policy requiring compulsory Irish; the rest of the curriculum was within a humanist tradition with a more limited emphasis on sciences.[2] O'Reilly also opined that 'official educational discourse was dominated by the perspective of Catholic teaching.'[3] A meagre attitude was applied to the funding of secondary level education in the 1950s and expenditure *per capita* was only one-third of other western countries. In 1961 the educational budget of Northern Ireland, with half the population of the Republic, was double in absolute terms that of the Republic's total educational expenditure so that spending per head was approximately four times greater in the North.[4] Consequently, the secondary system in the Republic was seriously underfunded by the government during the 1950s: capitation grants for secondary schools were at the same level in 1952 as they had been in 1924-25.[5] Furthermore, the *Irish Times* complained in 1956 that the government contributed nothing to the building or maintenance of secondary schools.[6] This policy of underfunding secondary education was – according to the *Irish Times* – 'apparently with the approval of the strong religious orders,' who valued their control over the curriculum more than the financial contribution from the state.[7] The proportion of young people in Irish secondary education in 1957 was the lowest in western

Europe.[8] There is no doubt that the extremely parsimonious financial regime imposed on secondary schools by the government throughout the 1950s was a major constraint on the range of subjects, sporting facilities and extra-curricular activities that St Andrew's College and other secondary schools could offer to pupils. Indeed, it is surprising just how much the school did enrich the lives of day-pupils and boarders, which is a tribute to the unselfish service of many staff over and above their normal teaching duties.

* * *

Every new experience in life is memorable – the anxiety of starting a new job, the first stirrings of love, or attending a new school for the first time. I was enrolled in St Andrew's College in September 1949 and on the first day of term I caught the number 8 bus from Dalkey into Ballsbridge, some eight miles distant. It was an era when parents were very trusting; there was no talk of paedophiles or muggers waiting to harm you or odd people seeking to spirit you away. Obviously they existed, but we were not warned about them. I alighted at Clyde Road wearing my new school tie and cap with a badge and the motto '*Ardens sed Virens*' – Burning yet Flourishing. I also wore short grey flannel trousers and long grey woollen socks as I strode up to the school, which was located in several adjoining four-storey Victorian terraced buildings. I walked nervously into the tarmacked playground (originally the gardens of two houses), which was dominated by a large mulberry tree. Against the wall parallel with Wellington Road was a bicycle shed roughly constructed with concrete blocks and an asbestos roof. On the opposite west side of the yard was the school hall, a large brick building penetrated by skylights with a stage at the south end behind which were wooden war memorials. At the north end of the yard, in former mews dwellings, were the science labs and the house of 'Sarge,' a former soldier, who checked the roll, rang the bell between classes and carried out maintenance. I was eight years of age and surrounded by boys, none of whom I had ever seen before.

Entering the playground for the first time engendered a feeling of uncertainty and solitude as I thought (incorrectly) that I was the only boy who was new and different. Nothing from my home or family had prepared me for this: I was truly on my own in a dauntingly large and strange place. Each day started with anarchy in the playground: groups of boys aged from 8 to 18 running around in gangs, laughing and chanting; many boys playing several different games of tip-rugby and football simultaneously, and cricket against the toilet wall in summer. Some pupils even dared to smoke in the bicycle shed. Every autumn playing conkers became the favourite activity in the playground. There were abundant chestnut trees in Dalkey from which we could plunder chestnuts. I had no idea how we absorbed the rules but if you managed to smash your opponent's conker you then added his score to your total.

No teacher ever supervised the playground at breaks and lunch-time; it was a matter of learning how to survive in an environment that was not inherently hostile, but where cruel teasing between boys occurred. Anything that made somebody different would be targeted for name-calling. It could be the colour of your hair, the type of shoes you were wearing, a fat physique, or an inability to play cricket – any characteristic that could be used to differentiate a potential rival. Fights did break out and bullying sometimes occurred, which frequently involved being ducked under a cold tap. I managed to survive the first day, no tears, no trauma, but a feeling of some excitement and uncertainty.

The classrooms were somewhat drab and cramped and clouds of chalk dust hung in the air. I carried a leather satchel from which I took out a new pencil box with a sliding lid, set square, ruler, compass and protractor, some of which we did not use in the Preparatory Department. There was no official uniform in 1949, apart from the requirement to wear a cap and a school tie. I wore short trousers held up by a belt with a buckle in the form of an S-shaped snake. Between 1949 and 1951 we were taught by Miss Phyllis Slator, a stern and dedicated teacher, whose hair was drawn into a bun and who wore spectacles, thick tweed skirts and a twinset, with comfortable, albeit not fashionable, shoes.[9] She was, of course, a spinster as career teachers of eight-year olds were at that time. We sat at ink-stained wooden desks and some of the learning was conducted by chanting jingles in a sing-song voice : 'Two hundred and twenty yards makes one furlong, eight furlongs makes a mile' – or 'Two pints makes one quart, four quarts makes one gallon.' Books with squared grid pages were distributed and these kept our sums in order down the page, the light blue lines squaring off the hundreds, tens and units. We also practised writing letters in an exercise book – rows of As and Bs through the alphabet; and I still recall the feeling of excitement when we advanced to starting 'joined-up writing.' We then used headline- books which required us to write out sentences onto a page of ruled lines beneath.

Later Miss Slator read out dictation which we would copy down. There were no biros allowed so we dipped our pens in an inkwell on the desk to load the pen with sufficient ink to write a couple of words at a time. My writing looked as if a drunken spider had crawled across the page; it remains almost unreadable when I make notes today.

We slanted our writing towards the 'east', calculated the price of carrots, and parsed our sentences. Much time was spent on learning the rudiments of addition, subtraction, multiplication and division. We learned our times-tables and, to my amazement, they were still there when I taught my own daughters their tables in the late 1970s! I recall the pleasure (and relief) of realising that I really enjoyed these elementary building blocks of mathematics. In the curriculum that we followed, there was little to awaken the slumbering imagination; much of the creativity had been stifled at birth, which was not the fault of the teachers. One day, however, Miss Slator brought in a vinyl LP of Beethoven's Symphony No. 6 in F major, the *Pastorale*, and played it to the class. Beethoven's masterpiece and his love of nature were inspired by Rousseau's vision of a new world. This was a transformational moment for me and at the age of nine sparked what was to become a life-long interest in classical music. Initially I liked romantic classical music with strong melodies and also the *bel canto* style of singing with characteristic smooth *legato*. It was to be a long journey from Beethoven to John Cage with his 'composition' 4'33, an orchestral piece in three movements that has no actual music. Although the BBC Third Programme was available from 1946, my parents did not listen to it and would have regarded it as too highbrow. They tuned into 'Your Hundred Best Tunes' on the BBC Light programme at the weekend and, since listening tended to be confined to the breakfast room where there was always a coal fire in winter, parental choice prevailed. Sadly, St Andrew's College in the 1950s did not have any formal music lessons or a school choir.

The headmaster of the school for the duration of my education at St Andrew's between 1949 and 1959 was a tall English gentleman, P J Southgate, a Cambridge-educated classicist. He was a benign presence who lacked leadership skills. He travelled to Clyde Road on his bicycle until he acquired a tiny Fiat from which he would unravel himself with difficulty each day. As one of my classmates recalled in 2019, 'the only time I ever met him was when he was at one end of the cane and I was at the other; and he then apologised for having to cane me.' The general consensus among the pupils who left in 1959 and 1960 was that he was a classical scholar who was a somewhat remote figure. It was an era when parents rarely met or contacted children's teachers directly and for most the only communication was a report at the end of each term.

When my cohort entered the Senior School at the age of ten, we were then required to attend the morning assembly. St Andrew's did not need to emphasise its Protestant (Presbyterian) ethos and its past connections to the British Empire, as evidenced by the lists of old boys on the war memorials who had been killed in the two World Wars. Few of us enjoyed this daily ritual which consisted of a Church of Ireland (Anglican) vicar or Presbyterian minister droning the prayers and Mr Southgate making any relevant announcements, such as admonishing boys who had been observed on the number 10 bus without wearing school caps. Such rules were irksome to many. I also ate school lunches, which I disliked. There was always a scramble both during and after grace to grab the best potatoes to partner a portion of ham or thin pieces of beef with rims of fat buried beneath thick gravy, or worse still, corned beef and over-cooked carrots. Cabbage was frequently on the menu and it was chopped and cooked – stalks and all – until it appeared on the plate as a lumpy, stringy mush. This was followed by such delights as tapioca ('frogspawn'), semolina, rice pudding with a splodge of raspberry jam, or a jam roll with thick, glutinous, (often) burnt Bird's custard poured over it. In those days there were no salads, fresh fruit, yoghurts or squeezed orange juice on the menu.

Academic achievement was not regarded as a high priority by most of us; being selected for the First XV at rugby and First XI at cricket were perceived as much more important. If a pupil was good at games he commanded respect from both teachers and pupils alike. In general, there was a relaxed approach to the teaching programme by the staff, which had the effect (almost certainly not deliberately) of encouraging pupils to think for themselves and to self-motivate, if, for example, they wished to try for a place at Trinity College Dublin. We respected most, but not all of the teachers. The majority of staff wore gowns when they taught, which set them apart from us and gave them an air of authority in the classroom, exemplified most clearly by Mr Sleath, an Oxford-educated mathematician, who always wore a gown. During the mid-morning break, the vast majority of teachers smoked in the staff room, which resembled a cinema of that era with dense clouds of blue smoke and a pervasive stench of tobacco. When they returned to the classroom at 11.30a.m., many would be holding a butt between two fingers and their thumb as they sucked the last atom of nicotine into their lungs. Others smoked pipes, which had the advantage (for them) of still being alight as they walked into the classroom; indeed 'Buster' O'Neill would simply shove the pipe, still alight, into his pocket.

The state's policy of compulsory Gaelic was implemented with the objective of creating an Irish-speaking society, a goal that was never achieved. English was too deeply embedded as the everyday language of the people and, moreover, was spoken in more countries than any other language. Most boys resented compulsory Gaelic so that the official state policy of coercion was in reality counterproductive and it remained a language only spoken by a few people in remote Gaeltacht areas. We read British comics, listened to the BBC more than Radio Eireann, not because the BBC was British but because it was more varied, interesting and exciting. The political establishment saw themselves as guardians of the Gaelic language, Gaelic games and the hegemony of the Catholic Church. It articulated a very narrow vision of Ireland and was ruthless in pursuit of it. The state withheld public jobs from those who could not prove their capability in Gaelic. The language strategy was a dismal failure and I cannot recall a time when I ever heard anyone in Dun Laoghaire or Dalkey speaking Gaelic in the street. It was the great Brian O'Nolan (writing under the pseudonyms of Flann O'Brien, Myles na gCopaleen and others) – a supporter of the Irish language – who castigated its defenders as 'the most nauseating phenomenon in Europe…. who are ignorant of everything, including the Irish language itself.'[10] O'Brien believed that the existence of the Irish language was essential for Ireland's cultural and literary future. He argued that it 'supplies that unknown quality in us that enables us to transform the English language and this seems to hold for people who know little or no Irish, like Joyce.'[11] Irish would have to survive as a second language.

The one great compensation with Gaelic at St Andrew's was that it was taught by a dedicated and charismatic teacher – Patrick 'Spud' Murphy – who had been appointed in 1938. He was genuinely interested in every pupil as they struggled to progress in learning a difficult language. The Department of Education's Irish syllabus placed more emphasis on the rules of grammar and less on spoken Irish. For example, we were required to write out 'The Deeds of the Day' in several different tenses and we also had to learn poetry by rote as part of the Gaelic syllabus. 'Spud' Murphy would then instruct the class to write out the poem from memory. While we were attempting this, he climbed to the top of the desk and gazed down upon us from a height of about nine feet. After a few minutes, he would utter the immortal words: 'there is a cogging boy in our midst.' This was followed by a long pause in order to allow tension to spread across the classroom like a bushfire before the unfortunate pupil was named, ordered to stand against the wall and told to 'Park 9321,' which meant that he was 'stuck' after school in Room 9 at 3.21pm. The first unfortunate boy was usually joined by several others. Alternatively, Murphy would ask each pupil in turn to recite the poem and many boys were ordered to stand out to the side before they had even attempted to start! He was truly dedicated and determined that pupils would succeed, even if his methods would be viewed today as somewhat unorthodox.

When a rumour circulated around the classroom that an inspector from the Department of Education was in the school and would be examining the Gaelic class, 'Spud' Murphy became visibly nervous. He would immediately rearrange the class by bringing all the more able pupils up to the front rows and then requesting that only those boys should raise their hands when the inspector asked a question in Gaelic. Like almost all the staff, Mr Murphy smoked and occasionally a (reliable) pupil was asked by Murphy to 'please nip up to Hayden's and get me 10 Woodbine's.' He was a master of shielding a cigarette in his hand. Murphy also taught us about life on the Blasket Islands in Kerry through Peig Sayers's autobiography, *Peig*, and Maurice O'Sullivan's *Twenty Years A' Growing*, which depict the declining years of a traditional Irish-speaking way of life. One year we were taken to see the Gaelic-language pantomime performed by the Abbey Theatre company at the Queen's Theatre. Unfortunately, exposure to a panto in Gaelic did not result in a large conversion rate to the state's linguistic policy aims. If someone had been invited to design a strategy to kill off the native tongue, compulsion would have been at its heart.

John 'Tadpole' Ruddock taught Maths. He was a pleasant and cultured teacher who, after he left St Andrew's to become Head of Villiers School in Limerick, did more to promote and develop an interest in classical music in Limerick than anyone in the past century. Although he was a congenial person when one met him later in life, he was not a great maths teacher and never made any meaningful attempt to relate the subject to the world of lived experience: we were given rows of figures to add, subtract, divide and multiply and algebraic equations to solve. The goal of all this was to do 'sums,' a process whose difficulty for us was correlated with its repetitive dullness. He lacked the patience necessary to explain maths problems to weaker pupils.

Yet, conversely, he opened up the world of classical music to me by organising visits to hear the Radio Eireann symphony orchestra under Brian Boydell. Classical music thereby became a passion for the rest of my life and it gave me great pleasure to tell him this when we met for the first time in 52 years at a St Andrew's dinner in 2009.

John Ruddock, in a more benign role, also took charge of cricket in the school. Cricket was to some extent in competition with swimming and life-saving in the summer term; this was in part due to Neville Ferguson who ran the swimming pool and life-saving and disliked cricket. When St Andrew's played Terenure College, Terenure's opening bowler- Kevin Flynn – was alleged by Ruddock to have a faulty bowling action that involved illegal 'throwing.' Hence, when we played Terenure College at home Ruddock knew that Flynn would open the bowling from the east end of the ground and so, when he walked out to the pitch with Brother Grace from Terenure, Ruddock was determined that he would occupy the square leg umpire position so that he could 'call' Flynn if he was guilty of 'throwing.' Flynn is more famous for scoring a magnificent try in injury time against England at Twickenham in 1972 that secured a memorable 16-12 victory for Ireland.

The principal Maths teacher of the 1950s was J R Sleath, an Oxford graduate, who during the decade I attended St Andrew's was the most outstanding teacher in the school. The classroom door opened and Sleath swept in with his gown flowing behind him. He was slim and always immaculately dressed, usually in a dark suit and Oxford college tie. As he moved briskly from the door towards his desk he would announce to a silent room: 'Please turn to page 46 problem 2.' He had a natural aura of authority so that he was listened to with respect and never needed to raise his voice in the classroom. He was a brilliant and dedicated teacher who sprinkled his lessons with practical examples such as: if a man is 5 feet 11 inches tall, how far away is the horizon at sea level? Homework was set regularly and marked rigorously. I respected him more than any other teacher in the school. Some teachers live in your memory less than others; some are there for all the wrong reasons. Mr Sleath is in my memory for all the right reasons.

Physics and Chemistry was taught by Rex Mullan whose major accomplishment at the school was to marry the matron, Miss O'Neill. He achieved little of any note. He sat behind his desk while conducting experiments and adopted a highly supercilious attitude towards us as we dawdled through light, gravity, mechanics and the periodic table. He was lazy and never set any homework. I was hopeless at Art and gave it up when I was 14 to sit in extra science classes during which time Rex Mullan was of little or no help.

A new school syllabus for teaching History was introduced after independence in order to promote a specific sense of Irish identity among pupils. Vincent Comerford has written how 'teachers were encouraged to tell the history of Ireland as a story of seven centuries of militant struggle against English domination.'[12] In relation to the teaching of history, the Department of Education's notes for teachers (in use until the early 1960s) suggested history was about articulating and illustrating 'sublime examples of patriotism in order to refute the calumnies of Ireland's enemies.'[13] Hence, a particular interpretation of Ireland's past as a Gaelic, Catholic-nationalist one provided the basis for history teaching, and the subject was also used to legitimise the restoration of Irish as a spoken language.[14] The influence of Rev. T J Corcoran, S.J. (Professor of Education at UCD) on the history syllabus that we were required to study in the 1950s was critical. Corcoran did not accept that history should be a secular discipline, but argued that the history curriculum should reverse British modes of learning, which were 'inimical to the to the study of the work and development of the Church of Christ.'[15] He asserted that the teaching of history in the Irish secondary school curriculum should reflect a Catholic spirit and outlook.[16] Hence, history teaching operated as a political project emphasising a monolithic nationalist, anti-British and pro-Catholic narrative. As a consequence, we worked our way through James Carty's (boring) books. I remember being very puzzled as to why the Civil War in 1922-23 was despatched in a single sentence. In a country still recovering from the tragedy of the Civil War, modern Irish history – apart from Easter week 1916 – was simply excluded from the state-sanctioned syllabus. In place of kings and queens, we were presented with over-simplified eulogies of past heroes (women did not feature) such as Owen Roe O'Neill, Brian Boru, Daniel O'Connell, Charles Stewart Parnell, Robert Emmett and Patrick Pearse. Not only were all the heroes Irish men, but every villain was English. In those days, only 30 years after independence, it is not perhaps surprising that the history books adopted only one perspective, that of ethnocentric Catholic- Nationalism and Anglophobia in order to conform with the ethos of the national syllabus, which incorporated a heavy emphasis on English injustices – of which there were many – perpetrated in Ireland. It was not until the 1980s that a number of authors – including Roy Foster, Conor Cruise O'Brien, Brian Fallon and others, began to challenge widely held historical myths and sought to initiate a more holistic, and non-partisan approach to Irish history. We were a generation too early to benefit from this revisionist approach.

The Geography curriculum determined by the state was dull and repetitive, involving roaming around the globe from Ireland to Britain, Europe, North America to Africa and Australasia. There was an emphasis on 'cape and bay' geography – having to learn the names of countries, rivers, mountain ranges, major cities along with climate data. I recall spending hours drawing a map of Australia on which we were asked to mark the state boundaries! Neville Ferguson, a conscientious teacher, adopted the traditional approach: 'memorise this list of capital cities and then learn the tributaries of the Shannon.' To some extent he was constrained by a very traditional and uninspiring syllabus which he failed to present in a stimulating way. However, his contribution to the school in other ways was immense. He was in charge of the boarders; he ran the scout troop; organised the excavation and construction of the swimming pool; ran films on Saturday nights; coached the first XV rugby team; and conducted the life-saving classes. The school was his life and his influence was all-pervasive. Charlie Duncan, who was a boarder, testifies that Ferguson made boarding a pleasure, like a home-from-home for the boys. He influenced everyone, usually positively, although he had favourites and bullied boys who did not play on the rugby teams or participate in life-saving classes. Boys who excelled at sport, especially rugby or cricket, were seldom punished severely. After Ferguson's tragic premature death from rheumatic fever in 1958, I was taught Geography during my final year by James Duke who adopted a more holistic view of the subject than Ferguson. Duke became Headmaster in 1967 and he oversaw the move to Booterstown and a major expansion of the institution from 271 pupils in 1960 to over 900 when he retired in 1991.

Latin lessons were dreary and uninspiring. The syllabus was heavily oriented towards grammar, including the thrill of learning declensions, conjugating verbs – '*Amo, amas, amat*' - and translating endless sentences from Latin into English and *vice versa*. Eventually we were judged fit to accompany Caesar on his adventures in Gaul without ever understanding the context of his French campaign; and later some of us moved on to Virgil's *Aeneid*. As we struggled to translate the dactylic hexameter, we were not told that this epic poem is one of the greatest works in Latin literature, telling the story of Aeneas, a Trojan who travelled to Italy, where he became the ancestor of the Romans.

We were never taught that it was a compelling founding myth that tied Rome to the legends of Troy. 'Buster' O'Neill taught Latin, although he probably spent more time discussing Philosophy since he was the teacher who was the easiest to distract from the delights of declining Latin verbs. He always wore the same double-breasted suit every day, complemented by a heavy pair of boots, which emitted a strange odour when he stood in front of the gas fire. He was frequently absent and, even when present, he was not a good teacher. My friend David Thomas always placed a yachting magazine on his desk and when 'Buster' rolled into the classroom he would demand the magazine and spend the rest of the class reading it since he owned a boat that he sailed out of Howth. Latin was also taught by Brendan Banks, who had trained as a Jesuit, but returned to civilian life and was arguably the most educated, but not the best teacher on the staff. His Latin classes morphed into fascinating insights on Roman history; and he also introduced us to oral Latin.

Initially French was taught by Kingsley Scott, a tall, gangly, languid, dark-haired and urbane person who cut a somewhat dashing figure in Dublin of the 1950s by driving a red MG sports car, wearing colourful sports jackets and corduroys and smoking Gitanes with the famous image of a gypsy dancer on the packet. A cultured person with a somewhat abrupt manner, he was an enthusiastic and stimulating teacher. I was unaware why he left the school's employment in the mid-fifties until I was astonished to read an article by him in the *Guardian* newspaper written from his home in Tangier around 1980. In the article he outlined the hostile climate towards himself and other gay people in the Ireland of the 1950s when homosexuality was seen as a threat to the post-war cult of family and domesticity. He was succeeded by R E Stiobhard (Irwin Stewart), a cosmopolitan person who was fluent in English, Irish, German and French. He also directed a Louis D'Alton play *'They Got what They Wanted'* in which, at the age of 13, I played the role of Sally Murnaghan. I discovered that performing as part of a group was good fun, and there was also the discipline of having to be word-perfect with one's lines.

The government's English syllabus also demanded much rote learning, and under our teacher, Mr George 'Bog' Taylor, there were grammar, syntax, parsing and Latin roots to be learned. This was not an inspiring process and yet I think it was essential. Since the millennium it's been impossible to walk down any high street in Britain or Ireland without encountering shops and businesses that have simply dropped the apostrophe, as in Hamleys, Selfridges and Harrods. The worst offender is Waterstone, the book shop, which was rebranded as Waterstones in 2012. There is also the sat/sitting issue, which used to be confined to football pundits, but has spread like a virus and I loathe it. We were taught by George Taylor that any continuous past action needed the present participle. Hence, 'I was sitting at my desk' is correct, whereas 'I was sat at my desk' is wrong. Moreover, I notice that many of my university students cannot tell the difference between a main and a subordinate clause or who are unaware that, when they utter the phrase 'I will have washed' they have used the first person singular of the auxiliary verb 'to be' followed by the infinitive of the verb 'to have' and then the past participle of the verb 'to wash' in order to form the future perfect of the verb 'to wash.' Consequently, I have thought more about George Taylor's tuition at St Andrew's in the past decade than in the first 50 years after I left school in 1959.

There was also a deep pool of great English literature in which to fish. We studied a Shakespearean play every year, which involved learning lengthy passages from major speeches; and there was also poetry to memorise. This I really enjoyed doing and it's surprising how snatches from these speeches remain in my head. However, the class was often dull as each boy was invited to recite the passage we had been set to learn for homework. Sadly, we were never invited to act the play in class with boys taking different roles. Mr Taylor proceeded at a glacial speed through each Shakespearean play so that we seldom ever completed it in the course of the academic year. Taylor did provide us with revealing insights into Shakespeare and poetry, but his impact was diminished by his vindictive and cynical nature; he seldom ever praised a pupil in class. We also strolled through the canon of great poetry from Milton to Keats and Wordsworth and, of course, Ireland's greatest poet, W.B Yeats. I still find myself repeating lines learned by rote and really appreciating for the first time their true meaning and majesty. Great poetry resides in the mind and never leaves. One former pupil recalled a year when Taylor informed the class that the Shakespearean play for the coming year would be *As You Like It*. He went home and when his parents asked him what Shakespearean play he would be studying he informed them that 'we can do whatever we like!'

We were a fortunate generation as schoolchildren don't learn poetry by heart these days, which is a great pity considering how easily small children can memorise it. When my granddaughter, Flora, sat Scottish Higher English in 2016, the only poems on the syllabus were a selection by Carol Ann Duffy and Edwin Muir; there was no Shakespeare play or any other drama and only one novel – *The Great Gatsby*. Moreover, from 2021, poetry will be dropped as a compulsory subject for the GCSE English literature syllabus in England. Today's children are not taught to appreciate our sensual intuitive language and phrases that have – as D H Lawrence said – their 'own blood of emotion and instinct' running through them.[17] Poetry, it seems, can be dropped from the curriculum as its meanings and purpose are lost. Why has this philistinism occurred? Larkin wrote poems to 'preserve things I have seen…both for myself and for others.' Betjeman wrote to capture forgotten and obscure artefacts in the landscape: Irish churches, the small towns of Ireland, railway stations, bungalows, tennis courts and sponge cakes. Nowadays teachers never stray outside the syllabus; those who taught me at St Andrew's frequently did so, usually to good effect. Now, all over Britain and Ireland the over sixties can quote Keats, Wordsworth, Yeats and Shakespeare while the younger age groups cannot and, as a consequence, have less appreciation of great literature.

In my schooldays, discipline was much more rigid than today; hitting children was a fundamental component of maintaining order and it was not illegal. Corporal punishment in schools was not banned in Ireland until 1982. Under the prevailing legislation, our teachers – who acted *in loco parentis* – were entitled to administer the same 'reasonable and moderate chastisement' as a responsible parent. Caning, or being clipped around the head, were seldom questioned, but accepted as part of the punishment regime at St Andrew's College. The threat of corporal punishment was used as a means of control and administered for even minor misdemeanours such as poor homework, giving cheek, cheating or disrupting the class. There were several teachers – including the headmaster, P J Southgate – who had the authority to wield the cane. It was an everyday fact of school life that even the young pupils could be hauled from their desks and made to stand facing a corner or at the back of the classroom until the end of the lesson, awaiting six of the best. I was a conscientious pupil, who always submitted my homework on time, and luckily I managed to avoid ever being caned during my decade at the school.

Corporal punishment in the classroom was resorted to by some teachers with scarcely a second thought. Some teachers had a habit of reacting spontaneously by giving pupils a clip round the ears if they misbehaved or failed their multiplication tables. One teacher had the uncanny ability to throw a wood-backed duster across the classroom to hit a boy at the back of the room. There were occasions when cuts to the head were inflicted. A more humiliating punishment was being grabbed by the cheek or ear, hauled out of the desk and dragged to the front of the class, often for the most trivial of reasons, or kicking a pupil if they left their backsides trailing over their seat. The whole class would be asked to raise their hands if they knew an answer to a question. Boys would often put their hands up out of fear, not knowing the answer, but not wanting to look stupid, and hoping they would not be asked. There was almost no appreciation of dyslexia, autism or other learning difficulties; the classroom of the 1950s was a difficult place for such children.

My parents – despite paying fees – played no role in the educational process at St Andrew's. They never discussed or questioned the content of the syllabus with me, the methods of teaching, the use of corporal punishment, or the vagaries of teachers' behaviour. They did not monitor if I had completed my homework; and they never articulated their expectations of me. Their interaction with the school was confined to the receipt of a (brief) written report on my progress, or lack of it, at the end of each term. As a schoolboy in the 1950s, I simply accepted the strengths and weaknesses of various teachers and tried to work around the shortcomings of certain staff. I was aware that there were weaknesses in the teaching as my twin sister, Sheila, in parallel with me, attended Alexandra College where she received superior tuition. The major source of my dissatisfaction, however, was not the school but the uninspiring, tedious and flawed syllabus that we were required to pursue by the Irish Department of Education.

I never regarded exams as something to become nervous about; I quite enjoyed the challenge of the difficult questions. I sat the State Intermediate Certificate exams in 1957 in English, French, Gaelic, Latin, Maths, Science, History and Geography. To my surprise, I achieved Honours in all subjects, which indicates that the standards set were somewhat less than demanding. Returning to school in September 1957, I quickly became utterly bored by the prospect of tackling the State Leaving Certificate over two years; the syllabus did not encourage creativity or spontaneity. After a fortnight, I informed my parents that I wished to sit the Trinity College Dublin matriculation exams. My parents accepted this without demur, even though the school made it clear that they would not teach the Trinity matriculation syllabus. Certain individual teachers, however, agreed to mark any mathematical problems or essays that I chose to attempt. Hence, Andrew Wilson and I sat the matriculation exams after a year in June 1958. In French and Gaelic we were required to take an oral as part of the exam. When I presented myself for the Gaelic oral and was ushered into the presence of Prof. David Green I was immediately discombobulated because I recognised him as a regular swimmer at the Forty Foot where I had only ever seen him – together with his long beard – in the nude. I recovered my equilibrium and he started to question me in the Connacht dialect, whereas I had been taught the Munster dialect by Mr Murphy, who hailed from Caherdaniel in County Kerry. He switched effortlessly into the Munster dialect and somehow I survived. The first question on the Geography paper – 'The desert is a beggar's mantle fringed with gold. Discuss' – was unlike anything I had encountered before. Quite how I managed to pass the Matriculation exams in all seven subjects still remains a mystery to me.

Several of us, usually Dave Thomas, John Keery and myself, travelled home together on the number 8 bus. We sat always amongst the smokers on the top deck where there was always a cacophony of coughing and throat clearing. On wet afternoons the upstairs windows of the bus were steamed up with a mixture of cigarette smoke, condensation from wet coats and body heat. As the bus bowled along through Ballsbridge, it passed the major landmarks of my life so far: Lansdowne Road; the IMCO building on Merrion Road that looked like the liner moored at the quayside in Fellini's film – *And the Ship Sails On;* Sandymount Strand where we encounter Stephen Dedalus mid-thought and mid-stride in the third chapter of *Ulysses;* – Blackrock College, where Ireland's greatest ever rugby player – Brian O'Driscoll – was nurtured; – Blackrock village and the Regal cinema, the Top Hat ballroom, Dun Laoghaire, the Adelphi cinema, the Bamboo café, the People's Park, Glasthule, the Astoria cinema, Sandycove and Bulloch harbour. The CIE Leyland buses in the 1950s had an open platform at the rear. As the bus travelled quickly down the hill of Sandycove Road towards my stop at Castlepark Road, I positioned myself at the back of the open platform, grasping the pole with one hand and my satchel with the other and, as the bus approached the stop, I would simply step off the platform backwards and hit the road running, hopefully fast enough so that I didn't fall over with the momentum. Meanwhile, the conductor on the platform – in full cooperation – would ding the bell twice and the bus would accelerate away without ever stopping. It is unimaginable that children would do this in today's safety- conscious culture, although conductors were phased out in 1986 when the Dublin buses became one-man-operated. Unlike the UK, there were no conductresses on the Dublin buses in the 1950s.

Neville Ferguson, our geography teacher, conducted life-saving lessons in the school swimming pool at St Andrew's College. When Ferguson was not teaching life-saving, the pool would be a screaming mass of adolescent boys swimming through the murky water in all directions with older boys jumping in on top of smaller ones and others diving off the boards. After pupils had passed a number of tests of the Royal Life Saving Society, the principal award was a day trip on a Sunday in Ferguson's green Morris Minor to Butlin's holiday camp at Mosney, some 30 miles north of Dublin, where we pupils performed a life- saving demonstration.

Billy Butlin owned nine holiday camps by the mid-fifties, which were extremely popular with their range of entertainments organised by their 'Redcoats' in a structured schedule of competitions and activities. Campers had a menu that included bingo, ballroom dancing, snooker, swimming, a boating lake, and a nightly variety show; and there were prizes for everything from lovely legs to knobbly knees and glamorous grandmothers. When Billy Butlin proposed to open his first holiday camp outside the UK at Mosney, County Meath in 1948, the local Fine Gael TD, Captain Patrick Giles, vented his anger in the *Catholic Standard* in an article headlined 'Holiday camp and Morals.' He opined that 'all holiday camps are an English idea and are alien and undesirable in an Irish Catholic country – outside influences are bad and dangerous.'[18] Unable to prevent Mosney from opening, Giles and some allies in the Catholic hierarchy secured a concession that a church would be built outside the main gate with a Catholic priest in residence acting as a moral policeman. This compromise was acceptable to Billy Butlin and the camp was opened in 1948 and operated successfully until 1982. The camp had similar specifications to those in Britain, including a boating lake, chalets, dining hall, an amusement arcade, theatre and swimming pool. It is easy to patronise Butlin and his glamorous granny and knobbly knee contests, but he provided regimented entertainment for a social class memorably described as the 'frayed collar worker.' It was to be many years before the package holiday industry relocated the knobbly knees from the Mosney Butlin's holiday camp to the Costa del Sol.

Butlin's swimming pool at Mosney was of the windblown open-air type that was treated but not heated. Our demonstration involved plunging fully clothed into the icy water of the swimming pool across which a chill north-easterly wind blew in off the Irish Sea. Following the demonstration, usually witnessed by small huddles of elderly campers dressed in transparent pac-a-macs, we were then free to use all the Butlin's facilities for a few hours, the highlight of which was a floor show in the theatre where the star attraction was a singer who, in those politically incorrect days of the late fifties, blacked up to perform Al Jolson songs.

My youthful enthusiasm for cricket was sparked primarily by listening to Test match commentaries on the BBC. John Arlott, poetic and politically liberal in a game steeped in conservatism, was not only the doyen of cricket commentators but also the best sport's commentator I have ever heard: lyrical, imaginative, enthusiastic, romantic yet authoritative, all delivered with his unmistakeable Hampshire burr, which became for many the defining sound of long summer days. Through the magic of John Arlott's commentaries I became interested in the nerdy aspects of cricket. The *Irish Times* published the English county cricket scores in detail every day in the 1950s and soon I was recording the batting scores of Dennis Compton, Len Hutton and Cyril Washbrook; and the bowling figures of Fred Trueman, Jim Laker and Tony Lock. Cricket is the perfect sport for people obsessed by numbers and soon I knew key statistics such as Don Bradman's Test average of 99.94, Dennis Compton's thrilling summer of 1947 when his cavalier batting style yielded 18 centuries in a season (a record that still stands) and 3,816 runs (also a record) at an average of 90.85

Playing cricket at school was a source of great pleasure to me. I was an opening quick bowler who batted at 4 or 5 and so was always involved in the game, however mediocre my contribution. Cricket is generally perceived in Ireland as a Protestant sport which, like many perceptions, is not accurate. We played against a number of private Catholic schools, including Blackrock College and the (Jesuit) Belvedere College. Indeed Belvedere, boasted the finest cricketer I have ever played against, arguably the greatest all-rounder Ireland has ever produced, Alec O'Riordan, left-arm pace bowler and middle-order batsman. On a match day at home to Belvedere, as their team walked into the Pavilion, there was only one anxious question on our lips: Is O'Riordan playing today?

Batting at cricket tested one's courage. Trying to remain calm and focused while facing the fast bowling of Alec O'Riordan – someone who could move the ball both ways off the pitch – on a less than perfect surface was a seriously challenging prospect. I really enjoyed the process of opening the bowling. It was exciting to grip the ball and walk back to the start of my run-up, while evaluating the batsman and the field placings. There was the rush of adrenalin as I ran in to bowl as fast as possible. Then there was the exhilaration of leaning my body back, pointing my left shoulder at the batsman, stretching out the left arm to its full extent, followed by whipping through the right arm and projecting the ball at maximum speed towards the batsman's off-stump. Cricket is also influenced by the fascinating vagaries of weather – whether the pitch was damp or dry, would it take spin, the pace of the ball off the pitch, or whether the wind would blow.[19] As an aficionado, I was aware of the Freemantle Doctor, the south-west wind that blew in consistently across the WACA ground in Perth and even influenced the selection of swing bowlers.

My best cricketing performances were achieved when I was young: at Under 14- level I took 48 wickets in eight single innings matches; while my best bowling figures were 8 for 11 against Avoca School. As I moved into senior school, my cricket form gradually deteriorated, although I still enjoyed the harmonious sound of ball on willow and the subtleties of the sport. It was also through cricket that I first became aware of the extent of social class division in England. Two initials were normal and young men armed with three were likely to be from a public- school background. Many of England's amateur gentleman test players of the 1950s – such as MCC Cowdrey, PBH May and NWD Yardley – had a kick start to life with the benefit of three Christian names and a public school education. Such strings of initials symbolised an affectation of pedigree and self-importance. In the two-class world of post-war cricket (amateurs and professionals), the professionals were finally given their initials on the scorecard at Lord's, but placed after the surname, whereas amateurs' initials preceded it. However, the two classes of cricketers continued for the most part to change in separate rooms. In May 1950, there was an announcement over the tannoy at Lord's when a young Middlesex pro was walking out to bat against Surrey: 'Ladies and Gentlemen, a correction to your scorecards: for 'F. J. Titmus,' please read 'Titmus F. J.'[20]

Rugby was perceived to be the leading sport at which to excel at St Andrew's. Every boy was expected to train on Monday and Thursday and there were also two matches per week against other schools on Wednesday and Saturday. From the age of 12 onwards I managed to gain selection for the school teams, playing at wing-forward. However, at a time when other boys seemed to be doubling in size every term and acquiring bulky torsos, I remained quite slim and light. Eventually, in my penultimate year (1957-58), I was also selected for the Leinster Schools trials. During my final year 1958-

59, I was chosen for the Leinster Schools trials again; and then subsequently I was selected twice to play in two Final Trials for the Leinster Schools team. Although I was disappointed to miss out on selection for Leinster, I realised that I did not deserve it for I was not sufficiently heavy or strong enough to play in the back row at provincial level. This was reinforced in our annual match against Belfast Royal Academy (BRA). We faced a BRA team in March 1959 that boasted two players – Sam Hutton and Ken Houston – who would subsequently play rugby for Ireland. As an open side wing forward, it was my job to mark Ken Houston, the BRA out-half. Houston was stocky, powerful, well-balanced and very fast. The first time I ran at him from the back of the lineout, he accelerated rapidly and I only just managed to tap tackle him. A few minutes later following a scrum I sprinted at him and he swerved and made an outside break, handing me off in the process by pushing my face into the mud while the remainder of my body collapsed in a heap. My only consolation came two years later when Houston, at the age of only 19, first played for Ireland against the South African Springboks. St Andrew's was a small school in the 1950s with around 220 pupils and in the later stages of the Leinster School's Cup we were unable to defeat the much larger private Catholic schools, such as Castleknock, Blackrock or Belvedere Colleges. On my last day at school in June 1959 I managed to compensate somewhat for the rugby disappointment by winning the 440 yards, 880 yards and one- mile races and the *Victor Ludorum,* Senior Championship Cup, at the annual school sports day.

Schools were very different then. No computers, whiteboards, modules or variety of subjects. St Andrew's College is the only school in Ireland under Presbyterian patronage and yet, somewhat paradoxically, it displayed a more liberal and tolerant ethos than many rival Protestant schools in the 1950s. This may partly explain why it was an attractive educational enclave for the children of foreign diplomats and also a healthy minority of Jewish pupils, even after the Jewish secondary school – Stratford College – opened in 1954. St Andrew's made a significant impression on me; it was an institution where we acquired much more than the principles and processes of a subject. It was a training ground for developing social skills, learning to get along with others, to make friendships and also how to cope with bullies. It was a setting where we experienced success and failure, where we were sometimes hurt and lonely, where rules circumscribed every day, and where teachers wielded a great influence upon one for life. One problem made teaching difficult:

since the school was small, there was only one class in each age cohort so that bright pupils shared the classroom with the academically less gifted. St Andrew's was a place where we learned about compassion, goodness, love, and other positive emotions. Most teachers created an atmosphere where pupils' curiosity could flourish, where we were allowed to think and question. The school tolerated the unconventional, the innovative and the eccentric. Also, there were the harsh lessons of life: failure in the exam hall or sports field, injustice in team selection, cruelty, name-calling and, above all, bullying, exposing our innermost insecurities. However, my recall is that bullying was not a major problem at the school in the 1950s, but it did occur occasionally.

The school's attitude towards public exams was relaxed in the late 1950s; students were not subjected to intense pressure to perform. The emphasis at St Andrew's in the 1950s was not primarily directed towards narrow academic achievement, but was oriented towards a more comprehensive concept of education embracing sport, scholarship and personality development. Having personally abandoned the state Leaving Certificate syllabus in favour of the Trinity College matriculation, I was from the age of 16 in a position where individual learning and self-motivation were essential. As a result, the St Andrew's system, with its understandable focus on the Leaving Certificate syllabus, forced one to become self-motivated and to study on one's own, which was an ideal preparation for university. In 1959, I was eager to move on to the Elysian Fields of Trinity College Dublin, although aware that I had many gaps in my knowledge and that I was naïve, poorly read and unsophisticated.

CHAPTER 4

Jiving in the Aisles

Four events were harbingers of change in the Ireland of the mid-to-late 1950s: the advent of rock 'n' roll; the arrival of Italian and Chinese restaurants; the development of a coffee- bar culture; and the first performance of *Waiting for Godot* by Samuel Beckett. The Marxist historian Eric Hobsbawm, reflecting upon the 20th century in 2002, opined to Prof. Peter Hennessy that 'the Fifties are the crucial decade. For the first time you could feel things changing. Suez and the coming of rock 'n' roll divide twentieth century British history.'[1] Although Ireland did not experience the humiliating loss of status that Suez visited upon Britain, it was impacted in 1955 by the film *Blackboard Jungle* in which Bill Haley and the Comets sang 'Rock around the Clock,' which reached number 1 in the hit parade in November 1955. The song – the first to sell a million copies in the UK – was also featured in the film *Rock around the Clock* in 1956. When this film was released in Ireland, I and many other young people jived in the cinema aisles bawling out the choruses. When Haley and his band appeared in person on the stage of the Theatre Royal, Dublin, in March 1957, the Gardai drew their batons in order to control some two thousand youths and Teddy boys. Bill Haley was unusual in that he was in his thirties and of flabby appearance with his hair sporting an absurd kiss curl. When I saw the film *Rock around the Clock*, I was more impressed by the Platters, who sang two of their greatest hits, 'Only You' (1955) and 'The Great Pretender'(1955), than I was by Bill Haley. The Platters were the earliest African-American group to break through as a major pop group propelled by the distinctive tenor voice of Tony Williams.

Bill Haley was soon superseded by Little Richard who recorded 'Tutti Frutti' in 1955 with a hard driving sound and wild lyrics. We loved jiving to it and singing the refrain 'A – wop – bop- a –loo- bop – a – lop – bam – boom.' Another black pioneer of rock and roll, Fats Domino, released two major hits – 'Ain't that a Shame'(1955) and 'Blueberry Hill' (1956). As black performers in the mid-fifties, their impact was limited amongst the white population of the USA. Pat Boone capitalised on this by releasing bland and uninspiring versions of 'Tutti Frutti' and 'Aint that a Shame' that targeted white radio stations and sold more than Fats Domino's far superior originals. Elvis Presley, however, was able to take the music of Southern blacks and present it to white audiences. His combination of a unique sound and hip movements projected four songs into the British charts in 1956, most notably 'Heartbreak Hotel' and 'Hound Dog.' As in the USA and Britain, critics were alarmed by the suggestiveness of Presley's performances. The term 'rock 'n' roll' was black slang for sex and the music was black music played for white audiences. It was to be decades later that I realised that the true king of rock-and-roll was Chuck Berry, who refined rhythm and blues into rock-and- roll and wrote his own classic songs, including 'Sweet Little Sixteen,' 'Johnny B Goode,' 'Memphis Tennessee,' 'Rock and Roll Music,' and 'Roll Over Beethoven.' Writing lyrics that focused largely on white teenage life, he electrified audiences with brilliant guitar riffs, swagger and exuberant showmanship, including his duck-walk.

During the late fifties it was the growing importance of the youth market that established the cultural values and social behaviour for the rest of the century. A singer who made a profound impact on me and my friends in the 1950s was Buddy Holly whose first single 'That will be the Day' reached number 1 in Britain and the USA in September 1957. He followed up with a string of even greater songs, including 'Peggy Sue,' 'Oh Boy,' 'Not Fade Away' and 'Rave on' in January 1958. Holly's style was characterised by vocal hiccups and alternations between his normal voice and falsetto, all complemented by brilliant guitar riffs. I loved this distinctive and influential rock music, which Holly wrote himself, and I had the octave range to mimic (only passably) his vocal style. Even today his songs seem so fresh and relevant. He changed the face of rock 'n' roll in a career that lasted only 17 months before his tragic death in an air crash in February 1959. Jiving to the pounding beat of Buddy Holly was just so enjoyable; it was the only dance form for which I had any talent whatsoever and wearing a pair of slip-on shoes and an open shirt I almost felt cool!

Overlapping with Buddy Holly was a great rock duo, the Everly Brothers. Their first recording – 'Bye Bye Love' – in the spring of 1957- was followed by three great hits in 1958 – 'Wake Up little Susie,' 'All I Have to Do is Dream,' and 'Problems.' Their beautiful close- harmony singing and acoustic guitar playing influenced the Beatles, the Beach Boys and Simon and Garfunkel. Don Everly sang the baritone part and Phil the tenor harmony, but their voices overlap in a subtle fashion. There was a purity and soulful quality to their two-part harmonies that was unique in popular music. There is no more beautiful and plangent sound than the voices of these two brothers in perfect harmony singing songs of yearning. In parallel with the birth of rock-and- roll, Lonnie Donegan, the Glasgow-born son of an Irish mother and Scottish father, who had previously played guitar and banjo in the Ken Colyer and Chris Barber jazz bands, released a Leadbelly song- 'Rock island Line'- which was to remain in the Top Twenty for 19 weeks in 1956. This song was responsible for igniting the skiffle boom of the fifties, a craze that was also popular in Ireland with skiffle groups touring dance halls around the country. My voice suited Donegan's music and I derived great enjoyment from singing songs such as 'Rock Island Line,' 'Cumberland Gap' and 'Grand Coulee Dam' on Geology field trips when at university.

The taste buds of the country also began to experience changes from the late 1950s. The Italians led the culinary invasion with restaurants and trattoria becoming established in Dublin and other cities by the mid- fifties. In the same period Chinese restaurants also began their march across the Irish urban landscape. The Italians and Chinese were followed by other culinary invaders from France, Greece, Turkey and India. Before the diffusion of Italian restaurants, eating out in Ireland was not a rewarding experience: menus were dominated by such delights as roast beef, pork chops, bacon and cabbage or watery cod accompanied by spuds and carrots that had been boiled to death. As a consequence, our family seldom ever ate out or stayed in a hotel before I went up to Trinity College in 1959, in part because there was virtually nowhere to go.

Dublin's first shopping arcade, Creation House, off Grafton Street, was opened in October 1958. During the same period the continental influence continued to grow with the arrival of bubble cars, such as Isettas and Messerschmitts, chic Vespas and Lambrettas and the sharp Italian mohair suit, which was lighter and smarter. Two innovations, however – one Italian and one American- combined to produce another harbinger of change on Irish high streets. In 1938, Achille Gaggia 'invented a piston system for forcing hot water at high pressure through finely ground coffee contained in a filtered holder'[2] to produce a smoother drink marketed in Ireland as expresso. Espresso bars sprouted all across Italy and the invention arrived on Irish shores in the early fifties. Previously in Ireland the coffee was either a boring powdered instant variety such as Nescafe, Maxwell House, or liquid camp coffee essence. The culture of the coffee bar became established in Dublin and was especially successful when the Espresso coffee machine was combined with an American invention, the jukebox. The Venetian café at the bottom of Clyde Road, Ballsbridge was beside the bus stop where I caught the number 8 bus from school home to Dalkey. The jukebox in the Venetian café (known to St Andrew's boys as 'the Venner') was a Wurlitzer, which imitated the style and appearance of a flashy American car. With its tailfins, chrome grills and windscreens, it was an unusual sight in fifties Dublin. Moreover, the coolest place to be seen in Dun Laoghaire at the time was the Bamboo café, which also boasted the essential Espresso coffee machine and jukebox around which students in their duffel coats sipped coffee and smoked. Its windows were always misted up which lent it an air of excitement as did the steaming coffee machine, the music and conversation. The coffee bar symbolised youth culture in the late fifties as it represented more sophisticated values for teenagers than anything else on the Irish high street. With a little imagination, they even resembled a film set in a 1950s Hollywood movie. As Hopkins wrote, 'one dallied over *Apfelstrudel,* Danish pastries, cheese-cake, chocolate torte dispensed by sophisticates in swinging skirts and large brass ear-rings or black-jersied gamines with Audrey Hepburn hairdos.'[3] It was much less sophisticated in the Bamboo café where we were happy to have a shilling in our pocket to spend on a coffee and the Everly Brothers latest hit on the jukebox.

Much of the teenage culture in Ireland was generated by either the United States or Britain. The success of rock-and-roll in Ireland depended on Radio Luxembourg, coffee bars, the jukebox, music magazines and record shops. The golden age of the jukebox in Dublin was the late 1950s – the time when rock- and- roll was dominated by Elvis Presley, Fats Domino, Chuck Berry, Buddy Holly and the Everly Brothers. By 1960, the 78rpm discs were being replaced by the more cost-effective 45rpm so that the jukebox could hold more records. The heyday of the jukebox was relatively brief and its surge in popularity did not extend beyond the sixties when pop radio stations, TV shows, rock concerts and the introduction of portable radios quickly challenged its hegemony. The advent of the audio cassette in the 1980s changed everything.

The other major indicator of change in late 1950s Ireland was the first performance of *Waiting for Godot*. Samuel Beckett had read Modern Languages at Trinity College Dublin and – while living in Paris – wrote the play, *En Attendant Godot*, in French. The first English production of Beckett's masterpiece, directed by Peter Hall, opened in London on 3rd August 1955. Brown has argued that *Waiting for Godot* 'in its tragic-comic angst caught a mood of near – desolation that helped to define the zeitgeist for a generation.'[4] Conversely, many of the English arts establishment were scathing about the play. John Gielgud 'loathed it;' Somerset Maugham called it 'two dirty old men picking their toenails;' the character actor Robert Morley concluded that the success of '*Waiting for Godot* 'means the end of theatre as we know it;' while Evelyn Waugh 'couldn't make head or tail of it.'[5] However, Harold Hobson in the *Sunday Times* and Kenneth Tynan in the *Observer* both acknowledged the play's remarkable originality and its London future was assured. Beckett was less fortunate with the BBC who, when he submitted his English translation, rejected it because the script contained 'too many Irish inflections and idioms.'

The first performance in Beckett's native city was two months later at the Pike Theatre on 28th October 1955 starring Dermot Kelly and Donal Donnelly. The play gains by being performed in an Irish idiom as the hibernicisims in the script are emphasised. Vivian Mercier famously wrote in the *Irish Times* that Beckett had 'achieved a theoretical impossibility – a play in which nothing happens, yet keeps audiences glued to their seats. What's more, since the second act is a subtly different reprise of the first, he has written a play in which nothing happens twice.'[6] It became the longest continuous run in Irish theatre history up to that time. When I first saw *Godot* as a fifteen- year old I could not understand why it rejected the accepted principles of drama: a sequence of actions, motives and conflicts leading to a resolution. It relies upon the core dramatic element of suspense – waiting and passing the time – and forces the audience to experience the uncertainty of Vladimir and Estragon, while raising fundamental issues about the nature of existence itself. It was only seeing the 2010 production in Edinburgh starring Ian McKellen, Patrick Stewart and Simon Callow that I fully appreciated the richness of *Waiting for Godot* and how it opens up vistas on so many different perspectives of life; that it is poetic, funny, and emphasises the attributes of stoicism, companionship, simply muddling through, and of what it means to be human. As Burt has written, 'the theatrical and existential vision of *Waiting for Godot* makes it the watershed 20th century drama…..as explosive, ground-breaking and influential a work as James Joyce's *Ulysses* is for modern fiction.[7] When the Royal National Theatre surveyed more than 800 playwrights, actors, directors and arts journalists in 1998 to nominate the most important play of the 20th century Beckett's *Waiting for Godot* headed the list with Arthur Miller's *Death of a Salesman* in second place.

The Irish hit parade was pioneered by the *Evening Herald* newspaper in February 1959 and the first chart featured Elvis Presley at number 1 with 'I Got Stung' followed by 'A Pub with no Beer' by Slim Dusty and, at number 3, Little Richard singing 'By the Light of the Silvery Moon.' In general, American artists were even more dominant in the Irish chart than the British ones. In order to listen to a chart programme in the early fifties, it was necessary to tune into Radio Luxembourg at 208 on the medium wave. Transistors had become available by the mid-fifties and one could then listen to the Top Twenty on Luxembourg while in bed! Luxembourg cultivated a more relaxed style of presentation with disc jockeys conversing in a non- patronising way on first-name terms with the predominantly teenage audience. Listeners were allowed to form the erroneous impression that all the presenters were sitting in the Grand Duchy, whereas, in reality, programmes were partly pre-recorded in the company's UK studios in London. Presenters such as Alan Freeman, Pete Murray, Keith Fordyce and others, having been DJs on Radio Luxembourg, relocated to London to work for the BBC. It was through such nocturnal listening on Radio Luxembourg that I first became acquainted with the great bands of the jazz and swing era in the thirties and forties, especially the swing bands of Chick Webb, Duke Ellington, Count Basie and Benny Goodman and great vocalists, especially Frank Sinatra, Nat King Cole, Ella Fitzgerald and Sarah Vaughan. Nat King Cole changed roles from being a jazz pianist of distinction into becoming a great crooner who produced definitive versions of songs such as 'Stardust,' 'Too Young,' 'Answer Me,' 'Mona Lisa' and 'When I Fall in Love.' It is now 55 years since his premature death at 45 and, listening again to his singing, I am struck by the unique velvety tone of his voice, the mesmerising phrasing, the hauntingly intimate way he caressed the words, and how he creates the feeling that he is singing directly to you. Despite facing blatant racism throughout his career, he conducted himself with great dignity and never abandoned his jazz roots.

There was a British Traditional jazz boom in the 1950s with a number of leading bands of which I preferred the Chris Barber Band, and also the

Humphrey Lyttleton Band, which played a mixture of Trad and Mainstream and enjoyed a great hit with 'Bad Penny Blues.' One evening in 1958 I rode my bicycle the nine miles to the Gaiety Theatre in Dublin to attend a Chris Barber concert with the man himself on trombone, Monty Sunshine (clarinet) and Ottilie Paterson from County Down supplying the vocals for an evening of infectious New Orleans jazz.

The British traditional jazz revival was but a pale imitation of New Orleans jazz and I clearly recall the first time I heard Louis Armstrong playing on the radio. I was instantly captivated by his sound and technique. He was uneducated – having dropped out of school at 11 – yet he became the greatest trumpet player of all time. Supremely inventive, his improvisations were sophisticated but also subtle and highly melodic; he was the first to create variations based on chord harmonies of the songs. Whenever I hear a trumpet playing, I can tell immediately if it's him. His influence on the development of jazz, including the development of scat singing, is immeasurable. How does one try to explain such talent except by listening to his 1928 Hot Five recordings of 'West End Blues' and 'Basin Street Blues' when Armstrong transformed jazz music into an art form. To listen to 'Hesitation Blues' and 'The Memphis Blues' – recorded with his All Stars almost three decades later in 1955 – is clear evidence of the imperishable nature of his genius.

* * *

Life was fairly dull in Dalkey in the 1950s. Everything seemed to be happening somewhere else in 1956: Elvis entered the US charts for the first time singing 'Heartbreak Hotel;' *The Goon Show* was live on the BBC; Marilyn Monroe married Arthur Miller; Britain and France embarked upon a disastrous invasion of the Suez Canal Zone; Grace Kelly married Prince Rainier of Monaco; the Russians launched the Sputnik with a dog on board in 1957; and the zeitgeist was elsewhere incorporating Martini cocktails, radiograms and television. However, my father purchased a Ford Consul in 1956. With a body designed by the parent US Ford company, the 1,500cc engine developed 47 brake horse power with a three-speed gearbox, which was synchronised only on second and top gears. It was painted azure blue, with the gear shift on the steering wheel and a bench front seat trimmed in PVC. I felt that modernity had finally arrived for us, although with a top speed of 72 miles per hour and fuel consumption of 26 miles per gallon, the car was positively pedestrian accelerating from 0 to 60 in a snail-like 23.2 seconds.

Together with my two best friends David Thomas and John Keery – with whom I am still close almost 70 years later- we engaged in discussions with our rector, Rev. Des Murray, with a view to establishing a scout troop in Dalkey, the 41st Dublin Dalkey Sea Scouts. Des Murray was short and stocky with a full head of dark hair. He always dressed as an Anglican clergyman, but instead of wearing a black suit he preferred a more subtle dark-grey, which differentiated him from the black-suited Catholic priests. Six of us met for the first time in St Patrick's Church Hall on 4 May 1956. Initially we were under the leadership of Des Murray, a role taken on in 1957 by Mike Stopford, a former merchant seaman and lay preacher. Mike, while not the most organised of people, was a Scoutmaster of integrity and decency who was a superb role model to the boys. He was ably assisted by David Sarratt, who became Scoutmaster in 1961. The troop made a large impact from the start by earning more money *per capita* in Bob-a –Job week in 1957 than any other troop in Ireland. The troop also acquired a clinker-built cutter with a lugsail in 1957 and each year we started to scrape and paint it on St Patrick's day. When I recently saw a photo of this boat from the summer of 1957, there were 13 of us on board and nobody was wearing a life jacket; and, moreover, there were no buoyancy aids. Bulloch harbour threw its arms around us, but once beyond its walls and into the open sea with the wind stretching the sail and the waves slapping against the clinker- built boat we were in a new, potentially exciting, environment, without life jackets. Yet we regularly rowed and sailed around Dublin Bay up to several miles offshore. Those trips were closely associated with the popular music of the day: in 1957 we were singing along to Buddy Holly's 'That'll be the Day' and 'Peggy Sue', the Everly Brothers 'Wake up Little Susie,' and Harry Belafonte's 'The Banana Boat Song.' The musical signature of the lovely summer of 1958 were the Everlys' songs 'All I have to do is Dream' and 'Wake Up Little Susie,' and under the influence of the late Stephen 'Spud' Murphy, Buddy Holly's 'Rave On' frequently rang out across Dalkey Sound.

We held our first camp in the summer of 1957 at Dromineer, a beautiful location on the shore of Lough Derg. My most vivid memory was that of Rev. Des Murray dressed in baggy white shorts with a fag hanging out of his mouth making 'thump,' a meal that was an archipelago of mashed potatoes, onion and corned beef. We were taught how to erect a tent, or build a shelter, and how to tie numerous knots and to send messages by semaphore. We were shown how to light a fire and cook a basic meal. The following year in 1958 we organised a summer camp in Dunmore East and several of us made the return journey up the River Barrow navigation in Mike Stopford's boat, which seemed like a trip up the Amazon as few boats, if any, had navigated the Barrow for decades. It was fun to operate the locks and to experience the boat rising or falling as the gates opened and the boat was raised or lowered to a different level. The boat glided slowly through the unspoilt pastoral countryside of Counties Waterford and Kilkenny. Eventually we had to abandon the boat at Graiguenamanagh due to torrential rain and severe flooding and an exciting if damp night was spent sleeping under the upturned boat.

I also accompanied John Keery on his First Class hike in 1958 and we camped beside the waterfall in Powerscourt demesne. The waterfall, surrounded by beech, oak, larch and pine trees is the highest in Ireland at 121 metres. It flows over schists – a metamorphic aureole of the Leinster granite batholith. We were entranced by the falling torrent cascading over the rock outcrops as it descended. The summer camp in 1959 was held at Morfa Nefyn on the Lleyn peninsula in Wales, travelling across on the mailboat to Holyhead in the company of gnarled emigrants returning to building sites across England. I loved being in the scouts; I had joined because I wanted to and not because my parents said that I should. I liked learning semaphore, how to tie complex knots, how to use a compass and read a map, and how to handle a boat at sea. Being in the Sea Scouts was great fun and, also, I believe that we absorbed important life skills as if by osmosis: personal responsibility, self-discipline, taking initiative, teamwork, leadership, awareness of high standards, and how to tolerate some people with whom one did not necessarily have a natural rapport.

I would occasionally frequent the Guild of Youth dances presided over by the Rev. Des Murray in St Patrick's Church Hall, Dalkey and our Scout troop would also organise a few record hops every year. Dancing to records – predominantly rock- and- roll in the late 1950s – was very different from doing the slow foxtrot, waltz or quickstep when accompanied by a small band. There was always a girl who would want to dance with you while hugging tight and you could then slip your hands down on her bottom. The last dance would be called and I recall an attractive 16 year saying 'yes you can take me home'. When I got outside, excited by the prospect of walking her home by the sea, I found that she had her best friend with her, who had not managed to pull a bloke at the hop, so I ended up walking them both home, having, as so often, misread the body language.

* * *

Due to the rigid implementation of the *Ne Temere* decree by Archbishop John Charles McQuaid, these dances were Protestant- only affairs and this certainly limited the opportunities to mix socially with the majority Catholic community. The *Ne Temere* decree was introduced by the Catholic Church on 19 April 1908 and, *inter alia,* made it conditional for the granting of a dispensation for a Catholic to marry a Protestant that both parties sign an agreement that any children would be raised in the Catholic faith. The decree was rigidly enforced. What was a source of deep hurt to the Protestant community was that the written promise to raise all the children as Catholics stemmed from the assertion that the Catholic Church was the one true church. The penalty for non-observance by the Catholic party to the marriage was excommunication. A further stipulation that caused upset was that any inter-church marriage had to be conducted by a Catholic priest in an unconsecrated building without religious celebration. An ethnic form of nationalism was emerging which Brown argued 'increasingly would establish Catholicism as a marker of Irish identity, setting in question the nationality of the country's Protestants.'[8] By the 1950s and 1960s, the age structure of the Irish Protestant population was old with a low marriage rate and low fertility. Walsh highlighted the *Ne Temere* decree as the primary factor behind the low fertility and declining numbers among the Church of Ireland community reporting that almost 30 per cent of all OD (other denomination) grooms and 20 percent of all OD brides married Catholic partners in 1961.[9] By contrast, mixed marriages accounted for less than two per cent of all Catholic grooms and brides. Walsh concluded pessimistically that ' any population that experiences a natural decrease over a fifteen year period ....between 1946 and 1961, is obviously in serious danger of eventual extinction.'[10]

The *Ne Temere* decree was clearly discriminatory and an unacceptable intrusion on personal choice; it was this Catholic ruling that impacted most upon those in the Protestant community by encouraging a high degree of social apartheid as Protestants had little option other than to confine themselves within their own social networks. This process was reinforced by the practice of the Catholic bishops of vetoing Catholics from attending any Protestant church services, Protestant schools and Trinity College Dublin. To make matters worse, the *Ne Temere* decree was granted the force of law by the Supreme Court. In the infamous Tilson case of 1950, the Supreme Court – in a departure from common law practice – upheld the verdict of the High Court and ruled against the right of Ernest Tilson (the Protestant partner) to determine the religious education of his children after his marriage to a Catholic woman had failed and the Court found in favour of the (Catholic) wife. Promises made by the non-Catholic partners in 'mixed' marriages to educate their children as Catholics were binding. Hence, the Irish state was not neutral as between the rights of its Catholic and non-Catholic citizens when Catholic Church interests were involved. Despite the manifest unfairness of the *Ne Temere* decree, good neighbourliness always prevailed in the Dalkey community and I never experienced a single sectarian incident or remark. The Church of Ireland population of Ireland declined steeply from 164,215 in 1926 to 89,187 by 1991. Since than there has been an increase of 44.7 per cent to 129,033 by 2011. This growth had been driven by Protestant immigration and by Catholics converting. Of the 137,048 Protestants who recorded their country of birth, only 69.2 per cent stated the Republic. Some 28,000 came from the UK, which accounted, therefore, for two-thirds of Protestant immigrants between 1991 and 2011.[11]

The influence of Protestants far exceeded their numbers in the population. Many of the writers who gave Ireland its great literary reputation were Protestants – from Jonathan Swift to William Congreve, George Berkley, Richard Brinsley Sheridan, Oliver Goldsmith, Maria Edgeworth, Edmund Burke, Oscar Wilde, Bernard Shaw, Sean O'Casey, WB Yeats, Bram Stoker, J M Synge, Elizabeth Bowen, Louis MacNeice, Samuel Beckett, William Trevor, Molly Keane, Derek Mahon and Michael Longley. Protestants could also claim their share of Irish Patriots: from Wolfe Tone and Henry Joy McCracken to Parnell, Robert Emmett, Roger Casement, Douglas Hyde and Erskine Childers. Protestants were also prominent in professions such as medicine, the law, banking, industry and business with household names such as Guinness's, Jacob's, Bewley's, Odlum's, Findlater's and many others providing employment.

* * *

Given that St Andrew's College was an exclusively boys school in the fifties (it became co-educational in 1973), the process of meeting girls was both nerve-racking and challenging. Our major source of teenage girlfriends was Glengara Park School in Dun Laoghaire. On Wednesday afternoon, if I was not playing rugby, David Thomas, John Keery and myself would cycle along the Metals in the hope that we would bump into Glengara girls on their bicycles whom we would then attempt to chat-up. We were gauche and I did not find this easy, but I do recall that it was all totally innocent. White Rock beach was a popular swimming location on Killiney Bay and – as I was soon to discover at Trinity College – it was an important geological site where the Devonian granite batholith (400 million years old), which outcrops for over 70 miles from Dalkey to County Wexford, makes contact with the adjacent Ordovician shales and a metamorphic rock – mica schist – was formed. A major reason why we frequented the White Rock was not geological but because, unlike the famous Forty Foot, there were swarms of teenage girls relaxing on the beach. To me the girls looked wonderful in a Jantzen swimming costume, with the famous emblem of a girl diving. There were even a couple of girls confident enough to wear a bikini, which reminds me of a priest in Sligo who, seeing one of his flock in a bikini, promptly told her to wear a one-piece costume in future, to which the girl responded: 'And now Father which piece would you like me to take off?'

There was a concrete bathing platform the size of a tennis court at White Rock on which young girls sunbathed in summer. I would sprint across this platform, perform a running dive into the sea and then execute a flashy 25-yard crawl, which, sadly, made no impression whatsoever on these girls. When we dived under the water at the White Rock, grains of mica schist glinted back at us from the sand, especially when the sun was out. We frequently whiled away the afternoon in this manner. A lot of time was spent doing, well nothing. Just drifting around. These were carefree teenage summers growing up in secure homes and in a community where we knew everyone else, surrounded by gorse-covered hills with shafts of sunlight glinting on the seawater at Vico; it was a near-perfect existence.

Dublin's love affair with the cinema began with a most unusual pioneer. Apart from his literary genius, James Joyce became an entrepreneur. He returned to Dublin from Trieste to open Ireland's first dedicated cinema, the Volta Electric Theatre on Mary Street in December 1909. Joyce's commitment lasted only seven months and he then returned to Europe. The cinema was overwhelmingly the popular art form of the time, the favourite recreation, together with ballroom dancing, of both the middle and working classes. The new state introduced the Censorship of Films Act of 1923 establishing that the censor's role was to ensure that 'all films submitted to him be fit for exhibition in public, unless he is of the opinion that all or part thereof is indecent, obscene or blasphemous, or is otherwise contrary to public morality.' The persistent focus of the censor on sexual content allowed issues of violence, horror or criminality to pass as suitable for Irish audiences. The first censor, James Montgomery, was particularly concerned about 'indecent dances' and costumes, double-meaning songs and gags, divorce, adultery, films that might lead to political or labour trouble and, above all, sex. He rejected Paramount's *Rumba* in 1935 noting that 'apart from the plot and indecent costumes, the Rumba is the most sexy thing that has wriggled its way into modern life from the lusts of the Jungle.'[12] Some of the cuts made by the censor were so blatant that they altered the plot of the film. The most notorious example was when the censor (Richard Hayes), in order to safeguard traditional Catholic values, cut key dialogue from the final scenes of America's greatest romantic film, *Casablanca*. The censor removed all references to the fact that Ingrid Bergman's Isla was married to Victor while she was involved in an intense relationship with Rick when in Paris. This would make her an adulterer, which was unacceptable to the Irish censor, but in removing the dialogue, Hayes decided to completely alter the film.

The peak year for cinema attendance in Ireland was 1956 when admissions totalled 52.1 million. There were over 50 cinemas scattered throughout Dublin and its suburbs in the mid-fifties. On a Friday or Saturday night queues stretched around the block as we stood there in the wind and rain. The queue edged forward until a self-important commissionaire dressed like an Argentinian admiral in a uniform boasting epaulettes, great scrolls of gold braid at the end of each sleeve, more up the outside leg and a twist on his peaked cap would come down the queue shouting: 'Two at 1s.6d', 'A single at 2s.6d.' When we eventually approached the head of the queue, the commissionaire would often stick out his arm and say: 'That's it, the house is full.' Then we would decide whether to try another cinema since there were three within a mile of where we lived in Dalkey in the 1950s. The nearest was in Glasthule, a dip in the topography between Dalkey and Dun Laoghaire into which the Council had poured low income residents, many of whom provided services for the large houses nearby. The Astoria in Glasthule was a small 750 seat cinema opened in 1940 where one was more likely to see continental films than elsewhere in Dun Laoghaire. The oldest cinema, the Pavilion, dating from 1903, overlooked the harbour. In the centre of Dun Laoghaire was the 1,621 seater Adelphi, which opened in 1948, closed in 1971 and is now an apartment block. While the entrances to the Adelphi and Pavilion were quite imposing – dominated by photos of current Hollywood starlets adorned with gleaming teeth – the auditoria were not much more than a hanger, with carpets on the aisles, the seats perched on lino and the whole building reeking of the smell of perfumed disinfectant, stale cigarettes and popcorn. The seating was stratified to maximise revenue with the cheap seats in the stalls at the front and more expensive at the rear. Conversely, on the balcony, the cheap seats were at the rear and the most expensive seats in the house were at the front. In Dun Laoghaire, it was always called 'the pictures' or 'the flics' but never 'the movies.' Every week there were three programmes of two films (the main feature and a support): Sunday, Monday to Wednesday, and Thursday to Saturday. Normally there was a continuous performance starting with the B movie – frequently a black-and-white western – followed by the Pathe news and then the main feature. A crimson curtain shielded the screen until the first film started at 2.00pm when the two halves of the curtain drew apart to wild cheers from the audience. The programme then just kept rolling until the stampede to beat the National Anthem at about 10.15pm.

Once settled inside a cinema in Dun Laoghaire film goers, especially in the afternoon performances, enjoyed reacting to the action on screen, calling out advice to the actors. Although this could be annoying at times, it was as nothing compared with when the major feature film would suddenly jump forward in the middle of a scene. This was clear evidence that the censor had cut a section of the action, which usually occurred during a mild romantic scene when it looked as if the actors might commit one of a large number of sins disapproved of by the Irish Catholic hierarchy. The censors were, however, very tolerant of violence and torture on screen.

Pathe newsreels – introduced by a crowing cockerel – were not censored and reached huge audiences in Ireland prior to the launch of RTE television in 1961. Their black- and- white items on British and overseas affairs brought the news into Irish homes vividly in a way newspapers struggled to match. There was a background of upbeat military- type music and a dynamic voiceover narrative spoken with upper-middle class English accents. Paradoxically, the activities of British royalty were followed avidly by nationalist Irish cinema audiences; while film of British troops under fire abroad reveals that in those days news reporters were actively supportive of British soldiers in difficult circumstances. This biased style of presentation was so unlike a 21st century Channel 4 news or BBC Newsnight, but in the 1950s it was acceptable. What has always surprised me is that the Irish authorities permitted these Pathe newsreels – incorporating blatant pro-British jingoism – to be shown in hundreds of cinemas across the land.

Cinemascope and stereophonic sound arrived and most westerns, swashbuckling adventure stories, slapstick comedy and musicals were in 'glorious technicolour.' Films about the Second World War also commanded large audiences, even in Ireland. Numerous British war films occupied the screens from 1950, including *The Wooden Horse* (1950), *The Cruel Sea* (1953), *The Cockleshell Heroes* (1955), *The Dam Busters* (1955), and *Reach for the Sky* (1956). The formula for most British war films was a standard one: plenty of action shots and heavy doses of stiff–upper- lipped British heroism in a great cause. The casting of these films not only reflected but deepened the British class structure with clipped military accents amongst the Oxbridge officer class, the occasional plucky Cockney private and, if the Empire was represented, it was usually (white) Australians or New Zealanders. Welsh, Scottish or Yorkshire accents were rarely heard. The No. 303 (Polish) Fighter Squadron achieved the best- scoring record in the Battle of Britain, despite flying slower and less manoeuvrable Hurricanes, but it was seldom, if ever, featured in films until *303 Squadron* was released in 2018, some 78 years after the Battle of Britain. The superior war films of the fifties subverted the myths of the Second World War: *The Cruel Sea*, *The Dam Busters* and *The Bridge on the River Kwai* all showed dissent in the ranks, in addition to the experience of suffering, injury and death.[13]

Although I did not actually see the *The Third Man* (1949) until 1959, it left an indelible impression on me that has never faded with every subsequent viewing. Based on a novella by Graham Greene, Carol Reed made extensive use of black-and-white expressionist cinematography involving unorthodox camera angles, combined with dark seedy locations to evoke the mood of post-war Vienna. When matched with great acting by Orson Welles and unique theme music on the zither, this is one of the definitive *film noir* movies. Reed did not want to use traditional Viennese waltz music. While filming in Vienna, he and the star actors Orson Welles, Joseph Cotton and Alida Valli, went to a wine cellar and heard Anton Karas playing the zither just for tips. Reed invited Karas to London to write and record the 'Harry Lime Theme', which became one of the most iconic film scores ever written. Different versions have sold 40 million copies worldwide.

The memory of certain films is so vivid that I can still remember where I first viewed them. This was true of Disney's *The Living Desert* (1953) and also

The Vanishing Prairie (1954), which I saw at the Adelphi, Dun Laoghaire. I was invited to David Burnett's 12th birthday party in March 1953 and we went to the Ritz cinema in Ballsbridge, a long, narrow auditorium opened in 1929, where I was thrilled by Gene Kelly, Donald O'Connor and Debbie Reynolds in *Singin' in the Rain*. This film incorporates some of the most brilliant dance sequences in the history of cinema. As a young boy one had no idea that it would come to recognised one of the greatest of all musicals. Similarly, I would never have imagined at the age of eleven that, as a fine example of positive change in Ireland, the Ritz cinema would become a Sikh temple.

I rushed to see any film directed by the great Alfred Hitchcock, one of the most influential directors in cinematic history, and so much more than his famous cameo appearances and obsession with platinum- blonde stars. He had a unique ability to engage the emotions of an audience by using the camera to mimic a person's gaze, thereby turning the viewers into voyeurs. We flocked to the Adelphi, Dun Laoghaire to see his films, including four that are frequently ranked among the finest of all time: *Rear Window* (1954), *Vertigo* (1958), *North by Northwest* (1959), and *Psycho* (1960). Later I managed to catch other Hitchcock classics, including *The 39 Steps*(1935), *Rebecca*(1940), *Shadow of a Doubt* (1943) – Hitchcock's own favourite – and *Strangers on a Train* (1951). *Vertigo* was not acclaimed after its release in 1958, but a *Sight and Sound* poll in 2012 ranked it as the greatest film ever made.

More controversial was Laurence Olivier's *Richard 111* (1955) in which he recut and altered Shakespeare's play, although his compelling, if melodramatic and camp performance, was stunning to an impressionable 14-year old. Later Olivier demonstrated his versatility as Archie Rice, a seedy comedian in decline, in the 1960 film of John Osborne's, *The Entertainer*. The Astoria was where I whetted my appetite for continental films, notably Jacques Tati in *Monsieur Hulot's Holiday* (1953) and *Mon Oncle* (1958) and Sophia Loren in *Aida* (1953) with her singing dubbed by the great soprano Renata Tebaldi. This was my first introduction to authentic opera as 13-year old and I fell in love with the art form, and especially Verdi's music.

The cinema in Ireland of the fifties was one of the few warm and comfortable places to woo girls. Around the age of 15 we became aware that that there was something different about the 'back row' of the cinema, but it was not until I was 16 that I dared to take a girl into this mysterious place. I would contact girls from a telephone box beside Buckley's Auctioneers on Sandycove Road, which smelt of stale cigarette smoke, but guaranteed that my stilted conversation would not be overheard by my parents and siblings. It was always more stressful if a parent of the desired girl answered the phone. The back row of the cinema was the closest we ever came to a feeling of sexual adventure, heightened by the fact that the seats creaked as couples kissed and struggled with their coats. Once settled into our seats the dilemma was then: should I hold her hand, or slide my arm around her, or even kiss her? I was 16 before I kissed a girl for the first time. Much of this for me was in the imagination rather than any real achievement. Amongst my peer group there was a lot more talk than action in sexual matters. 'How far did you go?' was of much greater interest to my peer group than my opinion of the film we had seen. Although we thought that we were in control, the reality was starkly different: the power was in the hands of the girls to limit the extent of sexual petting. Girls existed largely in our dreams. At the end, the lights went up, the seats clattered back, people shoved into the aisles to exit before the national anthem. We were out into the dark cold night and the spell was broken.

People smoked everywhere in the 1950s: at home, in the cinema, on trains and buses, at work, at sports events, in restaurants, and even in food shops. The most unpleasant environment was the cinema where a thick cloud of smoke wafted upwards through the projector light; and seats and walls reeked of stale tobacco. We were blissfully unaware of the dangers of secondary smoking despite the fact that the *BMJ* had already suggested a link between smoking and lung cancer in 1950. Some 70 percent of Irish men and 40 percent of women over 15 smoked in the 1960s and I felt marginalised as a non-smoker when at Trinity College. Filter- tip cigarettes and Audrey Hepburn-like cigarette holders projected an air of sophistication and security – both illusory. Living rooms in most houses in the 1950s had ashtrays available and new cars were fitted with ashtrays. Smoking 20 to 40 cigarettes each day was not considered unusual. It was so common that even as a non-smoker one did not notice the smell of smoke that penetrated clothes, curtains, carpets and hair. The pavement in Dalkey was strewn with cigarette butts, especially around bus stops. It was decades before the overwhelming evidence of the detrimental effects of smoking led to a gradual reduction in smoking so that by 2018 the percentage of Irish people who smoked had fallen to 24 percent for men and 21 percent for women.

In the mid – 1950s, my great friend, David Thomas, was given a new bright blue racing bike by his parents. Since it was new, it exuded the smell and sheen of modernity, similar to a new car. Although I did not acquire a new bike, I did visit Coombes' bicycle shop in Dalkey in order to search for a suitable one. Coombes' shop was a cornucopia of bicycle parts cascading down the walls and spilling over the floor, leaving only a small area between tyres, spare mudguards, lights, dynamos, bike frames and saddles where Mr Coombes himself could restore and repair bikes. I purchased a second-hand Raleigh racing bike from him that was fast and light with the requisite drop handlebars and the all-important set of Sturmey Archer three-speed gears, which were more reliable than the later derailleur systems. There were also bottle holders on the handlebars; and the pedals had straps so you could pull up with one foot while pushing down with the other. This was a real advance on my previous bikes and I thought at last that, even if not ahead of the zeitgeist, I was at least not far behind it. Because the bike was light, it conferred a freedom to venture much further into the surrounding Dublin and Wicklow mountains without needing to use a bus. Dave Thomas, John Keery and I would cycle the 32 mile round trip to the base of the 2,379 foot Djouce mountain in County Wicklow, climb it and be back home for supper. On one occasion, we climbed Great Sugarloaf mountain, a prominent quartzite peak, and camped the night on the summit; and on another we hiked through the night the 13 miles from Dalkey to a Scout hut in the Powerscourt demesne near Enniskerry. A lot of the time was also spent hanging around doing nothing very much: whiling away the hours sunbathing on White Rock beach while we discussed the merits, or otherwise, of various teenage girls. Such happy times.

* * *

The objectives of an Ireland Gaelic, Catholic and isolationist became an obsession of de Valera at the cost of ignoring the stagnant economy and soaring levels of emigration. However, despite all the efforts to revive Gaelic by de Valera and passionate language revivalists, Terence Brown asserted that the country remained a 'social province of the United Kingdom' and this was 'as true in the 1950s as it had been in the 1920s.'[14] De Valera's invoking of the Gaelic and Catholic theme of Irish identity was a defensive reaction to the fact that Ireland and Britain had much in common, or what Ferriter called the 'narcissism of trivial differences': exaggerating minor differences in order to mask the obvious similarities.[15] The rapid diffusion of both rock- and- roll, skiffle and fashions on a similar trajectory to the UK supports both Brown and Ferriter. English newspapers and magazines (if they were not banned) circulated widely; styles of dress were influenced by British tastes; many Irish fans travelled regularly to watch teams such as Liverpool, Manchester United, Leeds United, Arsenal and Celtic; mass emigration of Irish unskilled labourers to Britain in the 1950s underlined the close integration of the two economies; BBC radio could be received across most of the country and BBC TV in more populated areas; and the Irish and British economies were interlinked, a process later underlined by the Anglo-Irish Free Trade Agreement in 1965.

The 1950s was a period of unemployment and sustained emigration: a total of 412,000 people emigrated from Ireland between 1951 and 1961; in 1957 alone there were 78,000 unemployed in a year when emigration resulted in a net loss of population of 54,000. T K Whitaker, Secretary of the Department of Finance, published a report in 1958 that challenged the economic austerity that prevailed under de Valera's failed nationalist economic strategy and called for a Keynesian solution. This included greater state investment in productive industry, increased Central Bank power to direct investment by commercial banks, and, above all, encouragement of foreign investment by generous packages of government incentives. The radical change in economic strategy dates from the publication of Whitaker's report and the elevation of Sean Lemass to the position of Taoiseach.

By the time I became politically aware in the late 1950s, I observed that the Protestant population of South Dublin and Dun Laoghaire, in particular, were largely disengaged both from the majority Catholic population and from Irish politics. Most Protestants were very proud of their Irish background, but achieving better relations with Catholics was hindered by Archbishop McQuaid's authoritarianism and attempts to curtail the influence of Protestants in Dublin. The Dublin Protestant community was overwhelmingly middle-class and carried on behaving as it had always done by living in a parallel universe involving leisure interests that were favoured predominantly by other Protestants. Most notably these interests were: gardening, playing rugby, tennis, golf, cricket and hockey, watching rugby at Lansdowne Road, sailing in one of the three yacht clubs in Dun Laoghaire, playing bridge, dancing at Church of Ireland hops, rambling in the Wicklow mountains, and interacting socially with their friends, most of whom were drawn from the Protestant community. Almost all Protestants viewed themselves as Irish, but we did feel marginalised from a society whose dominant ethos was Catholic, Gaelic and republican; indeed there was a widespread view that to be Irish one had to be Catholic. Moreover, the Protestant community correctly objected to being (inaccurately) described as Anglo-Irish. There was a reluctance to become active in politics, or to be seen to rock the boat in any way providing that their way of life was not threatened. Most Protestants, therefore, either from indifference or feelings of alienation, made a point of keeping a low profile in public affairs. There was diffidence in the face of Catholic hegemony. Later, in the light of the deteriorating situation in Northern Ireland in 1969, 32 members of religious minorities in the Republic – including among others Bruce Arnold, Prof. WJ Jessop, Prof. WB Stanford, and Justice Kingsmill Moore – issued a public letter in which they acknowledged their reservations about the lack of provision for divorce and contraception, but strongly asserted 'the basic fairness of our political institutions and, what is more important, the basic goodwill toward us of the community of which we form a part.'[16] In the field of education, for example, the Protestant community was treated with generosity by the government. This is confirmed by the extent to which the government scheme to provide free secondary schooling for Protestant pupils in 1968-69 met the needs of that community, despite significantly higher costs than provision for Catholics due to contrasting population sizes and distribution.

If one term defined the Dun Laoghaire Protestant population it was respectability; this middle-class concept was often associated with moderation. It was not respectable to be loud, uncouth or outspoken in public. Glenageary Lawn Tennis Club – where my sisters and I all played between 1958 and 1963 – was notable for its social exclusivity. This was largely a consequence of the religious profile of the members, which was predominantly middle to upper-middle class Protestant (and a minority of upper-middle class Catholics) that created a posh and polite mileau where one's face had to fit. It also remained stubbornly closed every Sunday. When I queried this at the time, I was informed that it was because the grass courts needed a day of rest each week, so I suggested a Monday, but the policy of no play on Sundays remained intact. It was, however, also a social setting noteworthy for honesty and politeness over tea and cucumber sandwiches; a place where one could leave a wallet in the changing room and not have it stolen; and where shouting simply never happened across the hallowed turf. It was a club where Miss Joan Hunter Dunn, muse of John Betjeman's poem 'A Subaltern's Love Song,' would have been socially at ease. Similarly, the Royal St George Yacht club had a membership profile that was very similar to that of Glenageary Lawn Tennis Club.

* * *

The influence of middle- class respectability was strong and certain things, most notably sex, were not discussed. Inevitably, however, we picked up and used local slang and euphemisms, of which the term 'feck' was most prominent. Many Irish slang phrases have multiple meanings which may have developed to confuse British colonialists! For example, the word craic means fun and news. Hence, 'Where's the craic?' means 'Where's the fun at'? Or an entertaining event is said to be 'good craic.' The word 'grand' means 'magnificent' in English whereas in Ireland it means 'adequate, just fine' as in 'How are you?' 'I'm grand.' If, however, someone apologises, you may reassure them by saying 'No worries, you're grand.' Also, the word that my mother chose to describe me if I was being naughty or slow in obeying an order was 'bold.' The word bold means assertive and confident, but Irish culture thought otherwise and used it to describe a troublesome child. Irish swear words are often simple but more 'acceptable' minor modifications of English ones. For example, the word 'feck' has a number of meanings: you might be caught fecking (i.e. stealing) sweets in a shop, or you may tell someone to 'feck off' meaning 'go away'. The word in Ireland does not convey any sexual implications.

The American influence on Irish culture, whether manifested in crooners, rock- and- roll music and the increasing dominance of Hollywood movies in a country with no national TV station, was becoming pervasive in the 1950s; indeed it even extended to theatre when, as teenagers, we flocked to the Gas Company theatre in Dun Laoghaire to see the plays of Tennessee Williams and Arthur Miller. Few, if any, people in Ireland viewed this as cultural imperialism in the way that Richard Hoggart did in Britain in his classic book, *The Uses of Literacy*. Ireland in the 1950s was a theatre-conscious place and reviews were widely read and debated. Several of the actors we watched at the local Gas Company Theatre in Dun Laoghaire went on to earn international reputations including, Milo O'Shea, T P McKenna, Anna Manahan, Norman Rodway and Maureen Toal. The plays of Bernard Shaw also featured, unsurprisingly since he had lived in Dalkey as a child, and his plays addressed challenging themes, notably *Pygmalion* and *St Joan*. I was fortunate to see a great performance by Siobhan McKenna as St Joan at the Gate theatre. This play clearly influenced the award of the Nobel prize in Literature to Shaw in 1925.

The world famous Gate Theatre was co-founded in 1928 by Micheal MacLiammoir and Hilton Edwards and presented a rich variety of plays from the international tradition, including Ibsen, Chekov, O'Neill and Miller, and classic plays by Irish writers such as Goldsmith, Congreve, Sheridan, Wilde and Shaw. Together with their experimental and innovative productions, MacLiammoir's set and costume designs were also important elements in the success of the Gate. Moreover, Lord Longford always operated a policy of reserving one row at the back of the theatre for people who were not wealthy; these seats were available for a shilling in the 1950s. The Gate won its reputation by the sheer quality and style of its acting and the breadth of its repertoire. MacLiammoir was brilliant, intelligent, intuitive and multilingual (he spoke five languages) with a genuine visual flair; he was also sophisticated and cosmopolitan, an attribute sorely needed in the inward-looking Ireland of the time.[17] In a period when Ireland was cowering under the reactionary power of the Catholic Church, he and Hilton Edwards lived openly as a gay couple, and were known to Dubliners affectionately as 'The Boys.' MacLiammoir, a charismatic personality on stage where his extraordinary voice caressed the text, always dressed flamboyantly wearing full make-up at all times of the day and sporting a jet black hairpiece. With Dublin's other leading playhouse the Abbey devoted to rural Irish naturalism and the Gate to gay aesthetic, one local wag remarked that the two theatres offered a choice between 'Sodom and Begorrah.'

A 16 year old Orson Welles made his acting debut on the stage of the Gate in October 1931. The artistic brilliance of MacLiammoir and Edwards deeply impressed Welles and he remained in touch with them for many years; indeed MacLiammoir played Iago in Welles' film version of *Othello* in 1949. Welles returned to the USA in 1932 but appeared on stage in Dublin again in 1960 with his production of *Chimes at Midnight* at the Gaiety Theatre which my mother and I attended. It was an adaptation of *Henry IV* and *Henry V* in which Welles played Falstaff and also directed the play with his usual panache. Other distinguished actors who began their acting careers at the Gate included James Mason, Geraldine Fitzgerald and Michael Gambon. It was as a postgraduate student in 1964, together with Susan (who was resplendent in a stunning long dress) that I witnessed what to me was his most memorable performance as Oscar Wilde in his one-man production of '*The Importance of being Oscar*.' Based on the life of Wilde, MacLiammoir's stellar performance was a compelling theatrical tapestry revealing the wit, genius, triumph and tragedy of Oscar Wilde in an explosion of richness, boldness, passion and beauty. This was the crowning achievement of MacLiammoir and cemented his reputation not only as a renaissance man – dramatist, writer, poet and painter – but as Ireland's greatest and most glamorous actor of the 20th century.

After independence, Yeats was the dominant figure in Irish letters heralded as the founder of modern Irish literature. His international reputation as a poetic genius, having won the Nobel prize for literature, and his commanding position in the Abbey Theatre gave him great power over the careers of budding young playwrights who were overwhelmed by his personal formality and the fact that he was not, as Fallon opined, a clubbable man and certainly 'not a pubbable one.' He gave Irish writers an intellectual alternative to the dogmatic Catholicism or class-ridden Protestantism of their upbringing.[18] The other Irish writer to acquire an international stature comparable to Yeats was James Joyce. Joyce's writings are widely viewed as amounting to a damning judgement on his own country, which is seen as small, too narrow, too dominated by the Catholic church (which he had abandoned) to accept his cosmopolitan genius. As Fallon has asserted, Joyce has become the measuring rod not only for drab Edwardian Dublin and its rather provincial society, but for the totality of Irish history and culture since then.[19]

From 1941 to 1967 the artistic direction of the Abbey Theatre was largely controlled by Ernest Blythe, a period associated with dull kitchen farces and poor Gaelic pantomimes, several of which I endured with scant pleasure. The Abbey was forced to move to the Queen's Theatre in 1951 following a fire and it was there that I became familiar with O'Casey's three greatest plays, *The Shadow of a Gunman, Juno and the Paycock*, and *The Plough and the Stars*, all of which were first staged between 1923 and 1926 before O'Casey emigrated to England. O'Casey was a lower-middle-class Protestant whose father died when he was only six. He left a family of 13, who rapidly slipped into poverty. Although he was a Protestant, he clearly understood Catholic guilt and hypocrisy. He was a passionate socialist and nationalist who was the first Irish dramatist to write about the Dublin working classes. However, he became disillusioned with the Irish nationalist movement because its leaders put nationalism above socialism and so his great trilogy outlines a devastating case against revolutionary fervour. *The Shadow of a Gunman* deals with the impact of revolutionary politics on Dublin's slums; while *Juno and the Paycock* addresses the effect of the Irish Civil War on the working – class poor; and *The Plough and the Stars* is set at the time of the 1916 Rising. All three plays are tragic-comedies in which violent death is contrasted with the blustering bravado and patriotic swagger of characters such as Joxer Daly and Jack Boyle in *Juno and the Paycock*. *The Plough and the Stars* was not well received by the Abbey audience in 1926 and resulted in scenes reminiscent of the riots that greeted J M Synge's *Playboy of the Western World* in 1907. In the second act, a prostitute is seen lounging in a pub awaiting clients when three freedom fighters enter the stage. A riot followed and Yeats took to the stage and famously declared: 'You have disgraced yourselves again. Is this going to be a recurring celebration of Irish genius? Synge first and then O'Casey.' I saw all of these plays between the ages of 16 and 22 and the ironic juxtaposition of the comic and the tragic revealed the waste of war and the deeply corrosive effect of poverty, which made an indelible impression on me that I can clearly recall more than six decades later. It was also authentic Dublin, the accents, dialogue, wit and characters. When I saw O'Casey's trilogy for the first time, the casts featured such Abbey luminaries as Ria Mooney, Maire Keene, Harry Brogan and Philip O'Flynn.

Louis MacNeice, the brilliant poet who was both Irish and internationalist, lyrical and yet serious, published his great poem *Autumn Journal* in 1939. As the sense of international crisis deepened, MacNeice, whose west- of- Ireland father ministered as Anglican Bishop of Down and Connor, examines the economic and cultural stagnation in the North and South with a jaundiced eye, unequivocally viewing provincialism as the enemy. He was critical of the South's isolationist policies:

> Griffith, Connelly, Collins what have they brought us?
> Ourselves alone! Let the round tower stand aloof
>   In a world of bursting mortar!
> Let the school-children fumble their sums
>   In a half-dead language;
> Let the censor be busy on the books; pull down the Georgian slums;
>   Let the games be played in Gaelic.

MacNeice's ironic call of *Sinn Fein* ('Ourselves alone') is followed by a portrait of the insularity of the Irish Free State: the effects on children of teaching everything through Gaelic in state primary schools; the introduction of literary censorship; and unsympathetic housing development in Dublin. Each of these developments is seen by MacNeice as examples of the South's provincialism and isolationist self-regard. Casting his mind north to Belfast:

A city built upon mud;
A culture built on profit;
Free speech nipped in the bud,
The minority always guilty.
Why should I want to go back
To you Ireland, my Ireland?

MacNeice draws attention both to the sectarianism underlying the assumption that the minority in the North were always guilty, and the threat to free speech. He was critical of the intransigence of unionists and scornful of the unrealistic dreams of nationalists; indeed the Ireland described in his poem *Autumn Journal* in 1939 is a relatively accurate picture of the country in the 1950s as so little had changed North or South.

During the 1950s only the theatre was free from state censorship, although not from interference. Following the great success of *Waiting for Godot* at the Pike Theatre, Alan Simpson and his wife Carolyn Swift staged Tennessee Williams' play *The Rose Tattoo* in the first Dublin Theatre Festival in 1957 with Anna Manahan in the lead role and I went to see it with my mother. As Ferriter has opined, the production led to 'the most shameful episode of bullying in Irish theatre history' in which reputations, careers and a marriage were ruined.[20] The director of the Dublin Theatre Festival, Brendan Smith, received a letter from a group of self-styled zealots – The Irish League of Decency – complaining that the play promoted the use of artificial birth control. Simpson convinced Smith that this was untrue, although there was a stage direction that a contraceptive is thrown on the stage and in the Irish production this was deftly mimed because it was impossible to obtain a contraceptive. The play opened to great critical acclaim. In the second week of the run, the Gardai warned Simpson that he would be liable to arrest if he did not drop the play because it contained 'objectionable passages.' Simpson refused and was arrested and charged with having 'produced for gain an indecent and profane performance.' The case dragged on for over a year until Simpson was acquitted, but the cost in both money and reputation had taken a heavy toll on him. The Pike Theatre lost subscribers, never recovered and eventually closed. The real reason for the prosecution of Alan Simpson was more sinister: a battle between the state and Catholic Church over who was doing most in relation to the censorship of alleged unsuitable material. The case was not about *The Rose Tattoo* at all as the Minister of Justice sought to close it down before being seen to act after the Catholic Archbishop of Dublin Dr John Charles McQuaid demanded that he do so.

The sycophancy of certain politicians towards McQuaid was remarkable. Even civil servants requested permission from McQuaid to read Marxist literature when their duties as diplomats required it.[21] McQuaid, a Machiavellian schemer, rarely spoke out in public in matters of censorship because his lay allies, principally the Knights of Columbanus (a secret society) were vigilant and eager to implement his wishes. The biographer of McQuaid, John Cooney, argued that McQuaid's 'weakness is that he's totally obsessed with sex, and it's the imposition of a very severe code of sexual conduct, the opposition to filthy books'......snooping on people about their sexual mores, ...he's bringing Ireland more and more under a kind of spiritual terrorism.'[22] The case of *The Rose Tattoo* at the Pike Theatre was not about public indecency, but, as a consequence of it the marriage between Simpson and Carolyn Swift broke down, the livelihoods of two talented people were ruined and an innovative theatre was closed. Simpson used to say that 'we died so that Irish theatre could be free.'[23] This incident was a shameful national embarrassment and showed that Irish censorship was an insult to the country's many great literary achievements.

An incident of organized sectarianism occurred in the small Wexford town of Fethard-on-Sea in 1957 when Protestant businesses were boycotted by Catholics, apparently at the prompting of William Stafford, the local Catholic curate.[24] It was alleged that local Protestants had connived at the disappearance of Sheila Cloney, a Protestant mother, and her two daughters on 27 April 1957. Married to a Catholic farmer, Sean Cloney, she fled to Belfast due to her refusal to comply with the parish priest's insistence that she raise her children as Catholics and educate them at the local Catholic school. Local Catholics boycotted local Protestant shops.[25] The *Ne Temere* decree was the underlying cause of the boycott. To his great credit, the Taoiseach, De Valera, condemned the boycott 'as ill-conceived, ill-considered, futile, and unjust and cruel to confound the innocent with the guilty.'[26] In stark contrast, the Catholic bishops neither intervened nor condemned the boycott of the religious minority; indeed Bishop Michael Brown of Galway pronounced that the boycott was 'a peaceful and moderate protest.' An apology was eventually forthcoming from Bishop Brendan Comiskey of Ferns 41 years later in 1998, although his reputation was subsequently tarnished over his failure to respond adequately to allegations of sexual abuse in his own diocese.[27] As a

Protestant living in Dun Laoghaire at the time, I saw the 1950s as the nadir in terms of the apparent trend towards the realisation of a theocratic state where basic civil liberties and minority viewpoints were simply ignored in drafting legislation and in healthcare and social provision. What we did not realise at the time was that the Catholic Church had reached the peak of its triumphalism and intolerance towards any opposition, although its influence over policy-making remained significant until the 1990s when widespread scandals were exposed involving clerical sexual and physical abuse cases, which had been covered up, and the Catholic Church lost moral and social authority from which it has not recovered.

I have always liked athletics, partly because of my interest in records and numbers. Ireland was a very small country but for many years it produced a stream of Olympic quality class middle- distance runners. Ron Delany won the gold medal in the 1,500 metres at the Melbourne Olympics in 1956; and he inspired a number of 800 metre athletes who competed with distinction on the international stage in the 1960s: Noel Carroll, Derek McCleane (a former pupil at St Andrew's College), Frank Murphy and Basil Clifford. Later, Eamonn Coghlan won the World 5,000 metre title in 1983 and in the same year broke the world indoor mile record in 3:49.78, which is still the European record 38 years later.

During the 1950s it was a great pleasure to attend athletic meetings run on the grass track in Trinity College, but the country lacked a top-class athletics stadium. Billy Morton, an optician and secretary of Clonliffe Harriers, mounted a campaign to build a purpose-built athletic stadium. Largely as a consequence of his determination, the Santry Stadium was constructed and opened in 1958. Albie Thomas of Australia broke the world record for 3 miles in a time of 13:10.6 at a Santry athletics meeting on 8 July 1958. The British Empire and Commonwealth Games were staged in Cardiff in July 1958 and Billy Morton persuaded a group of Australian and New Zealand athletes to travel to Dublin for a meeting on 6 and 7 August. Albie Thomas agreed to act as a pacemaker in the mile and Herb Elliott would pace him the following evening in the two-mile race. An attempt on Derek Ibbotson's world mile record of 3:57.2 was planned. My father declined to come to the event so I cycled the 17 miles from Dalkey to Santry. The official capacity of the stadium was 17,500 but 22,000 people turned up and, in a typically Irish way, all were permitted to enter.

There was a palpable air of anticipation as the field lined up on that balmy August evening. As arranged, Albie Thomas led through the half mile in 1:58, despite the fact that on the second lap a mongrel dog joined the race (but did not trip anyone up) and then Elliott surged into the lead on the third lap. Merv Lincoln then made his move, a Sisyphean kick into the lead which lasted a mere 50 yards before Elliott swept past him approaching the bell, which was reached in 2:59. The great Australian was now about to create history. The 20-year-old Elliott recorded a final lap of 55.5 seconds to win in 3:54.5. Lincoln trailed in second some 12 yards behind, yet still broke the old world record in 3:55.9. This was one of the finest achievements ever in the history of middle distance running as demonstrated by the fact that Elliott had shattered Ibbotson's time by 2.7 seconds, which was the largest improvement in the world mile record in the 20th century. Delany, the local hero, never threatened, although he ran his best ever mile time of 3:57.5, as did Murray Halberg in fourth. Since Albie Thomas ran 3:58.6, it was the first time that five men had dipped below 4 minutes in a mile race. We were aware that we had witnessed something special, and it still feels that way over 64 years later. Elliott's record, seemingly unbeatable, was broken in 1962 by an even greater athlete, Peter Snell, when he ran 3:54.4 in Wanganui, a remarkable feat considering it was on a grass track. On the second night of that historic Santry meeting, Albie Thomas broke the world's best over 2 miles in 8:32.0

When you are very young anything seems possible and one's personal limitations have yet to emerge. One of the most notable effects of being a teenager is to become more and more aware of the numerous activities in life at which one not only lacks flair, but is quite simply useless. My father strongly encouraged me to become an engineer and to apply for the Engineering School at Trinity College Dublin. I was uncertain about this, given my incompetence at Meccano, model building, car and bicycle maintenance. There were no career advisers at schools in the 1950s, so I obtained some books as background reading, on the advice of the Engineering School. One of these was a book on Geology, a subject that we had not studied at St Andrew's. I was immediately captivated by the discipline and was soon searching the Trinity calendar to determine whether one could study it at Honours level at the university. I discovered that it was a recognised subject within the Natural Sciences Moderatorship. Consequently, I simply applied to study Natural Sciences on the strength of having read one elementary book on Geology as a preparation for an application to read engineering! Fortunately, I never regretted the decision.

* * *

Like most people of this era, I had received no sex education at all at the Church of Ireland or at St Andrew's College. My parents shied away from broaching the subject: politeness and reserve were the rule. There was no guidance at all for dealing with sexual feelings. Sex was seen as something secretive, not a topic to be discussed; it was the subject of rude jokes. Sex suddenly arrived, unbidden and unexplained for us to deal with as we saw fit. Our generation discovered sex by trial and error or via books such as Alberto Moravia's *Woman of Rome* being passed furtively around the classroom. There was always an undercurrent of indecent talk and sexual innuendo. Like most boys of our age in a single -sex school, we spoke out on the more subtle nuances of lovemaking with the bold confidence assumed by those anxious to conceal their ignorance. Given the severity of Irish censorship, the only breasts we ever saw featured in photographs in the *National Geographic* magazine. Nobody admitted that sex even existed, although the Bible was awash with it and bulls and rams were hard at work in the fields, self-loathing was tempered by sudden surges of self- love. Almost all of us were fairly innocent. Today's youth seem much more mature and uninhibited than we were. Amongst my close friends there was frequent speculation as to which (Protestant) girl in Dun Laoghaire had the best figure, a topic that fascinated us far more than declining Latin verbs. I thought that Mary, who lived a few doors away, boasted the most alluring figure in the area. The desk in my bedroom overlooked her back garden; Mary was a keen gardener and watching her tending her vegetables was a distraction. I was sent around to her house one evening to deliver a message and she opened the door and I had seldom seen a more voluptuous 16 year old in a Girl Guides uniform. A few weeks later she invited me to accompany her to a social function in the Presbyterian church. Looking back now over sixty years later I can scarcely believe that I was so shy at the time that I could only deliver a non-committal reply so that I never grasped the opportunity to date her. About a year later I struck up a friendship with Pat, who was a final year pupil at Glengara Park school. The problem was that she was a boarder and so it was difficult to arrange meetings apart from the occasional Saturday. She was a very thoughtful, gentle, compassionate girl of great integrity to whom I felt attracted. However, I was still paralysed by shyness and fear of rejection, something I did not overcome until after I enrolled at Trinity.

Masturbation was an issue that was rarely, if ever, discussed by boys at school and yet it was (presumably) widely practised. One was never told as a teenager that masturbation was a normal part of maturing, or that it was an effective way of relieving sexual tension; in 1950s Ireland, unsurprisingly, it was viewed as sinful. Even as we prepared for confirmation at the age of 15, the Rev. Des Murray did not directly allude to it other than to allege that it was deleterious to health (which it is not). His thinking may have been influenced by Robert Baden Powell, founder of the Boy Scouts, who used the movement as a platform against the alleged evils of masturbation asserting that 'the result of self-abuse is *always* that the boy after a time becomes weak and nervous and shy….he very often goes out of his mind and becomes an idiot.'[28] Archbishop John Charles McQuaid was concerned with temptation and was aware that 'the drawings of women modelling underwear used in Irish press advertisements actually revealed a *mons veneris* if one employed a magnifying glass.'[29] Pat Buckley, who studied theology at Clonliffe College, Dublin in the 1960s and ultimately became a rebel Catholic bishop recalled a corner of the College where those seminarians who had indulged in masturbation the previous night were sent: a small oratory off the campus chapel.[30] Buckley also maintained that some seminarians were issued with small whips for self-flagellation from which a number learned to derive sexual pleasure as it became their sexual outlet.[31]

During the summer before going up to Trinity College, David Thomas and I camped for a week at Dromineer on Lough Derg in order to sail in a regatta. Dave owned a Firefly dinghy and I enjoyed crewing for him in a series of races. We went to a dance where I met a French girl, Brigitte, who was more interested in dragging me outside to kiss me than in the actual dancing. One of my favourite singers at the time was Edith Piaf; I loved the emotional power of her soulful vibrato in songs such as 'La Vie en Rose,' 'L'Accordeoniste' and 'Milord' as she rolled her 'r's in her throat like nobody before or since. What was really surprising was that my French, which was extremely basic, was better than Brigitte's English and so we spoke in French, which is a more beautiful language than English in which to exchange words of affection. I was enchanted by this, but by the end of the week I was bored and mentally tired from my linguistic challenge and the limits of our conversations.

Amongst my friends in Dalkey Sea Scouts we talked constantly about the girls we fancied. I always did seem to have a girlfriend from about the age of 16 onwards: perhaps a girl I had danced with several times, or exchanged meaningful glances with, or someone I had taken home from a dance and no hand-holding or kissing ensued, even though I had imagined kissing her under a tree near her house. It was all very awkward and any hesitant kissing was accompanied by stilted conversation. Most girlfriends existed only in my dreams and nobody I knew at 17 was having sex – the ban on contraception in Ireland was a powerful deterrent. Sometimes girls became pregnant, although not amongst middle-class Dun Laoghaire Protestants.

When I reflect on teenage agonies, I feel relieved that I am not back there. Then I worried about having spots, not having a girlfriend, few male friends, nowhere to go on a Saturday night, sitting in my bedroom looking out the window, convinced that everyone out there was having a great time but me, wondering what to do in life and worrying whether I will discover anything that I am remotely good at, or if I will ever find any girl with whom I would be compatible. My luck changed on the 19 September 1959, however, a month before going up to university at Trinity College Dublin. I attended a party on White Rock beach near Dalkey. We climbed down the steep steps cut into the granite rock, crossed the railway bridge, gathered driftwood and lit a fire on the beach. I met a girl and I rapidly realised that intellectually she was more gifted than any of the other middle-class girls that were part of the local Protestant set. I cycled home with her over Killiney Hill to Ballybrack. She was of average height with curly hair and a pleasing figure; but above all, she was charismatic, eloquent, witty, well read and highly intelligent. She was the first girlfriend who was an excellent conversationalist and with whom I had really interesting discussions.

It was only a couple of weeks later after a date that we stood in the dark at the rear of her house. I felt awkward and my only thought was what move to make. I was not a novice at kissing, but my track record was not extensive. There was no room for a practice match here. She put her arms around my neck and tilted her face so that our lips met in pure joy. We kissed passionately in a way I had never been kissed before, and I can still recall the experience 63 years later, an unforgettable and liberating rite of passage. It could have gone on for ages, but her father suddenly emerged from the front door and berated me for bringing his daughter home late on the last number 59 bus! The Christmas parties and the dances were blissful as I had the girl with looks, personality and intellect wrapped around me. Talking to her was always so invigorating and stimulating and I counted the days until I would see her again to continue our conversations. I just could not stop thinking about her. She was my first serious girlfriend and one of the brightest girls I ever met. The seeds of our parting after seven months were sown largely by the pressures of the First year Natural Sciences programme at Trinity. Taking Physics, Chemistry, Maths, Geology, Zoology and Geography, with the additional burden of associated laboratory work, and needing to do well in the competitive exams to qualify for the Honours stream took priority, except at weekends.

CHAPTER 5

The Trinity Idyll

The dawn of a new decade heralded the gradual development of the consumerist society with many new products being launched on the market. New innovations in 1960 included the introduction of Blue Gillette Extra razor blades; the stripe in Signal toothpaste; 'ready – salted' crisps from Golden Wonder, a response to the blue bag of salt in Smith's crisps; plastic carrier bags; the first automatic dishwasher introduced by Miele; the Aston Martin DB4 and the Saab 96; bubble wrap; the electric toothbrush; fruit yoghurt; and Heinz Spaghetti Bolognese was the 'exciting new Italian dish'.[1] Other important innovations followed throughout the decade: the Jaguar E–Type, Renault 4 and coffee-mate in 1961; the Ford Cortina, Triumph Spitfire, After Eight Mints and Strongbow in 1962; the Hillman Imp and Instamatic cameras 1963; the Ford Mustang, Porsche 911 and Astro turf in 1964; the cordless phone in 1965; the Maserati Ghibli in 1966; the Ford Escort, Angel Delight and the Big Mac in 1967; the Renault 6 in 1968 and the Ford Capri and Austin Maxi in 1969.

The most common interpretation of the sixties was that it was an era of cultural renaissance that emphasised tolerance, freedom and love, and that it entailed a youthful uprising against war, racial discrimination and sexual repression. Green argued that the 'Sixties are as much a state of mind as a chronological concept' and in 1998 he asserted that 'as the century draws to a close, it is hard not to see the Sixties as the pivotal decade….seem[ing] to stand in the centre of it all, sucking up influences of the past, creating the touchstones of the future.'[2] This version of the sixties is a popular one, especially in the arts and publishing world. A British journalist David May wrote that: 'girls were incredibly beautiful, and luscious and they didn't have AIDS and didn't wear knickers. There was good music, dope, sex, and above all, there was not conforming.'[3] Another wag suggested that if you can remember the sixties, you weren't there. Even the Marxist historian Eric Hobsbawm called the sixties a 'golden age' of affluence and prosperity that 'generated a profound, and in many ways sudden, moral and cultural revolution, a dramatic transformation of the conventions of social and personal behaviour.'[4] Sandbrook suggests that 1963 in Britain marked 'an approximate crossover between the world of skiffle, duffel coats and expresso bars on the one hand, and the world of the Rolling Stones, mini-skirts and discotheques on the other.'[5] A similar shift occurred in Ireland, but, Dr John Charles McQuaid, Catholic Archbishop of Dublin, who had been the overwhelmingly dominant public figure of the fifties in matters of morals, culture and social policy, still retained a powerful influence over politicians in the sixties, and even attempted to orchestrate attacks on 'immoral' literature. However, the opening up of the country to inward foreign investment by the far-sighted Taoiseach, Sean Lemass, laid the foundations for subsequent social and cultural development and a more cosmopolitan outlook, although the process of change in the sixties was both complex and sluggish. In many areas of social and sexual reform the sixties in Ireland did not occur until the noughties.

* * *

The most meaningful event of my life, certainly educationally and socially, was in October 1959 when the small world of home and school was replaced by Trinity College Dublin and the Natural Sciences Moderatorship. With no grants available in the Ireland of 1959, it was extremely fortunate that an ancient world-class university existed only nine miles from Dalkey. Few people in Ireland attended university: the average number of first-time entrants to Irish universities in the 1950s was less than 1 percent of the 18 year old cohort. I was eager for serious academic learning and, although believing it would enable one to get a better job, I relished the concept of scholarship for its own sake; and the opportunity to read in a copyright library conferred an academic freedom that I had never previously imagined. One was quickly seduced by the architectural splendour of the campus, an oasis of calm and liberal values in the centre of a capital city, and by the scholastic opportunities on offer. We were young and full of optimism and we thought we were very grown-up, now that we were undergraduates of a major university.

Trinity is located at the very heart of Dublin within walking distance of all the legendary pubs, restaurants, shops, cafes, theatres and cinemas and yet the Dublin mountains could be seen from Fitzwilliam Street. The university is surrounded by a high wall which gives it a certain detachment from the surrounding city. It has the appearance of a large Oxbridge college and the main frontage – built in 1751 of sombre grey stone – echoes the classical curves of the Bank of Ireland opposite, which was the Houses of Parliament in pre-Union days, with the Liffey a short walk to the north and Grafton Street – the major shopping area – an easy stroll to the south. The imposing statues of Oliver Goldsmith and Edmund Burke command the front of the building confidently surveying Dame Street down which on the morning of my matriculation a gentle whiff of Guinness wafted on the westerly breeze.

Beneath the central pediment of the building was Front Gate seducing the viewer with glimpses of immaculate lawns, cobbles and buildings beyond into another world. Within Front Gate the College porters – dressed in tailcoats and black jockeys' caps – basically ran the University from a small office. Front Gate was the heartbeat of social and sporting life and was festooned with notices from a wide range of societies and sports clubs. Beyond Front Gate was an unforgettable sight: the magnificent cobbled eighteenth century Front Square, arguably one of the most magnificent squares in Europe, which contained, apart from rooms leading off staircases, a chapel (Church of Ireland, ecumenical since 1970), the beautifully proportioned Examination Hall and the austerely classical Dining Hall, both dating from circa 1790, the great Long Room of the University's copyright library (built between 1712 and 1732) with its barrel-vaulted ceiling and containing the celebrated manuscripts- the Book of Kells and Book of Durrow. Towards the East end of Front Square was a Victorian campanile whose bell was tolled to summon students to the Exam Hall. Forming the East side of Front Square – and facing manicured lawns – were the Rubrics, red-brick late seventeenth century buildings (the oldest in College) with a line of Dutch gables on top and tall hexagonal chimneys. On the north side of Front Square stood the Victorian Graduates Memorial Building (GMB) containing the reading rooms of the two debating societies – The Historical Society and the Philosophical Society – the Hist. being the oldest university debating society in the world, having been founded by Edmund Burke in 1753. We would pop into the reading rooms with their grubby windows and ancient leather chairs between lectures or at lunchtime to browse newspapers and magazines or to snooze between lectures.

Behind the GMB was a residential square, Botany Bay, with somewhat austere grey buildings overlooking asphalt tennis courts. As I wandered around it on that first day, I heard the voice of the 'Empress of the Blues', Bessie Smith, singing 'Nobody Knows when You're Down and Out' wafting across the quad from a first-floor window, and I knew immediately that I had arrived at a special place. To the east of the Rubrics lay New Square - built in the 1820s – with a pleasing Doric temple housing the University Press at its entrance, and the Museum Building commanding the south side. The Museum Building is an imposing mid-Victorian Gothic-Revival structure inspired by the Byzantine architecture of Venice. The exterior is built of limestone and faced with granite; while the main entrance hall houses large pillars, balustrades and bannisters constructed from numerous Irish marbles and Cornish serpentine, an ideal setting in which to study Geology. Its pioneering use of Connemara marble and Cork red limestone subsequently spread across the globe. Beyond New Square lay the sports' fields and most of the Science departments where I spent many hours in the first two years, including Physics, Chemistry, Botany, Zoology and Microbiology. The grounds of the university were segregated from the city by a high stone wall supplemented by sharply pointed iron railings. I had never before seen, or at least had not noticed, buildings that were clearly dedicated to a higher purpose, not to necessity or utility, not merely to manufacturing or shelter, but to something that might be an end in itself.

Trinity in the 1960s was a special place partly because of the multicultural nature of its student intake. While most other universities in Britain and Ireland were culturally homogenous, Trinity provided a diverse milieu of students from very different backgrounds. In October 1959, 981 students (43%) came from the Republic and rubbed shoulders with 600 (26%) from Britain, 365 (17%) from many other countries across the world; and 320 (14%) from Northern Ireland. By the time I graduated in 1963, the percentage of students from Britain had peaked at 34%. The cosmopolitan element added colour and variety not only to the College but to Dublin itself. The proportion of Catholics in the College in 1960 was 29%. Many of the Catholic students were British as the Irish Catholic church operated a 'ban' on Catholics attending the College. This ban prevailed despite the fact that Trinity first allowed Catholics to apply for admission as early as 1793, prior to equivalent changes in the universities of Oxford and Cambridge. All restrictions imposed on Catholics (and Presbyterians) were removed by 1873 and yet Trinity College continued to be confronted by the unremitting hostility of the Catholic Church, despite the fact that even Daniel O'Connell had sent his sons to the College.

Archbishop John Charles McQuaid, forbade the attendance at Trinity College by Catholic students, replacing strongly worded advice by fiat in 1944. A Maynooth synodal statute passed in 1956 used uncompromising language: 'We forbid under pain of mortal sin: (1) Catholic youths to frequent the College; (2) Catholic parents or guardians to send to that College Catholic youths committed to their care; clerics and religious to recommend in any manner parents or guardians to send Catholic youths to that College or to lend counsel or help to such youths to frequent that College. Only the Archbishop of Dublin is competent to decide in accordance with the norms of the Holy See, in what circumstances and with what guarantees against perversion attendance at that College may be tolerated.'[6] This made Archbishop McQuaid the sole judge of requests for permission from all the dioceses in Ireland. The statute came into force in 1960 and led to a reduction in Catholic admissions from 25 to 17 per cent.

McQuaid's Lenten Pastoral of 1961 recalled how Elizabeth I took 'active and permanent measures to impose on us a university formation to which death was in conscience preferable,' and declared that it was worth waiting another four hundred years, if necessary, for a fully Catholic university in Ireland.[7] Catholic friends from Britain studying alongside me at the time were incredulous at this extraordinary statement. The ban prevented Irish Catholics from enrolling at what was and still remains to this day – according to all the university league tables – the top university on the island of Ireland.[8] A witty Limerick expressed a certain tongue-in-cheek attitude to the ban: 'Said Archbishop McQuaid in a Lenten tirade/ You may plunder and loot, you may murder and shoot/ You may even have carnal knowledge/ But if you want to be saved, and not be depraved/ You must stay out of Trinity College.' A hint of rebellion against McQuaid's all powerful episcopal authority emerged in the sixties: McQuaid forbade Emmet Stagg to accept a job in Trinity in 1962. Stagg, however, defied him, as did the UCD academic Sister Benvenuta in 1965, when McQuaid demanded to see her lecture notes.[9] The ban on Catholics enrolling at Trinity College was not lifted until June 1970, two years before McQuaid retired as Archbishop of Dublin.

Entering Trinity College for the first time as a student in October 1959 – wearing the University's undergraduate scarf as a badge of pride – I was expecting that my fellow- undergraduates would be clever, certainly, but that they would also be original. In this mood of anticipation tinged with insecurity, I was conscious immediately that the British students (overwhelmingly English), who constituted almost one-third of the student body, spoke in posh Home Counties accents that indicated both a major public school education and wealth, in stark contrast to the sharp harsh accents of the Northern Irish contingent and the melodious tones of those from the Republic. A minority of the Northern Irish students could fairly be described as dour Presbyterians; but also amongst them in the 1960s were two who were destined to become among Ireland's greatest poets: Derek Mahon and Michael Longley. There were other exotic fauna also, notably Nigerians, Indians and Americans, some no doubt seeking the J P Donleavy *Ginger Man* experience. The English students were socially dominant displaying both self-confidence and sartorial elegance with coloured waistcoats, tweed jackets and cavalry twill trousers. The English girls were unattainably lovely with confident public-school accents and skirts that were short even before Mary Quant invented the mini in 1966. In contrast, the Northern Irish girls seemed quieter, less glamorous with fewer short skirts in evidence. While attending the social events of summer term, these English girls revealed their enticing shapes in cotton frocks vaporised by sunlight; it seemed not to matter in first year that they were unattainable.

Initially Irish students felt like interlopers in our own country. Most of the English students were older – having spent a 'gap year' abroad, or done National Service – and, more fundamentally, it quickly became apparent that they had also been to superior schools than I had with more in-depth individual tuition. Hence, they were older, more mature, better taught, more self-confident, wealthier (some even owned MG sports cars) and bolstered by substantial grants (we Southern Irish had none). How could we compete both socially and academically against the products of schools such as Eton, Harrow, Stowe, Rugby, Winchester, Ampleforth and Cheltenham Ladies College? A number of them subsequently informed me that they had schoolteachers with contacts in Trinity College who advised them and played a part in their application process. We lacked such support at St Andrew's College and we had to negotiate the detailed application protocol ourselves. They entered the university much better prepared than I was and I felt inferior, uncertain and somewhat in awe of these markedly self-assured students who came to study at a university that had a longstanding intellectual and social cachet. I was later to discover that the key advantage of a public school education was a confident self-belief which was a carapace that prevented them from being found out too quickly. One often had to know English public school educated students for years before realising that many of them were not especially bright. Some of those who had been at minor public schools manifested a sense of entitlement and snobbery and asserted themselves by braying at each other across Front Square. Conversely, I found that the students from Eton, Harrow and Winchester knew that they had been to the best schools and, consequently, were less likely to be arrogant and overbearing.

Despite the small size of the College in 1959 – some 3,000 students – Trinity was full of cliques. You could get in with the rugby set or the rowing one and be rowdy; or perhaps join the thespian set –Trinity Players – or the choral set, the debating set or the heavy drinking and carousing set. Almost all Dublin students lived at home; it was not possible for our parents to pay fees and also fund the additional cost of living on campus. This limited our participation in debating societies, sherry parties and lounging in the coffee bar during the day because, as students of Natural Sciences, we were required to attend not only lectures, but also practical laboratory classes most afternoons. This created a wide gulf between humanities students and the scientists so that social contact between them was minimal. This social apartheid was so marked that one of my best friends today was a contemporary at Trinity in the 1960s whom I never saw at the time. Much of the social life was generated by elites who either kicked a rugby ball, played cricket, acted in Players, or hung around those who did. What always surprised me was how the English contingent felt so at home in Dublin and really adored their four years at Trinity. Subsequently, I became friendly with some of these exotic specimens of the former colonial power; more importantly, I realised that it wasn't where you came from but how you behaved that mattered. I began to appreciate that many of them contributed in a major way to the cultural and sporting life of the university, although there was also a minority who – failing to qualify for Honours level courses – opted for a relatively relaxed life style on the General Studies programme. It was not until the second year that the advantages of the public- school education diminished and Irish students began to dominate scholastically. Several students who were contemporaries at Trinity had glittering careers after graduating, including Mary Robinson, first woman President of Ireland, who did more to promote the rights of women and the liberalisation of the state than anyone; Max Stafford-Clark, director of the Royal Court theatre, Michael Bogdanov, director of the English Shakespeare company, and, apart from Seamus Heaney, the greatest Irish poets of their generation – Derek Mahon, Michael Longley, Eavan Boland and Brendan Kennelly.

The typical Irish student of the early sixties, myself included, were serious-minded young men (there were few women) in a dark polo-neck and duffel coat, wearing the University scarf, carrying a gown (compulsory in lectures) and a pile of books on the way to the library, having just been to the coffee bar for an expresso. Nowadays, students do not parade around in a student scarf and gowns are no longer worn. The British students were overwhelmingly middle or upper-middle class, were basically conservative and presented little threat to the conventions of Irish life. Arriving at Trinity, I had no idea of a future career and I thought of myself as being there for the sheer pleasure of study for its own sake and mixing with clever people interested in scholarship. There was a minor jolt in the first Chemistry lecture when Mr Stuart, a taciturn Scotsman, scanned the steeply tiered and packed lecture theatre before declaring, without any nuance in his remarks: 'Have a look at the person on each side of you. Either you or he (no gender-neutral language in those days) will not be here next year.' Not only would such a statement probably cost him his job today, but it simply emphasised that around half the class would not qualify for the Honours programme at the end of the year. In those days issues of mental welfare were not on the agenda of major universities. It was a competitive environment: Trinity has granted you this opportunity, so get on with it.

I visited my tutor – Gordon L Herries Davies – in his office in the Museum Building during my first week on campus. I wondered what was in store for me. In response to my knocking, I received a firm response to enter. The small window of his office looked out on New Square which was swarming with students. A dark haired man of around 28 and of medium height and sturdy physique sat at his desk. He had a slightly ruddy complexion, no doubt a result of many hours spent conducting geomorphological research in the Wicklow mountains. Unusually for an academic in 1959, he was wearing a double-breasted suit. He was to be my tutor for the four years of my undergraduate degree. Gordon, who was a Manchester University graduate, became more flamboyant and eccentric over time as he was absorbed into the culture of Trinity College; but he was always very helpful, reliable and supportive of me as an undergraduate; and we maintained our friendship ever afterwards, although our research interests were totally different.

Initially, Trinity was almost overwhelming. Wherever I walked on this beautiful campus I became aware that many great scholars had studied at this ancient institution, most notably Jonathon Swift, Oliver Goldsmith, Edmund Burke, William Congreve, George Berkeley, Oscar Wilde, Bram Stoker, J M Synge, Samuel Beckett, William Trevor and Ernest Walton. There were also many of my contemporaries, including Micheal Longley, Derek Mahon, Brendan Kennelly and Mary Robinson who later distinguished themselves. In the mornings I attended lectures and in the afternoons there were practical classes in Physics, Chemistry, Zoology and Geology and more lectures. Amongst my fellow Natural Science students there was a fiction that nobody exerted themselves. Undergraduates, especially those from British public schools, pretended to toss off essays in a relaxed manner; the idea of achieving success without visible effort was widespread, although many worked hard in secret.

Food in Ireland during the early 1960s was notoriously dull and limited. Most diners did not stretch their taste beyond a plate of steak and chips with a bottle of Spanish red. Before attending a society meeting in TCD, a group of us would go to the Universal Chinese restaurant on Wicklow Street where I ate my first Chinese meals. Prices were reasonable, service excellent with some good coarse wines to wash down the food. As we were usually ravenous, our favourite meal was a 'Universal Special,' a dish of rice and noodles with a large fried egg perched on the summit that cost six shillings. The Universal was the place where I first ate sweet-and-sour pork. The taste and texture of the crisp golden balls of pork and the accompanying sauce is so memorable that it remains my favourite Chinese meal today. If one was meeting a girlfriend between lectures, then a famous Irish institution, Bewley's Edwardian Oriental café on Grafton Street, was a suitable venue for a good cup of coffee, partnered with a spicy cherry bun or a slice of delicious barmbrack. The tables of this Quaker-run institution were marble-topped and we sat in velvet-covered stalls or on old bentwood chairs while the aroma of roasting coffee beans permeated the entire restaurant in which were seated middle-class Dublin women in hats, tweed skirts and sensible shoes.

The other institution that became part of our lives at Trinity was the constellation of pubs encircling the University. Although some Dublin pubs were succumbing to the utter tedium of piped music, wall-to-wall carpeting and plastic flowers, it was still possible to locate genuine Dublin pubs such as those in the streets south of the College, including O'Neill's of

Suffolk Street, Slattery's, Neary's, O'Donoghue's – where the folk group 'The Dubliners' formed in 1962 – the Bailey, where the front door of Number 7 Eccles Street (the real life front door of the fictional home of Leopold Bloom and Molly) had been salvaged from demolition and cemented into the wall; and Davy Byrne's – where Leopold Bloom had a cheese sandwich and a glass of Burgundy on Bloomsday.

These hostelries, some of which boasted Leinster granite counters and a wealth of mirrors, employed barmen wearing white aprons deeply engaged in the ritual of pouring the perfect pint of Guinness. This involved holding the glass under the tap at an angle of 45 degrees until it was three-quarters full. The barman slowly straightened the glass and placed it on the bar to allow it to surge and settle for about a minute. When settled, the Guinness has a much darker appearance. The barman then lifted the glass, held it vertically as he topped it up until the head peeped over the rim of the glass, and he gently stroked off the collar of foam with an ivory palette knife until the drink was fully prepared and the ritual completed. The pint was now crowned with a half-inch high, white creamy head. Finally, like a priest presenting communion wine, the barman placed the perfectly prepared pint in front me. Draught Guinness in those days was served at the correct temperature; it did not taste as if it had just come out of the fridge. I loved the creamy depth of a pint of stout and the anticipation of watching the pint settle as the dark body of the drink gradually overcame the cream on the head. We said 'Cheers,' bent our elbows, swallowed several mouthfuls, wiped away the cream from our lips and relished its smoothness, the taste of hops in the mouth and the way it massaged the vocal chords on its passage down. It is widely acknowledged that Guinness tastes better in a Dublin pub than anywhere, not only because of the expertise of the barman pulling the pint, but also to the ambience and craic of the setting. Since living in Britain for fifty years, I have long since stopped drinking Guinness here as most barmen do not respect the need for the all-important 'settling time' to achieve the perfect pint.

These pubs provided the ideal location for us to converse, debate, develop ideas, lubricate friendships or engage with female students. The atmosphere was warm and friendly, a pint of Guinness cost 1/7 in 1960 (equivalent to 7p) and a bottle of plonk ten bob. I wore a Donegal tweed jacket – usually sporting leather patches – and corduroy trousers. The atmosphere was one of predominantly male bonhomie sustained by drink, thick smoke (70 percent of Irishmen smoked in 1960), and the unique conversational ability of Dubliners. It was such pleasure enhanced even more when spontaneous alcohol-fuelled singing broke out. If it was lunchtime, the pubs in the early sixties were required to close for 'holy hour' between 2.30pm and 3.30pm and we tumbled out into the daylight to attend a lecture or a laboratory session. Only this being Ireland, the 'holy hour' was not quite an hour as ten minutes was allowed for drinking up and this was later extended to twenty! There was, however, a strange anomaly in the Dublin pubs in the early 1960s: women were only permitted to drink half-pints.

Much time was spent in the circular Reading Room on campus where a respectful silence prevailed. Staff members spoke in hushed tones; and conversation by fellow students was admonished by a shush. There was a sense of awe about the place; after all, we were using one of the greatest libraries in the world: Trinity College Dublin, together with Oxford and Cambridge, are the only university copyright libraries in Britain and Ireland. When flirtations took place, they were silent and discreet, eyeing the female talent – of which there was an abundance – from under one's spectacles. There were opportunities to invite a girl to the coffee bar, but for at least the first year, the sophisticated public-school educated English girls, typically called Anastasia or Miranda, being both older and more mature, were simply unreachable, like the perfect apple high in a tree. Women were not permitted to live on campus in the early sixties and (theoretically) had to leave it by 10.00pm. Beyond the hallowed walls of Trinity, Ireland was a puritanical theocracy. Most Trinity students found flats or rooms in Ballsbridge, Ranelagh and Sandymount, below street level in Baggot Street, or basement flats in Wellington Road.

For the majority of Trinity students in the 1960s Irish politics were uninteresting, drugs were a rarity and sex a mystery. Sexually, the majority of Trinity students at the time were a relatively innocent lot and most, including me, were fumbling in the dark. Sex only really became universally feasible in the 1970s with the wider availability of contraceptives and sexual liberation. Trinity was like Oxford and Cambridge in the early sixties in that the male to female ratio was unbalanced: there were approximately four men to one woman. Hence, frequently one needed to look outside the hallowed walls of Trinity for female company. Consequently, after playing rugby on Saturday afternoons followed by a meal and a few pints of the 'black stuff', which was a male imperative, our favoured dance venue was Wanderers Rugby Club on Merrion Road. The girls would often be dancing with each other until the men arrived from the pubs. The room was invariably fairly dark and the dance floor crowded, which made it difficult to display one's skills at jiving (the only dance at which I had any expertise). Few experiences have surpassed the sheer joy of jiving with a slick partner to Chuck Berry's 'Sweet Little Sixteen', or Buddy Holly's 'Rave On'. During the dance, conversation was not urgently necessary – often limited to a narrow range of remarks on the size of the crowd and the quality of the band.

The dance hall at Wanderers had a unique aroma of hairspray, Brylcreem, Silvikrin lacquer, body odour and cigarette smoke and we were soon enveloped in a world of swirling couples, coloured lights and pulsating music. It was the era of rustling petticoats, stiletto heels and the Brigitte Bardot pout. Above all, the favoured female silhouette in the early 1960s was the creation of a conical bra which shaped breasts into sharply protruding cones that enabled a woman to add a cup size to her bust. The men eyed and evaluated the girls like cattle at a fair. The girls sat or stood around the sides of the dance floor waiting to be singled out and trodden on in the quickstep. Looking back I realise that it was a humiliating process for the women who had to tolerate being examined by men, many of whom were inebriated. I was nervous at the prospect of everyone looking at me when I walked up to a girl and invited her to dance under this public scrutiny. Hence, I tended to hold back as the first wave of men went 'over the top', selected a partner and took the floor. If one was refused, you then had to shuffle back to the lads crippled by the shame of rejection. It was important not to appear desperate but to say 'Would you like to dance?' with a somewhat nonchalant air. Despite being shy with girls initially, I was not often refused mainly because I was normally wearing a sports jacket or blazer and flannels and probably looked reasonably 'respectable'. The wallflowers who were not invited to dance looked sad, but tried to appear unflustered, and I have no real idea as to how they must have felt.

During the intermissions I would attempt to identify an agreeable looking girl through the dense clouds of cigarette smoke and hope to catch her eye and then look away. Then I would catch her eye again before walking over to put the question. After three numbers, the MC would announce: 'your next dance please'. Depending on the level of mutual attraction generated by my mediocre footwork and lack of real conversation, my partner would usually disappear or stay around for more if I said 'Would you like to stay on?' Mostly, the girls vanished into the smoky haze on the right hand side of the hall. The occasional Ladies choice could be awkward if I saw a girl whom

I didn't want to dance with steaming at full throttle towards me in the smoky atmosphere; one had to somehow shuffle around the floor for a few minutes making inane conversation until it was OK to say that you needed to go to the 'jacks,' hoping desperately she would not appear the following week. It was noticeable that the minority of pretty girls were never off the dance floor. It seems so churlish now to have been judging girls on superficial criteria like appearance, but that is how it was and how we behaved, although I knew that what I really desired was to meet someone of intelligence and learning, preferably in addition to having a great figure. I did not really enjoy or thrive in the dance hall setting. It is most suitable for people who are very good-looking and expert at dancing. I have never been either of these things. What I had going for me was a certain conversational ability and whatever little flair I had for that was nullified by the noise of the band and the crowd.

The underlying assumption was that this was the pick-up game. As the band usually commenced the last set with the Perry Como number 'Memories are made of This' and always finished the evening with 'Are you Lonesome Tonight' people became more concerned to find someone they could take outside for a few minutes. This might be initiated by complaining about the heat generated by the sweaty bodies in the dance hall and asking if she would like to go outside. Once in the car park, one made attempts to kiss the girl before trying (usually unsuccessfully) to open the buttons of her coat. It was not easy to be romantic while wearing a duffel coat on a freezing winter's night. As students, we were full of the passionate lust of youth, but nervous and somewhat awkward. Sex was on everyone's mind, but society did not sanction it. Even the older students at Trinity – men who had done National Service in Britain – had to yield to the law and customs of contraceptive-free Ireland. Drinking, conversing and going to the cinema were a form of sublimation. People's approach to relationships was constrained by doing what was socially acceptable; the fear of getting somebody pregnant and the terrifying prospect of boat trip to England for an abortion in an era when contraception was banned in Ireland was a constant source of panic and stress. There was also the stigma that unmarried mothers felt from their families and, above all, the church. For all the sexual frisson, Wanderers dances in the early 1960s were essentially respectable at a time when the country was ill at ease with sexuality. Recalling those dances from over 60 years ago, it is evident that I was interested in the whole person and not just to be hugged and kissed. Unfortunately, one rarely met anyone with whom one was likely to establish a deep relationship; it was more a rite of passage through which one was likely to pass and, in my case, frequently fail.

* * *

Sometimes events occurred that made me question whether the 1960s ever occurred in Ireland. In 1960 a plan had been hatched to link Trinity College's copyright library with the nearby National Library of Ireland on Kildare Street. A new building was proposed in the grounds of Trinity fronting onto Nassau Street and would be a shared facility, thereby saving the State money and eliminating duplication. It would have separate reading rooms for the two libraries and the collections would remain distinct, but books from each would be available to the readers of both libraries. The Taoiseach, Sean Lemass, who has a (justified) reputation as one of Ireland's greatest leaders, but who, nevertheless, on a simple issue to do with books and space wrote to Dr John Charles McQuaid on 31 March 1960 seeking his advice, thereby acknowledging the power of McQuaid by asking for his consent to the construction of a library extension. McQuaid vetoed the joint project arguing that the shared library extension at Trinity College might give the impression that Trinity College was somehow more prestigious than University College Dublin and McQuaid felt the chief university in a mainly Catholic community 'should manifestly be a Catholic institution.'[10] Lemass promptly abandoned the joint library concept and a few days later informed the Provost of Trinity that the government would provide financial support for the new Berkley Library, which subsequently opened in 1967.

* * *

The Geology lectures were attended by approximately 30 students in the third year and Geography attracted some 22, all of whom also studied Geology. When it came to matters of sex many of us were still inexperienced and shy while imagining (usually incorrectly) that most of our fellow students were leading highly charged passionate sex lives. Amongst the group studying both subjects Dave was a solid product of the Northern Ireland grammar school system. A good student, who eventually gained an upper class second degree in an era when they were very uncommon, Dave, for some inexplicable reason, seemed to exude a certain magnetism and had a unique ability to rapidly attract the prettiest girl at a party. He was socially smooth and seemingly irresistible to women, an attribute we only shared in our imaginations. At one time he was dating a former Irish international tennis star and they would play a game on the courts in Botany Bay, which she would win comfortably. He was far more confident and superior to the rest us in basic relationship matters, which usually has nothing to do with thought and everything to do with decisiveness.

The quality of teaching to which we were exposed varied considerably. The first year Physics course of three lectures per week was delivered entirely by the great Nobel prize winning physicist, Professor ETS Walton, a benign and humble don who entertained us with brilliant experiments which he conducted during the lectures; it is safe to say that today it is inconceivable that any first year Physics students in an Irish or British university would sit at the feet of a Nobel prize winner for the whole academic year. Much of the teaching in Chemistry and Zoology was dull and I never considered switching to either subject in the Sophister years. The Geology department was small with around five staff, but two of them – Prof. R G S Hudson and Prof Frank Mitchell – were Fellows of the Royal Society and this was clearly reflected in their research and teaching. The quality of teaching in the Geography department was highly variable: John Andrews was outstanding and his carefully prepared inspirational courses in Historical Geography were enhanced with touches of wry humour. A meticulous scholar, his most important book – *A Paper Landscape: the Ordnance Survey in 19th Century Ireland* – was published by Oxford University Press. John Andrews also had a major lifelong impact on me as he supervised my undergraduate dissertation. His supervision demonstrated to me that the bedrock of all quality scholarship is rigorous research, careful marshalling and analysis of facts, critically evaluating theories, and a willingness to consider alternative evidence and perspectives. It was to be many years later before I realised how great an influence John Andrews had been upon my development as an academic. Prof. Gordon Herries Davies, my tutor, who delivered an interesting course in Geomorphology, was an exuberant larger-than-life figure with a pleasing literary style that was both authoritative and entertaining. He who wrote a number of books of which the two most important were: *The Earth in Decay: a History of British Geomorphology*; and *Whatever is Under the Earth: the Geological Society of London, 1807-2007*. It was an important distinction that a geographer was invited to write the history of the world's oldest Geological society. The rest of the staff in Geography delivered courses that were highly descriptive and seriously lacking in intellectual challenge.

One pleasant dimension of the Geology syllabus was that we were required to attend a field course each year during the Easter vacation. We were based in Waterford in 1961 and the following year in Lisdoonvarna, County Clare. Clare was a unique landscape of wooded hills and lakes, consisting of grey karst limestone with the broad expanse of the Shannon to the south, and with wild flowers blooming profusely in the cracks of the limestone. Apart from the fascinating geological exposures that we studied, the highlight of these trips was the craic that we had each night after dinner. This period coincided with the ballad revival in Ireland, initiated by the Clancy Brothers and Tommy Makem. The Clancy Brothers were a sharp contrast to their rivals -The Dubliners- with their matching Aran sweaters and wholesome voices. Their finest asset was the sweet tenor voice of Liam Clancy, especially when he sang 'The Parting Glass,' and 'The Shoals of Herring.' The Dubliners were led by Ronnie Drew, who sang in a gravelly voice 'like glass being crushed under a door.' However, the great ballad singer of The Dubliners was Luke Kelly, a diminutive redhead with an exceptionally melodious and powerful voice heard to great effect singing 'Raglan Road' with words by the eminent Irish poet, Patrick Kavanagh. The most influential Irish musicians were the Chieftains, founded by Paddy Maloney in 1962, whose music is almost entirely instrumental, based on the uileann pipes, and when Derek Bell, a classically trained harpist, joined it lent an element of elegance to their sound. They became internationally famous when they recorded the musical score for Stanley Kubrick's film *Barry Lyndon* in 1975. Their music is played with a natural lilt: tempos were changed in mid- tune from reel to polka, to jig, to slow air and back again. They expanded the awareness of Irish music worldwide, which enabled other groups such as Planxty, the Bothy Band and the Fureys and Davey Arthur to flourish.

Having a reasonable memory at that time, together with the experience of singing around scout camp fires, I had a large repertoire of Irish ballads at my disposal. The after-dinner sessions on field trips were dominated by drinking and the singing of songs and I quickly realised – much to my astonishment – that I was expected to lead the singing and perform the solos and that, if I did not do so, it would simply not happen. Initially I was reluctant to do it, but when the Professor of Geology, Prof. RGS Hudson, personally requested that I lead the singing on the day in Waterford in 1961 when he was informed that he had been elected a Fellow of the Royal Society, it was impossible to refuse. Prof Dan Gill, a charismatic larger than life figure, but also someone who had taken more from alcohol than alcohol had taken from him, joined in the singing with gusto. I also have a clear recollection of Dave Naylor singing 'These Foolish Things' while accompanying himself on piano. The songs that I sang included a number of rousing rebel ballads commemorating battles and skirmishes (invariably lost) against the English such as 'The Rising of the Moon,' with its rousing opening lines: 'Oh then tell me Sean O'Farrell tell me why you hurry so;' 'Slattery's Mounted Foot,' 'Roddy McCorley,' the Antrim hero of 1798 who led a rebellion and was hanged on the bridge of Toome, and 'Kevin Barry,' the eighteen year old rebel, hanged by the British in 1920. One of the most passionate of all Irish rebel songs – 'The West's Awake' – was a brief history of Irish resistance in the face of the English invader from the Normans onwards. From the opening lines, 'Alas and well may Erin weep/ When Connacht lies in slumber deep,' the melody is slow, deeply passionate and powerful and builds to an emotional climax: 'Sing Oh hurrah! Let England Quake/We'el fight till death for Ireland's Sake.' The Irish rebels were usually portrayed as brave, patriotic and upright, but the songs tend to disregard the disparity in fire power as the English soldiers were armed with muskets in 1798 up against the Irish wielding pikes. Hence, the English were much better armed and organised but we definitely had the best tunes! I also enjoyed singing humorous ballads like 'The West Clare Railway,' 'A Jug of Punch,' 'Tim Finnegan's Wake,' 'The Mary Ann McHugh,' and moving songs such as 'The Real Old Mountain Dew,' 'The Parting Glass', 'The Travelling People,' and together with my late friend and Corkman, Dick Hill, celebrating the exploits of 'The Bould Thady Quill.' It was also the peak of the skiffle era and, fortunately, my tenor voice enabled me to sing the Lonnie Donnegan numbers such as 'The Rock Island Line,' 'Grand Coulee Dam,' 'Cumberland Gap', 'The Battle of New Orleans,' and 'Putting on the Style,' all accompanied by Jim Langrell on guitar.

These nights on field trips were some of the most enjoyable of my life fuelled by Guinness, great Irish ballads and by a zest for fun and enjoyment that is endemic in Ireland. When we frequented the pubs in Clare or Waterford, I loved the way that the singing was totally spontaneous and shared with the locals. An individual with a pint in hand would just burst into song; and when it was finished, another person would perform a song and the whole gathering would join in the choruses. We also organised and ran student field trips through the University Geographical Society when we would hire minibuses and head for places of interest such as Sligo, Connemara and West

Cork and the evenings would be full of singing, dancing and (sometimes) courting. For a shy Irish undergraduate, as I was, my (limited) ability to sing was an important social passport to acceptance amongst my peers at Trinity, including the large English public-school contingent.

We attended a field course on the Aran Islands, some 30 miles west of Galway in the open Atlantic, only two months before our Finals in April, 1963. The archipelago consists of one larger island, Inishmore, and two smaller ones – Inishmaan and Inisheer. As the cargo boat from Galway approached Inishmore, we could see the Twelve Bens of Connemara to the north-east, the sheer grey cliffs of Moher to the south-east, while to the west the Atlantic stretched out to the horizon and far beyond, the source of gales and rain that regularly lashed across these karst limestone islands. The boat anchored off the two smaller islands, which in 1963 lacked a pier. We watched the islanders scurrying down to the beach from their thatched cottages from which rose the unforgettable smell of burning turf. The men launched their flimsy currachs – made from thin canvas stretched over a wooden frame with a pointed bow in front – into the Atlantic surf and rowed out to the cargo boat. Every person had to be lowered from the ferry to the currach. The cattle were winched overboard with a system of straps and pulleys. Once in the water, the cow's halter was grasped by a man in a currach, the straps and pulleys were undone, and the cow swam as it was towed to the island. It was a mystery as to how cattle could be fattened there since the islands are composed of Carboniferous limestone, a landscape of tiny fields created by spreading copious quantities of seaweed on the ground. The mystique of Aran is personified by Dun Aonghasa, a hillfort on Inishmore at the edge of a 300 foot sheer cliff defiantly facing west into the wild Atlantic ocean. Constructed in the Bronze and Iron ages, and dating back to 1100 BC, the fort consists of four concentric drystone defence walls, while outside the third ring of walls is a system of stone slabs, *chevaux-de-frise*, with the edges and points upstanding to deter invaders.[11] At night in the pubs with their stone floors and barrels of Guinness there was the charming Irish ritual of sharing music and song with (some) visitors being expected to 'give us an auld song there Paddy.' On the islands, even on Inishmore, a sense of timelessness was my predominant emotion at the end of the week.

During our investigative work one was aware of walking in the footsteps of the eminent Irish playwright, J M Synge, who came to Inishmaan in 1898 and returned every summer for the next four years. He was prompted by

W B Yeats who suggested that Synge make the people of the Aran islands the subject of his creative work and that he should go there, absorb the culture and folklore and gather folk tales as raw material for his plays. Synge lived among the islanders and it is reported that he lay on the floor of his bedroom and listened to the flow of conversation of the locals below. Synge discovered his muse and wrote a series of plays, including *Riders to the Sea* and his masterpiece – *Playboy of the Western World* – in which he dramatised the wildness of expression and independence of spirit of the islanders. This was not a romantic vision of the Aran islanders as Synge sought to depict the people as they really were. A romanticised version was served up by Robert Flaherty's (fictional) documentary – *Man of Aran* – in 1934.

* * *

Much of the cultural and social change, including a boom in satire, that swept across the English speaking world in the 1960s originated at the Edinburgh Festival. The movement was initiated in 1960 at the Edinburgh Festival's production of *Beyond the Fringe* and its star performers Peter Cook, Jonathan Miller, Alan Bennett and Dudley Moore. All four were highly talented and intelligent. Despite being much younger than the others, Cooke (22) wrote most of the script for the Edinburgh show. British Prime Minister, Harold Macmillan, the Church, the RAF and the bourgeoisie were among the targets of *Beyond the Fringe*. The team took to the stage for the first time at the Lyceum Theatre in Edinburgh at 10.45pm on 22 August 1960 and the show ran for only a week; and yet it changed the face of comedy. The highlight was Peter Cook's parody of a party political broadcast by Harold Macmillan, such a sketch being extremely rare before then. When the show moved to London in 1961, Macmillan himself went to see it, as did the Queen. The initial reviews were mixed, although Peter Lewis in the *Daily Mail* emphasised the novelty, irreverence and intelligence of the show in which they 'proceed to demolish all that is sacred in the British way of life with glorious and expert precision.'[12] Subsequently, in the judgement of Michael Billington half a century later, 'if any one event marked a genuine cultural turning point – it was not the opening night of *Look back in Anger* in 1956 – it was the slightly shambolic first performance of *Beyond the Fringe* (which) 'exposed the widening gulf between the generations (and) helped to change our attitude towards authority forever.' *Beyond the Fringe* led to a boom in satire, challenging social and cultural norms: *That was the Week that Was* (1962), *Not Only but Also* (1965) and *Monty Python's Flying Circus* (1969) were all inspired by it. *That was the Week that Was*, or *TW3*, was first broadcast on 24 November 1962 ; the chief presenter was David Frost, who introduced and linked the items, but whose main characteristic was his extraordinary ambition.[13] Malcolm Muggeridge's wife, Kitty, said of Frost that 'he rose without trace.'

The British New Wave at the cinema began with Jack Clayton's film of *Room at the Top*, a serious examination of sex and social class. This inspired a new generation of writers from the north of England and the next successful New Wave film was *Saturday Night and Sunday Morning* in October 1960, based on Alan Sillitoe's 1958 novel in which for the first time in British cinema the working class were shown to be out for a good time, unconcerned about the disapproval of their social superiors.[14] New Wave films proliferated and audiences flocked to see *The Entertainer*(1960), *A Taste of Honey* (1961), *The Loneliness of the Long Distance Runner* (1962) and *Billy Liar* (1963). The landmark novel of early 1960 was David Storey's *This Sporting Life* set in the unrelentingly tough world of rugby league; the subsequent film was released in 1963 as part of the New Wave, with Richard Harris playing the anti- hero, Frank Machin, an appropriate role for Harris as he had played schoolboy rugby for Munster. The demand for provincialism was quickly exhausted, but the New Wave cinema had presented an honest satire of working class life.[15]

The BBC recruited a new Canadian producer, Sydney Newman in 1963 whose great innovation was *The Wednesday Play*, which commanded a regular audience of between eight and ten million viewers for challenging dramas tackling topics such as homelessness, abortion and political corruption. These plays, as Sandbrook suggested, 'were eventually regarded as classics of the genre.'[16] It is generally accepted that *The Wednesday Play* represented an apotheosis in terms of quality of writing and direction. Major dramas included Dennis Potter's *Stand Up, Nigel Barton*, and *Vote, Vote, Vote for Nigel Barton* (1965); Nell Dunn's *Up the Junction* (1965), which was directed by Ken Loach; and, especially, *Cathy Come Home* (1966), written by Jeremy Sanford and directed by Ken Loach, which focused on homelessness and drew an audience of twelve million. All of these plays were seen as controversial because they addressed social and political issues with uncompromising frankness and documentary-like realism.[17] Drawing on the techniques of the New Wave films of the early sixties, Loach used hand-held cameras and outdoor locations in grubby back streets.

Since I lived at home as an undergraduate until 1963, the acquisition of a television set in 1962 – after Telefis Eireann was launched – was an important event. It was to become a major factor in the process of liberalisation. During the 1950s conservative forces had fiercely opposed the introduction of television, despite the fact that households along the east coast and border counties could pick up BBC and ITV signals. For those living away from the BBC signal, the viewing began on RTE at 6.00pm. After switching on the TV, the viewer needed to wait for at least a minute for the valves to warm up and the screen to flicker into life. The TV had an aerial on the top with two antennae and we would engage in the repetitive processes of adjusting the 'vertical' and 'horizontal' holds, moving the antennae into different positions to improve the fickle reception and fiddling with the contrast. There was so much snow on the screen that watching the British Open golf meant that it was impossible to follow the ball after it left the clubhead. Sometimes if you coughed the reception would improve!

Before the opening night's entertainment on Telefis Eireann, the new service was duly consecrated by Archbishop John Charles McQuaid. The Catholic bishops were deeply suspicious of the medium arguing that television 'can do great harm, not only in the diffusion of the ideas of those lacking in deep or accurate knowledge of religious truth, but also in broadcasting programmes which offend all reasonable standards of morals and decency.' The bishops could count on the support of conservative politicians in the Dail, most notably the Fine Gael member for Laois-Offaly – Oliver J Flanagan – who famously declared that: 'Sex never came to Ireland until Telefis Eireann went on the air.' The Catholic ethos of the state was prominent on Telefis Eireann, as evidenced by the broadcasting of the Angelus daily.

Despite the Catholic Church influence, RTEs most famous programme – *The Late, Late Show* – hosted by Gay Byrne and launched in 1962 – developed a justified reputation for exploring controversial issues in Irish society and was highly influential in facilitating the process of liberalisation and social change; it became a fundamental part of the national conversation, although Gay Byrne did not perceive himself as a social radical. The 'Bishop and the Nightie' episode of the *Late, Late Show* occurred in 1966 when Gay Byrne asked a young woman if she could remember the colour of the nightdress she was wearing on her wedding night. She replied that she might not have worn any, which infuriated the Catholic Archbishop of Galway, Dr Michael Browne, who criticised the programme as filthy and immoral. The celebrated novelist Colm Toibin suggested that a whole generation of people would have lived and died in twentieth century Ireland without ever having heard any discussion about sex if there had been no *Late Late Show*. A group of priests wrote to McQuaid in 1968 about sex and the *Late Late Show* demanding that Gay Byrne be prevented from 'providing a platform for the vermin of England, France, USA or anywhere such vermin can be picked up.'[18]

Despite the insights and critiques of Sean O'Faolain and Frank O'Connor, the Censorship Board was still banning novels in the 1960s by writers, including Edna O'Brien and John McGahern. McGahern, arguably Ireland's greatest novelist of the past sixty years, married a Finnish theatre director, Anniki Laaski in 1965, the year his second novel, *The Dark*, was published and then banned in Ireland. On returning to Ireland, he was sacked as a primary teacher by the local priest and it later became clear that Archbishop McQuaid was involved in his dismissal. The general secretary of the Irish National Teachers Organisation, D.J. Kelleher, refused to take up his case. He met McGahern, having fortified himself with whiskey: 'If it was just the auld book, maybe – maybe – we might have been able to do something for you, but with marrying this foreign woman you have turned yourself into a hopeless case entirely.....when there are hundreds of thousands of Irish girls going around with their tongues out for a husband.'[19] With great dignity, McGahern discouraged protests on his behalf 'ashamed, not because of the book, but because this was our country and we were making bloody fools of ourselves.'[20] The banning of McGahern's major novel and his sacking by the Catholic Church heralded the liberalisation of the censorship laws. Attitudes were changing at last and the decisions of the censors were patently ridiculous; and in Ireland, 'ridicule kills more painfully than moral denunciation.' Ireland's writers and poets were and still remain its greatest asset internationally and yet they were subjected to the kind of treatment which should have been reserved only for pornographers.

* * *

My younger brother Brian started playing golf when he was eleven in 1958 and from the start displayed a precocious talent for it; he possessed two great assets – an ability to hit the ball vast distances and a cool temperament. He ultimately played off scratch, and even at 60 he retained a handicap of two. I did not pick up a golf club until the summer of 1961, at the end of my second year at Trinity, when I started to play with Brian at Carrickmines Golf Club, having joined as a student member. Brian taught me much about the game and we truly bonded together on the golf course. Carrickmines is set in the foothills of the Dublin mountains with glorious views of Dublin Bay, the Hill of Howth, Bray Head and beyond. The course has areas of the original heathland turf and an abundance of gorse, hawthorn and bracken, while to the west the gorse-strewn hillsides slope upwards to the Dublin mountains. To play golf here was such an experience that it has dwelt in my mind all my life. It was beautiful at all seasons of the year: in summer when the bracken was green and sweet smelling; in autumn when it was golden brown and the Dublin mountains were clothed with purple heather. It was loveliest of all in spring when the rough bordering the fairways was sprinkled with cowslips and carpets of bluebells glowed in nearby woods. On some days the weather was unrelenting: gales, rain and sleet blown horizontally into our faces as we attempted to control the ball. On sunny days in summer, however, the expanse of freshly-mown turf was caressed by a gentle breeze enhanced by the songs of numerous skylarks overhead; I heard them as they rose and rose into the sky, pouring out their notes like tinkling bells.

I fell in love with golf there recognising that it was a game where one strived for a perfection that was ultimately unachievable. I had two lessons from the professional, Jimmy Barrett and slowly improved. I only discovered many years later that Jimmy Barrett had often played with Samuel Beckett, who had been a star cricketer at Trinity College. Beckett, when he could find nobody to play with at Carrickmines, used to follow one ball after another, enjoying (not surprisingly) being out on the course alone.[21] This was also to become a feature of my golfing career. Beckett played to seven handicap and also represented Trinity College at golf. I would have relished playing with him since I played off six handicap and we would have been well matched. Golf for him was all 'mixed up with the imagination' with the impact on him of the Irish sea, which one could see from the course, and the landscape of the Dublin mountains.[22] When Beckett could not sleep decades later in France, he would play over again in his mind the holes on the charming bracken and heather course, something I only discovered this year when I read James Knowlson's biography of the great playwright. Amazingly, playing Carrickmines in my head is something that I have also done many times, although I have not actually played the course for 50 years.

The membership of Carrickmines reflected that of Glenageary Lawn Tennis Club, that is to say predominantly middle and upper-middle class Protestants. Glancing at the list of men and women captains and presidents since 1980, there was only one name of the seventy listed that started with an O apostrophe! On one occasion I was invited to join a four-ball which included a gentleman who had retired to Dublin after many years of service as an administrator in India at the time of the Raj. On the third hole he sliced his drive into deep rough. I joined him in the search for his ball whereupon he told me that when he golfed in India this situation never arose because he always had a caddy and an 'olligolli,' a person who walked ahead and stood approximately 200 yards from the tee. If he drove the ball into the scrub or rough, the 'olligolli'- whose main qualification for the job was the possession of a prehensile toe – was than able to surreptitiously move the player's ball to a more favourable lie.

Christy O'Connor Senior was a golfing hero to both Brian and I and we saw him win a number of professional tournaments. I can clearly visualise the great man walking down the fairway in a relaxed style, the hunched shoulder sloping to the right from the thousands of balls he had hit in practice. Unlike many modern players, O'Connor, or 'Himself' as he was known in Ireland, played quickly without delay: the cigarette was dropped on to the fairway, the club selected and – following a practice swish – he would unleash that beautifully smooth, wristy, languid swing which projected the ball into the centre of the green. He was one of the most inventive shot-makers in the history of golf with an extraordinary ability to imagine and execute outrageous recovery shots. His only weakness was an inconsistent putting stroke. The great Gary Player recently stated that: 'O'Connor and Sam Snead were the two greatest natural players the world has ever seen.' A brilliant player in wind and rain, having spent his early years in Bundoran, there was an aura and charisma about O'Connor that developed as a result of the many tournaments he won with an irresistible charge on the final round. The *Guardian's* esteemed golf correspondent, Pat Ward-Thomas, wrote of O'Connor in 1964: 'There is no one in these islands who is less daunted by the prospect of victory than he.' When cheers arose from a part of the course, spectators assumed that O'Connor was making a move and the crowd stampeded across to support the local hero like a pack of wolves chasing its prey. Brian and I were fortunate to witness some of his great triumphs: in the 1959 Dunlop Masters at Portmarnock, he trailed the Irish amateur Joe Carr after three rounds, but shot a 66 to win by four strokes;

at the Irish Hospitals' tournament at Woodbrook in July 1960, he returned a 64 in the final round to tie Ken Bousefield and then recorded a 63 to Bousefield's 71 to win the playoff; at the Carroll's International tournament in 1964 he won again defeating Roberto de Vicenzo in a playoff. Finally, and most dramatically, in the Carroll's International tournament in 1966 at Royal Dublin, O'Connor shot a 66 in the final round, but only overhauled Eric Brown by playing the last three holes in 5 under par- eagle, birdie, eagle – to win by two strokes. There were many other great victories, including the World Seniors title twice in 1976 and 1977.

* * *

To my astonishment, I managed to achieve First Class honours grades and was top of the year in both Geology and Geography in the first part Moderatorship exams at the end of the Third year at Trinity in 1962; the marks from these exams accounted for 30 percent of the final degree assessment. Since I had decided that getting rich was not on my agenda, my hope was to do a PhD for which I would need a First Class degree in order to win a postgraduate scholarship. Hence, during the final year I became a bit of a nerd, working my way through most of the prescribed reading lists, writing a dissertation that was too long, and worrying about deadlines. My greatest good fortune was my memory which permitted me to memorise complete references (something I can no longer do) and to recall passages from books and research papers, to see them on the page and to synthesise them with other material. This was not a great talent, but it was useful in preparing for exams. When I began to revise for finals, I gradually reduced my files of notes for each of the six exams to both sides of an A4 sheet on which I wrote quotations, references and summaries of complex arguments with a few bullet points. I carried these sheets around and read them on trains and before going to bed during the fortnight before the exams. I also played golf at Carrickmines on the evening before the first exam! We sat six papers and after I selected which questions to answer I scribbled a few notes sketching out the structure of each answer and my key insights. The notes for subsequent answers were augmented as I wrote each essay. Afterwards I was satisfied that I had done my best and I needed to await the verdict of the examiners. A couple of weeks later we were subjected to a *viva voce* exam by a Professor from Manchester University. During the final year several members of staff told me that they expected me to get a First, which was very flattering, but it also made the process more stressful. Achieving a First in finals was a relief and a research scholarship was forthcoming. However, the university offered me a Teaching Assistant post which remunerated me more than a scholarship. In retrospect, it was not the best decision as I was given too much teaching and preparation to do which left insufficient time to develop my PhD thesis over the following two years.

During the Final Year I was romantically involved with Patricia, a Scottish medical student at the Royal College of Surgeons in Dublin. Pat was an intelligent girl with a sharp intellect who was a good hockey player and could jive superbly. The main problem was that at the time – but not in later life – she was a practising Catholic and sex in early 1960s Ireland was still a taboo subject. The Irish experience of the sixties reveals a strong continuity with the past and, because of the conservative influence of the Catholic Church (and Presbyterianism in Northern Ireland) the sixties era of liberation and hedonism was largely postponed. After completing my Finals in June 1963, we went on holiday for a week touring the Scottish Highlands in her black Morris Minor car. Driving around the north-west of Scotland and staying in B and Bs or caravans every night was quite stressful. Being with a Catholic girl then required patience and forbearance. I knew for several reasons, however, that our relationship was not sustainable. The sexual revolution of the 1970s – representing a process of liberation- allowing young men and women to experience physical pleasures free from consequences or guilt came a decade too late for my Irish generation.

After graduating, it was time to move on and, having obtained the post as a Teaching Assistant at Trinity, I moved into a flat in Hatch Street with Jimmy Patterson, a Geology graduate, and Charles Morley, a mature Geology PhD student. I spent periods of time in County Tipperary during 1964 and 1965 collecting data and conducting interviews as part of my doctoral dissertation on Central Place Theory. I purchased a 350cc AJS motor cycle in 1964 to replace my Vespa scooter. Early in the morning with little traffic on the road from Clonmel to Carrick-on Suir and with a south-westerly wind behind I topped over 100mph on several occasions. One afternoon I was zooming down into Clonmel from Knocklofty and, as I approached the level crossing on the main Limerick to Rosslare railway line, I noticed that one level crossing gate was open and the other was shut. I shouted up to the signalman to ask him why one gate was open and one shut? 'Ah well' he said 'I'm half expecting the Limerick train.' On another occasion, I popped into a chemist shop owned by an O'Farrell. When I informed the owner that we shared the same name, he asked me where I was studying for my higher degree and when I told him that it was Trinity College Dublin he responded by asking whether I had difficulty obtaining permission from Dr. John Charles McQuaid to attend Trinity. I told him that I had not sought McQuaid's permission as I was not a Catholic. He then summoned his wife from an adjoining room to inform her that I was the only non-Catholic O'Farrell he had ever met. As I was leaving his shop he said: 'Please God you'll return to the true faith before you die.' I was pleased that I had not told him that my grandfather had trained for the priesthood, lapsed, became an atheist and married a Presbyterian from County Cavan!

In the Spring of 1964 I participated on a field study visit to Clifden in Connemara where I first struck up a relationship with Julia, a very pretty English student whose grandfather had been Governor General of the Bahamas. Her background was an upper-middle class Labour supporting family living in Ruislip with a very large country house on the south coast of England at West Wittering. We enjoyed some exciting times cruising around the environs of Dublin with Julia on the back of my motor bike. After spending the summer of 1964 in County Tipperary collecting data for my thesis, I flew to Gibraltar in September where Julia and I spent a two- week holiday together in Marbella. Following this trip we returned to stay with her elderly mother in Ruislip from where we drove to their large summer house in West Wittering for a short holiday. This was an epiphany of major consequence for I discovered that Julia's mother was a very intelligent and politically engaged person who was an excellent conversationalist. Unfortunately, it was not possible to combine her intelligence and personality with Julia's calm and beauty.

During my second year as a Teaching Assistant, earning around £400 per annum, I moved into a room in the Graduates Memorial Building in the Front Square of Trinity. In reality it was a bed-sit with the walls painted in a dull cream colour. The window commanded a splendid view of the cobbled Front Square and the campanile, although in 1964 few of the college buildings had been restored or cleaned. There was a tiny kitchenette, bed, built-in gas fire, desk and chair all adjacent to the Iveagh bathhouse and the luxury of enormous baths with limitless supplies of hot water. In October 1964 I started dating Susan, who was the daughter of a Methodist minister from Yorkshire, and we developed a very close and exciting relationship; she was good fun, but also extremely kind, thoughtful and unselfish, frequently cooking me excellent meals in her flat on Wellington Road.

During the summer vacation of 1965, I spent many weeks in County Tipperary travelling around on my AJS motor cycle while collecting data for my PhD thesis. The AJS, like many other British manufactured bikes of the time, was highly unreliable and breakdowns were a regular occurrence. Needless to say, I did not have the expertise to conduct any but the most basic of repairs. While staying in Birr, County Offaly in July 1965, I went to Morning Prayer in St Brendan's Church of Ireland church. The service was attended by the Earl and Countess of Ross and a smattering of Colonels and Squadron leaders. When the service reached the first prayer, the rector – Dr Francis Bourke – dedicated it to 'Great Britain and the Commonwealth,' followed by one for 'Queen Elizabeth' and finally 'other nations of the world,' with no specific reference to nation in which we were located. I was astonished since our country had been independent for 44 years.

Trinity was tolerant, scholarly, benign, a place that somehow managed to embrace both the very bright and the less bright, the wealthy English and the native Irish, and to tolerate and celebrate both the idle and the industrious, providing that the idle made a contribution either on the rugby pitch, in debating – at which the College excelled – or perhaps on the stage of Players – all were accommodated within the liberal, free-thinking mileau. Almost any amount of eccentricity was acceptable as long as it was not publicised. Outstanding sportsmen, such as the captain of the First XI cricket team, were allowed to repeat a year, if necessary, and would go on to be awarded a Cricketer's Third or a General Studies degree. This tolerance is encapsulated beautifully by the experience of Laurie Howes, who graduated in 1964 in Economics and Political Science, but disliked having to study Statistics and Economic Geography. He went to see his tutor, Mr Fitzgibbon, intending to switch to a Pass degree in General Studies. Mr Fitzgibbon listened intently to Howes and then delivered his immortal advice: 'But it doesn't matter what you read at Trinity. The important thing is…. being here!'[23] Being here was much more than just attending lectures but was about meeting the rich mixture of students who made up the cosmopolitan community that was Trinity, which was unique in 1960s Ireland and extremely rare in Britain. I was never especially keen on the ancient rituals at Trinity such as the long Latin grace on commons, the formality of wearing gowns in lectures and the Fellows hierarchy, which I found dated, pompous and reeking of smug self-satisfaction. However, since graduating and subsequently working in five British universities I have come to love Trinity more than any other institution, not only for its tolerance and conviviality, but also because it boasted the most talented, diverse and interesting student body I have known, complemented by a group of academics at whose feet I sat ranging in quality from a Nobel prize winner in Physics (ETS Walton), two FRSs in Geology (Prof R G S Hudson and Prof Frank Mitchell) to some academics who were barely fit to manage the College wine list.

I was captivated by Trinity College. I enjoyed the challenge that it presented; and I relished the opportunity to enrich my life. Two great benefits of a Trinity education were that one learned how to learn and that one also imbibed much from the people that one met. There was a tidal wave of social change about to occur in the mid-sixties of which we were unaware as we enjoyed just being at Trinity. We were the last generation of students before the Vietnam War, Paris 1968, the Troubles in Northern Ireland, the Prague spring, international terrorism, the end of apartheid and climate change. Those far-off days were truly golden; Trinity remains the most transformational experience of my life. What we students of the 1960s only obliquely apprehended was that all was about to change, that the golden era had ended. Now when I return infrequently to Trinity I find that Front Square is packed with tourists queueing to see the Book of Kells – more than one million a year- and that the University is also hiring out the space in Front Square for other activities. Where is that glorious institution of my past? It looks even more timeless and beautiful. Is it possible that it still does not matter what one reads, but that the important thing is simply being there?

CHAPTER 6

North of the Border

There were many strands to my life in the 1960s: graduating from Trinity College; starting work and research at Trinity; moving to the Northern Ireland to a lecturing post at Queen's University Belfast; becoming engaged to Susan; completing a PhD; the joy of getting married in 1967; the pleasure of furnishing a flat; publishing research papers for the first time; becoming politically active, especially participating in the civil rights movement in Northern Ireland; making new friends and playing golf. After two years teaching and initiating research on my PhD at Trinity College, it was time to consider moving on as nobody on the staff there had expertise in the subject area of my thesis, Central Place Theory. I applied for a Junior Lecturer post at Queen's University Belfast and – much to my amazement – after a gruelling interview process, I was appointed. Arriving in Belfast on the train from Dublin in September 1965 to take up the position at Queen's University, I was immediately struck by how foreign it seemed; it reminded me of an English city like Manchester or Leeds with narrow tentacles of red-brick terraced housing radiating westwards towards Divis mountain, unlike any town in the Republic. The narrow side streets were crammed with small Victorian terraces with walled-in yards and back–alleys. There were no front gardens and no trees shaded the streets. Union Jacks were flying prominently; the RUC wore bottle- green uniforms and carried guns in holsters; and the accents were sharper and less melodious than those of the South.

Reaching the university, I was impressed by the main building, dating from 1849 and designed by Sir Charles Lanyon in a style borrowed from the Gothic and Tudor character of medieval universities, especially Magdalen College, Oxford. Having settled into my new office in the north wing of the main building, my next task was to sort out accommodation. The University accommodation office suggested that I should opt for digs in a three- story terraced house in Lawrence Street within walking distance of the university. My room was on the top floor and its main feature – in the absence of any central heating – was the intense cold once the winter weather arrived in November. Four other people resided in the house and there was always a scramble to gain access to the only bathroom every morning. Miss Maguire, the kindly landlady, provided breakfast and supper every day and sharing the mealtimes with four Ulster folk was a rapid learning experience in how to tiptoe around the boundaries of sectarian sensitivities. As Seamus Heaney wrote:

> And whatever you say, say nothing.
> Smoke-signals are loud- mouthed compared with us:
> Manoeuvrings to find out name and school,
> Subtle discrimination by addresses
> With hardly an exception to the rule.

I remained in Lawrence Street for a term before being appointed Sub-Warden of a Hall of Residence in Upper Crescent, close to the university. Robin Glasscock, an avuncular academic colleague, was most helpful in advising me about the duties of a Sub–Warden. I ran a relaxed regime at the hall where I stayed until I married in July 1967.

Although my starting salary at Queen's University was only £1,100 per annum, my next priority was to purchase my first car. The Morris Mini Minor, designed for BMC in 1959 by the brilliant Alec Issigonis (he had previously designed another classic car, the Morris Minor) had become 'the motoring icon of the Swinging Sixties.' It bucked the norm with its short bonnet (accommodating the east-west layout of the engine), front-wheel drive, small ten- inch wheels at each corner, fuel efficiency and affordability. It was extraordinarily small, yet spacious inside with its pull wire instead of a door handle and quirky windows which one slid open by hand. The Mini went on to become an icon of classlessness, the most popular British car of all time, selling more than 5 million. It was also fashionable and, consequently, I marched into the Great Victoria Street branch of the Bank of Ireland, which was managed by a former school friend of my father's, Stewart Dick, and he immediately lent me £370 pounds – one third of my annual salary – with which to purchase a car. One of my colleagues, Noel Mitchel, very kindly spoke to a friend at the garage and he reduced the price by £50 so that I paid a total of £496 for a new red Mini. It was the only time I have ever borrowed from a bank and it was one of the few occasions when I was in tune with the zeitgeist in terms of consumption behaviour! I was not yet free to drive in Northern Ireland as I had acquired my Irish driving licence at the age of 18 through the onerous process of paying one pound at the post office. Hence, before being let loose on the roads in the North, I was required to pass a driving test after some six years of driving in the South. Sadly, the Mini was poorly manufactured and mine rusted and leaked within a year.

The Geography department at Queen's University Belfast was welcoming and was led by Prof. Emyr Estyn Evans, who had moved to Queen's in 1928 to establish the department and is regarded as the father of Irish geography. Prof. Evans was a gentle and kind leader who commanded great respect as a result of his international scholastic reputation. He straddled the disciplines of geography, folklore, anthropology, history, and archaeology with an approach that was not restricted by disciplinary boundaries. He chaired the large staff meetings and listened to even the lowliest of Junior Lecturers, such as myself, with patience and understanding. After leading a major archaeological survey of Northern Ireland in which he discovered many unrecorded megalithic monuments, Evans became interested in peasant culture and folklore and published a number of classic books on the subject illustrated with his own line drawings. Some of these books – notably *Irish Folk Ways*, *Irish Heritage* and *The Personality of Ireland* – are still in print, although written over 60 years ago. He identified the conflict between native and newcomer as 'the clash that struck the sparks of Irish culture.'

The Geography department was sufficiently large that there were clusters of staff with cognate interests who regularly met over coffee or lunch to exchange ideas and references; and there were a number of research students who contributed substantially to the stimulating intellectual environment, which was also reinforced by a steady stream of visitors to the department who frequently presented a research paper. The Geography department at Queen's was unquestionably the pre-eminent one in Ireland. Prof. Ronnie Buchanan was a source of invaluable impartial advice to me about the university and Ulster culture; Prof Fred Boal, who did pioneering research on ethnic spatial segregation in cities, was an important influence upon me. Although our research topics were different, he was a key role model for me and we shared a concern for rigorous methodology as the quantitative revolution was changing Geography to the discomfort of some of our colleagues. There was some tension between the staff interested in topics such as economic geography, urban geography and migration, and the geomorphologists and glaciologists who were less persuaded by the charms of statistical modelling and complex sample designs. I also formed a close working relationship with Mike Poole, who was a contemporary, and when we had both completed our doctorates, we collaborated on a couple of research projects.

I knew that I wanted an academic career; but I harboured serious reservations as to whether I had sufficient ability to succeed. I lacked confidence as a researcher and even as late as 1969 I was contemplating whether to become a schoolteacher. This is reflected in the fact that of my first seven research papers I submitted only one to a leading international journal. Looking back now I realise that the issue was simply the absence of a mentor as, for the final two years of my PhD while working at Queen's, I did not have a supervisor. The problem was resolved by the appearance on sabbatical leave of Prof. Morgan D. Thomas of the University of Washington. Morgan was a true scholar, who had flown on bombing missions over Germany in the Second World War, and was editor of a prestigious journal, *Papers of the Regional Science Association*. He was very gifted conceptually and, despite the age difference, he and I became friends and he attended a paper I presented on Central Place Theory. Afterwards, he called me into his office and gave me feedback on the presentation, which nobody had ever done before, and told me that I was perfectly capable of publishing in the leading international journals. Never patronising, always helpful, he became my academic mentor during his sabbatical year at Queen's and his support was critical at a key moment in my career. When I subsequently moved to work at Cardiff University in 1973, he called to see me each year when he returned home to Swansea to visit his relatives.

Although I had done some lecturing at Trinity College, I shouldered a much greater load at Queen's. The most taxing, at least initially, was to lecture for two hours to a night class of part-time students on dark winter Friday nights. These teachers, civil servants and others drove into Queen's from all across Northern Ireland and arrived shivering in their coats. I admired them, although I was shocked to discover that they were all older than me. However, we soon struck up a rapport and I managed to survive the year.

A notable feature of the syllabus at Queen's was the system of First year tutorials whereby a small group of seven or eight students attended each week to discuss a range of topics. What shocked me was the discovery that if two students came from the same small village or town in Northern Ireland and one was Catholic and the other Protestant they would never have met before attending my tutorial class. This happened frequently and underlined just how segregated the lives of the two tribes were: different schools, churches, sports, youth organisations and social activities.

* * *

Belfast in 1965 was a city of dingy pubs and cafes, drab terraced streets, endless rain and rundown threadbare hotels. People wandering around in shabby raincoats under a dull sky evoked the mood of a place worn down by high unemployment and austerity. Sundays were even more bleak as cinemas, dance halls, pubs and even children's playgrounds were closed under the powerful influence of evangelical Protestantism. By noon on a Sunday the churches had emptied and nothing was happening; the city was lifeless and the red-brick gospel halls and mean terraced houses were frequently blanketed in drizzle as a dull melancholy set in. I was a Protestant living in a Protestant middle- class area of south Belfast, but I was a southern Protestant and a nationalist and so I felt alien. Northern Protestants had a direct manner of speaking and a sharp sense of humour which I really liked, but, unfortunately, many were very anti-Catholic.

This was my first experience of living in the UK and I soon became aware that there were major social, economic and cultural disparities between regions of the country. In the mid-sixties the differences between London and Belfast became even more marked. The first colour supplement launched by the *Sunday Times* in February 1962 had featured photographs of Jean Shrimpton on the cover. Shrimpton, the photographer, David Bailey, the designer, Mary Quant and the painter David Hockney were on the verge of major international celebrity; the affair between David Bailey and Jean Shrimpton, who became the world's top model for several years, was followed by Bailey's marriage to the alluring French film star, Catherine Deneuve. Mary Quant's fashion shops were a mecca for the pioneers of the new age; her key innovation was the miniskirt, which she launched in September 1965, the month I arrived to work in Queen's University Belfast, where the sight of a miniskirt at the time was as rare a swallow in winter. The peak of the Swinging London phenomenon – according to historian Jerry White – lasted from 1963 to 1967: 'its temples were the boutique and the discotheque...its high priests the pop star, the fashion designer, the model and the photographer; its emblems the miniskirt and the haircut.'[1]

Swinging London involved a subtle synthesis between the worlds of art schools, design, music, culture and fashion, a combination of attributes that simply did not exist in Belfast or other British cities in 1965. The musical accompaniment was truly seminal: the Beatles' ground-breaking album '*Revolver*' and the Beach Boys classic '*Pet Sounds*' were both released in the summer of 1966. Drug taking – especially cannabis and LSD – became widespread; inhibitions about pre-marital sex disappeared in a wave of permissive indulgence, homosexual as well as heterosexual; and the transformations in relation to sex, clothes, relations between generations and the attitude to authority were dramatic.[2] David Bailey later admitted that Swinging London was 'a very elitist thing for 2,000 people living in London,'[3] which constantly reinvented itself, facilitated by drugs. Terence Conran opened Habitat on the Fulham Road in May 1964; it became the iconic shop of the decade in the UK with wooden chairs from Italy, pine furniture from Scandinavia and trendy kitchenware all targeted at affluent middle-class couples. Conran did not open any stores in Belfast in the 1960s.

The 1960s was also a period of liberal social reforms in Britain under the Wilson Labour government. The legislation was implemented by Roy Jenkins, a highly enlightened Home Secretary. Capital punishment was abolished in 1965, abortion legalised in 1967, and in July of the same year the Sexual Offences Act decriminalised homosexual acts in private between two men. The Lord Chamberlain ended theatre censorship in 1968, divorce laws were eased in 1969, flogging in prisons was abolished and majority verdicts for English juries introduced. Hence, the 1960s had also witnessed – under Jenkins' leadership – more liberal social reform than any decade before or since. However, by the autumn of 1967 the optimism and the glamour of the Swinging Sixties had vanished. Even when Swinging London was at its height, sterling was under constant attack in the foreign exchange markets, and, finally, on Saturday 18th November 1967, the government devalued the pound by 14 per cent against the dollar, and to compound the national humiliation, Prime Minister Harold Wilson went on TV and infamously proclaimed that 'it does not mean that the pound…in your pocket has been devalued.' The spotlight left London in 1967 and lit up San Francisco's Summer of Love where young activists – motivated by black civil rights and anti-Vietnam war protest movements – carried flowers to demonstrate their peaceful intentions.

Although other British cities, such as Manchester, Leeds and Glasgow were only marginally influenced by the Swinging London phenomenon, there could not have been a greater contrast than that between the glamour of Swinging London and the grey, drab face of Belfast in thrall to strict nonconformism. Belfast seemed another world from the mini-skirts, boutiques, bistros, pop stars, designers and models of mid-sixties London; there was no prospect of bumping into Jean Shrimpton or Julie Christie while strolling along Royal Avenue. It was not just geographically but also culinarily far from the bright lights of Swinging London (and also, to a lesser extent, Dublin) where avocados, courgettes, kiwi fruit, sophisticated wines and continental cheeses were becoming more available. Such delights had not reached the shops in Botanic Avenue, Belfast, even in the late sixties. The one innovation of Swinging London that did hit the streets of Belfast was the mini-skirt, although whether the hems rose quite as high as in London is less certain. Apart from this, life seemed to go on much as before as indeed it did in provincial Britain; some of the so-called liberation was little more than media hyperbole and much of its sophistication was no more than passing fashion. In Ireland it could legitimately be maintained that the 1960s did not begin until the 1970s.[4] Jonathon Green asserted that this was also true of Britain: 'The sixties, as widely celebrated, is chronology as pure myth. Everything in the myth pertains to sex.....the real revolution would not emerge until the seventies.'[5] For all the publicity in the media about drugs, sex, rock -and – roll and flower power for most people in Ireland and Britain life was much more mundane: DIY was one of those trends in the sixties that spread to all parts of the country; and activities such as wallpapering, painting, plumbing, dressmaking and gardening became very popular. I was only passably competent at one of these, gardening. Hunter Davies argues that 'the big noticeable change in the sixties was one of attitude and deference, rather than drugs and sex.'[6] For myself, I cannot pretend that I was remotely the epitome of fashion in the sixties, apart from owning a red Mini.

Popular music of the 1960s was dominated by the Beatles.[7] Following a successful spell in Hamburg in 1960, the Beatles obtained their initial booking at the Cavern, near Liverpool's decaying docks.[8] After winning a recording contract with Parlophone records – where the group came under the wing of George Martin – their second recording, 'Please Please Me' reached number one in the charts in March 1963; while their fourth single – 'She loves You'- became their largest selling single ever in August 1963. When the Beatles came to play in Ireland in November, 1963, it was three days after they had starred at the Royal Variety Performance, which was watched by 26 million people on ITV.[9] They played two shows at the Adelphi cinema in Dublin and then travelled to Belfast to play at the Ritz cinema. When McCartney played Dublin many years later people texted mobile messages to a big screen and the one that prompted most laughter was 'Greetings to everyone who was at the Adelphi in 1963 – and the GPO in 1916'[10] Both events certainly rocked Dublin.

The unique success of the Beatles was due to a number of key factors: their approachable, witty personalities; their guitar-based sound; their knack of spotting trends before their rivals did; and their sheer melodic flair and song-writing ability, especially that of McCartney.[11] Their initial success in the United States is beyond rational explanation. They were almost completely unknown in the USA at the end of December 1963 when 'I Want to hold your Hand' was released there. By the 17 January 1964 the song had reached number one in the American Top Hundred and the Beatles had become the most famous group in the world.[12] During the spring of 1964, the Beatles accounted for almost two-thirds of all records sold in the United States, and in April they had twelve records in the *Billboard* Hot 100, including all the top five. What was so impressive was how their music developed during the seven years that they were writing and recording: each album represented a major development, experimenting with new instruments, sounds and harmonies. Hunter Davies suggested that 'Eleanor Rigby was possibly the best poetry we would hear in 1966.' However, for those of us who were Seamus Heaney's colleagues at Queen's University, the major poetic event of 1966 was unquestionably the publication by Faber and Faber of his first poetry collection, *The Death of a Naturalist*, marking the auspicious debut of one of the century's greatest poets. His poem 'Docker' hints that communal strife was merely slumbering in the back streets of Belfast and Derry.[13]

> That fist would drop a hammer on a Catholic-
> Oh yes, that kind of thing could start again.
> The only Roman collar he tolerates
> Smiles all round his sleek pint of porter.

The only rock group to challenge the hegemony of the Beatles was the Californian-based Beach Boys who created a unique sound drawing upon the music of jazz-based vocal groups, rock and roll, and black Rhythm and Blues. Their music reflected a southern Californian youth culture of cars, surfing and romance. The group's 'California Sound' became prominent through the success of their 1963 album *Surfin USA*. Between 1961 and 1964 the band – in which Brian Wilson was composer, arranger and producer- recorded a string of top-ten singles. The Beach Boys then abandoned surfing themes – Wilson did not surf himself – for more elaborate orchestrations and more personal lyrics. In May 1966, a highly innovative recording – *Pet Sounds* – was released and the Beach Boys became one of the most important bands in the history of rock. Paul McCartney acknowledged that *Pet Sounds* was a primary impetus for the Beatles' album *Sergeant Pepper's Lonely Hearts Club Band*. Later in 1966 'Good Vibrations' became their first number one in Britain and it is now recognised as one of the great masterpieces of rock music. The quality that appealed to me most about the Beach Boys' music were the harmonies that made the band unique; their purity of tone was facilitated by the genetic proximity of their voices.

* * *

Some changes were afoot in Northern Ireland, notably the construction of a motorway between Belfast and Dungannon which began in 1962; and new small self-service supermarkets were opening. Unemployment was high and the economy was over-dependent on public- sector employment, and it still is. Moreover, although Northern Ireland was peaceful in the mid-sixties, the problem of two politically and religiously divided communities living uneasily side by side remained unresolved. Even in Dublin little had changed. Archbishop John Charles McQuaid, on his return from the Vatican Council on 9th September 1965, announced to his flock: 'Allow me to reassure you. No change will worry the tranquillity of your Christian lives'. As Kerrigan has pointed out, it was not liberals who caused the Catholic Church problems over the following decades, it was practising Catholics making choices such as easing censorship and taking the pill.[14]

Northern Ireland was something of a cultural desert in the sixties, far removed from the swinging capital city. Queen's University, to its great credit, did much to improve the situation by organising the Belfast International Arts Festival every year where we flocked to hear music ranging from Bach's Brandenburg Concertos to Johnny Dankworth and Cleo Laine, then at the peak of her extraordinary vocal powers. The festival was the brainchild of a student, Michael Emmerson, who started it in 1962. Emmerson also founded the Queen's Film Theatre (QFT) in 1968, which screened art- house, indie and world- cinema films selected on grounds of artistic merit rather than commercial appeal. A lecture theatre was converted into a 250-seater cinema; the seating, designed for students slumbering through a lecture, was notoriously uncomfortable, but this seemed a worthwhile price to pay in order to view classic art- house movies. Hence, I donned my duffel coat and, together with Susan, we queued at the QFT to see the latest sub-titled films from Federico Fellini, Ingmar Bergman or movies of the French New Wave directors, including Francois Truffaut's *Jules et Jim* and Jean Renoir's *La Grande Illusion.*

The QFT was also the venue where I fell in love with the Hollywood *film noir,* the stylised crime dramas with a low- key black and white visual style in which a private eye and a *femme fatale* of questionable virtue are the typical character types. Humphrey Bogart, after ten years cast as a villain, emerged in 1941 in John Huston's *The Maltese Falcon* as Sam Spade, a tough yet vulnerable detective. Raymond Chandler, whose mother came from Waterford where Raymond spent his summer holidays, became the most celebrated author of the hardboiled novels that were transformed into classic *film noir* movies, most notably *The Big Sleep* (1946) and *The Lady in the Lake* (1947). He also wrote the screenplays for *Double Idemnity* (1944), *The Blue Dahlia* (1946) and *Strangers on a Train* (1951). Other classic *films noirs* that we saw during this period were John Huston's, *The Maltese Falcon* (1941), *Key Largo* (1948) and Orson Welles' *A Touch of Evil* (1958). My favourite is *The Big Sleep,* featuring classic *film noir* characteristics of low-angle shots, shots through curved or frosted glass; stark light/shade contrasts and dramatic shadow patterning, a style known as chiaroscuro, adopted from Renaissance painting. Bogart and his screen and life- mate, Lauren Bacall starred in the famously convoluted plot with a brilliantly clever, wry and humorous script drawn from Chandler's book. Hollywood's most celebrated gumshoe Philip Marlowe (Humphrey Bogart) embarks on an obscure investigation involving blackmailers, drug pushers and pornographers, but what really matters is his pursuit of the wisecracking Lauren Bacall as his client's daughter, which results in some of the most urbane innuendo in cinema. Women were more than a minor love interest in *film noir* movies. Lauren Bacall was an actress who was sexy yet remote and sceptical, who would perch on a bar stool, slide one leg over another while lighting a fag, make a witty remark and then blow the smoke into the face of the hero. Neither the director, Howard Hawks, nor the cast knew whether the chauffeur killed himself or was murdered . A cable was sent to Chandler who told a friend in a letter on 21 March 1949: 'They sent me a wire...asking me, and dammit I didn't know either.' Set against foggy mean streets, this *film noir* is a masterpiece.

One film that was released in 1968 but which I did not see until years later was Sergio Leone' epic – *Once Upon a Time in the West*. This is an exceptional western: strange, mysterious and almost existential. It has a fine cast: Jason Robards as a maverick gunslinger, Henry Fonda, cast against type as the villain, Charles Bronson adding menace as the Harmonica man, and Claudia Cardinale. The opening sequence of around eight minutes is one of the greatest in cinema history: there is no dialogue, just natural sounds – dripping water, a fly buzzing, the wind moaning through a squeaky weathervane accompanying the approaching sound of a distant train as three gunmen lounge on the station platform. The musical score for the film was the apotheosis of the brilliant career of Ennio Morricone ranging from Cardinale's tender, wistful leitmotif to the evocative haunting harmonica of Charles Bronson.

* * *

During my first term on the staff of Queen's University I joined the Northern Ireland Labour Party and volunteered to canvass for them in the Stormont election of 25 November 1965. I campaigned in Belfast Willowfield constituency, an area of south-east Belfast dominated by Victorian red- brick terraced housing with a population that was working class and lower-middle class and overwhelmingly Protestant. Many street corners in the constituency boasted Evangelical and Pentecostal gospel halls. All of them had a quotation from the Bible hung on the front wall or framed behind glass. There were severe warnings about the importance of being 'saved' and the 'judgement' or consequences of not doing so that would follow – being 'damned to hell' as an 'outcast from the fold.' This was the working-class Bible belt of East Belfast. It was a unique experience for me as this brand of evangelical Protestantism did not exist in the Dun Laoghaire of my youth.

I knocked doors in Willowfield on behalf of Martin McBirney, who was a QC and a resident magistrate. McBirney was a Protestant who had read Law at Trinity College Dublin, and, unusually in Northern Ireland, was married to a Catholic. He was an engaging polymath who wrote plays and documentaries for the BBC and he introduced me to the work of one of the giants of poetry, Louis MacNeice, with whom he had been friendly. During the election campaign, I was puzzled by how infrequently we encountered any canvassing activity from the Unionist party. The reason became apparent the night before the election when the local Orange flute bands appeared and marched triumphantly around the constituency playing loyalist tunes, such as 'The Sash.' When I started to argue the case for McBirney on the doorstep that night the most common reaction was: 'Who's our man?' meaning, of course, the Unionist candidate. The Unionist, William Hinds, won 65 percent of the vote and Martin McBirney 35 per cent. The Unionist party successfully cut across regional and class boundaries and simplistic appeals to the Union flag and Orange solidarity produced a positive response. What was so striking to me was that the Unionist fold included working – class Protestants from the back streets of Belfast, middle- class office workers, businessmen and the landed gentry. Martin McBirney subsequently served as the Senior Crown Prosecutor for Belfast and on one occasion succeeded in having Ian Paisley convicted and jailed; he also worked as a lawyer for the defence on civil rights cases. At 08.20am on 16 September 1974, McBirney was shot dead while making breakfast in his kitchen in Belfast, a murder attributed to the IRA. Worse was to follow as his sister-in-law, on being told of his death, suffered a fatal heart attack. When I learned of his murder I had been in Cardiff for a year, having left Ireland in 1973. I cannot understand how such a decent, talented and humane man could be assassinated in such a brutal way.

I enjoyed playing golf with Todd Davies and Colin Latimer at Malone Golf Club on the beautiful parkland course in south Belfast. When playing there on lovely June evenings I would hear the strident and menacing sound of Lambeg drums as Orangemen in the nearby fields practised for the 12 July Orange parades. I was selected to play for one of the Malone Club teams and the captain whispered to me that I was the first person whose name began with O' who had ever represented the club. No wonder I questioned why I sometimes felt alien in a place only 100 miles from Dublin. I loved the challenge of playing golf, but as for the 'golf club set' I never felt a part of it when I was a part of it. I did not excel at the 19th hole at any of the golf clubs of which I was a member, whether in Dublin, Belfast, Portrush, Bridgend or North Berwick. The general climate of opinion in club bars was predominantly sexist: women in those days did not have the same membership rights; while politically the predominant attitude was right-wing Conservative with which

I felt decidedly uneasy, and I was always anxious to slip away as soon as possible.

The division of Ireland dates from the seventeenth century when the most fertile land was confiscated from Irish Catholics and given mainly to Scottish Presbyterian settlers. The Protestants of the north under Edward Carson pledged to defend their privileged position in the UK and were prepared to use force to prevent the establishment of a Home Rule parliament in Ireland. The boundary of Northern Ireland was defined in 1921 when the Unionists and the British government carved six northern counties out of the nine county province of Ulster based on a sectarian headcount: the defining characteristic of the new entity was that it was 63 per cent Protestant and 36 per cent Catholic, thereby guaranteeing that nationalists were permanently excluded from power. The area was then designated as Northern Ireland and was granted a parliament at Stormont; the rest of Ireland became a Free State and, in 1949, an independent Republic.

Socially Ulster Protestants were friendly and very hospitable to me, but even though I was known to have been raised as a Church of Ireland (Anglican) in Dublin, it was not wise to directly confront them across the dinner table on any issues related to identity or religion. I felt politically divided from Ulster Protestants, who were overwhelmingly unionists, and theologically separate from Ulster Catholics, who were predominantly nationalists. Despite the comfortable majority enjoyed by Protestants in Northern Ireland, the Unionist party perceived the Nationalist minority as 'the enemy within,' as 'loyal to the half-crown but not the crown,'[15] while the widespread use of slogans such as 'No Surrender,' reflected an uncompromising and defensive mindset. This led successive Unionist governments to implement a ruthless series of measures to ensure that their power would be permanent. The institutions of law and order were partisan: judges and magistrates were almost all Protestants, many of them associated with the Unionist party. Protestants outnumbered Catholics in the Royal Ulster Constabulary (RUC) by more than nine to one, while the armed auxiliary security forces, the B Specials, were exclusively Protestant and had access to handguns, rifles and submachine guns. Under the Special Powers Act, the police could make arrests and searches without a warrant, intern suspects without trial and prohibit meetings and publications. Catholics were outnumbered in the Civil Service by nine to one; and there were also no Catholics in the Stormont cabinet, in the top ranks of the RUC, the Civil Service Commission and other important public bodies.[16] Whole industries in the private sector, such as shipbuilding and heavy engineering, had workforces that were more than 90 per cent Protestant so that the unemployment rate amongst Catholics was generally more than double Protestant unemployment. Some of us also suspected that Queen's University was not administering fair employment policies in the 1960s. The British government was presented with a damning report on employment practices at the University in 1989. At the end of the 1980s when 39 per cent of the population of Northern Ireland was Catholic and 45.6 per cent Protestant, the Fair Employment Agency's report on the university, which employed 3,000 staff, showed that 79 per cent of the Northern Ireland employees were Protestants and only 21 per cent Catholics.[17]

The Orange order had deep roots in the fabric of the state: an Orange lodge was established within the RUC; Orangemen made up the bulk of the B Specials, who in some areas were based in Orange halls. The Orange Order was also represented on the ruling council of the Unionist party and Unionist Party meetings were held in Orange halls. The tone for this was set by the politicians. Some Prime Ministers made directly anti-Catholic statements in public. The Prime Minister, James Craig, told the Stormont parliament in April 1934 that: 'All I boast is that we are a Protestant parliament for a Protestant state.' The Orange Order became deeply embedded in the power structures of the state: between 1921 and 1969 only three of 54 Unionist cabinet ministers were not members of the Order. Catholics, however, were not actively persecuted by the authorities; the Catholic Church ran its own schools and hospitals and nationalist newspapers, especially the *Irish News*, were free to openly criticise the Stormont government; but the representatives of the Catholic nationalist community were deliberately excluded from power with no means of redress.[18]

I quickly became aware of the ways in which the Unionist Party maintained its dominant position. The most egregious policy was gerrymandering of electoral boundaries designed to replace Nationalist with Unionist control. For example, blatant boundary rigging occurred in Derry/Londonderry so that 7,500 Unionist voters returned 12 councillors and 10,000 Nationalist voters returned only eight, ie it required double the number of votes to return a nationalist councillor. In order to maintain Unionist hegemony, the Stormont government abolished proportional representation in 1929 and replaced it with the first-past-the-post system. Nationalists lost their majorities in 13 of 24 councils they had originally controlled. In local government elections, only ratepayers or their spouses could vote which deprived a quarter of the electorate of a vote and Catholics were overrepresented among the disenfranchised. Furthermore, housing allocation was also highly politicised: many Unionist councillors were reluctant to build homes in Catholic areas. In 1963 the Unionist chairman of Enniskillen housing committee was unequivocal: 'we are not going to build houses in the South Ward and cut a rod to beat ourselves later on. We are going to see that the right people are put in these houses, and we are not going to apologise for it.'[19] Housing policy in certain areas, such as Fermanagh or Dungannon, was discriminatory, but in many parts of Northern Ireland it was fair. Whyte argued that discrimination in housing was less widespread than in public employment.[20]

Friendships, marriages, neighbourhoods and schools remain as stubbornly religiously segregated now as they were when I first moved to Northern Ireland to work 57 years ago in 1965. This has left two communities – Protestants and Catholics – frozen in separate but parallel lives. Tom Garvin noted that people tend to talk past each other: 'an eerie symbol of this is provided by the fact that Catholic and Protestant deaf children are actually taught different sign languages.'[21] There is no common identity to unite them so that even a dialogue of the deaf is not possible. The Good Friday agreement in 1996 adopted the two communal identities as if they were fixed and immutable and constructed the power- sharing political architecture on the two separate foundations. Such a strategy has maintained the peace for 26 years, but, when combined with a lack of government commitment to both integrated schools and housing, has greatly constrained the possibility of developing normal political discourse and change in the future. On the issue of national identity in 2014, 75 per cent of Protestants self- identified as British, 25 per cent as Northern Irish and only 2 per cent as Irish; while 68 per cent of Catholics identified as Irish, 15 per cent as Northern Irish and 9 per cent as British.[22] Politics is the fundamental underlying basis of the division and conflict, while religious denomination is its form. Although Ulster Protestants passionately identified themselves as strongly British, when they are outside Ireland many become self-consciously Irish.

The huge Belfast Orange parade commemorating King William of Orange's victory over King James II at the Battle of the Boyne in 1690 takes place every July. I watched it for the only time on 12 July 1966 from a vantage point on the Lisburn Road. Union Jacks adorned every house and bunting was strung across the street. In Sandy Row arches had been erected across the street entrances displaying large portraits of the Queen and images of William of Orange and Lord Edward Carson, the founding father of the state, who was, ironically, a Dubliner educated at Trinity College. The kerbstones along the streets in loyalist areas were all painted red, white and blue. There was pageantry, colourful uniforms, bowler hats, sashes and tasselled banners that identified every lodge. Young baton twirlers hurled their batons aloft and unfailingly caught them, and there was fervent, if repetitive, music from the flute bands. There was also explicit anti-Catholicism and anti-Irish sentiment and a sense of superiority on full display, accompanied by a hint of menace from the pounding of the Lambeg drums. Despite my Church of Ireland upbringing in Dalkey and the fact that my paternal grandmother's family had links with the Orange order in Balieborough, County Cavan in the 1930s, I felt like a total stranger witnessing the swaggering triumphalism on display and the implicit message that they were inheritors of the land of Ulster as God's promise to them. What surprised me even more was that numerous Church of Ireland clergymen address the Orangemen (few women march) at the Demonstration Fields on 12 July each year.

Captain Terence O'Neill became Prime Minister of Northern Ireland in 1963. O'Neill, who had been educated at Eton and served with the Irish Guards, sounded like a member of the English gentry, but lacked empathy and a populist touch. He was not hostile to Catholics, although he patronised them in an interview with the *Belfast Telegraph* in 1969: 'If you treat Catholics with due consideration and kindness, they will live like Protestants in spite of the authoritative nature of their church.'[23] O'Neill prioritised economic development, including rationalising the railways, clearing slums, establishing a second university, creating a new city and initiating a motorway. O'Neill's reforms, however, did little to improve the lot of nationalists. Many of the multinational companies attracted to the province located in Belfast or other eastern towns with Protestant majorities, such as Antrim, Portadown and Ballymena. When a new city was built, it was located in a mainly Protestant area and named after a former Unionist Prime Minister, Craigavon. A new university was established and Catholic Derry, where Magee College already existed, was the obvious location but was passed over in favour of the much smaller Protestant Coleraine. All of these initiatives fuelled the resentment of Catholic politicians. Arguably O'Neill's major achievement was inviting the Taoiseach, Sean Lemass, to visit him in January 1965, the first time any Taoiseach had ever made the 100 mile journey to Stormont. Years of hostility and mistrust were overcome as North and South sought to embark upon a period of economic cooperation. Sadly it did not materialise.

Among our closest friends in Northern Ireland were two Quakers, Desmond and Dr. Joyce Neill. Joyce became first chair of the Northern Ireland Family Planning Association (NIFPA) in 1965. In a divided society Joyce Neill was fearless in challenging the organisations that attempted to hinder the work of NIFPA. For example, in November 1965 the BBC in Belfast informed her that it was not permitted to include an announcement about meetings in relation to family planning clinics as it came under the category of 'open advocation of controversial causes.' Neill responded, 'I find it hard to believe that the BBC considers that the subject of family planning is controversial today. The need for controlling the size of families is freely admitted by the RC Church; the only difference of opinion is on methods approved – a difference which our association has publicly respected.'[24]

Joyce Neill was not only content to develop a comprehensive network of family planning clinics in Northern Ireland but was also prepared to assist those seeking such a service in the Republic. She obtained the name of a female doctor in Dublin, Dr.W, who was 'willing to give advice on oral contraceptives' and pass it on to the British Family Planning Association 'for anyone who takes up residence in the Irish Free State.... Things might be made unpleasant for her in Dublin if public attention was drawn to her activities.....Our clinics in Northern Ireland are, of course, willing to help anyone from the Free State who come to us, but the journey is often long and expensive.'[25] The birth control issue in Northern Ireland was a delicate one: striving to avoid offending the Catholic population while also dealing with Evangelical Protestant opinion based on puritanical attitudes towards anything to do with sex. The Catholic church, both North and South, succeeded in creating a power-base within homes in a country where the family unit was paramount. It also sought to link matters of contraception and abortion. Eamonn McCann noted that: 'If there is one thing that Catholic and Protestant reactionaries can unite on, it's that young people mustn't be allowed to enjoy sex.'[26] Consequently, in the late sixties some individual local health committees refused to support the establishment of family planning clinics in the North. In April 1968 Joyce Neill wrote to the *Belfast Telegraph* complaining that the financial assistance to establish a clinic at Belmont in Derry had been refused and she pointed out that 'no-one visiting a family planning clinic is persuaded to use methods conflicting with her conscience.'

Finally, 'Councillor Brown... need have no fears that family planning will never be a serious rival to dancing at the crossroads.'[27] Joyce Neill continued throughout the worst of The Troubles to provide this vital service in Northern Ireland and recalls many moving incidents, including an exhausted mother fearful of further pregnancies saying: 'Isn't it a terrible thing, doctor, to be only content when the blood is flowing from you?'[28]

Cross-border cooperation is now a fashionable topic but in the sixties – because it was illegal to import and supply contraceptives to the Irish Republic – any cooperation was mostly *sub rosa*. When a clinic opened in Dublin, Joyce Neill, a redoubtable Quaker, began to smuggle contraceptives across the border from Northern Ireland. Initially they were transported via the Belfast to Dublin train, which became known as the 'contraceptive express.' Vigilant customs inspectors at the border forced Joyce to start using cars which were less frequently searched than the train. On one occasion she transferred the contraceptives into her daughter's hockey bag in order to avoid arousing the suspicion of the customs' officers. For a time Dublin patients sent prescriptions to the International Planned Parenthood Federation (IPPF) in London and they posted the contraceptives back to the Republic. However, the Customs began to identify the packets and to ban them. Joyce Neill solved the problem by organising for the IPPF to post the contraceptives in bulk to her in Northern Ireland. She then split up the individual packages and drove over the border – usually the 183 mile return journey to Letterkenny in County Donegal – purchased the necessary stamps and posted them individually, thereby avoiding the Irish customs.[29] Intrauterine devices were also illegal in the Republic so any Southern patient who opted for it was vetted and advised in Dublin and then travelled to Joyce Neill's clinic in Belfast for insertion. These patients could be fairly confident that they would not arouse the suspicion of customs officers on the return rail journey!

The most anticipated musical event of 1967 was the release of the Beatles latest LP, *Sergeant Pepper's Lonely Hearts Club Band*. *The Times* theatre critic Kenneth Tynan hailed *Sergeant Pepper* as 'a decisive moment in in the history of Western civilisation,' while *The Times Literary Supplement* described the lyrics as the 'barometer of our times.' However, as Sandbrook opined 'less intellectually ambitious reviewers ...registered not excitement and ecstasy but simple bafflement.'[30] *Sergeant Pepper* was a most original pop album with its continuous stream of sound, sitars, studio banter, farmyard noises, circus vaudeville, gentle ballads and raw rock music. It was a collage of different musical genres from Edwardian brass bands to American blues; the strongest motif was that of the late Victorian or Edwardian music hall.[31] This album proved that the composing partnership of Lennon and McCartney was richly talented combining brilliant musical originality and – unlike other pop groups – trying new sounds and instruments complemented by clever and witty lyrics. After recording *Sergeant Pepper,* the Beatles lost interest in further studio sessions and ultimately it was Lennon's devotion to Yoko Ono that caused the breakup of the group.

* * *

During the early months of 1967, I was frantically completing my doctoral thesis, while also preparing to marry Susan who was teaching in a secondary school in Newtonabbey. By modern standards we were young to be marrying as Susan was just 23 and I was 26. After my doctorate was conferred at Trinity College Dublin on 11th July, 1967, the marriage ceremony conducted by Susan's father on 29 July 1967 at Manchester Road Methodist church in Burnley was a lovely event, despite the overcast drizzly day. My parents flew over from Dublin for the wedding and were intrigued to visit a post-industrial landscape in Lancashire where cotton had once been king. Our honeymoon was spent in Yugoslavia where Tito was still all-powerful. Susan's English phrase book contained what to me as an Irishman was a very amusing statement in Serbo Croat: 'I am an English woman, please let me pass.' One day we hired a pedalo and headed out across the bay of Kotor. When we were almost a mile offshore, a swimmer executing a beautiful crawl style suddenly called out – 'there's a Dublin man in the boat' to which I responded – 'there's a Cork man in the water.' After returning to shore, we quickly struck up a friendship with Paddy and Betty Hayes, who were great fun and teased us mercilessly about being on honeymoon. Paddy was the chief executive of the Ford motor company in Cork.

On return from honeymoon, we moved into a university – owned flat on Mount Charles, a leafy tree-lined street close to the main campus. The flat was part of a Victorian terraced house and the layout was inconvenient as the building had not been converted so that there was incomplete separation of living quarters. Our flat occupied space on three floors: on the second floor was the kitchen and a dark bathroom with a lavatory as old as the building itself, with a chain and a wooden seat; a bedroom and sitting room occupied the third floor, with another two bedrooms on the fourth. The sitting room boasted two sash windows which overlooked a communal garden and the gated entrance to the quiet street. In order to access the flat, we had to pass by the kitchen and bathroom area of the flat below, thereby compromising the privacy of the occupants. It only worked if everyone was quiet and respected the privacy of other flat- dwellers. There was no central heating; indeed the only heating was a gas fire in the large sitting room so that in winter the remainder of the flat was icy cold. Moreover, a cool box outside the landing window was the sole means of preserving fresh food as neither a fridge, washing machine or dishwasher were provided; and yet somehow Susan managed to provide a stream of varied and delightful menus so that I gained a stone in weight within a year! Clothes were taken to a laundrette on Botanic Avenue. Despite the somewhat spartan conditions, there were compensations: the rent was £17 per month and the location of Mount Charles was only three minutes walk from the university and close to the Botanic Avenue shops. Susan and I derived much enjoyment hunting for antique furniture at auctions and antique shops in Belfast and Bangor.

We would always have two bottles of sherry -one dry and one sweet-available for visitors. Dry sherry was a favoured drink in university circles in the sixties. We did not have beer available in the flat, and I generally did not go to pubs, except for a quick drink in the golf club after playing a round. Moreover, we did not have a supply of wine in the flat as we did not drink it with supper on a regular basis – even at weekends – until the 1970s. There was a thriving informal social life based around staff and research students at the Geography Department and, indeed, it was more welcoming and friendly than any of the other six departments where I have worked during my career. If the Queen's department had been located in Dublin, Edinburgh, Glasgow, Cardiff or Bristol, I greatly doubt that I would have ever moved elsewhere. If we were having some of my university colleagues and their partners for supper, I would pop down to Botanic Avenue and buy two bottles of wine, usually Liebfraumilch, a semi-sweet, low quality German white, or Chianti in a straw covered bottle, the medium sweet Portuguese Mateus Rose – thought to be the height of sophistication and the preferred wine of the Queen – or a French red, Hirondelle, meaning 'swallow', a pun I only got when drinking the second bottle! The type of wine we drank evolved over the decades, with dry white now being the most popular, apart from when I really wish to splash out £25 to purchase Chablis or a wonderful bottle of Chateauneuf-du-Pape, especially since visiting their vineyard in the Rhone valley north of Avignon.

* * *

Meanwhile, Trinity College Dublin was again under reactionary pressure in 1967 when Donagh O'Malley, Minister of Education, announced that he intended to merge Trinity with UCD to form one university in Dublin. The Report of the Commission on Higher Education (1967) contained a written submission from Dr Michael Tierney, President of UCD. Tierney stated that he viewed Trinity as a rival institution claiming parity with UCD and presenting itself as a university suitable for Catholics. Archbishop McQuaid controlled five academic chairs – all funded by the taxpayer – at UCD: Moral and Social Sciences, Ethics and Politics, Logic and Psychology, Education and Sociology. All of these chairs were occupied by Catholic priests, essentially nominated by McQuaid, while there was a particular vigilance about the possible infiltration 'of all kinds of terrible people and in particular by the ideas of those two brilliant Jews, Karl Marx and Sigmund Freud.'[32] Furthermore, even in the 1960s, the distinguished academic, John Whyte, author of the seminal *Church and State in Modern Ireland*, was instructed not to write the book when on the staff at UCD as it would be an interference in the affairs of the Dublin diocese, an incident which shows that 'bullying and denial of academic freedom were an integral part of clerical politics at Ireland's largest university while McQuaid was still Archbishop.'[33] Dr Tierney made some remarkable assertions about Trinity considering it to be a 'foreign body' whose whole tradition 'is something we can never assimilate into national life;' the 'ideal solution,' would be to 'close down Trinity College' and to found a new University of Dublin at Belfield, the site of UCD; and the only future he could envisage for Trinity was as an 'enclave for Protestants.'[34] The sheer arrogance and ignorance of Tierney in recommending that Trinity should be closed down because it was allegedly a 'foreign body' that could not be assimilated into the national life revealed an extraordinarily narrow vision of the nature of the Irish state and society. Tierney was at one time identified with the corporatist and syndicalist ideas that were associated with Mussolini's regime in Italy, and the teachings of papal encylicals that criticised state centralisation.[35] O'Malley's merger plan was controversial and when he tragically died suddenly in 1968, aged only 47, the project died with him.

In television, as the 1960s progressed, New Wave realism became less fashionable but other classic TV programmes emerged. We enjoyed the *Forsyte Saga* in 1967 and Lord Clarke's acclaimed series *Civilisation* (1969). *Dad's Army*, a comedy about the wartime Home Guard, was launched in 1968 and ran until 1977. Writers Jimmy Perry and David Croft brilliantly conceived a class-reversed relationship between Captain Mainwaring, the local bank manager, and Sergeant Wilson, his deputy at the bank. Mainwaring (played by Arthur Lowe) is a patriotic self-made man who appoints himself head of the local Home Guard and whose tedious pomposity camouflages his social insecurity. Wilson, beautifully realised by John Le Mesurier, is a diffident upper-middle- class public-school educated clerk with a slightly dubious love life who quietly questions Mainwaring's judgements. The rest of the platoon is populated with rich characters, many armed with their own catchphrases, such as Corporal Jones 'They don't like it up 'em' and 'Don't panic,' while panicking himself. An episode of *Dad's Army* is still shown every Saturday night on BBC2, over fifty years after the comedy was first broadcast in 1968. Its popularity also reflects a love for nostalgia for an age of corner shops, village fetes, church bells tolling, good neighbourliness and a class-ridden hierarchical society.

By the late 1960s, the Rev.Ian Paisley had emerged as O'Neill's rival for popularity amongst unionists. Paisley founded his own Free Presbyterian church in 1951. As Tim Pat Coogan wrote, with 'his husky oratory, raw sex appeal and powerful personality and physique' he was a 'dominant figure bestriding the political landscape of Northern Ireland with the Bible in one hand and both eyes on the ballot box.'[36] Paisley became increasingly prominent as 'the Big Man,' the uncompromising charismatic spokesman for militant Unionism and anti-Catholicism. His career encompassed the pulpit, politics, protest marches, rallies, and two periods behind bars. In 1966 he launched the *Protestant Telegraph*, which ran sensationalist stories like 'Love Affairs of the Vatican,' and 'Priestly Murders Exposed.'[37] Having attended a 'service' of his at the Ulster Hall one Sunday night, I quickly recognised that he was a superb orator who could mesmerise an audience with fiery rhetoric and strong imagery; above all, he had an uncanny ability to rouse and exploit the anxieties of the urban working- class and rural Protestant communities, which was a crucial factor in his rise to prominence and gave him all-important political momentum. He formed the Democratic Unionist Party in 1971 and it eventually eclipsed the Unionist party in popularity.

New articulate politicians of a nationalist hue, notably Gerry Fitt, MP for West Belfast from 1966, John Hume and Austin Currie, were determined that Catholics would no longer be treated as second class citizens. They were all linked to the formation of the Northern Ireland Civil Rights Association (NICRA) which campaigned to achieve several objectives: legislation to prohibit discrimination; fair electoral boundaries and housing allocation; the disbanding of the B Specials; one man one vote in local elections; and repeal of the Special Powers Act. We were unaware for years later that the IRA did aid in the creation of the civil rights movement and 'did so with the explicit intention of bringing down the Northern Ireland state.'[38] The movement, however, was taken over and dominated by thousands of people seeking non-violent, non-sectarian reform of the state rather than its overthrow. Meanwhile, the pace of reform by the O'Neill government was slow and insufficiently radical because he was afraid of losing the streets to Paisley. Both Harold Wilson and his Home Secretary, Roy Jenkins, failed to act 'because they were fatally complacent.'[39] Remarkably, Jenkins displayed little interest in Northern Ireland affairs and never bothered to visit the province. Indeed, at the Labour Party conference in 1968 Northern Ireland was not even on the agenda.[40]

* * *

In March 1968, I purchased another cult car – a Morris Minor convertible – from Prentice's garage in Belfast. Although originally dismissed as a 'poached egg' by Lord Sheffield – founder-owner of Morris Motors – it was another brilliant design by Alec Issigonis. There was no chassis but an all-in-one body shell with independent front suspension and rack and pinion steering that made the car easy to drive. There was a saying that if you drove over a penny in a Morris Minor you knew whether you'd gone over 'heads or tails' side up.[41] The first Saturday afternoon Susan and I took the new car for a spin with the hood down and the heater on and, as we sailed into Newtownards, it started to snow on us. Unsurprisingly, I was unable to get the hood back up and so we were cold, wet and plastered with snow on arrival back in Belfast.

The summer of 1968 was blessed with glorious weather and we spent three weeks with Susan's sister Helen and her family in a house overlooking a beautiful beach on the Fanad peninsula in County Donegal. As one crossed the border into Donegal beyond Derry, I was always anticipating the first whiff of turf smoke on the wind, its unique pungent smell instantly carrying me back to the holidays of my youth. The following summer in 1969 – after attending my younger sister Judy's wedding in Connemara – we drove to Goleen on the Mizen Head peninsula in West Cork where we rented a cottage from our university friends, Dick and Sue Hill. Mizen Head extends its long arm out into the open Atlantic north west of the Fasnet Rock lighthouse; it was a beautiful landscape tinged with sadness and poverty. There were numerous abandoned cottages surrounded by rusting farm machinery and small fields choked with weeds from where the residents had emigrated to Boston or Birmingham. The shop windows in the small nondescript towns were dusty and offered little of interest to the visitor, while the few dingy hotels had paint peeling off the walls. The Celtic Tiger was, as yet, dormant. While walking on the jetty at Crookhaven, I saw what appeared to be a drunken sailor wobbling towards me. When I asked if he needed some assistance, he replied that he had just arrived having sailed single-handed 3,000 miles across the Atlantic. Later that same evening – 16 July – we crammed into Sonny Sullivan's pub to watch the moon landings.

* * *

The distinguished poet Derek Mahon wrote of a time before The Troubles in Northern Ireland that 'If a coathanger knocked in a wardrobe/ That was a great event.' This was about to change dramatically. NICRA scheduled a civil rights march in Derry on 5th October 1968. William Craig, hardline Minister for Home Affairs at Stormont, banned the march, but some 4,000 activists turned up. Baton-wielding RUC officers attacked the marchers in Duke Street and men, women and children were beaten to the ground, including the politicians Gerry Fitt and Austin Currie. Images of Gerry Fitt's bloody head and shirt were flashed around the world on TV. A subsequent report concluded that he had been struck 'wholly without justification or excuse,' and that the RUC had 'used their batons indiscriminately' and with 'needless violence.' The unprovoked assault by the RUC had the effect both of enraging the Catholic community and conferring credibility on the civil rights movement.[42] Moreover, the Westminster convention of not debating Northern Ireland affairs finally ended. Four days later on 9 October some 2,000 students and some academic staff from Queen's University Belfast (including myself and my colleague Mike Poole) marched to the centre of Belfast in protest at police brutality in Derry. Shortly after the start, the RUC re-routed the march away from Shaftesbury Square where Paisley was holding a counter- demonstration. Our march was halted by an RUC cordon in Linenhall Street and a three- hour sit-down protest followed during which time we were abused and spat on by loyalists. Following this protest, the students returned to the campus and a radical faction of the civil rights movement – the People's Democracy – was formed.

Terence O'Neill announced some reforms on 22 November 1968, including appointment of an ombudsman; limited voting reforms; a new system of housing allocation; and a future review of the Special Powers Act. To Catholics it was too little too late, especially as the changes did not include one-man-one vote, while amongst Unionists it went down as appeasement to disloyal Catholics. It was against this background of protest and counter-protest that Susan and I, together with her brother, John, joined a civil rights march that took place in Armagh on Saturday 30 November 1968. We drove to Armagh and there was a carnival atmosphere as we set off for the centre of the town among several thousand marchers singing 'We shall Overcome.' Suddenly, the march came to an abrupt halt before a line of RUC men blocking the street. Beyond them another row of police was visible standing in front of a large crowd of union-jack waving loyalist counter-demonstrators led by Ian Paisley and Ronald Bunting, who had been allowed to commandeer the centre of the town. A lawful civil rights march had been stopped from completing its agreed route and a loyalist mob had been allowed to take over the centre of Armagh. Many of the loyalists were armed with more than 200 weapons, including sharpened pipes, bill-hooks, scythes, pickaxe handles, cudgels and at least two guns. The atmosphere became more hostile and loyalists attacked the BBC and ITN film crews. As so often on these occasions, the RUC stood facing the civil rights demonstrators – who were unarmed – with their backs to the loyalists, who were armed. John Hume advocated restraint and so we turned back. Later in the afternoon some locals broke windows in a bus full of loyalists; and the RUC started beating everyone in sight with their batons in an indiscriminate attack.[43] A familiar narrative was being played out: loyalist triumphalism and aggressive policing of civil rights demonstrators leading to increasing frustration.

O'Neill resigned in April 1969 and was replaced by his decent but uninspiring cousin, James Chichester- Clarke, yet another Unionist leader from the landed gentry. On 12th August 1969, 15,000 Orangemen marched in Derry to commemorate The Apprentice Boys relief of the city in August 1689. By early afternoon, young Catholics were hurling stones and nails at the RUC men guarding the barricades set up to keep the two sides apart and these skirmishes quickly escalated into what became known as The Battle of the Bogside.[44] Fierce rioting raged for several days and brought the province close to full-scale civil war. One British journalist reported that what shocked him most was the RUCs ' threats, the religious tauntings – and all coming from a peace-keeping force.'[45] When police at one stage broke through the barricades, a Protestant mob ran in after the RUC and attacked Catholic houses. Both in Derry and Belfast there were many reports of RUC and B Specials acting in concert with loyalist rioters during battles with Catholics.[46]

The situation in Belfast deteriorated rapidly and for the first time serious trouble broke out within earshot of our flat. On the night of 14 August 1969, hundreds of loyalist rioters rampaged into Catholic areas throwing incendiary devices into each home. In Conway Street they torched 50 Catholic houses; in Bombay Street they burned more than half the properties; and in Percy Street a mob of 200 Protestants hurled petrol bombs into the Catholic school and neighbouring houses.[47] Meanwhile the RUC, who had failed to protect the burnt-out Catholic communities, was engaged in a gun battle with IRA men near Divis Flats where the RUC opened fire with machine guns and killed a nine year old Catholic boy who was lying in his bed.[48] A total of eight people were killed, four by the RUC and one by the B Specials. From our flat we could clearly see houses and shops in flames and hear the noise of gunfire, petrol bombs, rioting and sirens blazing; it was deeply disturbing.

These catastrophic events led to decisive action by James Callaghan, the Home Secretary, who ordered British troops on to the streets of west Belfast on 15 August 1969. The troops were welcomed by Catholic residents who plied them with tea, sandwiches and cake. On 27 August Callaghan visited Belfast and Derry where he was warmly received by the Catholic communities. He handled a very difficult situation with great skill, courage and understanding; he refused to be swayed by bigotry from either side. Crucially, in October, he announced that the RUC must be reorganised and disarmed; and the paramilitary B Specials abolished and replaced by the Ulster Defence Regiment under British Army control. The damage caused by the violence was profound. Almost 200 homes – mostly Catholic – had been destroyed and some 1,800 families, mainly Catholics, had been forced to flee from their homes. The following day I walked down Bombay Street and Conway Street with my colleague Mike Poole to witness a scene reminiscent of the Blitz: smoke rising from uninhabitable burnt-out houses; bullet-marked flats; armoured cars and helicopters overhead; and soldiers moving cautiously through litter-strewn streets. The rioting eventually petered out by Sunday 17 August. More ominously, the firebombing led to the formation of the Provisional IRA later in 1969, splitting the Republican movement and creating the Official and Provisional wings of the IRA, the former being Marxist and the latter being traditionalist Catholic republicans. This projected Gerry Adams and Martin McGuinness into the ascendancy. The subsequent Scarman Report into the disturbances found that the RUC officers were 'seriously at fault on at least six occasions during the rioting.' RUC officers were on Conway Street when its houses were set alight but 'failed to take effective action.' The rioting exacerbated the bitterness between the two communities and destroyed the relationship between the Catholic citizens and the RUC.

As the months passed, the Troubles settled into a deadly pattern that became so familiar on TV screens across the world night after night: a city of dirt, poverty and religious bitterness; relentless rows of shabby red-brick terraces, some of them bombed and bricked up; barbed wire and walls of corrugated iron protecting institutions; the British army in armoured cars and personnel carriers driving around the dark and seedy back streets; soldiers and police in riot gear carrying riot shields, batons and CS gas; many school-age children hurling stones, bricks and petrol bombs at the security forces; homes, pubs and shops being firebombed; police raiding, searching and damaging properties; walls of corrugated iron protecting vital installations; and always lurking in the background the menacing, hidden presence of paramilitaries from both loyalist and republican organisations. To wander into the 'wrong' street, depending on your surname or having an accent like mine, could literally mean death.

Sandbrook and other historians suggest that the sixties are best understood not as a dramatic turning point but as 'stage in a long evolution stretching back into the forgotten past.'[49] He argues that the continuity of national history was much stronger than the transient whims of fashion: 'for all the Minis and mini-skirts, the sex, drugs and rock and roll, Britain in 1970 was still fundamentally the same country it had been twenty, thirty or a hundred years before.'[50] He draws upon Orwell to suggest that 'national character is continuous, it stretches into the future and the past, there is something in it that persists as a living creature.'[51] Sandbrook's conclusion may be true when considering England (and possibly Scotland and Wales) but it most certainly does not apply to the events and changes that I witnessed occurring in Northern Ireland during the sixties.

CHAPTER 7

The Centre cannot Hold

The events of the early 1970s – high inflation, strikes, the IRA bombings, loyalist paramilitary terrorism, and the major recession induced by the 1973 OPEC oil price shock – seemed such a marked contrast with the carefree, optimistic culture of the swinging sixties. The 1970s was a period marked by unusual fashions: jeans and sweaters, flares and high heels, parka anoraks, and flowing maxi-dresses, long-haired footballers, men in donkey jackets, sheepskin coats and corduroy jackets, long sideburns and wispy beards and women in dungarees. It also witnessed the birth of the women's liberation movement, the growth of package holidays, the popularity of sitcoms, the explosion of pornography, the virus of football hooliganism and rapidly deteriorating industrial relations as Britain's industries struggled to compete. It was in the early 1970s, not the 1960s, that young single women began to take the Pill, the feminist movement developed, gay liberation first made headlines and ideas of progressive education percolated into classrooms.[1]

Our first beautiful daughter, Catherine, was born in the City Hospital, Belfast on 23 February 1970. In keeping with the prevailing attitudes at the time in Belfast, I was not permitted to be present at the birth. This was a wonderfully exciting event and Susan, who had stopped teaching a month earlier, immediately demonstrated that she was an excellent and devoted mother. I resigned my position at Queen's University in June 1970 and moved to a research post at CIE – the Irish national transport company – responsible for bus and rail travel in Ireland. We purchased our first house in Gosworth Park, Dalkey for £7,000, which given the prices in Dalkey now, seems like a purchase from medieval times. Susan was fully occupied by interrupted nights, feeding Catherine, changing nappies and settling into a new house. We were anchored. We had fun planning and developing a new garden with advice from my mother; I renewed my membership of Carrickmines golf club and enjoyed playing regularly with Charles Watson; and it was great to see Dave Thomas frequently and to become friendly with his brother Michael and his wife Heather who lived two doors away. My mother would occasionally take Catherine for a walk in her pram and would always be accompanied by her secateurs with which she would snip off cuttings and pop them under the blankets. It was lovely being back in Dalkey, which is not only a charming place but a state of mind, respectable, tidy, with its feet in the Irish sea. It did not become really fashionable until the 1990s when various celebrities moved to live there, including musicians, Bono, The Edge, Van Morrison, Enya and Chris de Burgh, the film star Pierce Brosnan, film director and novelist, Neil Jordan, Maeve Binchy, and grand prix drivers Damon Hill and Eddie Irvine.

A new R and D department had been established in CIE and two of us – myself and John Markham (a statistician) – were given responsibility for designing and conducting a major research project on modal choice behaviour for the journey to work in Dublin. Substantial resources were made available. I enhanced my knowledge of statistical methods working in partnership with John Markham; we were in complete harmony concerning both our approach to the research and attitudes to analytical rigour; and, moreover, we became lifelong friends. After a year, however, it was clear that the scope for further research of this type was limited. A major problem was lack of leadership: none of the managers of the R and D department had a proven research track record. Furthermore, I missed the academic freedom of the university environment. Although I loved Dublin and Dalkey, I realised that contentment in work was more important to me than residential location. I managed to obtain a lecturing post at the New University of Ulster at Coleraine. Susan and our 18-month-old daughter, Catherine, moved there in June 1971, while I remained working in Dublin until September. I drove up from Dublin to spend the weekends with them.

* * *

Meanwhile, the British army imposed a curfew of the Falls Road area in July 1970 and considerable damage was done to hundreds of houses as the Black Watch soldiers ransacked rooms, kicked in locked doors and ripped up floorboards.[2] The Provisional IRA then escalated the conflict by exploding bombs, murdering soldiers and intimidating local residents. The tougher military line from the British army coincided with Labour losing a general election in June 1970 with Heath and Maudling replacing Wilson and Callaghan. Maudling was less forceful, lazier and less engaged than Callaghan and knew little of the province's problems. Moreover, by the early 1970s Maudling's 'mind was coarsened by drink (and) his attention distracted by corrupt business interests.'[3] He also committed a political gaff when he spoke of 'an acceptable level of violence;' and he is reported to have told a stewardess on a flight back to London after some difficult meetings in Belfast 'What a bloody awful country. For God's sake bring me a large Scotch.'

Unionist Prime Minister James Chichester-Clarke introduced more reforms, including one man one vote and changes in police and housing, but the Unionist grass roots were hostile demanding ever tougher security measures. Meanwhile, in the Republic, following an illegal attempt to import arms for the north, two cabinet ministers – Neil Blaney and Charles Haughey – were charged with conspiring to import arms and ammunition into Ireland. The case against Blaney was dropped and Haughey was acquitted by a Dublin jury with 'few believing the whole truth emerged.'[4] The Provisionals escalated the conflict in Northern Ireland in March 1971 by luring three young Scottish soldiers to a lonely road on the outskirts of Belfast where they were shot in the back of the head by an IRA unit. Chichester-Clark flew to London to demand tougher security measures, but when Edward Heath offered only extra troops, Chichester- Clark resigned. He was succeeded by Brian Faulkner, an ambitious businessman and heir to a shirt-making company, but the security situation deteriorated even further.[5] Having built his reputation with the use of internment in the 1950s, Faulkner saw it as a solution which would halt the violence.[6] Internment was a drastic measure for any UK government to contemplate as it meant abandoning the rule of law and legal procedures. The UK government conceded to Faulkner on 5 August, 1971, but Heath insisted that the process 'should be seen to be impartial in its application and 'it would presumably be desirable that those interned should include a certain number of Protestants.'[7] This was advice that Faulkner totally ignored. Acting on intelligence supplied by the RUC, British troops arrested a total of 342 men – all Catholics – in a series of dawn raids on 9 August 1971. Some of those arrested were not IRA men as the RUC's files were out of date; and many others had not been active in the IRA for years. Consequently, a hundred people were released after just two days. Internment without trial, accompanied by interrogation without the benefit of civil rights, left the minority Catholic community even more alienated from the state.

As news of the mass arrests spread across Northern Ireland, anger quickly turned to violence: in a mere two days seventeen people were shot dead (equivalent to 612 on a UK population basis), ten of them Catholic rioters shot by the British army, while mobs forced people out of their homes. Nationalist groups attacked Protestants in the Ardoyne, many of whom fled their homes having set fire to them to prevent Catholic families taking them over.[8] Reginald Maudling, who had spent the day relaxing by his swimming pool in Hertfordshire, repeated Stormont's spin that internment had been a great success, overlooking the fact that it completely destroyed the hearts and minds campaign the army had been conducting for two years by alienating the Catholic population without adding to the effectiveness of security measures.[9] In 1971, the Ulster Defence Association (UDA) was founded; it barricaded off its own 'no-go' areas and by 1972 it was murdering twice as many civilians as the IRA.[10] My weekly commute from Coleraine to Dublin between June and September 1971 involved driving through Tyrone and south Armagh, the latter being home to the Provisional IRA South Armagh Brigade. The area became known as 'Bandit country', a somewhat unfair vilification by the media of the local community, although British rule was tenuous there during the Troubles. Driving through this area after internment was not a relaxing experience and I planned my journeys to avoid the area after nightfall.

Many internees suffered violent beatings which the British government denied, arguing that this was merely IRA propaganda, but it was true. The fact that two intelligent politicians – Lord Carrington and Maudling – had approved the proposed methods of interrogation is a sign that British politicians viewed the conflict through a colonial prism.[11] Five years later the European Commission of Human Rights found Britain guilty 'not only of inhuman and degrading treatment but also of torture.' Also, Faulkner was criticised for the fact that not one loyalist had been detained, confirming that it was as much a political device as a security measure.[12] Internment underlined that the most significant thing about British attitudes to Northern Ireland was the sheer indifference of the British mainland population. Even as the troubles worsened in 1972 – the peak year for deaths – Northern Ireland receded as a political issue.[13] After internment, Northern Ireland experienced the bloodiest period in its history: civilians, paramilitaries and soldiers were being killed almost every day by the autumn of 1971. The situation reached a new low on 4 December 1971 when the Ulster Volunteer Force (UVF) planted a 50 pound bomb in McGurk's bar in Belfast and fifteen people were killed. The Stormont government and the British army flatly denied that loyalists were responsible, claiming that forensic and intelligence evidence showed that the IRA were to blame; but UVF culpability was confirmed years afterwards when a member of the organisation confessed and was jailed for life.[14]

The most controversial single incident of the Troubles occurred in Derry on 31 January 1972 when a march of civil rights activists took place to protest against the internment of Catholics. At the barricade on William Street a group of teenagers started throwing stones at the British army. Around 4.00pm the Paras in C and Support Companies were ordered to move into the Bogside. The Paras claim they were under heavy fire from the Rossville Flats and that over 200 shots had been fired at them; yet no other witnesses saw gunfire, and no guns, bullets or bombs were ever recovered from the scene.[15] The Paras fired more than 100 rounds into the melee of fleeing marchers, killing thirteen unarmed civilians (another died later), seven of them teenagers. Most were shot from behind. Simon Hoggart wrote that they were the troops 'most hated by the Catholics' and an unnamed officer said they were 'frankly disliked' by other British officers.[16] To make matters worse, there was an attempt by the British authorities to create an alternative explanation. Lord Widgery's inquiry reported in 1972 whitewashed the Parachute regiment by asserting that while some the shooting had 'bordered on the reckless,' their actions had been essentially justified.

The incident stimulated yet more violence and law and order collapsed. In February 1972, the two wings of the IRA killed seventeen people, including ten innocent civilians. There were reports of bombings and shootings every day and the *Sunday Times* concluded that 'carnage and mutilation (had become) the accompaniment of daily life.'[17] For the first time in Northern Ireland I became conscious that my strongly Catholic names and Dublin accent were not the ideal combination of characteristics for a relaxed life in the Protestant stronghold of Coleraine. Following this sustained upsurge in violence, Ted Heath prorogued Stormont and imposed Direct Rule on 28 March 1972. Willie Whitelaw was installed as Secretary of State for Northern Ireland. He was the epitome of one- nation conservatism: a Scottish landed gentleman and a popular consensus politician. At his first press conference Whitelaw, when pressed about Bloody Sunday, replied: 'I do not intend to prejudge the past,' which *The Times* journalist Robert Fisk thought was 'one of the most glorious sentences ever uttered by a politician in Ulster.'[18] Whitelaw met the leaders of the Provisional IRA in secret in July 1972, but no progress was made.

Republicans killed Protestants while loyalists murdered Catholics: a total of 42 people lost their lives in a nine day period in July 1972 – killed by the IRA, UDA and British army. A new low had been reached: many paramilitaries forsook military targets and sought to terrorise by murdering ordinary men, women and children in the cause of a united Ireland or a Protestant state. In one hour on a sunny Friday afternoon, 21st July 1972, the Provisional IRA exploded 22 bombs in the centre of Belfast in the space of 65 minutes after a series of hoax warnings. A total of 9 people were killed and 130 seriously injured (some terribly mutilated), including 77 women and children, amidst scenes of such carnage, with some people blown to pieces, that the number of dead was unclear for some time.[19] The killing continued night and day and by the end of 1972 – the bloodiest year of the Troubles – there had been 2,000 bomb explosions, more than 10,000 shooting incidents (an average of 30 per day), 5,000 people badly injured and 479 people killed. These statistics are equivalent to 71,000 bombings, 345,000 shootings, 177,500 people injured and 17,400 deaths in one year in the UK.

Both republicanism and nationalism (as expressed in the Republic) subscribed to the notion that partition was an unnatural British imposition on a nation which history intended to be one; and, if Britain withdrew, unionists would quickly see sense and agree a settlement with their fellow countrymen.[20] Conor Cruise O'Brien, historian, diplomat and politician dismissed this nationalist fantasy. Cruise O'Brien, as Seamus Heaney remarked, contributed 'some kind of clarity in Southerners' thinking about the Protestant community in the North. And it's not enough for people to simply say 'Ah they're all Irishmen' when some Northerners actually spit at the word Irishmen.[21] According to historian John A Murphy, Dr Cruise O'Brien 'with characteristic pungency and courage, masterfully exposed the wooliness of Southern attitudes towards Northern Ireland and in particular the ambivalence of Southern thinking – or more accurately, feeling – about the Provisional IRA.'[22] Willie Whitelaw published a Green Paper, *The Future of Northern Ireland,* in 1972 in which he argued that Northern Ireland should have a devolved government with a guaranteed role for the minority; and for the first time, Britain recognised that any settlement must acknowledge Northern Ireland's position within Ireland as a whole and be 'acceptable and accepted by the Republic of Ireland.'[23] Later Whitelaw managed to broker a power-sharing executive, giving the Unionists six seats, the SDLP four, and the non-sectarian Alliance one seat. Whitelaw's proposals were problematic for many Unionists.

The department at the New University of Ulster was under the leadership of Prof. Frank Oldfield, an expert in quaternary research, environmental change and radioisotope dating. Our research interests were radically different, yet I enjoyed working with him as he was a man of decency and integrity who believed in academic freedom and did not interfere in any way with one's own research agenda. Founded in 1968, the New University of Ulster when I arrived in 1971 was establishing itself and Oldfield was trying to develop a School in which he inherited a core of staff previously employed at Magee College in Derry. Staff were friendly at NUU but inevitably I made (unfavourable) comparisons with my recent experience at Queen's University Belfast. There was a lack of top class research scholars on the staff at NUU and I realised that it was not a sufficiently stimulating intellectual environment and that ultimately I would seek to move. The situation was exacerbated by the deteriorating security situation which made it more difficult to recruit quality academic staff from Britain and elsewhere and to retain them, and by our desire not to educate children in a sectarian educational system.

On the night of 27th May 1972 a heavily pregnant Susan woke me at 3.00am to drive her to the Mary Rankin nursing home in Coleraine in our Morris Minor soft top. I completed the 5 minute journey, dropped her off – fathers were still banned from attending a birth – and returned only to receive a phone call from Dr Holly as I entered the house to inform me that Susan had given birth already and that our second daughter, Margaret, had arrived. In September 1972, we moved to a house in Portstewart overlooking the golf course and the ocean from the windows of which in winter we could see the snow-covered Paps of Jura rising out of the sea like ice-cream cones some sixty miles distant to the north-east, while to the north–west the Inishowen peninsula in County Donegal thrust north into the Atlantic. The coastline between Portstewart and Portrush was rocky and bleak with few trees as the wind blew ceaselessly. One day as I opened the driver's door on our Morris 1100 car, the wind snatched the door and bent into a perfect L shape, reminding me of Derek Mahon's poem – *North Wind: Portrush*:

I shall never forget the wind
On this benighted coast.
It works itself into the mind
Like the high keen of a lost
Lear-spirit in agony
Condemned for eternity.

We became devotees of the thoughts and suggestions that Dr Benjamin Spock outlined in his book *Baby and Child* . His key idea was that children of 1970s parents would be more relaxed and comfortable in company with more freedom of expression than I had as a child. We still wanted, however, for the children to learn to behave in ways that did not disrupt family life. Therefore, we insisted on mealtimes and good table manners, learning to wait before speaking, listening when others were talking, and remaining seated at the table until the meal was finished.

I have happy memories of this period in Northern Ireland. I enjoyed playing golf on the magnificent Royal Portrush links with, amongst others, Billy McAfee. On one occasion I was playing with Bill and his father-in -law, who owned a shop in Portrush. Suddenly, away to our left down the fairway Bill's father- in- law spotted two tour busses heading for the centre of town whereupon he immediately picked up his ball and scurried away at speed with the parting comment – 'there's £200 for me on those busses.' Susan and I also enjoyed bracing walks on the windswept beach at Portstewart; weekends spent in Portsalon on Lough Swilly in Donegal; day trips to Ballycastle along the basalt coastline of north Antrim; strolls along the Bann pushing Margaret's pram; developing life-long friendships with Joyce and Desmond Neill, Peter and Susan Leyshon and Judy Hegan; golden memories of watching a flickering black and white TV in the Leyshon's house as the British and Irish Lions defeated the All Blacks in 1971 for the only time in a Test series in New Zealand, with a near neighbour on our road in Coleraine, Willie John McBride, at the heart of the Lions pack.

Before leaving Northern Ireland for South Wales I received shattering phone call from a doctor in Dublin to inform me that my mother had been diagnosed with pancreatic cancer at the age of only sixty – two. She who had a lifelong record of excellent health had contracted the cancer with the poorest prognosis of all (which still hold true today). During the last year of her life I flew over to Dublin from Cardiff as frequently as possible both to see her and also because I had a research contract with the Industrial Development Authority. It was an era when the word cancer was not openly discussed; people communicated with meaningful looks rather than specific medical information. However, we all knew that there was only one possible outcome. My mother bore this most painful of cancers with incredible stoicism. When I visited her for the last time in March 1974 she lay in her bed pale, weak and emaciated and yet composed and accepting of her fate. She was a very private person but being there with her in conversation for the last time was a deeply moving experience. She asked me to promise her that I would stay in regular contact with my siblings; I have tried to honour this promise over the past forty-seven years. Her death a week later was the first of someone I had really loved. I was tearful for the first time in my life. I felt not only bereaved but also convulsed by regret and guilt. Why had I not written to her more often? Why had I not shown her more appreciation and love for what she had done for me? We never discussed matters of faith and ideas about life after death. The feeling of acute loss fades over time and transforms into a deep longing and regret. Occasionally I receive reminders of her even almost fifty years later. Attending an alumni dinner at St Andrew's College in 2019, one of my school friends suddenly told me unprompted how lovely my mother had always been to him when he came over to play.

CHAPTER 8

A Welcome in the Hillside

We moved from Northern Ireland to Wales in March 1973, travelling via Dublin in order that my mother, who was then terminally ill, might spend some time with our two daughters, Catherine, 3, and Margaret, 9 months. What sort of Britain were we moving to in March 1973? Was it a land of flares and high heels, parka anoraks and flowing maxi dresses, sheepskin coats, long sideburns and shaggy beards? It was a country in which Enoch Powell – because of his views on immigrants – was the most popular politician in the land – a country that had just joined the EEC which had the highest divorce rate in Europe and was blighted by the cancer of football hooliganism. Or was it a country whose class system pervaded almost all aspects of life? A Gallup poll of moral attitudes in January 1973 revealed that two-thirds of the population favoured the death penalty, 50 per cent thought both that the Bible was literally true and that chastity was a virtue, and one in four believed in innate white superiority. Moreover, it was not until 1968 that the Family Planning Association permitted some of its branches to give contraceptives to unmarried mothers. I was unaware that we were about to live through the collapse of consensus politics in Britain, the erosion of the post-war state, the decline of the Labour party, the three-day week, power cuts and endless strikes.

Based on the advice of our two close friends Susan and Peter Leyshon, who were raised in Bridgend, we decided that it would be preferable to live there and to commute by rail to the university in Cardiff since Bridgend was a stop on the mainline between London Paddington and Swansea. The town itself was no architectural masterpiece and on wet days – of which there were many – it presented a shabby image to the world. There was a profusion of plastic-fronted shops, scabby paint, grimy hamburger joints and the tasteless Rhiw shopping arcade – opened in 1972 – in which old cigarette packets and litter swirled around and whose major redeeming feature was a lively market. The infrastructure was dilapidated. The concrete edifice of the new Co-op store – a rectangular monstrosity on stilts – was already cracked and discoloured and was a metaphor for Wales in the 1970s: a major new store opening followed quickly by a seedy and tacky reality. The number of chapels was dwindling; cinemas were closing; and the coalmines and British Steel were shedding workers. The aspirational Britain of *The Lotus Eaters* and *The Antiques Roadshow*, microwave ovens, the Atari game console and Habitat was clearly elsewhere. The major and crucial compensations were the nearby coastline and the warmth and friendliness of the Welsh people of all age groups. It was always a pleasure to hear the lilting accent; every sound is firmly stressed by the Welsh emphasising both ends of the word; and they also separate out all the syllables and linger long over the pronunciation, as in won-der-ful or round-a-bout.

We rented a cottage near the sea for a couple of months in the charming hamlet of Southerndown, which overlooks the Bristol Channel to the west. It was April and most evenings around 8.00 pm I walked to the edge of the cliff to watch the rim of the setting sun slip down below the sea in the west. We were fortunate to purchase a house in Bridgend and we moved into it in May 1973. It was a semi-detached 1920s property with a 75-yard- long back garden, which was a perfect haven for the children with a paddling pool, slide, climbing frame and Wendy house. The house was located on Merthyr Mawr Road – the most desirable and pleasant residential area of Bridgend – where there were hints of the Arts and Crafts movement in the half-timbered black-and- white gables on many properties, stained glass porch windows and widespread use of pebble dash. The trend for making house 'improvements' or 'modernisation' in the 1970s yielded evidence of indifferent design, such as the use of concrete blocks to rebuild walls in front gardens and substituting UPVC doors for wooden ones. Merthyr Mawr Road was a lovely environment in which to raise young children, although it was not part of the museli belt; a sighting of the *Guardian* newspaper was as rare as a heatwave in summer.

Suburban ambition for social mobility was expressed in the stripped pine and wood furniture that became very popular in the mid-seventies. Shops like Habitat sold home-made looking tables and chairs in bulky stripped pine that were actually mass -produced. Upwardly mobile couples complemented the furnishings by covering their walls with textured Laura Ashley wallpaper, while in bathrooms synthetic tiles imitating mosaics or marble were common.

The effect was often claustrophobic, which is why the 1970s were a byword for bad taste everywhere.[1] Most houses on Merthyr Mawr Road had a number, but around one-third had names. It was not the type of neighbourhood where one would expect to find a house called 'Dunroamin', but a number of owners (or previous ones) had named them after some rural idyll. Hence, houses built on Merthyr Mawr Road displayed on the gate or beside the porch names such as 'Somerset Lodge', 'Cherwell', 'Birkhill Lodge', and 'Glenview', suggesting that the owners had either hailed from Somerset, or had spent a pleasant holiday in the northern Cotswolds (Cherwell), Birkhill in Angus, or a remote Scottish glen.[2] Some residents may have been motivated by a desire to add value to their property, or simply by pretentiousness as the most common nomenclature was a name which suggested that the house was located in several acres of leafy woodland: 'The Firs', 'The Beeches', 'The Rowans', 'The Oaklands' and 'Woodlands'. Sadly, there is no woodland of firs, beeches, rowans, oaks or other trees on Merthyr Mawr Road.

* * *

The Department of Town Planning (later City and Regional Planning) occupied a Victorian red-brick building in Park Place, close to Queen Street, the main shopping street of Cardiff. Other departments of the university were scattered across the Cathays Park area of the city. In December 1898, the local council had purchased 59 acres from the Marquess of Bute and it was subsequently developed into an attractive civic area. A number of elegant Edwardian Portland stone buildings were erected, including City Hall, Museum and National Gallery of Wales, Cardiff Crown Court and several university buildings. Later extensions to the Park in the 1960s and 1990s remained faithful to the original exterior designs.

I fulfilled an appointment with Prof. Anthony Goss, Head of Department, on my first day at the university. I was immediately discombobulated when he informed me that members of staff were expected to conduct assignments for his Planning consultancy firm in London, which would boost our salaries. When I politely refused his offer and told him that, apart from my lecturing and administrative commitments, I would be devoting my time to pursuing my own research programme and grant applications he was visibly surprised.

Later in the afternoon, I was summoned to see the Vice-Chancellor, Prof. Aubrey Trotman-Dickenson, and as I walked through the architectural splendour of Cathays Park to his office I was pondering as to why he would wish to see a new 32- year-old lowly lecturer. As I was to discover, Trotman-Dickenson, or 'T-D' as he was affectionately known, was something of a legend and his commitment to the institution was total; it was reported that he even came into his office on Christmas day. He owned and personally maintained several flats in Cardiff which were let to students. It was also rumoured that he owned the tea and coffee machines in the university and could be frequently observed switching off the lights in the buildings. On that March day in 1973, in a way I had not done with Goss, I immediately warmed to 'T-D' as in a brisk and business-like manner, he quickly informed me that his goal was to seed a number of new research-active staff – including myself and others – into several departments in order to rapidly develop their research profile. His aims were clearly very different than those of Goss and he informed me then that I would be welcome to apply for promotion to a Senior Lectureship within a year. By 1974, I had published 17 research papers in refereed journals and my application was successful. This caused problems in the department, however, as there were several other staff who were much older and more experienced than me, had been strongly supported for promotion by Prof. Goss, but who were again unsuccessful. A frigid atmosphere prevailed in the staff common room as people began to realise that Trotman-Dickenson was not likely to sanction the promotion of staff who were not publishing research in refereed journals. Goss could not bring himself to congratulate me and simply told me that I now had to shoulder a higher administrative burden, to which I responded by volunteering to be responsible for UCAS undergraduate selection.

One notable characteristic of Prof Goss's tenure as head of department was that he spent a proportion of the working week in London running his planning consultancy firm. Frequently, he would travel to Cardiff on the sleeper train. Such an arrangement was unsustainable in the long term and Goss eventually resigned. He was replaced by Prof. Michael Bruton, who came from the University of Central England. He quickly established himself as a decisive leader prepared to take decisions. These decisions were not necessarily popular with all members of the staff, who were a heterogeneous group drawn from a wide variety of backgrounds from architecture through geography, sociology to economics. Prof Bruton's previous experience had been in planning practice and former polytechnic institutions where research was not a key priority. Early in his tenure as head of department, he asked me for a copy of my most recent research paper which happened to be: 'An Analysis of Industrial Closures: Irish experience, 1960-1973,' published in a five star journal, *Regional Studies*, (1976), 10, 433-448. I was summoned to his office, where he informed that 'this was not the sort of research he wanted people in his department to be doing.' I thanked him and ignored his advice. The department quickly developed its research reputation and several staff became distinguished scholars, including Richard Davies, Phil Cooke and Paul Longley. The first ever Research Assessment exercise was launched in 1985 and departments were required to submit a total of five papers by different staff members. Mike Bruton, who had quickly adjusted to the new reality, invited me to submit one paper and he was very happy to accept a later publication of mine in *Regional Studies*. Although the department was increasingly successful and a few of us – Phil Cooke and myself – were winning grants from the Economic and Social Research Council – it was never a friendly and harmonious working environment.

* * *

Following the UK's entry into the EEC in January 1973, Prime Minister Ted Heath declared in the autumn of 1973 that Britain's problems were the problems of success. This optimism was rapidly deflated. At one moment the prospects were good with the harmonies of the Beatles still echoing in the background and Keynesian demand management in the ascendant. Soon all was gloom; the airwaves were filled with punk rock and monetarism had become the new orthodoxy. Inflation and industrial unrest were the agents of change. With sterling falling on foreign exchange markets, the Chancellor, Anthony Barber, slashed £500 million from public spending in May 1973 and raised the bank rate to 11.5 per cent. The consequences for us, having stretched our borrowing capacity to the limit in order to buy a £16,000 house in Bridgend, was that the mortgage payments were raised within one month of moving into the property.

After the Yom Kippur War in 1973, OPEC countries raised the price of oil from $2.40 to $11.65 by the end of the year, a rise of 385 per cent. Immediately Western economies descended into a deep recession between 1973 and 1975, which was characterised by stagflation – a deadly combination of high inflation and high unemployment. The Bank of England introduced the tightest credit squeeze in memory raising the bank rate to 13 per cent (a record) in

November 1973. House prices, land values and share prices collapsed. Our mortgage payments rose again. The National Union of Mineworkers imposed an overtime ban on 12 November 1973. In response, the government banned electric advertising, street lighting in South Wales was cut by 50 per cent, the speed limit was reduced to 50 miles per hour, electric heating was forbidden in workplaces, floodlighting was banned at sports events, offices were ordered to turn down their thermostats to 65 degrees Fahrenheit and the BBC and ITV ceased broadcasting after 10.30pm each night. Nothing like this had been witnessed in Britain before in peacetime.

A miners' strike commenced in December 1973. The government then introduced an emergency budget slashing public expenditure by 4 per cent, the largest spending cut in modern history, while Slade's 'Merry Xmas Everybody' urged people to 'look to the future now/It's only just begun.'[3] These measures were complemented by Ted Heath's drastic decision to impose a three-day working week on industry from January 1st 1974, while shops – unless deemed essential – were limited to opening either in the mornings or the afternoons. Even clergymen took to the airwaves to debate the morality of family members sharing baths; and the government minister for energy – Patrick Jenkin – urged people to 'clean their teeth in the dark' only for the press to find five lights blazing in his north London home.[4] The miners voted for an all-out strike in February and Heath responded by called a general election, which simply underlined the power of the unions: in 1976 half the public thought the leader of the Transport and General Workers Union (TGWU), Jack Jones, was the most powerful man in the country.[5]

Harold Wilson defeated Ted Heath in the election in February 1974, but with no overall majority, and although only 57, he was drinking heavily, enduring poor health, and failed to provide strong leadership. He was not a leader but a tactician with bourgeois tastes, including listening to Gilbert and Sullivan, playing with his children's Meccano set, golfing and reading Arthur Bryant and Agatha Christie. The new Wilson government compounded the effects of the reckless Barber boom and inflation was nudging 20 per cent by the summer of 1974. The government's attempt to spend its way out of stagflation through increasing public spending was foolhardy and led to more wage inflation and the humiliation of a bail out by the IMF. We had arrived to live in Britain at the moment when it became increasingly obvious that the country was in relative decline characterised by industrial inefficiency, over-powerful trade unions, incompetent managers and poor public services.

Wilson called a second election in October 1974 and managed to scrape back with a small majority of 3 seats. A month later five people died in the Guilford pub bombing, and worse was to follow on 21 November when 21 people were murdered and 182 injured in the Mulberry Bush pub in Birmingham. Both attacks were carried out by the Provisional IRA. Under pressure to arrest the bombers, the police beat confessions out of six Irishmen who spent 16 years in prison for a crime they did not commit. Former Labour MP Chris Mullan courageously lead a campaign for their release. Four innocent Irish people were also imprisoned for 15 years for the Guilford bombings until their sentences were overturned. The horror of the Birmingham bombing led to Irish people being refused service in shops, thrown off busses and threatened in pubs, but serious attacks were rare. Personally, I have never encountered any anti – Irish feeling in Britain.

Meanwhile, pay awards escalated alarmingly. Bernard Donoghue, Labour's advisor, criticised Michael Foot for saying that a 30 per cent settlement was OK because it was the 'going rate.' Donoghue commented that: 'if any rate that is the going rate is OK, then any going rate must be OK – so why not 50%.'[6] Inflation was now out of control reaching an all-time record of 33 per cent in April 1975 and unemployment had more than doubled in a year, but Prime Minister Wilson was reluctant to do anything that might upset the unions. The British car industry was in steep decline. British Leyland's productivity was far below overseas levels and its new models were unreliable, especially the Austin Allegro. Labour relations were abysmal (at some plants, such as Cowley and Longbridge, there were stoppages almost every day); and BL's management 'was notoriously incompetent.'[7] British Leyland, therefore, was a metaphor for the lack of competitiveness, poor industrial relations and decline of British industry in the 1970s. This was the world into which our third daughter, Bridget, arrived in February 1975, but it was an especially enjoyable experience for me as it was the first time that I had been able to attend a birth of one of my three daughters as fathers were excluded from witnessing births in Northern Ireland. Moreover, she was delivered by a nurse from Donegal, who was charmed by Bridget's red hair, a colour that had skipped several generations from my paternal grandfather. Susan then shouldered the major child-rearing responsibilities, which she conducted with complete dedication.

The two important political events of 1975 were the Common Market referendum of 5 June which recorded a large 2 to 1 majority for remaining in the EEC, and the election of Margaret Thatcher as leader of the Conservative party. Dismissed by the head of her Oxford College as a 'second-class chemist', she was never invited to weekend dinners because 'she had nothing to contribute.' 'Methodism, science and suburbia' Simon Jenkins wrote 'armoured her in self-confidence and self-righteousness'; and while her colleagues deplored what they perceived as socialism's inefficiency, she viewed it as a moral outrage.[8] She was narrow of outlook, inflexible and lacked a sense of humour and irony. She was heavily influenced by her father, Alfred Roberts, the son of a shoemaker, who raised himself by dint of hard work and ultimately owned two grocery shops; there was, however, no hot running water or inside lavatory in the Roberts' family flat.[9] She espoused a philosophy and morality about the individual and the nation that appealed to some and generated deep hostility in others; she never won the support of more than one-third of the electorate. When she married a rich businessman, Denis Thatcher in 1951, the Grantham grammar schoolgirl transformed herself into a Home Counties Tory by adopting a contrived posh accent – following voice coaching – sending her children to private schools and abandoning Methodism for membership of the Church of England.

* * *

Bridgend was an enjoyable place in which to raise three young daughters. It was a compact town with the primary and comprehensive schools and shopping all within walking distance and with easy access to the nearby countryside and beaches only four miles distant. Welsh people were easy-going, warm and friendly, if occasionally somewhat parochial in their outlook. At weekends in summer, we enjoyed walking with the girls on the open common land above St Brides Major and watching our kite rising and plunging in the upper air; roller skating on the promenade at Porthcawl in the autumn as the sea slammed against the wall sending spray on to the pavement, and then visiting Luigi Fulgoni's café for ice creams; taking the girls to Llangeinor for swimming lessons; travelling with the Lewis family every July to Herefordshire to spend the day picking strawberries and raspberries in warm sunshine after playing cricket with their three boys at Raglan Castle; driving to Rhossili Bay on Gower to collect whinberries each September; taking the girls to see Santa Claus in the Co-op in Bridgend, a Santa Claus with a wonderful South Wales valleys accent! I also created a lily pond in the back garden in which golden orfe and frogs thrived, while dragonflies visited on summer days. Along the lane at the bottom of the garden elderberries grew profusely. With the girls all helping, we collected elderflowers each May from which Susan made tasty elderflower champagne. Then on autumn days we returned to the lane and the children – sporting purple fingers and faces – harvested bucketfuls of elderberries. Susan then boiled the berries with sugar and, after sieving through a muslin cloth, the purple wine was bottled and stored to be administered to anyone with colds during the winter. We enjoyed picking wild blackberries in the former Prisoner-of –War camp in Bridgend where there was an abundance of sprawling briars laden with juicy berries. The brambles were tall with sharp thorns and most of the berries were ready for picking in early September. The three girls rode their bicycles around and around the prison huts while Susan and I picked the berries. The internal walls of some huts were decorated with graphic drawings of sweethearts who were left behind in Germany. A number of the prisoners, after they had completed their work assignments following the war, chose to settle in South Wales rather than return to Germany.

On a fine weekend in summer, we would take the girls to the beach at Ogmore-by-Sea where the crumbling fossiliferous Jurassic cliffs stand proudly facing west into the Bristol Channel towards the Tusker Rock and seagulls were borne up the cliff face on updraughts. The beach was bisected by the glistening Ogmore river estuary. Out at sea, ships nudged slowly westwards, while to the south the coast of Somerset and Devon thrust into the western approaches. When the tide was out, we searched for ammonites and the girls played on the coal-streaked sandy beach across which the tide advanced rapidly. When the tide was high with a south-west wind driving the surf, each retreating wave created a unique sound as it sucked back off the shingle at the top of the beach. As the tide rose over the expanse of sand, the temperature of the water moderated and swimming was a joy. On a fine day in August 1980 I ran into the sea in order to dive through a wave and swim out into the bay. However, I ran straight into a submerged rock and hurt my foot. I travelled to Como in Italy the next day to read a paper at a Regional Science conference. When I returned, an X ray confirmed that I had broken two toes!

Since fireworks were banned in Ireland, I had never experienced the thrill of Bonfire Night until our children were sufficiently old to enjoy it. In 1978, I purchased a large box of fireworks from the newsagent's, which contained an exciting collection of Catherine wheels, squibs, sparklers, penny bangers,

Roman candles, golden fountains, silver rain, and rockets in brightly coloured cardboard tubes. When it was dark, we assembled on the patio at the back of the house – together with our friends Marg and Ed Williams. I arranged the Catherine wheels by nailing them to the garage door and I had carefully pre-prepared the rockets for vertical lift-off by placing them into milk bottles. I had also built a huge bonfire at the bottom of the vegetable plot with a suitably attired guy on top wearing some of my old clothes stuffed with (*Guardian*) newspapers. I always started the fire by soaking some newspaper in petrol in order to rapidly generate a fierce blaze which then filled the air with wood smoke and sparks. It was now time to ignite the fireworks. I lit the touchpaper on the fireworks and started with the Catherine wheels. This was when events did not always follow the script. Sometimes the Catherine wheel failed to ignite and after a short period I would approach carefully, prod it and try to light it again. After several Catherine wheels had successfully started by spinning *in situ* on the garage door, they suddenly dropped on to the patio and began to race around between the three girls while crackling and spitting out showers of sparks. This caused a mixture of panic and high excitement, enhanced by the fact that it happened every year. I always saved the rockets until last. Having lit the touchpaper, the rockets accelerated into the dark void but, instead of upwards into the night sky, they always climbed to about six feet and then shot away on a horizontal trajectory parallel to the ground flying across several neighbouring garden fences before exploding into a multi-coloured shower of sparks leaving glittering trails behind. My unique rocket displays became so well known that the families within 100 metres of our garden would all assemble in the certain expectation that they would witness a rocket streaking across their fence to explode into a multitude of colours directly in front of them

Christmas was always a magical time with our three young daughters. We had two variegated holly trees in the front garden from which some locals helped themselves from time to time. There was a tree with Christmas lights and Susan, who always tried to make each Christmas special, helped the girls to make some new decorations with gold and silver paper and then they hung them on the tree. These new decorations would cluster in three different parts of the tree depending on the relative heights of the girls that year. On Christmas Eve we would all listen to the Festival of Nine Lessons and Carols from King's College, Cambridge and Susan and I enjoyed singing along to them. One of the real pleasures of Christmas was carol singing in Bridgend or Cowbridge while collecting for Amnesty International. When Catherine and Maggie had reached the age when they no longer believed in Santa Claus but Bridget did, they still pretended that he came down the chimney and consumed the mince pies and cake that, in reality, I had enjoyed on Christmas Eve. While the children played with their new toys and Susan prepared a wonderful Christmas meal, I went down the back garden to the vegetable patch to pick brussels sprouts. I also enjoyed the ritual that I inherited from my father of pouring a very large measure of Jameson's whiskey over the Christmas pudding and setting fire to it. How the children screamed when they watched the flames engulf the pudding.

* * *

The choice of television programmes in the 1970s was still limited to only three channels –BBC1, BBC2 and ITV – each with its own distinctive schedule of programmes. When we moved to South Wales, we upgraded our TV to colour. Looking back, it seemed like a vintage period for TV quality, although there was some dreadful dross on ITV and even occasionally on *Play for Today*, seen by some as a vehicle for left-wing propaganda. There were a number of excellent series, including *I Claudius, Tinker Tailor Soldier Spy* (starring the brilliant Alec Guinness), *Dad's Army, Life on Earth, Porridge,* and *The Two Ronnies*. Dennis Potter, arguably the greatest television dramatist, wrote a number of outstanding plays, most notably, *Pennies from Heaven* (1978). His plays combined fantasy and reality, the personal and social. He was the most innovative dramatist on British television who made extensive use of flashbacks and non-linear plotting. In *Pennies from Heaven,* Potter mixed the reality of the drama with a dark fantasy content as the characters mimed old recordings of popular songs. Arthur, a travelling sheet- music salesman played by Bob Hoskins, hopes that the lyrics of the music will become reality. Potter created a contrast between the cheerful lyrics and the dreary lives of the characters. This is a drama of style and substance, conjuring up the atmosphere of mid-1930s England, a setting that complemented the original recordings of the Depression era songs- especially those of Al Bowlly – in order to heighten the dramatic tension. The way that the songs are integrated into the action still seems revolutionary over 40 years later. This production led on to other Potter classics, most notably, *Blue Remembered Hills* (1979), *The Singing Detective* (1986) and *Lipstick on your Collar* (1993) . *The Singing*

Detective – starring Michael Gambon – was Potter's greatest masterpiece in which the line between fantasy and reality becomes blurred by interweaving narratives and timelines. It is arguably the most vivid representation of the workings of the human mind ever shown on TV.

All three of our daughters were interested in reading, especially Beatrix Potter, C S Lewis and Enid Blyton, although in Bridget's case the story always had to feature animals. However, their cultural lives were defined above all by television. The quality and choice of programmes available was exceptional: while *Blue Peter* and *Jackanory* aimed to provide an entertaining and educational experience, they were complemented by the adorable *Bagpuss, Ivor the Engine, Mary Mungo and Midge, Bill and Ben the Flowerpot Men* and *The Magic Roundabout,* all of which were so professional that even parents enjoyed them. Susan was always diligent in rationing the amount of time that the girls spent watching childrens' TV and she made sure that they had a constant supply of books to read. Being raised in a house with a large garden, they were able to play imaginary games with numerous Cindy and Pippa dolls, to ride their tricycles, to exercise on a climbing frame, and bounce on a space hopper (which I also enjoyed).

The garden was large enough to enable me to practise my golf short game by pitching balls over a line of fir trees across the garden. Great fun. Beyond these trees I prepared a large vegetable plot on both sides of a central path. The soil was fertile and the South Wales climate of warm spring and summer weather combined with copious supplies of rain was ideal for growing vegetables. There were blackcurrant and gooseberry bushes and I grew a wide range of lettuces, radish, spinach, dwarf beans, runner beans, peas, leeks, broccoli, brussels sprouts, broad beans, beetroot, cabbage, courgettes, leeks, onions, potatoes (which the children loved harvesting), raspberries and strawberries. The one vegetable which I totally failed to cultivate successfully was carrots. The Bridgend Agricultural Show was held each July and I used to submit a number of entries under the names of the children. To my utter amazement we managed to win a few prizes every year, which I reckon was largely a tribute to the fertility of our soil rather than any skill of mine. The 1970s also witnessed the frozen food revolution which we became a part of in 1976 when we acquired a freezer, thereby enabling us to store surplus fruit and vegetables from the garden.

* * *

It was an era when light entertainment was popular and there were still performers around who had trained and performed in music halls. Les Dawson was a lovable comic with the flexible face, perfect timing and a world-weary, deadpan style of delivery. He portrayed a working- class man with pretensions above his station with humour often based on his relationship with his mother-in-law. He was a talented pianist: he would start playing Beethoven's Moonlight Sonata and then throw in a few hideously wrong notes (but not destroy the tune) without appearing to realise, while smiling at the audience. My favourite comedian of the period, however, was Dave Allen who was born in Dublin and christened David Tynan O'Mahony. Having broken into the comedy circuit in Britain, his agent told him to change his name as he believed (correctly) that most British people could not pronounce O'Mahony. He became the most controversial comedian on British television in the 1970s and 1980s. Unafraid to take on taboo topics, he frequently highlighted political hypocrisy and his disregard for religious authority. He pioneered solo joke-and-story telling while sitting on a stool smoking and drinking, interspersed with sketches that frequently lampooned the Catholic Church. Routines included sketches showing the Pope (played by Allen) and his cardinals doing a striptease to 'The Stripper' music on the steps of St Peter's, while another featured aggressive priests beating their parishioners. His performance was relaxed and intimate with an air of charm as he spoke with a twinkle in his eye. He was a classic Irish story-teller with an observational rather than joke-driven style. As such, he was a major influence on the alternative comedians of the 1980s. While most found this innovative Irish comedian gentle, rueful and whimsical, Mary Whitehouse thought he was 'offensive, indecent and embarrassing' because he satirised the Catholic Church. Such judgements by Whitehouse merely served to enhance his reputation.

There were numerous sitcoms on British television in the 1970s, many of which were both formulaic and forgettable. As Sandbrook has argued, the most common class theme of the 1970s sitcoms was not that between working-class old and new, or even between middle class and working- class, but between different kinds of middle- class identity.[10] The Good Life, for example, a somewhat dated sitcom, explored the subtle differences between two middle-class families – the conservative Leadbetters and the environmentally conscious Goods. My favourite sitcom was Fawlty Towers (closely followed by Father Ted) – written by John Cleese and Connie Booth. It addresses the subtleties of the British class system with characters ranging from the tense, aggressive, snobbish hotel-owner Basil Fawlty, with his military moustache, rudeness and incompetence at languages to his lower-middle class, acerbic, ambitious and bossy wife Sybil, with her extravagant hairdos and crude laugh. Much of the comedy arises from Basil's snobbery and attempts to attract a 'higher class of clientele,' his fawning attitude towards the aristocracy, his dislike of foreigners and the working classes and his impatience leading him to argue with guests. The plots are complex and farcical involving coincidences, misunderstandings and cross-purposes. The hotel itself was a metaphor for Britain's economy and society in the 1970s with its shabby appearance, cheap furniture and virtually non-existent service culture.[11]

Suburban social life in 1970s Britain was brilliantly satirised by Mike Leigh in *Abigail's Party*, his *Play for Today* in 1977, a comedy of manners in which the aspirations of an *arriviste* lower-middle- class couple are forensically explored. Alison Steadman brilliantly portrays the hideous Beverly, a former cosmetics demonstrator and social climber, sexual predator and snob. She hosts a drinks party complete with fake leather sofas, beige wallpaper, bowls of nibbles, Bacardi and coke with a Demis Roussos record playing on the turntable. Meanwhile, her estate-agent husband, Laurence, contemplates his unread volumes of Shakespeare. Beverly is in reality insecure and childless and the play is a vision not only of social climbers seeking to impress their neighbours, but of all the vices of 1970s suburbia: 'its materialistic one-upmanship, its sexual voraciousness, its lack of community and feeling, its aggressive individualism.'[12] It was a golden age of television and in 1978 London Weekend Television launched a new series, *The South Bank Show*, as its new arts programme, presented imaginatively for several decades by Melvyn Bragg.

A brilliant satirical comedy, *Yes Minister*, written by Anthony Jay and Jonathon Lynn, was launched in 1980 starring Paul Eddington as Jim Hacker, a dim and cowardly minister of administrative affairs (and later Prime Minister) unable to take decisions and totally obsessed with opinion polls and his own promotion prospects. He was constantly outmanoeuvred by his permanent secretary, Sir Humphrey Appleby, superbly played by Nigel Hawthorne who frustrated all Hacker's policy ideas with consummate ease. The writers used the diaries of Richard Crossman, a former Labour cabinet minister, as inspiration. Jonathan Lynn declared that they 'deployed a traditional comic formula of the servant who is more able than his master – the same ploy as

Jeeves and Bertie Wooster.'[13] As I pen this in the winter of 2021, *Yes Minister* is being repeated again – over 40 years later on BBC2 – and it is as fresh, witty and relevant as it was back in 1980.

* * *

After a couple of years in Bridgend Susan started to attend Quaker meetings and the children went to the Quaker Sunday school where dedicated Quakers provided a stimulating experience for them. One day I stumbled across a book sale which was raising money on behalf of Amnesty International and discovered that most of the local Amnesty group were also Quakers. I joined the Amnesty group and remained a committed member for the next decade before moving to Scotland. After a few months, I was elected as Chair of the local group and we responded to a request from the multi-denominational Cowbridge United Free Church to form a larger Bridgend-Cowbridge Amnesty group which met alternately in Bridgend and Cowbridge. This was an excellent initiative as the group acquired some dedicated members from Cowbridge and we were able to raise more money for Amnesty through flag days and book sales. It was also a source of friendship among like-minded, dedicated people. As a result of joining the Amnesty group we became very friendly with Ed and Marg Williams and, despite a 20- year age gap between us, Ed and I had many shared interests, including politics and classical music. They were the only other *Guardian* readers that I knew on Merthyr Mawr Road. It was the era of cassette tapes which, although the sound quality was mediocre, made it easy to record and share favourite pieces. When we went on our annual summer holidays with the girls, I recorded music on to tapes so that each of the three girls had a section of the tape especially for them. This was surprisingly popular.

We started drinking wine on a regular basis during the 1970s. For a brief period we joined the ranks of those who made wine at home. I purchased glass jars, plastic funnels, tubing and thermometers. The resulting wine, needless to say, was virtually undrinkable. British consumption of wine rose almost 450 per cent between 1970 and 1990, a trend largely confined to the middle classes. Initially, the range of wines available in the local Spar grocery in Bridgend was limited to brands such as Blue Nun, Mateus Rose, Liebfraumilch and Black Tower. There was a time lag as tastes became more discerning before quality wines appeared on the shelves. One of our closest friends during the 1970s, Gwyn Bevan, was a bachelor at the time and, when he came to South Wales to stay with his parents, he visited us on the Saturday night, always bringing a bottle of Hungarian Bull's Blood, a dry red blend that was regarded as a quality wine at the time. This was the era when a snobbish Basil Fawlty commented that it is 'always a pleasure to find someone who appreciates the *boudoir* of the grape. I'm afraid that most of the people we get in here don't know a Bordeaux from a claret.'

One of the great gastronomic mysteries of my lifetime was not the growing popularity of wine and the phenomenon of real ale, but that water was the truly fashionable drink of the early 1980s. By 1981, some 500 million gallons of Perrier, Evian and Malvern Water were sold and a year later Britain spent £50 million on mineral water. Even serious newspapers commented on the merits of drinking water: the *Guardian* reviewer liked Harrogate Sparkle: 'freshly brisk, with a touch of stimulating impatience, though perhaps a little thin and nervous.'[14] Bottled water usually costs a thousand times more per litre than tap water yet sales in Britain were worth £1.6 billion in 2018. Bottled water often originates from public sources and is then filtered before being bottled. Hence, British tap water, which is strictly regulated, is some of the cleanest in the world; and even though the Consumers' Association reported that bottled water was no better for you than tap water, sales rose inexorably.[15] Then there is the issue of plastic waste and the fact that 3 litres of water are needed to produce a litre of bottled. Filtering tap water to reduce the minerals is probably the safest water available.

During the 1970s we organised our holidays in Ireland around my research commitments for the Industrial Development Authority and Shannon Development who had both supported my research with a series of grants. Hence, each year from 1974 to 1977, inclusive, I took the car over to Dublin to do research and a week later Susan and the children would travel by train from Bridgend to Fishguard and catch the ferry to Rosslare where I would meet them. In 1974 we spent two weeks in a tiny semi-detached chalet at Ballyferriter, west of Dingle, where we enjoyed magnificent views of the 3,127 foot Mount Brandon to the north east when it was clear of rain and mist. We were joined for several days by our friends Susan and Peter Leyshon who drove down from Northern Ireland with their children in a VW camper van. There was an eccentric man wandering about in this remote rural area and one day he removed some of our towels and clothes from the washing line. When we raised this with the owner of our chalet, he responded by saying that 'We all have to forgive him…he's quite harmless, but he knows all about the history of the world.' This was a lesson in the tolerance that a remote community extends towards eccentrics. The following summer in 1975 Susan again travelled to Ireland alone with three girls by ferry to Rosslare, which was a remarkable feat as Bridget was only six months old, Maggie was three and Catherine five. We rented a cottage at Ballyconnelly near Clifden in Connemara. Bridget slept in a drawer and Susan washed her nappies in the adjoining lake. Every day Catherine and Maggie enjoyed watching our neighbour, Mrs O'Malley, pulling up her skirt and wading out to an island in the lake to feed her hens, who were safe there from predation by foxes. Sadly, the weather was frequently wet and windy, although we had one lovely day on the beautiful coral beach at Mannin Bay.

We rented a house on Achill Island, county Mayo, in the summer of 1976. On the first morning I walked to the nearest shop, which functioned as a general store, post office and pub, and asked for the *Irish Times*. The owner replied 'Would that be today's *Irish Times* or yesterday's you'd be wanting?' When I replied in a slightly bemused voice 'Well today's of course,' he responded by saying that 'In that case, if it's today's paper you want, you'll need to come back tomorrow.' The Irish telephone system was archaic at that time as I discovered when dropped into the same shop to make a long-distance call only to be informed that you could not phone off the island after 10.00pm at night. Again we had indifferent weather on Achill, but all changed when we returned to Wales to enjoy the rest of the long hot summer of 1976.

* * *

James Callaghan had succeeded Harold Wilson as Prime Minister in March 1976 and proved to be a better Prime Minister than Chancellor or Home Secretary. A man who had left school at 16 before serving in the Royal Navy during the war, Callaghan was elected as a Cardiff MP in 1945 and became a junior minister of transport in Attlee's government. In this role he made his most durable contributions to the life of Britain: the introduction of cats-eyes and zebra crossings to the nation's roads. The summer of 1976 was the hottest that Britain has ever known. Every day from June 23 to July 7 the temperature reached a minimum of 90F (32.2C) with 5 days above 95F (35C). Britain faced the worst drought since records began: crops wilted in the fields; fish died in their thousands; the heatwave devastated frogs, toads and newts;

and the baking sun parched parks, golf courses and cricket pitches across the country. Heath fires broke out and across South Wales – more affected than any part of Britain – firemen also battled raging forest fires. The government rushed a Drought Act through the Commons in August and Callaghan appointed the Sports Minister, Denis Howell, as 'Mr Rainmaker.'[16] Inviting reporters to his house, Howell announced that his main plans to save water included putting a brick in the toilet cistern. He advised people not only to fill their baths to a depth of only five inches and to report 'abuses and misuses' by their neighbours, but he also announced that he would share baths with his wife, which led to the most popular T-shirt of the summer bearing the slogan – 'Save Water, Bath with a Friend.' In South Wales, a ban on car-washing was introduced on pain of a £400 fine and the water was cut off at 2.00pm every afternoon and not switched on again until 7.00am the following morning. This prompted Mid Glamorgan council – not the most enlightened educational authority in Britain – to close 220 schools an hour early at 2.00pm each day.

For me, as I recall the glorious summer weather of 1976, it will be forever associated with the Test match series between England and the West Indies and the extraordinary batting of the great Sir Vivian Richards, who averaged 118.4 in the tests and made two double centuries as the West Indies thrashed England. Richards was imperious, 'arguably the most destructive batsman the sport has ever seen' who had struck the fastest century in test cricket (56 balls) and could intimidate opponents before he had even received a ball. In an era when all cricketers wore helmets, Viv strode out to bat wearing only the famous West Indies cap – the symbol of his superiority – a reminder that no bowler, however fast, not even Lillee or Thompson, could threaten him. There was a swagger to Richards as he sauntered to the crease that engendered a hum of expectation around the ground. He could quite simply destroy any bowling on any wicket at any time since he had the ability of the truly great to perform at his peak on the really big occasions. He was notorious for punishing bowlers who sledged him so that many opposing captains banned their players from doing it. Greg Thomas of Glamorgan sledged Viv in a match at Taunton after he played and missed telling him: 'It's red, round and fast. Now try playing it.' Richards hit the next ball for six out of the Taunton ground into a river. Turning to Thomas he said: 'You know what it looks like, now go and find it.' Apart from the weather and the glorious sight of Viv Richards batting in his prime, 1976 was a dreadful year with riots at the Notting Hill carnival, the IRA bombing campaign in Britain, the Jeremy Thorpe affair, and widespread football hooliganism.

Above all, however, the plight of the economy loomed over the sun-parched fields of Britain. At British Leyland(BL), the most famous shop steward of all, Derek Robinson (known as 'Red Robbo' in the tabloid press) is credited with causing 523 walk-outs at the Longbridge plant, costing an estimated £200m in lost production.[17] BL was simply unable to match the products of its competitors, especially Ford, whose Escorts and Cortinas were icons of the era. A study in 2004 named two BL models from the 1970s – the Austin Allegro and Morris Marina – in the top five worst cars of all time, ahead of the Lada.[18] The Austin Allegro was not only ugly, but boasted a square steering wheel, looked more aerodynamic in reverse and had atrocious reliability that earned it the sobriquet 'All- Aggro.' The Morris Marina, launched in 1971, but based on the Morris Minor of 1948, had the cornering stability of a blancmange, prompting James May to suggest that at least one Morris Marina should be preserved in a museum 'as a warning from history.' I managed to avoid ever purchasing one of these two cars, but I did own a Hillman Imp from 1966-67, a notoriously unreliable car that needed a new gearbox, which cost me a month's salary in 1966.

Denis Healey raised interest rates to 13 per cent, but the pound continued a descent to $1.63 by 27th September 1976 from $2.00 12 months before, and mortgage rates rose again to 12.25 per cent.[19] After a courageous speech at the Labour conference, Healey later negotiated the largest loan ever approved by the IMF that heralded cuts of £1 billion in 1977-78 and £1.5 billion a year later. The IMF crisis was a national humiliation and exposed Britain's lack of competitiveness – from its overvalued currency and financial indiscipline, to its abysmal industrial relations, a product of the greed of the trade unions and careless and low-calibre management; it was an era of remarkable selfishness leading to steep falls in Britain's world shares of the car, shipbuilding and steel markets.[20] Government spending peaked in 1975-76 when it accounted for 49.9 per cent of GDP. Denis Healey then cut public spending by 1 per cent per year for five years to 44.8 per cent of GDP, a feat that no other chancellor has ever matched.

* * *

My period living in Wales coincided with a golden era for Welsh rugby with legendary stars like Gareth Edwards, Barry John, Gerald Davies, JPR Williams and Phil Bennett. Between 1969 and 1979, they won three Grand Slams, and two Triple Crowns, although they have not defeated the All Blacks for 69 years since 1953. Being at Cardiff Arms Park on match day is a unique experience, even though between 1973 and 1985 Ireland lost every game in Cardiff, except 1985 when we won the Triple Crown. The pride of the Welsh in their national game, the passion of the singing and sense of tribalism was palpable in affirming their identity, especially when England came to town. After leaving South Wales for Scotland in 1986, Ireland only lost one of the subsequent 13 matches in Cardiff in the 24years between 1987 and 2011, a truly remarkable away record. Bridgend also had a strong rugby team in the 1970s and I would often attend matches at the Brewery Field to see players such as JPR Williams, Steve Fenwick and Gareth Williams. During our stay in Bridgend, Welsh cultural identity became more self-confident: the Welsh Language Act of 1967 had given Welsh equal status in law and government; bilingual road signs became the norm, although they make road signs more difficult to read; the BBC launched the Welsh-language station, Radio Cymru in 1977; and a Welsh language TV channel S4C opened in November 1982.

* * *

In the 1970s, before the internet, it was impossible to discover whether self-catering properties were well furnished and clean. When we went to Donegal in the summer of 1977, the property that we rented was both uncomfortable and grubby. My father, who by then had been widowed for three years, stayed with my twin sister, Sheila, in her holiday house on Lough Swilly and this enabled him to spend some time with our daughters. He took Margaret for a drive in his car and – having slid back the roof – allowed her to stand on the back seat with her head projecting into the wind, an incident she recalled when appearing as the guest on *Desert Island Discs* in 2021. The weather was again predominantly windy, damp and cool and we decided on the return journey that we would holiday in France in 1978.

It was our first visit to France with the children and we loved it. We rented a gite near Quimper in Brittany and I enjoyed the delights of eating out in restaurants, attempting to speak French, swimming off the glorious beaches of Brittany and playing boule with Catherine. A great highlight was watching the parade at the Fete de Cornouaille in Quimper. This was a showcase for Breton culture in all its diversity with Bretons all dressed in traditional costumes. Quimper was packed and the historic town vibrated to the Celtic rhythms featuring Breton bands (bagards) composed of bagpipes (biniou), bombards and drums. The bombard is a woodwind double- reed instrument with a powerful trumpet-like sound usually accompanied by bagpipes, which play an octave above the bombard; the bombard calls and the biniou responds. This was a good holiday, but not for Bridget, then three, who fell and split her head which required several stitches.

During 1978, despite the economic woes, there was a consensus that James Callaghan – calm, cheerful and authoritative – reigned supreme over Mrs Thatcher in the House of Commons; and even a Conservative papers such as *The Times* conceded that he was a 'champion of moderation, common sense and national unity.'[21] The key decision facing Callaghan was whether to call an election in October 1978 or to wait until the spring of 1979. Most advisors and the cabinet favoured an autumn election and were astounded when Callaghan decided to postpone the election until the spring of 1979. He was determined to pursue a pay norm of 5 per cent which was regarded as completely unrealistic. The portent of what was to come was set in June 1978 when the government's pay review body awarded deals worth 30 per cent to senior judges, top civil servants, and the chairmen of nationalised industries. What the ensuing Winter of Discontent – a phrase that was already part of the language from Shakespeare's *Richard 111* – proved 'was not that a 5 percent pay policy was dead, but that *any* incomes policy was dead, whether 5 per cent, 7 per cent or even 10 percent.'[22] Road haulage drivers went on strike to claim 35-40 per cent; local authority manual workers, NHS auxiliary workers and the miners all put in for a 40 per cent increase. All pretensions to an incomes policy were abandoned.

There was severe weather in early January 1979 with blizzards and deep snow accumulations, the most severe winter weather I had ever experienced. Bridgend was engulfed by 12 inches of snow, followed by freezing rain; and the roads were littered with abandoned cars. The snow smoothed the fields and bushes and all the branches of the trees and shrubs; it also made all the land silent so that individual sounds – such as a bird calling – were startling and clear. Road conditions worsened as pickets blockaded the nation's only supplier of rock salt. The lorry drivers' strike prompted panic buying in supermarkets causing food and petrol shortages. Buses were cancelled and on

15 January train drivers walked out bringing the entire network to a standstill. Pickets in Hull refused to release supplies of chemotherapy drugs and materials for penicillin. Meanwhile, Callaghan flew to the Caribbean island of Guadaloupe for a summit meeting with the USA, France and West Germany. A week later he arrived back at Heathrow and delivered an ill-judged press conference. Adopting a reassuring emollient tone that had served him well over the years, he misjudged the mood of a cold and anxious nation with serious consequences. The following day Rupert Murdoch's *Sun* newspaper printed a devastating headline: 'Sun-tanned premier Jim Callaghan breezed back into Britain yesterday and asked : 'Crisis? What Crisis?' Callaghan never used those words and yet the expression became associated with him instantly and came to symbolise his premiership in popular memory, an early example of fake news.

On Monday 22 January 1979, the unions called for a Day of Action in pursuit of a minimum wage of £60 per week. Around 1.5 million people walked out in the largest industrial action since the General Strike of 1926. Over the following two weeks the unions launched a programme of continuous action: talks to resolve the rail dispute broke up; snow fell on untreated roads in freezing temperatures; rubbish piled up on the street because dustmen were on strike; public services were unable to cope; 999 calls went unanswered; many hospitals only accepted emergencies due to picketing by porters and cleaning staff; the dead lay unburied in hospital morgues; and dustmen, hospital porters, ambulance drivers, caretakers, canteen staff, maintenance men and bus drivers followed the road hauliers out on strike. Hundreds of schools closed for weeks for want of a caretaker; and Liverpool gravediggers refused to bury the dead, with the result that 200 corpses had to be embalmed and stored in a disused factory. These unburied bodies became the nadir of irresponsible trade unionism. During January and February 1979 almost 30 million working days were lost. Bridgend was paralysed by snow and strikes and many parents – unable to travel to work – simply enjoyed playing with their children in the snow. Teachers' unions demanded a 36 per cent pay increase, and civil servants a mere 26 per cent.[23] Other union leaders were shocked by the tactics of Alan Fisher and the NUPE union, especially when hospitals were picketed. The British state had never seemed so irrelevant[24] and yet Susan managed somehow to cook a regular flow of delicious meals for the family.

The Winter of Discontent decimated support for the unions amongst the public; and pollster Bob Worcester reported in March 1979 that 94 per cent of trade unionists supported Mrs Thatcher's proposal to have compulsory ballots before strike action.[25] In 1979 the number of working days lost due to industrial action was 29.4 million – the highest on record. The Winter of Discontent was nothing to do with socialism and everything to do with greed and lack of concern for the sick, weak and vulnerable. Ironically, by the beginning of May 1979, when the public was asked by Gallup who would make the best Prime Minister, Callaghan – avuncular, likeable and shrewd – was 19 per cent ahead of Thatcher and even four out of ten Conservatives thought he would be the better PM. The militant and selfish behaviour of the unions cost Labour the election and it was a symptom of Britain's lack of competitiveness, low productivity and lamentable industrial relations. Callaghan was a much more effective and honest Prime Minister than Wilson; most tellingly, Callaghan was also more highly regarded by his political opponents than Wilson.

Mrs. Thatcher, who was not interested in books, ideas or the arts, was a remarkably divisive person: she could be strident, jingoistic, humourless, blinkered and annoying; but was also courageous, pro the EU and more pragmatic than those on the left realised. President Mitterrand famously said that she had the eyes of Caligula and the mouth of Marilyn Monroe. Despite this, one-third of trade unionists voted for her in 1979. Her priorities were monetarist policies to cut inflation by controlling the money supply, to reduce government spending and the size of the public sector, to curb the power of unions and free up the labour market. In Geoffrey Howe's first budget in 1979, he cut the top rate of income tax from 83 to 60 per cent and the standard rate from 33 to 30 percent . Interest rates, however, were raised from 12 to 17 per cent in six months to curb a spending boom fuelled by the tax cuts. The Conservatives actually increased the tax burden but redistributed it by cutting taxes for the wealthy and raising VAT from 8 to 15 per cent. Public spending, which Healey had reduced to 44.8 per cent of GDP, actually rose under Thatcher to 48.5 per cent .

The 1980s witnessed major changes on Britain's high streets. Supermarkets evolved into superstores, cinemas became multiplexes and building societies transformed into banks. Out–of –town shopping centres grew rapidly in the 1980s, a process that accelerated the decline of the high street. In 1982, Tim Waterstone invested his £6,000 redundancy payment from W H Smith and established his first bookshop in London. The 100th shop was opened in

Reading in 1991 and, by 1992, it had become the largest bookseller in Europe. At the time of writing in 2021, Waterstones operates 283 shops across the country. Other shopping innovations – such as video rental stores – sprouted on all high streets in the 1980s, but the development of widespread streaming services, such as Netflix, led to mass closure and few video rental shops have survived.

Britain was in recession by the summer of 1980 with inflation at 22 per cent, mortgages 15 per cent and unemployment subsequently increased to 3.2 million by 1982. The country was in sharp relative decline and sterling lost a third of its value in 1981. Britain endured a period of economic and social crisis that exceeded anything in the post-war era. Thatcher's new government at the end of its first year delivered higher unemployment, race riots in the cities, higher inflation, higher public spending, another sterling crisis and a large transfer of wealth to the highest earners. The UK lost one-quarter of its manufacturing capacity during Mrs Thatcher's first term, while the government operated no incomes policy, no pay norms and no deals; unions and management were to reach pay deals without government interference. Opposition to Thatcherism was overwhelming both in artistic circles and on university campuses.

* * *

Music may move or energise or induce calm; it may make one laugh or cry or ponder; or it may simply induce wonder. As Clemency Burton–Hill has so beautifully expressed, the greatest musical compositions are 'engines of empathy, they allow us to travel without moving into other lives, other ages, other souls.'[26] My passion for classical music and its capacity to express what it means to be human gradually seeped into my consciousness over a number of years. However, one specific event in 1979 was to have a major impact. I was invited by the EEC Directorate General for Regional Policy to conduct a research project on the Mobilisation of Indigenous Potential. While on a visit to Brussels to discuss this research in April 1979, I was transfixed by a piece of choral music being played in a restaurant; I obtained the details and purchased a recording of *Spem in Alium*, a 40 – part motet by Thomas Tallis. Listening spellbound to *Spem in Alium* was like entering an exotic garden laden with fruits that I had never tasted before; it opened up the glorious world of polyphonic choral music from the sixteenth century that I had not properly explored. My view of Tallis's genius has simply deepened over time. Somehow, despite remaining a devout Catholic all his life, Tallis had the ability to create masterpieces in whatever was the currency of the day, and these styles changed frequently in his lifetime. First, it was the traditional Latin Catholic music of Henry VIII's reign; then it was the severe chordal style of Edward VI's reign whereby church services had to be sung in English and must give 'to each syllable a plain and distinct note;'[27] then it was back to Latin and Catholic composition again under Queen Mary; and finally, it was the compromise style of Elizabeth whom he served for 26 years and who left him unhindered to produce some of his greatest music. *Spem in Alium,* composed circa 1570 for eight choirs of five voices each, is so brilliant that it seems scarcely feasible that one mind could create it without a computer as individual voice lines act freely within the elegant harmonic framework. Individual voices sing and are silent in turns, sometimes alone, sometimes in choirs, sometimes calling and answering, sometimes all together. To write for 40 voices which do not repeat themselves in consecutive motion and not to lose control of the whole colossal edifice is a monumental achievement. For a modern choir *Spem* remains the ultimate severe technical challenge to bring off. By contrast, during the reign of Edward VI, Tallis wrote some of the greatest Anglican music ever composed, of which *If ye love me* is a supreme example of a four- part Anglican motet.

The discovery of *Spem in Alium* unlocked the treasure trove of great polyphonic music from continental Europe. During the course of the Counter Reformation at the closing sessions of the Council of Trent in 1562- 63, concern was raised about the intelligibility of polyphonic music and whether it obscured the words of the mass and ought to be banned outright. This was the impetus behind the attempt by Giovanni Pierluigi da Palestrina to prove that a polyphonic composition could set text in such a way that the words could be understood and the music still be complex and beautiful. His *Missa Papae Marcelli* was performed before the Council and met with such acclaim that polyphony was allowed to remain. Another great Renaissance composer whom I treasure is Tomas Luis de Victoria, but someone to whom I constantly return is Claudio Monteverdi, who straddles the Renaissance and Baroque. He wrote one of the earliest operas, *L'Orfeo* in 1607 and numerous madrigals, but for me his first venture into religious music – *Vespero della Beata Vergine, 1610* – a setting of the evening vespers on Marian feasts, is a truly great original composition. Composed while working for the Duke of

Mantua, the vespers, according to Sir John Eliot Gardiner, 'is the richest and most substantial single work of church music prior to Bach's Passions.' This work is heroic in its scale and goes far beyond any other sacred music of the day; it forms a continuous liturgical sequence and an artistic whole, all the more remarkable for its diversity.

Now that I am 81, I have strong preferences in classical music that have evolved over many years. I realise that my list is eclectic and is also influenced significantly by the music we have sung for over 20 years in the Heriot-Watt University choir, the repertoire for which was chosen by our wonderful, charismatic musician-in-residence, Steve King. Since coming under Steve's influence, I have realised that the human voice is so expressive and flexible, especially voices intertwining in duets, trios, quartets and choirs. Choral singing in harmony transports me into a different world. To be in a choir striving to achieve the correct key and tempo demands deep concentration. As Bragg has observed, 'the music and the voices weave around your brain transforming it, and you become part of this... community of sound.'[28] Steve King introduced the choir to many inspirational choral pieces, including *Locus Iste*, a beautiful motet by Bruckner; a glorious setting of the nativity – *O Magnum Mysterium* – by Morton Lauridsen, Palestrina's *Sicut Cervus*, *Angelus Domini* by Franz Biebl and Victoria's *Ave Maria*, amongst many others. The music of J S Bach features most prominently for me because he is the most important figure in not just classical but all music. He wrote over 3,000 pieces while holding down several jobs, not to mention a couple of wives and twenty children. The essence of what makes Bach the greatest is, I think, how he combines technical precision with brilliant counterpoint and profound emotion. My separate list for Bach includes the cantatas, the six cello suites, the Goldberg Variations, the Brandenburg concertos, the B Minor Mass, the cantatas, Concerto for two violins in D minor, the Four Orchestral Suites, The Christmas Oratorio, the Preludes and Fugues from the Well-tempered Clavier Book 1, the Magnificat, and the St John and Matthew Passions.

Other music that resonates with me whenever I hear it includes, *inter alia*:

>   the operas of Mozart and Verdi ;
>   all Beethoven's symphonies (the greatest in the canon) and piano concertos;
>   Biebl's *Ave Maria*

> Brahms' symphonies;

> Chopin's nocturnes and piano concertos;

> Handel's oratorios, especially Messiah, operas, and Concerto grossi (Opus 6);

> Faure's Requiem;

> Mozart's piano concertos, symphony no. 41, and Solemn Vespers; Mozart's Clarinet Concerto in A Played by Jack Brymer, whom I saw play it at the Orangery in Margam Country Park;

> Tchaikovsky's symphonies 4, 5 and 6;

> Rachmaninov's Vespers;

> Schubert's Impromptus played by the legendary Alfred Brendel;

> Richard Strauss *Der Rosenkavalier* and the *Four Last Songs* sung by Jesse Norman, evoking a mood of serene acceptance of death, their melodic lines soaring upwards as a valedictory musical statement;[29]

> Debussy's *Suite Bergamasque* and *Deux Arabesques*, representing musical innovation with novel harmonies and melodies;

> Allegri's *Miserere*, with one group singing a simple Miserere chant as another weaves theirs around it;

> Part's *Spiegel im Spiegel* in which he adopted a minimalist and meditative direction and a more spiritual 'tittinabular' style to create a haunting reverie in F Major and 6/4 time;

> Berlioz's *Symphonie Fantastique*;

> Liszt's *Les Jeux d'eau a la Villa d'Este* from *Annes de Pelerinage*

> Gershwin's *Rhapsody in Blue*, a piece that combines classical music and jazz, a composition so inventive from its unique opening clarinet glissando that it defines the jazz age.

One wonderful attribute of classical music is that one is on a permanent path of discovery throughout life. For example, in December 2020, I heard for the first time a glorious Christmas motet on Radio 3 – *Nesciens Mater* – by Jean Mouton (1459–1522), a French priest and Renaissance composer, which is characterised by beautiful continuous vocal lines – flowing like a silk garment – with melodic imitation. In this technical masterpiece, one half of the choir sings the same music as the other but a fifth higher and two bars later, a tour de force of Renaissance polyphony.

I have been fortunate to see many great conductors perform at the Edinburgh Festival, including, *inter alia*, Bernard Haitink, Claudio Abbado and the Berlin Philharmonic and Charles Mackerras. However, the greatest single conducting performance I have ever witnessed was by Gunter Wand and the NDR Symphony orchestra playing Brukner's 8th symphony. It was in 2000 at the Edinburgh Festival and Wand was then 88 years of age and required two members of staff to help him on to the stage. The performance was magisterial with a powerful sense of purpose: he knew where he wished each movement to go and he guided it unhurriedly and monumentally with perfect tempo and controlled momentum that generated both intensity and power. The sheer structural grandeur of the music and the beautifully paced contrasts of epic struggle with interludes of simplicity, were utterly thrilling.

Among great singers, I have always adored Maria Callas who had a huge, penetrating, voice, a dramatic soprano with a dark top that was sublime yet imperfect. She could express the pain and suffering of the character she played like no other soprano. I found that once I had heard Callas sing a part, it was difficult to enjoy any other artist – no matter how great – afterwards, because as Sir Rudolph Bing opined 'she imbued every part she sang with such incredible personality and life.' Turning to tenors, ever since I was a teenager and first heard his recordings on the radio I have always been of the opinion that the Swede Jussi Bjorling has the greatest voice of all tenors: the effortless and flawless vocal technique, the beauty of tone, the thrilling upper register, and wonderful interpretive skills are unique. He possessed an unusually beautiful voice; his timbre displayed clarity and warmth; his sound was flexible, smooth and even throughout the whole range; and his upper register was glowing and resonant. He was the ultimate embodiment of Italian *bel canto* singing who never strayed into affectation or melodrama. Luciano Pavarotti in an interview in 1988 stated that 'I would more than anything else wish the people compared me with Jussi Bjorling.'

Classical music is clearly a minority taste and so BBC Radio 3 is one of the great justifications for public service broadcasting as it has an audience of around 2 million. I find Classic FM – the alternative to Radio 3 – quite annoying. Selecting the more 'tuneful' movement from symphonies or concertos – usually the slow ones – and presenting them in the banal style of a disc jockey is demeaning to great music. Examples of this presentational style include: 'This was a big hit for Mozart in 1786,' or describing Johann Pachalbel as a 'one-hit wonder' with his Canon and Gigue in D Minor. It is actually a wonderful composition – a complex conversation between three violins, a cello and eight bars of music repeated 28 times. I dislike Classic FM for its conservative safety and unwillingness to challenge the mind of the listener. The popular passages of the same list of compositions are repeated *ad nauseam*, especially on their flagship programme – The Hall of Fame Hour – based upon listeners' votes for their favourite three pieces of classical music each year. It is presented like Top of The Pops – 'And next it's *The Lark Ascending* at number 2, having moved up four places since last year.' I feel annoyed when they play an abridged version of a Beethoven or Mozart movement, cutting it short to squeeze in an advert for private health insurance. Presenters are upbeat and cheerful as they compere Relaxing Classics at Seven, which is presented as a form of massage for the weary mind. As I write this in December, 2020, I visited the Classic FM website and was invited to click on an option for 'Ten relaxing pieces of Christmas music to keep you warm, sink into our soothing Christmas soundworld.' Thank goodness for Radio 3 where the presenters are experts who are deeply knowledgeable about the music and from whom one is continuously learning.

* * *

In the summer of 1979 we travelled to Brittany and Normandy and rented tents from Canvas Holidays on two sites. The first was at Lannion in north Brittany and for the second week we moved to a camp site in the Chateau de Martragny in Normandy. Canvas Holiday tents were luxurious by the standards I had been accustomed to in the sea scouts. Bridget, age 4, managed to swim the width of the swimming pool for the first time. We visited the Bayeux tapestry and Bayeux cathedral; and we also explored the sites of the D day landings on Gold beach, the Mulberry harbour at Arromanches and the Omaha beach to the west. Later we visited the Pointe de Hoc, a promontory with a 100 foot sheer cliff overlooking the sea, being the highest point between the American landings at Utah beach to the west and Omaha beach to the east. The battery at the top was fortified by six guns and an infantry division. Three companies of the US Army Ranger Assault Group were landed at the foot of the cliff and fought their way up under sustained fire using ropes, ladders and grapples. At the end of the mission, the original landing force of 225 men was reduced by 60 per cent to around 90 rangers. Two days later we were returning from France by boat and eating in the cafeteria when we were joined by an elderly

American couple. Amazingly, he was a decorated veteran Ranger making his first trip back to visit Pointe de Hoc since he had scaled it under fire on D day some 35 years earlier; this was a humbling experience.

The period living in Bridgend coincided with the peak of my interest in playing golf. I became a member of Southerndown golf club which was located on a Jurassic limestone heathland plateau, rising over 200 feet above sea level. The course commanded splendid views west into the Bristol Channel and benefitted from a well-drained turf and an ecology characterised by typical heathland vegetation of gorse, bracken and heather. Most of the holes faced either east or west and consequently the course was challenging to play in a strong south-westerly gale, of which there were many. Looking out across the Bristol Channel the sky often reached down and touched the sea. The sun was usually a rumour, while to the north rain clouds frequently enveloped the South Wales valleys. I played regularly with Grahame Hodgson – a former Welsh rugby international full-back – Paul Main and Ron Stockford. We were evenly matched as all of us played off 5 or 6 handicap, but our strengths and weaknesses varied. Both Grahame and Ron were longer than me off the tee, Paul was very consistent, while my (limited) skills were confined to accuracy with fairway woods and pitching. All of them were superior to me at putting. We competed with each other but always in a very good spirit; and I managed to win a number of club competitions. In September 1976 – playing in a gale force wind – Paul Main and I tied for the Dunraven Bowl and we could not be separated on the back nine, last six or last three holes. I noticed that whenever I won or did well in competitions it was usually on a windy day and I reckon that my experience of playing at Carrickmines in the foothills of the Dublin mountains and at Royal Portrush on the Antrim coast helped as it was absolutely necessary to be able to manoeuvre the ball in stormy conditions. There are few greater pleasures in life than on the rare occasions when I managed to strike a three wood off the fairway with all my power, all my control, all my calculation and the ball did exactly as I wanted by flying over a series of bunkers to find the heart of a green 210 yards away and to roll up just 10 feet from the hole. Then I usually missed the putt. I have fond memories of the camaraderie and friendship at Southerndown golf club. Recently I spoke with Ron Stockford – now 88 years of age – and he generously reminded me of how smoothly I used to strike a 4 wood 200 yards into the greens to which I replied that it was only because my two iron play was so hopeless.

My father, who had been widowed for six years since my mother died in 1974, led a slightly restless existence following her death. In 1974 he moved to Surrey to rent a flat next door to my twin sister Sheila's family in Surrey, but returned to Ireland within a year to a flat near Killiney. Later, in 1979, he moved to a flat near the sea in Monkstown where he lived for some six months before he died of a heart attack in March 1980 at the age of 68. He had endured angina and heart trouble for more than a decade and he was quite lonely when he died as none of his four children lived in Dublin at the time.

The 1980s seemed so different from the carefree 1960s that had been the land of the Beatles, Swinging London, the Mini and Mary Quant's mini-skirt. The Beatles had broken up a decade ago, mini-skirts had fallen out of fashion, the Mini had been succeeded by the (dull) Austin Metro and Swinging London had long since disappeared. Idealism had faded and life seemed harder. For my daughters, the greatest challenge at the time was trying to solve the Rubik's cube. The BBC broadcast an adaptation of Malcolm Bradbury's brilliant novel, *The History Man*, in 1981 with Anthony Sher in the role of the left-wing self-regarding Marxist sociology lecturer, Howard Kirk, a composite of various academics Bradbury had known. Bradbury's black comedic satire was published in 1975 and Bradbury recognised that by 1981 the Kirk figure had changed. 'They probably voted for Mrs Thatcher in the last election and now, instead of Left-wing politics, they are into jogging and tap dancing. My students are much more motivated about their work and are working twice as hard.'[30] This mirrors my experience at Cardiff University at the same period, although Bradbury may have exaggerated somewhat for effect. Not all students were small 'c' conservatives and the tone of student debate was still left-leaning, from boycotting South African goods to participating in CND marches to Aldermaston. What was unarguable was that Mrs Thatcher inspired more opprobrium across the universities of the land than any previous prime minister.

Michael Foot, a passionate orator and fine writer, became a reluctant leader of the Labour party in 1981. The intellectual Foot was the perfect person to deliver a lecture on his great literary hero Jonathan Swift (on whom he had written a biography) but he did not have the attributes necessary to lead a major political party and didn't 'look' like a potential prime minister. The Conservative government announced the deployment of US Cruise missiles at RAF Molesworth and the US air base at Greenham Common in June 1980 and, boosted by Foot's election to the Labour leadership, CND staged huge rallies at Greenham Common. Unilateralism broke free of beards, duffel coats and sandals and nuclear disarmament had become fashionable and cool.[31] It was a movement dominated by the middle classes, but Mrs Thatcher always suspected that the peace movement, although heavily influenced by Quakers, was a front for the Kremlin.[32] The CND, however, never commanded the support of the majority in the UK for scrapping the deterrent.

* * *

In preparation for our summer holiday in 1980, we purchased a large family tent and a trailer and travelled from Portsmouth to Le Havre heading for the Dordogne. Our visit coincided with a heatwave and temperatures hovered in the mid-30s, which was much too hot for Susan. Hence, we moved north and relocated to a camp site near Chateaurault where we spent the remainder of the holiday. A couple of weeks later our eight year old second daughter, Margaret, became ill with a severe headache. A few days later, her hands started to shake involuntarily and she was unable to pick up a pencil. Messages from her brain were no longer able to direct normal movements and a tremor had developed in her leg, arms and head. The GP, Dr. Evans, visited and quickly called in a genial consultant physician, Dr Trevor Jones, who realised the seriousness of her condition and arranged for her to see Dr Wallace, paediatric neurologist at the University Hospital of Wales, Cardiff. It was with a deepening sense of worry that we entered Dr Wallace's consulting room and she began to take a case history, to conduct blood tests and to carry out a lumbar puncture and a CAT-scan. Margaret remained in the hospital for week with a nurse on duty by her bed 24 hours a day.

The illness was diagnosed as acute cerebellar encephalitis, which attacks the areas of the brain that are fundamental to timing and precision of movement. The illness is associated with headaches, impaired coordination in arms and legs; frequent stumbling and an unsteady gait; uncontrolled eye movements; problems with eating and performing fine motor tasks; and poor balance and reflexes. After around a week, Margaret was discharged home, but it was soon clear that her condition was continuing to deteriorate and to exhibit ever more severe symptoms. This is not what Dr Wallace told us to expect and on a Friday afternoon in September 1980 we drove Margie back to the hospital in Cardiff. Susan and I could sense that Dr Wallace was both surprised at the worsening in Margie's condition and seemed uncertain about what to do.

Finally, she left us for a few minutes and returned to request that we bring Margaret back on the following morning – a Saturday – when Dr Wells, the senior neurologist, would come in specially to see her. As we reached the car park, I realised that I had left my jacket in her office so doubled back to collect it. When I was alone with Dr Wallace for a few moments I asked her if she was deeply concerned about Margaret's deterioration. She replied that she was gravely ill and she was particularly worried that the ataxia would impair the swallowing function. I hurried back to the car, but did not tell Susan about my conversation. The following morning I carried Margie to the car, lay her down – limp as a rag doll – on to the back seat and drove to the hospital, leaving Susan to care for Catherine and Bridget.

Having been introduced to Dr Wells, I waited alone for almost an hour while he carried out an examination. When he and Dr Wallace reappeared, Dr Wells took complete control and I was immediately impressed with his knowledge and professionalism. For the first time I felt that I was talking to an expert on acute cerebellar encephalitis. He told me that Margie's symptoms would continue to worsen before stabilising and slowly starting to recover over a period of many months. There was an air of authority about him and I felt confident that the path of the illness would unfold as he stated. Subsequent events proved that he was totally correct. Margaret remained in hospital for several weeks and her symptoms did deteriorate initially – as he had predicted – and then gradually stabilised.

On her return home Margaret embarked on a long period of recovery and rehabilitation. When she arrived home she had lost the ability to walk, to run, to hop and skip, to ride her bike, to swim, to feed herself, to catch a ball, to climb the stairs, to write and to draw. She spent months being wheeled in an outsize buggy. There were endless sessions at the Physiotherapy Outpatients department at Bridgend hospital. The treatment she received from the staff and patients there are a major reason why she eventually made a good recovery. There were also exercises and stretching that had to be practised regularly at home to counteract muscle wastage. I supervised these exercise sessions twice daily; I recall wrapping a glass bottle (Hungarian Bull's Blood) in a blanket, placing it under her knees and cajoling her to lift her ankles again and again. I took her to the Blind School swimming pool in Bridgend in the evenings in order to relearn how to climb up a step; I encouraged her, again and again, to lift her trembling foot on to the submerged step in the pool as the water offered support for the wasted muscles of her limbs. Later she tackled the more demanding task of lifting her foot over the shallow step at the back door. What I sought to achieve – not always successfully – was to transmit a determination to succeed to this emaciated, trembling, weak but so courageous child of eight. I made graphs of her progress and her many attempts to recover the ability to write. The medical staff were pessimistic about her prospects of walking properly, swimming, or holding a pencil. Dr Wallace argued that Margaret would need to attend a special school, which Susan and I were utterly determined to avoid and, largely due to the physiotherapy treatment, she returned to her primary school within a year. The period of her illness was undoubtedly the most stressful and challenging experience of my life.

Margaret was home-schooled for a year and spent hours on her own during which time she read voraciously. Sometimes I wonder whether this traumatic experience for her and the long aftermath recovering at home influenced her personality since she became a quirky little girl. One weekend I had invited a Chinese PhD student of mine to the house for the day. On the Monday following Susan was collecting Margie from the playground when her teacher, Mrs Jones, told Susan that Margie had raised her hand in class and asked Mrs Jones – 'Have you ever been kissed by a Chinaman?' A few weeks later Canon Richards, the rector of the local Anglican church – which none of us ever attended – called at supper time and we spent an hour listening to his boring platitudes. When he was eventually leaving the house, Margie looked up at the tall, stooped, bald figure and asked – 'Why have you come?' In the summer we made a special trip to Bristol zoo and Margie spent a long time staring through a thick glass partition at a chimpanzee before asking – 'Daddy is that monkey thinking?' Finally, one day when digging the vegetable plot Margaret asked me 'Daddy what's behind the sky?'

In 1981 we again holidayed in France, renting a gite at Erdevan in the south of Brittany near to the Quiberon peninsula. Each summer I prepared a tape with an appropriate selection of music for each of the three girls. By the 1980s they had begun to express their preferences more firmly. I realised that I was destined to listen to the tape for hours on end as we travelled to our holiday destination so, if possible, I tried to include their choices that were least likely to become irksome. In this way I was introduced to two performers whom I really enjoyed, Tracy Chapman and, above all, Mark Knofler and Dire Straits. Chapman, a folk singer-songwriter, released a memorable album including the classic songs 'Fast Car' and 'Talking 'bout a Revolution.' Mark

Knofler formed Dire Straits in 1977 when he was teaching at an art college. The group's first hit in 1978 – 'Sultans of Swing' - incorporating extraordinary guitar riffs – was composed by Knofler. From 1980 he wrote and recorded longer songs with more complex arrangements, including the hits 'Romeo and Juliet' (1981) and 'Money for Nothing' (1985). Knofler drew from various influences, including country, folk, blues, rock and jazz. The album *'Brothers in Arms'* was released in 1985, entered the UK album chart at number 1, spent 228 weeks in the chart and sold 4.3 million copies. It became the biggest-selling album in the UK in the 1980s; and was also a number 1 album in the USA selling 9 million copies there alone, and a total of 30 million worldwide. The album spawned several chart singles, including 'Money for Nothing,' 'So Far Away,' 'Brothers in Arms,' and 'Walk of Life.' Knofler is a wonderful lyrical guitarist and his brilliant riffs contrast with the economy of his songs. According to *Classic Rock* in 2018, Knofler was 'peerless as a craftsman and virtuoso, able to plug into rock's classic lineage and bend it to sometimes wild forms.' His songs were 'taut mini-dramas of dark depths and dazzling melodic and lyrical flourishes.'

During the French holiday of 1981, I read Joyce's modernist masterpiece, *Ulysses,* which remains the most stimulating and unique book I have tackled. From this time on, I began to read more widely for pure pleasure. Favoured authors included James Joyce, John McGahern, Philip Roth, John Updike, Roddy Doyle, Colm Toibin, Annie Proulx, Tim Winton, Sebastian Barry, David Lodge, Malcolm Bradbury, Molly Keane, William Boyd, Kate Grenville, Jonathon Coe, Ian McEwan, Muriel Spark, William Trevor and my daughter, Maggie O'Farrell. There is no hierarchy implied here, although one unquestionably exists. There is also the occasional single novel that lingers in the mind forever. One such is *Good Behaviour* by Molly Keane, a black social comedy about the Anglo-Irish in the 1930s, that is preoccupied with what is unsaid, a society in which feelings are expressed obliquely and grief ignored; a masterpiece that is witty, sardonic, but also lethal and understated as it tolls the death knell for Anglo-Irish society. Another classic is *Stoner* by John Williams, a beautiful, incredibly moving, sad book executed in faultless prose in which Williams elevates one academic's story into something universal.

Obviously being Irish one has a real connection and appreciation of the greatness of W B Yeats and Seamus Heaney. Yeats is the most protean poet since Shakespeare: a poet who ceaselessly reinvented himself and his art amid the turbulence of the world.[33] Many are deeply moved by the wonderful lyricism and imagery of Yeats' love poems inspired by his unrequited love for Maud Gonne; his greatness as a lyric poet is unassailable. As Edna Longley has argued: 'no modern poet has done more than Yeats to reinvent the English lyric.'[34] There is so much more to him than that. He was immersed in the relationship between politics and the individual at a deeper level; his later poems address this relationship with remarkable insight.[35]

> And what if excess of love
> Bewildered them till they died?
> I write it out in verse –
> MacDonagh and McBride
> Connolly and Pearse
> Now and in time to be,
> Wherever green is worn,
> Are changed, changed utterly:
> A terrible beauty is born.

The imperishable genius of Yeats – who won the Nobel Prize for literature in 1923 – lies predominantly in his later poems. After Irish independence, Yeats played a key role in the Irish Senate between 1922 and 1928 by fighting censorship and the domineering Catholic cultural ideology that marginalised southern Protestants. Yeats' poetry plumbs depths that do not yield to science or philosophy. Virginia Wolf met him when he was 65 years old: 'wherever one cut him, with a little question, he poured, spurted fountains of ideas. And I was impressed by his directness, his terseness. No fluff and dreaminess.'[36] Thom Gunn recalls that the 1950 reprint of Yeats' *Collected Poems* ended the idea that 'Eliot was *the* modern poet....suddenly here was someone with a lot more vigour, a bigger range;' while Ezra Pound regarded Yeats as the 'only poet worthy of serious study.'[37]

Seamus Heaney, from Mossbawn in County Derry, has been described by John Sutherland as 'the greatest poet of our age.'[38] Heaney was awarded the Nobel Prize for Literature in 1995 for what the Nobel Committee described as 'works of lyrical beauty and ethical depth, which exalt everyday miracles and the living past as Heaney drew much inspiration from the bogland, small fields and the eel fishermen of Lough Neagh surrounding his father's farm.' Heaney was noted for the extraordinary depth and warmth of his personality and, as Colm Toibin wrote: 'in a time of burnings and bombings Heaney used poetry to offer an alternative world.'[39] Andrew Motion, a former British poet laureate, called him 'a great poet, a wonderful writer about poetry, a person of truly exceptional grace and intelligence.'[40] Like Yeats, Heaney's poetry has also inspired politicians, including Bill Clinton and Joe Biden.

I also began to read autobiographies and memoirs, several of which have not only impressed me, but also altered my approach to life in distinct ways. Denis Healey's – *The Time of my Life* - is the finest autobiography written by a British politician in the 20th century: a serious, intellectual reflection on British politics, leavened both by his humour and knowledge of music, painting and literature deployed throughout to illuminate the politics, with a heavy emphasis on W B Yeats. Clive James, Australia's renaissance man, published several volumes of memoir, of which the first, *Unreliable Memoirs*, is the finest. This hilarious volume covers his childhood in Australia and is overflowing with life and original humour. The book is charmingly written, irreverent and insightful as it addresses family, love, life choices and self-acceptance with perfect comic timing. As James himself admits 'nothing I have said is factual except the bits that sound like fiction.' The former Labour cabinet minister Alan Johnson's memoir, *This Boy,* is a wonderful account by a self-effacing politician of growing up in poverty in the 1950s. Johnson lived in condemned housing – declared unfit for human habitation – a cramped flat with no central heating, no electricity and no running water. Without a hint of self-pity, Johnson wrote a beautifully observed tribute to his 16 – year -old sister, Linda, who embraced the adult's burden of responsibility and fought to keep the family together when she was still only a child. *This Boy* is the deeply moving testimony of a humble man achieving great success against all odds. The great John McGahern published *Memoir* in 2005 just one year before he died. This spell-binding, profoundly beautiful book is a story of cruelty, bereavement (his mother died) and childhood torment at the hands of his father during childhood and adolescence in Leitrim. In mesmerising, luminous prose McGahern outlines a tale of grace in the face of the abuse of power that is rooted in the thin soil of Leitrim.

* * *

In the mid-seventies we were so constrained for money that I undertook on one occasion only to paint the outside of the house, including all the windows, doors and gutters. This was a painstaking job that took a couple of months effort after work, much of it perched up a ladder. By 1981 we could afford to hire a painter and we commissioned a local painter, Len, to do the job. Len was a lovely man, but he had a rather old fashioned view of the gender division of authority. On his first day on the job, Susan popped out to give him a coffee and she asked him to paint the window sills a particular shade. Len responded by telling Susan to 'Go in and mind the house and I shall discuss it with Patrick when he returns from the university.' When I arrived home I asked Susan what shade of colour she wanted and then proceeded to tell Len. I also told him that Susan knew far more about the practicalities of house decoration than me, but he was unbending and said he would only ever take his instructions from me. Hence, every day for the following two weeks I would arrive home, go through the convoluted ritual of asking Susan what instructions she had for Len, and then would proceed to inform him.

* * *

The increasingly leftward orientation of the Labour Party prompted four prominent politicians – Roy Jenkins, Shirley Williams, David Owen and Bill Rodgers – to found the Social Democratic Party (SDP) on 25 January 1981 by issuing the Limehouse Declaration. The policy statement was pro the mixed economy, the welfare state, the EU, and the Atlantic alliance. As Sandbrook opined, the SDP was 'less a party than a dinner party, a social club for people who had a new hatchback in the drive, a home computer in the sitting room and a prep-school prospectus on the kitchen table,' while Peter York called them 'Volvo people' who helped 'with the washing up;' the SDP always seemed more comfortable as 'the voice of the wine bar than the party of the chip shop.'[41] At the Liberal conference in the autumn of 1981 the delegates endorsed an alliance with the SDP. In the 1983 election, the Tories with 42.4 per cent of the vote won 397 seats, Labour with 8.5 million votes won 209 seats and the Liberal-SDP Alliance won 7.8 million votes but only returned 23 MPs. As always in Britain, the lack of a fair voting system was a major factor undermining the attempt to build major lasting success for a third party.

The despair induced by mass unemployment in the early 1980s spawned a dramatic response from Alan Bleasdale when his creation – *Boys from the Blackstuff* – was featured on BBC2 in the autumn of 1982. This was a devastating critique of Thatcherism and is remembered above all for the anti-hero, Yosser Hughes – driven by violence, greed and hatred (played by Bernard Hill) – with a pronounced Scouse accent and fixed stare menacingly repeating 'Gizza job, go on, gizzit, gizza go, go on, I could do that.' There was, however, one positive item of cultural progress in the autumn of 1982 when Moira Stuart, she of the mellifluous voice, became the first black woman to read the BBC news. In the autumn of 1981, in stark contrast to *Boys from the Blackstuff*, Granada broadcast an adaptation of Evelyn Waugh's 1945 novel, *Brideshead Revisited* starring Jeremy Irons as Charles Ryder, Anthony Andrews as the dissolute and aristocratic Sebastian Flyte and other theatrical luminaries, Claire Bloom, Laurence Olivier and John Gielgud. Anthony Burgess proclaimed it to be not merely the 'best piece of television ever made' but 'even better that the book.'[42] I do not agree with the latter; to me it's Waugh's finest novel. The TV adaptation is very faithful to the book and looks beautiful conjuring up as it does a lost world of wealth and privilege. The acting, notably by Irons, Gielgud and Nickolas Grace was outstanding, the photography is lush and the score by Geoffrey Burgon is both tasteful and haunting. However, viewing it again in 2020, I found that I was bored by the languid pace of the production and its surfeit of champagne lunches with plovers' eggs and the realisation that little seems to have changed regarding the entitlement of the Oxbridge elite.

Cold weather became established over the UK in January 1982 with bitterly cold easterly winds which blew in dry, powdery snow. It snowed continuously for 36 hours and the strong wind caused the powdery snow to form huge drifts up to six metres high, the heaviest snowfall I have ever experienced. The M4 motorway in South Wales was impassable and many other roads were blocked. An eerie stillness settled over Merthyr Mawr Road as the snow fell on the trees soundlessly and the trees twinkled under the street lights. The holly trees in our front garden had donned a white garment and great slabs of snow lay on the roofs. The schools were closed for two weeks, long queues formed for bread and milk and the road was impassable for several days. We built an igloo on the back patio using cloches as a framework and every time the children scurried into the house they stamped the snow off their feet and shook the flakes off their hair.

The Falkland Islands, with a population of 1,854 are 300 miles off the coast of Argentina and had long been a disputed territory. They were invaded by Argentinian troops in March 1982. Diplomatic efforts were made to try to secure an end to the invasion, but Mrs Thatcher – whose opinion poll ratings were extraordinarily low – adopted a bellicose attitude from the start. The restoration of her political credibility was clearly a factor in the decision to send a huge task force of 10,000 troops half-way around the world to recapture these rocky outcrops. A mood of passionate jingoism gripped the UK and the task force set sail for the South Atlantic on 5th April 1982. War fever gripped the country and the *Sun* newspaper was by far the most bellicose using the notorious headline GOTCHA when the cruiser General Belgrano was sunk with the loss of over 300 lives. It also ran a daily 'Argy-Bargie' joke column and offered £5 and a tin of non-Argentinian corned beef for every entry. Their most outrageous pun, referring to the latest breakdown in diplomatic negotiations, was: 'Stick it up your Junta.' The commander of the task force, Admiral Sandy Woodward, thought that the editor of the *Sun*, Kelvin McKenzie had crossed the line and deplored the 'lunatic nationalistic pride' of the tabloids.[43] *Private Eye* lampooned the *Sun* by printing a mock *Sun* front cover, including the offer 'Kill and Argie and win a Metro.'

In three weeks, Britain had secured victory over an inadequate conscript army. Invited to comment after the Argentinian surrender, Mrs Thatcher replied 'Rejoice! ..Just rejoice at the news and congratulate our forces.' She continued to celebrate the victory by personally taking the salute at the victory parade in London, making an early visit to the Falklands, and constantly referencing it in speeches for years to come. Looking back, to me it seems remarkable that such a jingoistic atmosphere was stirred up in Britain over a few windswept rocky islands near the Antarctic with fewer than 1,900 inhabitants. Given that there are hundreds of uninhabited islands off Scotland, it would have been relatively simple to resettle the tiny population of the Falklands on one of them and they would have enjoyed both the NHS and a warmer climate. Mrs Thatcher did not display a universal distaste for Latin American dictators since she had a lengthy friendship with General Augusto Pinochet, the ruthless ruler of Chile.

In the summer of 1982, we travelled north to Northumberland for two weeks holiday in a rented house near Alnmouth. The house was neither clean nor comfortable; it was almost impossible to evaluate holiday properties at that time by simply looking at drawings in a brochure. The holiday was further compromised by the weather. Although an anticyclone prevailed and the rest of the UK basked in glorious sunshine, we were subjected for ten of the 14 days to a haar or sea fret off the North Sea, which at best embraced the coast in a sea fog with a cold onshore breeze and at worst resulted in fog and thick drizzle all day. Four years later when we moved to live in North Berwick, a beautiful seaside resort on the coast near Edinburgh, we were to experience again what R L Stevenson wrote of Edinburgh in 1879 : 'She is liable to be beaten upon by all the winds that blow, to be drenched with rain, and to be buried in cold sea fogs out of the east.'[44]

The mood of triumphalism over the recapture of the Falklands changed the political climate in favour of Mrs Thatcher and she won a general election with a landslide majority of 144 in June 1983. This resounding electoral mandate enabled Thatcher to pursue her privitization agenda: BT, Jaguar cars, British Gas, the National Bus Company, the British Airports Authority and British Airways were all floated on the stock market, to be followed by Rover Group, British Steel and the electricity industry. By the end of the 1980s there were more shareholders than trade unionists in Britain, many of whom had bought shares.[45] Universities were undervalued by a narrow-minded Thatcher government that was more interested in the skills required for business success than in knowledge for its own sake. In the early 1980s major cuts in real funding were made to university budgets and thousands of jobs were lost. The average cut between 1980/1 and 1986/7 was 12.5 per cent with the most severe one of 46.3 per cent suffered by the University of Salford.[46] To Mrs Thatcher the universities represented a privileged elite that was managerially incompetent, uninterested in wealth creation, and protected by the University Grants Committee. Consequently, universities remained under pressure throughout the 1980s and research programmes were underfunded. Paradoxically a government dedicated to the principle of individualism became obsessed with state control of not only universities but also unions, local authorities and the media.[47]

In March 1984, Thatcher's government – via the National Coal Board (NCB) – announced a programme of pit closures that would result in 20,000 men losing their jobs. Arthur Scargill, the miners' leader, announced a national strike and called on all National Union of Mineworkers (NUM) members to withdraw their labour. At the time the South Wales coalfield employed 21,500 miners and 99.6 percent of them joined the strike, a proportion that had only reduced to 93 per cent by the end of the action a year later. Thus began the most famous dispute in British industrial history that seemed doomed to end in defeat from the outset because Scargill refused to ask the miners through a national ballot, whether or not they wished to strike. This defined the strike as illegal, thus cutting off the NUM from other trade unions, the Labour Party and public opinion outside Wales. The lack of a ballot also meant that miners' families were deprived of benefits and ultimately the strike was doomed. Mrs Thatcher denounced 'the enemy within.' The miners were split and many of them, especially in the Nottingham coalfield, worked through the dispute, despite the attempts to stop them by Scargill's pickets. Violent confrontations between flying pickets and the police characterised the year long strike and the number of working days lost exceeded 26 million, making it the largest since the 1926 general strike.

The miners' strike impacted detrimentally on the education of our three daughters. The boilers at the local Brynteg Comprehensive school were fired by coal from the South Wales coalfield; and Mid Glamorgan Education Authority did not import coal to replace the local supply. Therefore, when the temperature of the classroom dropped below 18 degrees centigrade, the children were sent home, which happened during the winter of 1984-85. Furthermore, the schools made little or no provision for learning at home when the school was closed. There was a period of two weeks in January 1985 when the children were totally confined to home.

The most controversial incident of the year long strike occurred on 30 November 1984 when a taxi driver, David Wilkie, was murdered while driving a miner, David Williams, in his Ford Cortina to Merthyr Vale pit, with two police cars and a motorcyclist outrider escorting him. They followed the same route each day. Two striking miners dropped a 21kg concrete block and a concrete post on to the taxi from a bridge 27 feet over the A465 Heads of the Valley road north of Rhymney. Mr Wilkie, the taxi driver, died at the scene of multiple injuries. Wilkie had two children under thirteen by a previous relationship, and a fiancée with whom he had a two- year- old daughter and who was also pregnant with a baby, born six weeks after his death. The two miners – Dean Hancock and Russell Shankland – were convicted of murder in May 1985 and sentenced to life imprisonment; but a campaign was started to mount an appeal on the grounds that they should have been charged with manslaughter. Many of our Welsh friends in Bridgend, including those on the political right, supported clemency for the two convicted miners. This surprised me and indicated that a sense of community solidarity in a fruitless cause like the miners' strike overwhelmed their rational judgement. The convictions of the two miners were changed to manslaughter and their life sentences reduced to eight- year terms, of which they served only four. In March 1985, the 63 per cent of miners who were still out staged simultaneous marches back to their pits, having endured the greatest defeat the unions had faced for over fifty years. The closure programme that had triggered the strike was now implemented and within a year some thirty-six mines were closed, with huge job losses. The financial costs to the nation were heavy: between three and five billion pounds were spent opposing the strike, in addition to the costs of closures and redundancies that followed.[48] The labour force in the South Wales mines, once 250,000 men, had fallen to fewer than 5,000 by 1989.

After almost 14 years, I decided that it was time to move as the department in Cardiff, although increasingly successful by most key metrics, was not an especially friendly environment with internal divisions and a lack of enlightened leadership. I was never assimilated there and always felt something of an outsider. The mood of the time is the most difficult thing to recall as a chronicler and, although I was very happy living in Bridgend, the department at the university was not a congenial place. Hence, we set a course north to Edinburgh in June 1986. After I was offered a Professorship by Heriot-Watt University, I was invited to see Vice-Chancellor Trotman–Dickenson and he informed me that I was the fifth member of staff in his 18 years as Vice-Chancellor in Cardiff who had managed to obtain a Chair in another university, an 'indicator' that he clearly monitored carefully!

CHAPTER 9

Epilogue

Time changes perspective. As a teenager, one longed for a year to last for eternity, whereas in adulthood I remember how a single academic year seemed to stretch ahead forever. From the 1970s, there were three children to nurture, new friendships being developed, a large garden to be tended, and an evolving research agenda to be tackled. A comfortable rhythm developed. I used to think that when the girls went up to university – two to Cambridge and one to Edinburgh – that there would be no more worries. Life does not work out like that. As long as one is alive and they are still around, you remain a parent and still worry about them. Relationships change and mutate within families, but the network of genes holds us together even in difficult circumstances.

I am fortunate to have all three daughters and their families living nearby in Edinburgh, some 20 miles distant. Our oldest girl, Catherine, and her husband Roddy live with their youngest daughter, Flora, who is a final-year medical student at Edinburgh University, while their eldest daughter, Mary, who graduated from Glasgow University in medicine in 2019, has a flat near to the Meadows in Edinburgh. After we moved to North Berwick in 1986, Catherine helped us to restructure the garden; and subsequently she has developed a beautiful garden in Edinburgh. She and I shared a passion for watching Wimbledon every year, which was lovely for me as I am always alone when I am watching Six Nations rugby internationals, athletics or the Open golf championship. Catherine was also very empathetic and companionable as a teenager and enjoyed adult conversation with Susan and me. Margaret lives on a cobbled road in The Grange, south of the city centre. She and her husband Will have three children – Saul, who is 19, and their daughters – Iris and Juno – aged 13 and 10. Bridget and her husband, Nick, both of whom are vets, also live on the south side of Edinburgh with their two daughters Ella and Rosa, aged 12 and 10. Since Margaret and Bridget's daughters are very close in age, they visit each other to play and enjoy sleepovers. They are good friends, frequently in each other's houses, and often holiday together as families. It is especially rewarding to have grandchildren that range in age from 26 to 10. In normal circumstances we would see them all frequently, but Covid 19 has changed everything during the past two years. My life would be far less rich without children and grandchildren, who keep me in touch with modern trends and appliances.

I don't really worry or ever get depressed. Any anxiety is almost exclusively associated with a computer – related problem or a failure to purchase an item on the internet. Here Bridget or my grandchildren are especially helpful in explaining how mobiles and laptops function and in the affection that they inspire. As I become less able to do things I would like to do – hearing less, seeing less, joints hurting more, friends and siblings dying, it would be easy to become pessimistic about life, making the later years drearier. Declining energy is one of the most tedious aspects of being old. Young people help to combat this and, moreover, nowadays they are more mature and sophisticated than I used to be and relate better to their elders.

My waking hours are marked by considerable daydreaming; and so much of my inner life makes no appearance on the stage of this memoir: disappointment, irritation, boredom, routine, frustration, persistent doubts, political despair and sudden delight. How much time is wasted in thinking of people I would like to disengage from, or admonish, or erase from my life, or with whom I would like to forge a closer friendship? Now there is much less time ahead of me than behind and so it is more valued; I no longer wish to hear Marvell's lines 'At my back I always hear/Time's winged chariot hurrying near.' I am fortunate to have survived malignant melanoma three times. Yet, as I age, I am aware that my walking speed has slowed considerably and that I am inconvenienced by osteo-arthritis in several joints. Fortunately, I was able to learn skiing at Glenshee – tutored by Bridget – after we moved to Scotland in 1986. Bridget is a beautifully balanced skier – whom I never actually saw fall – in contrast to her father who at 50 was very enthusiastic, if a bit too intrepid. We enjoyed five ski holidays together in Austria between 1988 and 1992. Bridget, who is a dedicated vet, has a unique ability to solve all my computer problems over the telephone without seeing my laptop, which remains a total mystery to me.

My short-term memory has deteriorated: I am unable to remember what I did last week, or yesterday, or what I have planned to do tomorrow, yet paradoxically events and people from 60 years ago are more clear in my mind. Forgetting what I am about to do is increasingly common. I often walk downstairs from my study and when I reach the kitchen I am unable to remember why I came down. I return upstairs to my study and then suddenly I recall the purpose of my journey. My normal memory is fine, unless I am distracted by other things. I do not forget appointments, promises, work, answering emails, or making phone calls. I always have a list of jobs for the day on my desk and I tend to achieve them. I can sometimes recall something that I was unaware I had remembered, especially music. Poems and chunks of Shakespeare that I learned at school come back to me; and I can sing many pop songs from the golden era of the 1950s and 1960s, often remembering the name of the girl I was jiving with at the time, although she probably does not remember me.

I do derive much satisfaction out of work, in which I can become totally absorbed. I published my most recent research paper in 2019 when I was 78 and continued supervising doctoral students until I was 79. If I manage to write something during the day, it induces a degree of satisfaction and I feel justified in going for a good walk. The day has a shape and purpose to it, even if I edit out most of what I have written when I read it again in the cold light of the following day! As writing this book has progressed, I realised with increasing conviction that of greater interest than who I was, which is not exceptional, or what I achieved, which is modest, was what I observed and how I influenced others. I have deliberately avoided writing about my academic career during which I published more than 110 research papers in refereed journals, several monographs, four books and many conference presentations, most of which would be of no interest to the general reader. I also served as Pro Vice- Chancellor of two British universities for a period of nine years between 1995 and 2006 during which time I frequently wrote and delivered laureations for honorary graduates and graduation addresses. If I had been able to innovate just one important thing – a motet to rank alongside Tallis or Palestrina, an anthology of memorable poetry, or a cure for certain cancers – it would have been better than all the years of graft and publishing in academic journals from my first paper in 1965 to the last in 2019, 54 years later. My academic reputation will fade rapidly as subjects evolve and mutate. If I have any semblance of reputation left it will be for insisting on the importance of analytical rigour; too much empirical research in the social sciences is undermined by flawed data collection and erroneous statistical analysis and modelling.

One of the few pleasures of being over eighty is that I have been young, while the young have not been old.[1] I know what it's like. I can look back on life and reflect upon opportunities I did not take, the girlfriends I missed, research opportunities forsaken and the jobs rejected. Despite living in the UK now for 56 years – including 50 in Britain – I have never felt anything other than Irish. I have never contemplated obtaining a British passport, even more so since the disastrous decision of the UK to leave the EU. How was it that a once – great nation committed such wilful folly? O'Toole has argued that Brexit is 'fuelled by fantasies of 'Empire 2.0,' a reconstructed global mercantilist trading empire in which old white colonies will be reconnected to the mother country', but it is also 'an insurgency.....a revolt against intolerable oppression' that 'requires both a sense of superiority and a sense of grievance.[2] The decision of UK voters to leave the EU has left me feeling betrayed and has impacted upon my sense of identity. As Britain has become more xenophobic since the EU referendum vote of 2016 I feel more attached to Ireland.

When I meet Irish people in Britain, I feel a sense of community with complete strangers with whom I have nothing else in common other than our nationality. If I converse with an Irish person for an hour, I find that I slip back into a stronger Dublin accent and start using Irish phrases and idioms. I get a lump in my throat when I listen to John McCormack sing a Handel or Mozart aria; or when I hear Seamus Heaney read one of his poems. Nostalgia for something I have lost is a part of this, a void to be filled. I greatly miss the beauty of the Dalkey and Dun Laoghaire area of my childhood, especially the granite walls and kerbstones, the fanlights above the Regency and Georgian doorways and the quiet lapping of seawater at high tide at the Forty Foot bathing place. Above all, I miss the warmth and friendliness of Irish people, the opportunity to engage almost anyone in conversation in a shop, on a bus, or in a pub and to relish their eloquence, wit, banter, endlessly renewable conversation and capacity for enjoyment. There is also a feeling of pride in the constant flow of great literature that pours out of such a small country. There has been significant progress in race and gender equality, but greater equality in incomes, wealth and educational opportunity have not been realised. Above all, I am proud that Ireland has voted by referendum to change the constitution and the law in several crucial ways. First, Irish legislation on homosexuality in 1993 became, at a stroke, more liberal than that in Britain.[3] Second, divorce reform was introduced in 1995 and, subsequently, in 2015, Ireland became the first country in the world to introduce, by direct popular vote, equal marriage for any 'two persons without distinction as to their sex.' After abortion became legal in Britain in 1968, at least a quarter of a million Irish women travelled to Britain to terminate their pregnancies. As O'Toole has argued, this achieved what Catholic Ireland always wished to do – to construct two parallel universes, two truths: there was no abortion in Ireland, unlike in godless Britain.[4] Eventually, abortion reform was introduced following a referendum in 2018 with a 67 percent majority in favour. These referenda and other legislation have turned the closed, conservative, rigid Catholic country of my youth into one of Europe's most liberal and tolerant states.

Notes

1 The Emergency

1   Nicholson A (2001) *Sea Room: an Island Life*, p.30

2   O'Farrell Thomas, Notebook, cited by Nicholson, *op.cit.,* p. 125

3   Fanning R (1983) *Independent Ireland*, pp.124-5

4   Walker B (2012) *A Political History of the Two Irelands*, p. 91

5   *Ibid.,* p. 91

6   Fallon B (1999) *An Age of Innocence: Irish Culture, 1930-1960,* p.8

7   *Irish Times*, 27 May 1941

8   *Irish Times*, 28 May 1941

9   Fallon, *op.cit.,* p.215

10 Girvin B (2006) 'De Valera's Diplomatic Neutrality,' *History Today*, 56(3), p.50

11 Department of Justice Memorandum 'Admission of One hundred Jewish Children' April 1948

12 Reid L E (2018) 'The Emergency in Ireland during World War 2', p.3

13 Gray Tony, (1994) *Ireland this Century*, p. 165

14 O'Brien Flann (1964) *The Dalkey Archive*, p.7

15 Holroyd M (1988) *Bernard Shaw*, Vol. 1, p.28

16 Quoted by Randall D (2019) *Suburbia*, p. 16

17 *Architectural Review*, (June, 1955) quoted by Kynaston D. (2010) *Family Britain 1951-57*, p.420

18 Gray, *op.cit.,* p.173

19 *Ibid.,* p.174

20 List partly inspired by Kynaston D (2007) *Austerity Britain, 1945-51*, p.19

2   Will Anything ever Happen?

1   Daly M E (2006) *The Slow Failure: Population Decline and Independent Ireland, 1920-1973*, p.184, quoted by O'Toole F (2021) *We Don't Know Ourselves: a Personal History of Ireland since 1958*, p.14

2   Leonard Hugh (1979) *Home before Night*, pp. 72-3

3   Sandbrook D (2005) *Never had it so Good: a History of Britain from Suez to the Fifties,* pp. 381-2

4   Gelly, David, 'Blown up, Deaded but not Forgotten,' *Observer*, 26th May 1991

5   Kynaston D (2009) *Family Britain 1951-57*, p.434

6   Sandbrook, *op.cit.*, p.67

7   Potterton H (2004) *Rathcormick*, p. 124

8   Brown T (2004), *Ireland : a Social and Cultural History, 1922-2002*, p. 99

9   I am grateful to Dr David Thomas for supplying information about the importance of the Dun Laoghaire Water Wags in the world-wide development of one design yacht racing.

10   Whyte J H (1971) *Church and State in Modern Ireland*, p. 223

11   Fallon B (1999) *An Age of Innocence: Irish Culture 1930-1960*, p. 187

12   *Irish Times,* 12 April, 1951, quoted in Brown T (2009) *The Irish Times: 150* Years *of Influence*, p.203

13   Ferriter D (2012) *Occasions of Sin: Sex and Society in Modern Ireland*, p.127

14   *Ibid.*, p.333 and p.356

15   Flynn G M (2003) *Nothing to Say*, p.6

16   Ferriter D, *op.cit.,* p.460

17   O'Toole Fintan (2021) *We Don't Know Ourselves: A Personal History of Ireland since 1958*, p.526

18   For example, at the Westbank Orphanage in Greystones under the evangelical regime of born-again-Christian Adeline Mathers, who ran the institution for 50 years, 'children were deprived of food, whipped and beaten and also trafficked illegally north of the border (See *The Journal.ie*, 6 July 2014) . Westbank was closed in 2002.

19 Ferriter, *Occasions of Sin, op.cit.*, p.xii

20 Connery DS (1968) *The Irish*, p.174, quoted by Ferriter, *Occasions of Sin, op.cit.*,p.195

21 Fallon, *op.cit.*,p.196

22 Brown, *op.cit.*, p.186

23 Ferriter, *Occasions of Sin, op.cit.*, p. 308

24 *Ibid.*, p.308

25 *Ibid., p. 308*

26 Brown, *op.cit.*, p. 184

27 *Ibid.*, p.189

28 O'Faolain S (1943) 'Silent Ireland,' *Bell*, VI, (5), p.460, quoted by Brown, *op.cit.*, p. 189.

29 O'Faolain S (1943) 'The Stuffed Shirts,' *Bell*, VI (3), p.183, quoted by Brown, *op.cit.*, pp. 189-190. For an excellent analysis of O'Faolain's campaign against Irish book censorship, see Brown *op.cit.*, Chapter 6.

30 *Irish Independent*, 15 February 1962, quoted by Garvin T (2010) *News from a new Republic: Ireland in the 1950s*, p. 196

3 Schooldays

1 O'Leary E (2018) *Youth and Popular Culture in 1950s Ireland*, p. 15

2 O'Reilly B (2012) 'Education Policy in Ireland since the 1940s, *Italian Journal of Sociology of Education*, 1, p. 242

3 *Ibid.*, p.248

4 Walker B W (2012) *A Political History of the Two Irelands*, p.42

5 Garvin T (2010) *News from a New Republic: Ireland in the 1950s*, p. 169

6 *Ibid.*, p.177

7 *Ibid., p.*177

8 *Ibid.*, p. 178

9 Many of the insights and anecdotes in this chapter are derived from a meeting of ten old boys of the school recorded on 12 October 2019 at Gleeson's pub in Booterstown. Those present from the 1959 cohort to whom I am deeply grateful included: David Burnett, Charlie Duncan,

Peter Fisher, David McCleane, Jo Pinkster and Andrew Wilson; and from the 1960 cohort: Melvyn Boyd, Terry Forsyth and David Thomas.

10   Clissman A (1975) *Flann O'Brien: a Critical Introduction to his Writings*, p. 238

11   *Ibid.*, p.238

12   Comerford R V (2003) *Inventing the Nation: Ireland*, p.81, quoted in Walker *op. cit.*, p.15

13   Travers Pauric, 'History in Primary school: a Future for our Past,' *History Ireland*, 4(3), Autumn, pp.13-16, quoted by Ferriter D (2005) *The Transformation of Ireland*, p.430

14   O'Callaghan J (2011) 'Politics, Policy and History: History Teaching in Irish Secondary Schools, 1922-1970.' *Etudes Irlandaises*, 36-1, p.1

15   *Ibid.*, p.5

16   Corcoran T J (1923) The new secondary programmes in Ireland: the teaching of History,' *Studies*, 12, p.258

17   Lewis Roger 'Poetic Injustice,' *The Oldie*, October, 2020, p.31

18   Corless D *Irish Independent*, 24th June, 2

19   Semple P (2002) *Believe it or Not: a Memoir*, p.57

20   Kynaston D (2010) *Family Britain, 1951-57*, p.137

4   Jiving in the Aisles

1   Hennessy, Peter (2006) *Having it so Good: Britain in the Fifties*, p.49

2   *Ibid.*, p.14

3   Hopkins H (1964) *The New Look: a Social History of the Forties and Fifties in Britain*, p. 460

4   Brown T (2015) *The Irish Times: 150 Years of Influence*, p.188

5   Kynaston D (2010) *Family Britain 1951-1957*, p.516

6   *Irish Times*, 18th February, 1956

7   Burt D S (2007) *The Drama 100: a Ranking of the Greatest Plays of All Time*, pp.43-44

8   Brown T (2009) *The Irish Times: 150 Years of Influence*, p. 71

9   Walsh B M (1970) Religion and Demographic Behaviour in Ireland, ESRI Paper No. 55, pp.27-28

10   *Ibid.,* p.34

11   Central Statistics Office (2004) quoted by Wikipedia 'Protestantism in the Republic of Ireland.'

12   National Archives of Ireland, Film Censor's Office, 98/29/4, Reject Book 1935-53, 10 May 1935, quoted by Ferriter, D (2009) *Occasions of Sin: Sex and Society in Modern Ireland,* p. 212

13   Sandbrook D (2005) *Never had it so Good: a History of Britain from Suez to the Fifties,* p.203

14   Brown Terence (2004) *Ireland : a Social and Cultural History, 1922-2002,* p. 205

15   Ferriter D (2005) *The Transformation of Ireland,* p.364

16   *Irish Press,* 2 October,1969

17   Fallon B (1999) *An Age of Innocence: Irish Culture 1930-1960,* p. 142

18   *Ibid.,* p.41 and p. 56

19   *Ibid.,* p.60

20   Ferriter D (2009) *Occasions of Sin: Sex and Society in Modern Ireland,* pp. 313-314

21   Cooney J (1999) *John Charles McQuaid: Ruler of Catholic Ireland,* p. 229

22   *Ibid.,* quoted in Ferriter, *Occasions of Sin, op.cit.,*pp. 338-39

23   Ferriter, *Occasions of Sin, op.cit.,* p.314

24   O'Corrain D (2006) *Rendering to God and Caesar: the Irish Churches and the two states in Ireland, 1949-73,* p. 94

25   *Ibid.,* p. 94

26   *Ibid.,* p.96

27   Ferriter ,*The Transformation of Ireland, op.cit.,* p.738

28   Baden Powell R (1908) *Scouting for Boys*

29   Cooney, *op.cit.,* p.282, quoted in Ferriter D (2012) *Occasions of Sin: Sex and Society in Modern Ireland,* p.353

30   Ferriter, *Occasions of Sin, op.cit.,* p.353

31   *Ibid.,* p.353

5　The Trinity Idyll

1　Kynaston D (2015) *Modernity Britain 1957 – 1962*, p.470 and p.695

2　Green J (1998) *All Dressed Up: Sixties and the Counter –Culture*, pp. ix, xiii

3　David May quoted in Green D (1998) *Days in the Life: Views from the English Underground, 1961-71*, p.425

4　Hobsbaum E (1994) *Age of Extremes: the Short Twentieth Century 1914-1991*, p.319

5　Sandbrook D (2005) *Never Had it so Good, A History of Britain from Suez to the Beatles*, p.xxv

6　Luce J V (1992) *Trinity College Dublin: the First Four Hundred Years*, p.196

7　*Ibid.*, p.181

8　Even in the few cases where McQuaid granted permission to attend Trinity, the student was required to observe a list of safeguards as follows: (1) regular and frequent attendance to religious duties; (2) avoidance of all societies that may propagate ideas contrary to the Catholic faith or morals; (3) in cooperation with the priest in charge of the case, to engage in the study of the Catholic teaching on those subjects on the course that have philosophical or theological implications; and (4) to habitually consort with Catholic companions, see 'Faith of our Fathers: my Fight to study at Trinity, *Irish Independent*, 2 March, 2014.

9　Foster R F (2007) *Luck and the Irish: a Brief History of Change 1970-2000*,p.39

10　Kerrigan G (1998) *Another Country: Growing up in '50s Ireland*, p.209

11　Marsden P (2019) *The Summer Isles: a Voyage of the Imagination*, p. 79

12　Carpenter H (2000) *That was Satire that Was: the Satire Boom of the 1960s*, p.107; *Daily Mail*, 24th August, 1960

13　Sandbrook, *op.cit.*, p.584

14　Kynaston, *op.cit.*, p.476

15　Sandbrook, op.cit., p.210

16　*Ibid.*, p.397

17　*Ibid.*, p.398

18 Toibin Colm, 'Gay Byrne: Irish life as Cabaret,' Cranebag, (1984) 8(2), quoted by Ferriter D (2005) *The Transformation of Ireland*, p.602; and Ferriter D (2012) *Occasions of Sin: Sex and Society in Modern Ireland*, p. 398

19 McGahern J (2005) *Memoir*, pp. 250-1

20 Ferriter D (2012) *Occasions of Sin: Sex and Society in Modern Ireland*, p.385

21 Knowlson J (1997) *Damned to Fame: the Life of Samuel Beckett*, p. 33

22 *Ibid.*, p.61

23 Howes L (2009) 'Castaway,' in Balfour S *et al* (eds) *Trinity Tales: Trinity College in the Sixties,* p.76. For a delightful description of the architecture of Trinity College, see Lewis J (1987) *Playing for Time*, pp.40-44

6   North of the Border

1   White Jerry (2002) *London in the Twentieth Century*, p.345 Levy Shawn (2002) *Ready, Steady, Go! Swinging London and the Invention of Cool*, p.353

2   Morgan K O (2001) *Britain since 1945: the People's Peace*, p.259

3   Sandbrook D (2006) *White Heat: a History of Britain in the Swinging Sixties*, p.275

4   Ferriter D (2012) *Occasions of Sin: Sex and Society in Modern Ireland*, p.337

5   Green J (1993) *It: Sex since the Sixties*, p.9

6   Davies H (2017) *A Life in the Day*, p.73

7   Norman P (1981) *Shout: The True Story of the Beatles*, pp. 30-32

8   Sandbrook D (2005) *Never Had it so Good, a History of Britain from Suez to the Beatles*, p.491

9   *Ibid.*, p.719

10 *Irish Times*, 4 November, 2013

11 Sandbook, *White Heat, op.cit.*, p.103, p.115

12 *Ibid.*, p.109

13 Parker M (1994) *Seamus Heaney: the Making of the Poet*, Palgrave Macmillan, p.71

14   Kerrigan G (1998) *Another Country: Growing up in '50s Ireland,* p.150

15   Taylor P (2000) *Loyalists,* pp.13-28

16   McKittrick D and McVea D (2012) *Making Sense of the Troubles,* p. 13

17   *Irish Times, 25* August, 2016

18   McKittrick and McVea, *op.cit.,* pp.18-19

19   *Ibid.,* p.14

20   Whyte P 'How much Discrimination was there under the Unionist Regime, 1921-1968?' in Gallagher T and O'Connell J (1983) *Contemporary Irish Studies,* p. 17

21   Garvin T (1994) 'Dialogue of the Deaf', review of Andy Pollak (ed.),*The Opsahl Report on Northern Ireland, Irish Review,* 15, Spring 1994, pp.123-5

22   Coakley J (2014) 'Public Opinion and the Future of Northern Ireland,' Working Papers in Conflict Transformation and Social Justice, Queens University Belfast, p. 21

23   *Belfast Telegraph,* 10th May 1969, quoted in Sandbrook, *White Heat, op.cit.,* p.355

24   Public Record Office of Northern Ireland (PRONI) D354, NIFPA, D. Hearle, BBC Belfast, to Joyce Neill, 12 November 1965, and reply 23 November 1965, quoted by Ferriter D. (2012) *Occasions of Sin: Sex and Society in Modern Ireland,* Profile Books, p.369

25   PRONI, d3543, NIFPA, Joyce Neill to Mrs. Pullen, 5 February 1966, Quoted in Ferriter, *op.cit.,* p.370

26   McCann E (1998) *War and Peace in Northern Ireland,* column of 5 September 1991.

27   Neill, Joyce to editor of *Belfast Telegraph,* 19 April 1968, quoted in Ferriter, *op.cit.,* p.371

28   Neill Joyce, 'Family Planning in Northern Ireland,' unpublished manuscript, p.24; and confirmed in personal conversation with Dr. Neill.

29   *Ibid.,* p.21; and personal conversation with Dr. Neill

30   Sandbrook, *White Heat, op.cit.,*p.437

31   *Ibid.,* p.439

32 Garvin T, (1998) 'The Strange Death of Clerical Politics in University College Dublin' *Irish University Review*, 28(2) Autumn/Winter, 308-15

33 Cooney J (1999) *John Charles McQuaid: Ruler of Catholic Ireland*, The O'Brien Press, p.28

34 Luce J V (1992) *Trinity College Dublin: the First 400 Years*, p. 196

35 Fallon B (1999) *An Age of Innocence: Irish Culture 1930-1960*, p.180

36 Coogan Tim Pat (1996) *The Troubles: Ireland's Ordeal 1966-1996 and the Search for Peace*, p.53

37 Quoted in Coogan, *op. cit.*, p.55 and Sandbrook, *White Heat*, *op.cit.*, p.357

38 English R (2003) *The Armed Struggle: the History of the IRA*, p. 82

39 Sandbrook, *White Heat*, *op.cit.*, p.737

40 Rose P (2001) *How the Troubles came to Northern Ireland*, pp. 77-78, 1785, 178; quoted by Sandbrook, *White Heat*, *op.cit.*, p.737

41 Kynaston D (2008) *Austerity Britain*, p. 301

42 Sandbrook, *White Heat*, *op.cit.*, p.739

43 O'Hagan S. *The Guardian*, 22nd April 2018.

44 Sandbrook, *White Heat*, *op.cit.*, p.749

45 Limpkin C (1972) *The Battle of the Bogside*, p.19

46 Sandbrook, *White Heat*, *op. cit.*, p.753

47 *Ibid.*, p.753

48 *Ibid.*, p. 753

49 *Ibid.*, p.794

50 *Ibid.*,p.794

51 Orwell G 'The Lion and the Unicorn: Socialism and the English Genius', quoted by Sandbrook, *op.cit.*, p.794

7 The Centre cannot Hold

1 Sandbrook D (2010) *State of Emergency: the Way we Were, Britain, 1970-1974*, p. 10

2 McKittrick D and McVea D (2012) *Making Sense of the Troubles*, p.71

3 Sandbrook D (2010) *op.cit.*, p.228

4   McKittrick and McVea, *op.cit.*, p.74

5   Sandbrook, *op.cit.*, p.242

6   McKittrick and McVea, *op.cit.*, p.77

7   Sandbrook, *op.cit.*, p.243

8   *Ibid.*, p.245

9   *Ibid.*, p.245-46

10   Beckett A (2010) *When the Lights Went Out : What really Happened to Britain in the Seventies*, p.116

11   Sandbrook, *op. cit.*, p.248

12   McKittrick and McVea, *op.cit.*, p.80

13   Sandbrook, *op.cit.*, p.250

14   McKittrick and McVea, *op.cit.*, p.87

15   Sandbrook, *op.cit.*, pp. 480- 481

16   *Ibid.*, p. 482

17   *Ibid.*,p.485

18   *Ibid.*,p.489; *The Times* 3 December 1973

19   McKittrick and McVea, *op.cit.*, p.100

20   Brown T (2004) *Ireland: a Social and Cultural History, 1922-2002*, p. 271

21   'Unhappy and at Home,' interview with Seamus Heaney by Seamus Deane, *Crane Bag*, vol.1, no.1 (1977), p.64, quoted by Brown, *op.cit.*, p. 273

22   Murphy J A (1978) 'Further Reflections on Irish Nationalism,' *Crane Bag*, vol.2, nos.1 and 2 p.157, quoted by Brown, *op.cit.*, p.273

23   McKittrick and McVea, *op.cit.*,p.102

8   A Welcome in the Hillside

1   Sandbrook, (2010) *The State of Emergency: the Way we were, Britain 1970-1974*, p.337

2   I am grateful to my friends Susan and Peter Leyshon who kindly collected the data on house names on Merthyr Mawr Road, Bridgend.

3   Sandbrook (2010) *op.cit.*,p.591

4   *Ibid.,* pp.597-98

5   Sandbrook D (2012) *Seasons in the Sun: The Battle for Britain, 1974-1979,* p.11

6   Donoghue B (2005) *Downing Street Diaries,* Vol 1, p. 352

7   Sandbrook (2012) *op.cit.,* pp. 262-263

8   Campbell J (2000) *Margaret Thatcher,* vol 1: *the Grocer's Daughter,* pp.31-32, 47,50; Jenkins S (2006) *Thatcher and Sons: a Revolution in Three Acts,* p.47; Sandbrook (2012) *op.cit.,* pp.238-239 and p.672

9   McSmith A (2011) *No Such Thing as Society: a History of Britain in the 1980s,* p.21

10   Sandbrook (2010) *op.cit.,* p.51

11   *Ibid.,* p.52

12   *Ibid.,* p.345

13   *The Times,* 9 August 1984, quoted by McSmith, *op.cit.,* p.138

14   Sandbrook D (2019) *Who Dares Wins: Britain 1979-1982,* p.131

15   *Ibid., p.*131

16   Sandbrook (2012) *op. cit.,* pp.597

17   Turner A (2008) *Crisis? What Crisis? Britain in the 1970s,* pp.190-91

18   *Ibid.,* p.192

19   Sandbrook (2012), *op.cit.,* pp.475-476

20   *Guardian,* 26 and 27 September 1978, quoted in Sandbrook (2012) *op.cit.,* p.698

21   *The Times,* 25 May, 1978, quoted in Sandbrook (2012) *op.cit.,*p.700

22   Sandbrook (2012) *op.cit.,* p.714

23   *Ibid.,* p.756

24   *Ibid.,* p.759

25   *Ibid.,* p.759

26   Burton- Hill C (2017) *Year of Wonder: Classical Music for every Day,* p.7

27   *Ibid.,* p.249

28   Bragg Melvyn (2022) *Back in the Day,* p.32

29   Burton – Hill, *op.cit.,* p.246

30 *Daily Express, 25 October, 1982*

31 *Guardian,* 8 June, 1981

32 Sandbrook (2019) *op.cit.,* p.405

33 Longley E, *The Times Higher,* 7 October, 2003

34 *Ibid.,* p.568

35 Healey Denis (1989) *The Time of my Life,* p.568

36 *Ibid.,* p.569

37 Quoted by Longley, *op.cit., The Times Higher,* 7 October, 2003

38 Sutherland J. *Guardian,* 19 March 2009

39 Toibin Colm, *Guardian,* 30 August, 2013.

40 Motion Andrew, *BBC News,* 30 August, 2013

41 Sandbrook (2019) *op.cit.,* pp.429

42 *Ibid.,* p.616

43 Turner A (2013) *Rejoice! Rejoice! Britain in the Eighties,* p.110

44 Stevenson R L (1879) 'Edinburgh: Picturesque Notes.'

45 Turner, *op.cit.,* p.228 and 229

46 Morgan K O (2001) *Britain since 1945: the People's Peace,* p.480

47 *Ibid.,* p.481

48 Turner, *op.cit.,* p.187

9   Epilogue

1 Davies Hunter (2019) *Happy Old Me,* p.ix

2 O'Toole Fintan (208) *Heroic Failure: Brexit and the Politics of Pain,* p.3

3 Foster R F (2007) *Luck and the Irish: a Brief History of Change 1970-2000,* p.3

4 O'Toole Fintan (2021) *We Don't Know Ourselves: a Personal History of Ireland since 1958,* p.33

Acknowledgements

Excerpts from 'North Wind,' 'A Swim in Co. Wicklow,' and 'Beyond Howth Head,' by Derek Mahon from *The Poems 1961-2020* (2021) are reproduced by kind permission of the author's estate and the Gallery Press. www.gallerypress.com. Excerpts from 'Autumn Journal' by Louis MacNeice from *Collected Poems* (1979) are reproduced by kind permission of the Estate of Louis MacNeice and David Higham and Associates. Excerpts from 'Whatever you say, say Nothing' and 'Docker' by Seamus Heaney from *Death of a Naturalist* (1966) and *North* (1975) are reproduced by kind permission of the author's estate and Faber and Faber.

Many friends, to whom I am deeply indebted, have read parts or all of the text. They offered many valuable suggestions on perspectives, style and interpretation. I would like to thank a number of former pupils of St Andrew's College in the 1950s who kindly participated in a group discussion in October, 2019. Gratitude, therefore, is extended to Melvyn Boyd, David Burnett, Charlie Duncan, Peter Fisher, Terry Forsyth, David McCleane, Jo Pinkster, David Thomas and Andrew Wilson. In addition, both David Thomas and John Keery kindly read and commented upon the complete draft of the memoir. I am deeply indebted to MaryJane Bennett who completed the copy edits with extraordinary attention to detail. Many other people, too numerous to mention individually, kindly supplied numerous comments and corrections on issues as diverse as fashions in the 1960s and details of sports events at St Andrew's College. Finally, I am grateful to the members of my family who supported me throughout the lengthy process of writing this manuscript.

Step Change
Total Quality

Step Change
Total Quality

Achieving world class business performance

Second edition

Paul Spenley
Director,
Pera International, Swindon, UK

Illustrations by Angela Spenley

CHAPMAN & HALL

London · Weinheim · New York · Tokyo · Melbourne · Madras

Published by Chapman & Hall, 2-6 Boundary Row, London SE1 8HN, UK

Chapman & Hall, 2-6 Boundary Row, London SE1 8HN, UK

Chapman & Hall GmbH, Pappelallee 3, 69469 Weinheim, Germany

Chapman & Hall USA., 115 Fifth Avenue, New York, NY 10003, USA

Chapman & Hall Japan, ITP-Japan, Kyowa Building, 3F, 2-2-1 Hirakawacho, Chiyoda-ku, Tokyo 102, Japan

Chapman & Hall Australia, 102 Dodds Street, South Melbourne, Victoria 3205, Australia

Chapman & Hall India, R. Seshadri, 32 Second Main Road, CIT East, Madras 600 035, India

First edition 1992
Reprinted 1993 (twice)
Second edition 1995
Reprinted 1996

© 1992, 1995

Originally published as *World Class Performance Through Total Quality: A practical guide to implementation* - © 1992, Paul Spenley. Published by Chapman & Hall

Printed in Great Britain by St Edmundsbury Press, Bury St. Edmunds, Suffolk

ISBN 0 412 64270 0

A Catalogue record for this book is available from the British Library

∞ Printed on permanent acid-free text paper, manufactured in accordance with ANSI/NISO Z39.48-1992 and ANSI/NISO Z39.48-1984 (Permanence of Paper).

To my wife Judy and family

Contents

Foreword

To achieve and sustain a competitive advantage in today's global market place, companies need to provide products and services of outstanding quality to their customers. This means achieving operational excellence in their organization as a matter of course rather than the occasional high spot in performance which is typical of most organizations.

Total Quality has traditionally been associated with continuous improvement and is aimed at providing a company culture where improvement is the norm. Unfortunately, it is generally recognized that this can take a long time.

Step Change Total Quality is about making a series of breakthrough improvements in operational performance in a short time, before implementing the longer term culture of continuous improvement to hold the gains. Continuous improvement is, of course, an excellent policy but if your competitors have embarked on a similar path, your relative competitive position may be substantially unchanged. To make real gains requires step changes in performance and also, perhaps, operating culture.

Nearly all the companies I know who have successfully introduced a process of radical change have one thing in common – total commitment from the top team to Step Change Total Quality. The challenge is tough, demanding new skills and careful management of risks, but I think you will find that the rewards are well worth the effort.

Ronald Armstrong
Chief Executive
Pera International

Preface

The response to the first edition of the book has been extremely encouraging, and I am grateful for the many positive comments received. In particular, it was felt that an extra section demonstrating success through case studies would strengthen the impact of the book, and I am pleased to be able to include some world class case studies in this second edition.

During 1993 we were asked by the CBI to help spread best practice in TQM implementation, and undertook a national tour with the theme 'Achieving World Class Performance Through Total Quality'. The case studies are of an unusually high standard, representing large and small companies in many different businesses. The constant theme of all the case studies is the achievement of significant business benefit from a determined and practical approach to the implementation of Total Quality.

In addition to the case studies, the following quotes serve to provide a much needed inspiration, whether just starting down the TQ route, or looking for a new direction to reactivate a TQ approach which has lost its initial enthusiasm.

QUOTES SECTION

1. 'The problem that the UK faces is that most directors do not understand that TQ is about total business performance – they still think it is about product quality. It is, in fact, about turning companies around, and achieving step change improvement'.

      Jaap Kooger, Operations Director, DuPont Europe.

2. 'Customer perception – internal and external – is all there is'.

      Ken Sanders, Managing Director, Texas Instruments.

3. 'The greatest threat to the successful implementation of TQM in an organization is if the chief executive and senior management team fail to generate the necessary enthusiasm, commitment and fanaticism themselves in order to sustain the relentless momentum of this never-ending journey. Regrettably, so many only pay lip service to the issue, and regard TQM as a responsibility that can be delegated down to middle management'.

      Malcolm Diamond, Managing Director, TR Fastenings Limited.

4. 'The whole future of UK manufacturing depends on the quality of its people – and TQ is an important part of that commitment. It has helped us, in the short term, to survive this recession, and I am absolutely convinced that without it we would not be around in ten years' time'.

      John Palmer, Managing Director, Firsteel Group Limited.

5. 'Our belief is that quality is fundamental to continued success. To us, it is first and foremost a leadership issue – it has to be a management-led release of creativity, not a management-imposed comformance to standard.'

      Geoff Hutt, Quality Director, AT&T ISTEL UK.

6. 'Total Quality Management is about company performance. It is not an option for British Companies – without it they will neither compete nor survive'.

      Eric McCoy, Managing Director, Ransomes Sims & Jefferies.

7. 'Management must demonstrate its belief and commitment to the TQ process; it must demonstrate its leadership and the priority it gives to the process. Management is responsible for implementing, executing and measuring the results of the process changes. Finally, management is responsible for sticking with it'.

Ken Sanders, Managing Director, Texas Instruments.

8. 'Staff want to see and believe – they don't only want to hear. Therefore senior management must be pragmatic about TQ; they must demonstrate their commitment by finding a platform which offers tangible short-term benefits, from which to launch continuous improvement'.

Barry Thornton, Quality Improvement Manager,
AE Turbine Components Limited.

9. 'Without customers you are not in business. The way in which customers are esteemed is essential to the success of any organization; all products and services should be based on them; all thinking should start with them'.

Bill Hughes, Chairman and Chief Executive, Grampian Holdings plc.

Preface
to the first edition

TOTAL QUALITY MANAGEMENT (TQM) –
A COMPETITIVE EDGE

In the context of the European and Western manufacturing challenge being set by the 'Far Eastern Machine', it is of critical importance that manufacturing competitiveness is improved in Western companies.

The ability to export successfully is becoming even more critical to the economic well-being of developed countries worldwide. The Japanese domination of the motor cycle, automobile and domestic consumer markets has had a significant impact on the balance of payments in Western Europe and the USA. All the signs are that Japanese companies are ready and able to enter other markets aggressively, through takeovers, acquisitions and off-shore manufacturing facilities.

In Western Europe, the creation of the 'Single Market' in 1992 has provided major opportunities for companies to increase their market share. Unfortunately, many companies in the West have shown an inability to succeed even in their market when faced with tough, well-organized opposition, such as that from the Far East. There is very little time left for Western companies to catch up – the challenge is becoming more fiercely competitive daily. The time to improve competitive edge may be too late for many companies, as the European frontiers are dismantled and the Japanese companies continue to build off-shore plants in Europe. For example, it is a fact that companies are increasingly being forced to achieve world class manufacturing capability in order to compete and, in many cases, survive. Also, these pressures are not restricted to manufacturing activities – they apply to service industry activities just as strongly.

The ability to respond to these domestic and worldwide challenges is the differentiator between survival and extinction. Total Quality Management (TQM) is the means to establish that differentiator in your company. Whatever your business, the principles outlined in this book are always valid, and so are the key actions that need to be taken.

Product or service?

There is an artificial view that all companies can somehow be divided into either manufacturing or service 'sectors'. In my experience, it is wrong to compartmentalize companies into manufacturing or service sectors: all companies are different whatever sector they are supposed to fit into and I have seen more fundamental differences between 'service' companies than between manufacturing and service companies.

In fact, the so-called service sector comprises businesses that are as diverse as any manufacturing versus service comparison. Similarly, many people consider all manufacturing companies to be the same when clearly, depending on their size, product and industry sector, they are as diverse as service sector companies. To make things even more complicated, manufacturing companies contain many 'service' functions, such as Finance and Personnel, which do not fit neatly into the so-called manufacturing area.

Fortunately, as far as TQM is concerned, deciding which sector your company belongs to is not important – it is not even relevant. The biggest single piece of advice I can give to a company in any sector is to ignore your label as part of the manufacturing or the service sector and get on with the implementation of TQM, following the basic principles outlined. Every company I have ever worked for or worked with has been different and, for successful implementation, the total plan has to be customized carefully to the particular company.

The problem is one of perception – perception that service companies have nothing to learn from manufacturing companies, for example. In practice, it is enormously beneficial to talk to other companies who are implementing TQM, whether they are in your sector or not. You will find that the problems they have encountered or are tackling are surprisingly similar from company to company. Beware of the people who would convince you that somehow a company in your own sector must be the model to follow – they may be following the wrong principle entirely!

Another perception is that it is somehow easier to implement TQM into a company that manufactures a product. This view is basically and fundamentally wrong; I do not subscribe to the view that TQM has to be implemented differently into the service sector than the manufacturing sector – it is absolute rubbish. In many cases, it is more difficult for manufacturing companies to implement TQM, because they already have an established quality system which is product-based. This is an absolute requirement of course, but it causes confusion when moving to the broader-based, more business-orientated Total Quality principles. I have seen some manufacturing companies struggle for a long time to get their staff to understand Total Quality principles simply because of the narrow focus on product quality. In service companies there is no such constraint and, in effect, there is a blank sheet of paper called Quality which in many ways makes for an easier management task.

The direction is clear – all the principles outlined in this book are totally applicable to your company, whatever your 'sector'. This book shows that it is the company processes which are improved by the application of TQM, by ensuring that everyone understands their role and has the culture and the techniques needed to implement continuous improvement. There is not a different set of principles for service companies. Implement TQM correctly and it does not matter what sector you come from; remember that there are no two companies the same anywhere in the world!

I am absolutely convinced, after many years of experience in implementing TQM into companies from both service and manufacturing sectors that the basic principles contained in this book are right. These principles need to be followed carefully, but with recognition that the implementation plans must be configured and tailored to the specific requirements of the individual company. My sincere thanks are due to my colleagues and to the people in the companies I have had the privilege to work with who really make these ideas work.

PART ONE

Introduction to Total Quality Management (TQM)

CHAPTER ONE

Total Quality Management – worldwide effect

It was not so long ago that the USA and the UK were dominant in world markets – mainly due to the post-war hunger for consumer goods such as motor cars, motor cycles, televisions, fridges etc. It is also true that goods made in Japan were synonymous with a poor or cheap quality image.

Today it cannot be disputed that the Japanese nation have achieved a position of superiority in many markets throughout the world. This has been achieved by reversing the early image of shoddy goods to that of quality goods attaining a universally accepted position in the market where Japanese goods are recognized as being 'quality products'.

This reputation for quality has enabled Japanese companies to increase market share at a rapid and enviable rate. For example, in the UK motor cycle marketplace, the Japanese invasion succeeded to the tune of an incredible 94% by the mid-1980s from a figure of less than 30% in the late 1960s. The figures in the motor car market were even more impressive whereby in the same period, their market share rose from less than 0.5% to the tariff-constrained 11% of the mid-1980s.

Of course, companies like Nissan have established successful manufacturing operations worldwide, in order to further increase their market share, and are showing the capability of totally dominating the automobile market worldwide by the end of this century. Their world-beating achievements are remarkable and it is essential to understand the reasons for the Japanese success in world markets – a success based on the application of Total Quality Management (TQM).

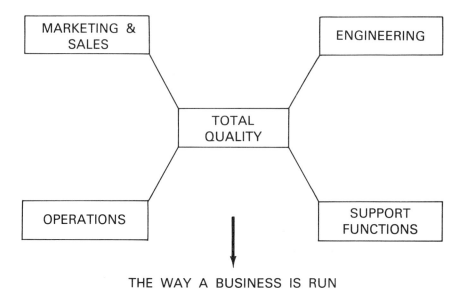

THE WAY A BUSINESS IS RUN

Figure 1.1   World class performance through Total Quality.

THE JAPANESE 'SECRET'

Immediately after the Second World War, Japanese goods had a reputation for shoddiness and cheapness that kept their competitive position in the bottom half of the world trade league table. This was mainly due to the devastation of their industrial base as a result of the war.

Also there was a management methodology modelled on the methods of F.W. Taylor who is often referred to as the 'Father of Scientific Management'. F.W. Taylor began his work in the early 1900s in the USA and could be said to be the world's first work study expert. He revolutionized work practices and productivity effectively by thinking of workers as 'human machines' designing the work equipment and expecting the workers to meet them without question. The only incentive for the workforce was considered to be their wage packets. This principle of management led to the use of piece-work payments and to the use of Inspectors to check output. This use of people as human machines revolutionized output, but at a reduction in the quality of output.

In the early 1950s, Taylor's methods were a fundamental tool in manufacturing industry worldwide and helped enable the USA to rapidly meet the huge post-war demand for goods such as cars or televisions. The Japanese recognized that they could not compete using the same Taylor management methodology but without the huge advantage the USA had in having an established industrial base, and began to develop an alternative strategy.

In the early 1950s, Japanese 'study tours' became a feature of many Western companies' lives, whereby the most successful companies were scrutinized in incredible detail in order to

Figure 1.2 The human machine.

define 'industrial best practice'. At the same time two eminent quality 'gurus' from the USA, Dr Edwards Deming and Dr J.M. Juran, were invited by the Japanese to help with the principles of quality control and their application in Japanese industry. This work formed the basis of a national drive, co-ordinated by the Japanese Union of Scientists and Engineers (JUSE), to improve quality control in Japanese companies which by the mid-1960s had achieved a cultural change in the methods and attitudes prevalent in Japanese industrial society.

Over the last 20 years the fundamental principles taught by Juran and Deming have been refined and built upon and applied with increasing success by Japanese companies. The outdated Taylor management principles have been replaced with a Total Quality management methodology where all employees receive education and training, and are encouraged and expected to contribute to the company objectives.

The establishment of the TQM methodology (or TQC, Total Quality Control, as it is referred to in Japan,) is the real secret of Japanese success. It has taken many years for the Japanese to develop and apply TQM. In many companies in the Western world, Taylorism is still the management methodology being used. The inability of many companies to realize that their management practices are the root cause of their lack of competitiveness in world markets is the key factor that will allow Japanese companies increasingly to dominate world markets into the 21st century.

QUALITY: A CULTURAL CHANGE –
COMPANY OR COUNTRY?

There are many views on the cultural aspects of achieving TQM in a company. Some company executives feel that it is impossible to achieve a change in culture away from the old values of Taylorism to the new TQM total employee involvement principles. To support their rejection of TQM they point to the fact that the Japanese have a totally different historical culture from Western countries. Underlying this view is the absolutely un-

Figure 1.3   Company culture not country culture.

deniable fact (to them) that it is easy to manage the Japanese because 'they are used to doing what they are told'.

This explanation conveniently fits their current management thinking of 'telling people' – never asking – always viewing 'management' as experts. 'How easy it would be if all people would do as they were told.' The belief is that their Japanese managerial counterparts go round the organization telling their employees what to do all the time – the only difference is that the Japanese employees never question but do as they are told.

This view is defended most volubly by those managers who have never set foot inside a Japanese company or taken the trouble to study best management practice worldwide. It is a view that completely ignores the professional approach to the implementation of TQM that is adopted by successful Japanese companies. It also conveniently overlooks the fact that there are many Japanese companies who have also failed to successfully adopt TQM principles, but these companies are not successful and are therefore not known outside Japan.

How can the success of Nissan in Washington, County Durham, UK, be explained away as a country culture? This factory has successfully produced the Nissan Bluebird car to a higher quality standard than has been achieved in the equivalent

Japanese Nissan factory. The principles of TQM are the same whether it is an organization in Japan or in the UK, USA, Europe or any other developed country in the world. However, it would be foolish in the West to copy to the letter the application of TQM as in Japan. Much more time has to be spent in obtaining the understanding and acceptance of employees in the Western world in general, in order to obtain whole-hearted commitment. This is mainly because of the distrust and lack of communication between management and workers, built up generation upon generation by bad management practices, based on F.W. Taylor's principles of the early 1900s.

This atmosphere and culture cannot be removed overnight, but it can be removed over a period of one to three years, depending to some extent on the size of the organization, but mainly on management understanding and commitment. The culture of the company is set by the company, not by the country, more definitely it is set by the management of the company – no one else can have as big an effect on its employees.

TQM: A COMMERCIAL ADVANTAGE?

TQM is becoming synonymous with successful companies – it is increasingly being used as a public relations tool to persuade customers that the company can be relied upon to produce products and services that will meet customer requirements and therefore provide satisfaction.

There is no doubt that there are more TQM conferences, magazines etc. than ever and that there is a drive for many companies to be featured as successful TQM implementors in commercial and government publications. The danger is that some companies may want to jump on this particular bandwagon before a real TQM implementation has been achieved. If this is the case, it is inevitable that sooner or later the company will be 'found out', and will never get a second chance to take advantage commercially of TQM exposure even when implementation has been achieved. Those companies that are prepared to show visitors around their plants, and who are prepared to discuss failures as well as successes, are more likely to be TQM companies.

A quick and easy way to test TQM understanding is to ask a simple question:

How do you know you have TQM?

This question should be asked of the CEO or senior management and will generate a large number of responses!

The most definite answer I can offer is as follows:

- Every employee understands and is committed to the objectives of his department/area.
- Every employee knows who his intended customer and supplier is by individual name.
- Every employee has agreed requirements with his customer/supplier.

When this definition is understood in an organization, it is possible to audit and monitor the success of TQM by asking employees the relevant questions. It is even more revealing to use this definition to find out if a company, particularly a supplier, has TQM! This is achieved by asking the above questions of a secretary, receptionist, driver, goods-in clerk etc. Only then, will it be possible to check that management TQM claims are true!

CHAPTER TWO

The management methodology

TQM – THE WAY A BUSINESS IS RUN

'TQM is the single most important management methodology available today to achieve and maintain a competitive edge against worldwide competition.'

Put simply, there is little value in the Executive Board of a company arriving at a set of business objectives, for example to increase market share, introduce new products, increasing margins, reduce operating costs, implement flexible manufacturing systems or CIM, if there is no clear management methodology for achieving these business objectives.

This is not to deny the importance of setting clear business objectives through focussed market research or any of the other Business School and MBA methodologies that have been refined in the West over the past 20 years. Clearly all of the expertise that goes into providing a business strategy is of critical importance to the success of companies fighting on a world scale. There is no shortage of these skills in the Western world, indeed it has been suggested that there are more MBAs in one single American company (not named!) than in the whole of Japan. It would be wrong to assume from this that the MBA skill is not a valuable acquisition to a company. The need for a business strategy is of critical importance to the identification of key business objectives and the ability to fight successfully against competition worldwide.

However, what has been missing from Western companies,

Figure 2.1 The importance of everyone working together in the chain.

typically, is the utilization of a management methodology to implement the business strategy. TQM provides the management methodology which must form part of the total company business strategy, has been thought through, fully understood and implemented from the top down via the TQM process. This requires a fundamental change in culture for many companies in order to achieve a new and improved way of doing business. It is a corporate company culture where all employees understand what is required of them and are encouraged to contribute – as individuals and as members of Quality improvement teams – to the achievement of business objectives.

TECHNOLOGY

Technology when utilized fully and focussed to support business objectives can be a competitive advantage. Unfortunately it is very often the case in the West that technology has been utilized for its own sake instead of as part of a total business strategy.

It is a startling fact that in the period from the mid-1950s to the

mid-1980s, UK scientists won 26 Nobel Prizes for scientific innovation, whilst the Japanese won only four. This is an enlighten-
ing statistic since the period is the exact time that Japanese
industry successfully took major world markets. If technical
edge was available to the West before Japan, why didn't Western
companies take greater advantage? Again the answer lies in the
inability of those companies to implement clearly their business
objectives because of the lack of a TQM management methodology.

The Japanese were not misled by the exhortation to 'Automate
or Die!' which was the clarion call in the early 1980s. Unfortunately this became 'Automate and Die' for many companies
who, through poor implementation, failed to realize the benefits
of their investments in automation.

It would be short-sighted to ignore the results of a survey
conducted for the British Institute of Management (managing
manufacturing operations in the UK 1975–1985) which showed
that manufacturing efficiency improved only marginally between 1975 and 1985. It is foolish to ignore the fear that Western
commerce and industry may fail to optimize the business benefits that the successful application of technology can provide.
One of the problems is that technology is exhorted for its own
sake by many people who are not directly involved with the running of a company.

Industrial leaders are rarely the champions of FMS, CIM, IT or
other technology 'buzz words'. This mantle is taken on by consultants, academics, and of course the 'technical elegant expert',
in companies – the people who like technology for its own sake
'if it moves, automate it!' Yet industrial leaders are the only
people who can really make technology work, since successful
application involves all the people in the organization. It cannot
be left to technical experts – success depends on people's understanding, acceptance and commitment. Total quality management provides the management methodology for industrial
leaders to harness the benefit of appropriate technology in line
with, and as a key part of, implementing the business strategy.

THE HUMAN FACTOR

'Acceptance and understanding is a pre-requisite to obtaining whole-hearted commitment!'

If it were possible to obtain the whole-hearted commitment of every employee in pursuit of the company mission statement and business objectives wouldn't this be a factor in beating the competition? All successful sports teams demonstrate whole-hearted commitment – it is a major feature of a winning team. Why should companies be any different from sports teams and what is the differentiator that makes a company or a sports team world class?

The answer to this question fundamentally of course is its people. It is difficult to understand why so little attention is given to a management methodology that will achieve the whole-hearted commitment of all employees. The achievement of this objective is the most important aspect of a total company strategy. People are the differentiating factor between achieving world class capability and being also-rans. People are responsible for developing, implementing, controlling and maintaining the processes, methods and systems which companies use to provide products and services to their customers. To ensure these procedures, methods and systems work successfully it is essential that all the people fully understand the things they do, why they do them and of course help to specify, modify, implement and control their work.

It is necessary for each person to have an appreciation of his or her individual part of the total process and therefore of the effect this contribution makes to the total. This statement might appear crushingly obvious; it is hardly world shattering. However, it is my belief that the lack of understanding people have of their process as an integral and essential part of the total, is at the heart of inefficiency and a lack of competitivity in business. Examples are the design engineer who does not understand the requirement of designing a product that can be successfully put through the manufacturing process, the salesman who sells products that cannot be made, or the systems analyst who

cannot understand the requirements of a factory stores manager
– always assuming he asks him in the first place!

There are, unfortunately, too many examples of compartmentalization where the total requirement is not understood
and when individuals do not understand or address their contributions to the total business needs. This compartmentalization can be seen in the functional 'Empires' built around
design, manufacturing, sales, marketing and so on. Worse still,
in some cases these functional empires begin to see each other as
the competition instead of concentrating on the real competition! This of course is akin to shooting yourself in the foot before
having to face the real enemy! There are no prizes for working
out who wins.

What is needed is a methodology to ensure employees recognize the need to work for, and with, each other against a common enemy – the competition. This task is fundamentally a
management role in providing the leadership and example for
the rest of the employees to follow. It demands a common
understanding of what needs to be achieved by the company,
and a recognition that the company is the employees, all of
whom have a key role to play, both as individuals and as members of teams. This requires all employees, as stated previously,
to have a clear understanding of what they need to contribute as
individuals and as part of a department, division or organization
with clearly stated and agreed objectives.

If management understand the employees are the key to competitive advantage, then the old traditional barrier between
management and employees will begin to be dismantled. The
company is its employees whether they are called managers or
not, and all have a vital role to play in achieving and maintaining
competitive advantage.

COMMITMENT TO PEOPLE: THE KEY TO
COMPETITIVE ADVANTAGE

In this chapter it has been highlighted that Western companies
have successfully developed technology but failed to optimize a

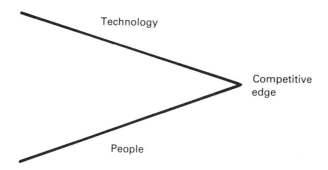

Figure 2.2   TQM links people and technology to activate the business strategy for competitive advantage.

business benefit. It is also true that they have developed many excellent business strategies but failed to implement these strategic plans successfully. The elements of a company strategy have frequently failed to include the third key factor – people. Without the understanding that people are a key factor in the implementation of the business strategy, companies will fail to achieve competitive advantage.

Indeed as technology and business strategies become more and more easily available to companies worldwide, the only differentiating factor will be the people.

BUSINESS REQUIREMENTS

By definition of the marketplace we expect in the 21st century, Western companies need to achieve world class capability.

Put simply, this means the ability to meet customer requirements better than the competition can. These requirements vary depending on the marketplace and the individual customer, but it is a fact that universally customers are demanding better quality of service, as well as quality of products. This means companies have to achieve competitive edge through business 'drivers' which reflect customer concerns.

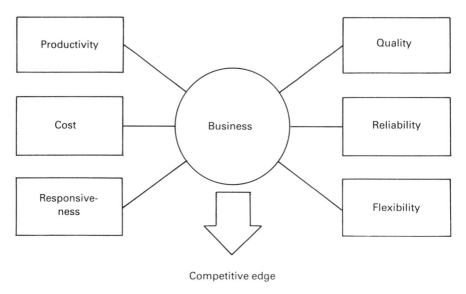

Competitive edge

Figure 2.3   Business 'drivers'.

INVESTING IN PEOPLE

A good test of a company's commitment to investing in the people it employs is the training budget. Very often, the money budgeted each year for education and training is only a few per cent of the investment made in technology. This is akin to buying a Rolls Royce without bothering to learn how to drive! For example, the UK national average for 'off the job' training is about one-and-a-half days per employee per year. In Japan, the figure is in excess of ten days per employee per year. Most significantly, in Total Quality training, Japanese managers are given more training than the rest of the employees. This is to ensure that the management fully understand the TQM principles, tools, techniques and methodology, so that they are respected by the people who work for them and can make a personal contribution to the company quality improvement process.

It is important to understand that training in TQM is a con-

Company course	Trainees	Time	Outline of contents
Total quality basics	All new employees	½ day	What total quality is. How it is applied in the company. Quality improvement teams.
Quality assurance	All new professional staff	2 hours	What quality assurance means. How to assure quality (prevention). Quality assurance structure.
Tools and techniques	All employees	1 day	Tools and techniques. How to use. Problem solving process.
Total quality for supervisors	All people with supervisory responsibility	½ day	Role of supervisor. Team leadership.
Total quality for managers	All managers	1 week	Role of manager, quality assurance, team leadership, problem solving, tools and techniques.
Improvement team leader course	All team leaders	3 days	Role of team leader. Problem solving process. Tools and techniques.
Outside company courses	Assigned by managers	½ day to 1 week	Provided by external experts.

Figure 2.4 Japanese company TQM training schedule.

tinuous process for all employees and not a 'one-off' investment for a year. If this 'one-off' approach is adopted, then the TQM training will be seen as a programme, not as a process. It is essential to avoid the use of the word 'programme' because this indicates lack of understanding that TQM is a continuous improvement process. A programme has a beginning and an end – continuous improvement is never-ending.

Figure 2.4 shows a typical training schedule for Total Quality as practised by successful Japanese companies. It is a useful exercise to compare your company's Total Quality training with this schedule and measure the real commitment to the Quality Improvement Process.

CHAPTER THREE

TQM principles

SIMPLE PRINCIPLES

The principles of TQM are a set of commonsense beliefs that determine the individual's actions in everyday life – not just at work! It is a fascinating effect of TQM that individuals do apply TQM to their non-work lives, particularly when affected by poor service in a restaurant, hotel or transport. The reason for this is that the focus and awareness of quality is increased through the understanding and application of TQM principles and meaning.

Perception of quality

One of the biggest problems faced by a company in implementing TQM throughout the organization is the understanding of what is meant by the term 'quality'.

It is essential that the company has only one definition of quality which everyone can understand and that makes sense. Unfortunately quality means different things to different people. For example, the media, advertisements and everyday conversations portray quality as meaning 'excellent', 'luxurious' and 'expensive' – all subjective terms. The trouble with this concept is that quality means anything that you want it to! In business, quality is associated with 'quality control' – the inspection of people's work in order to make sure it meets the Quality Control Standards. This approach suggests to the people in an organization, that the only department responsible for quality is the Quality Control or QC department.

These definitions, or to be more accurate, perceptions, of what quality means to the people in an organization have to be changed. It is essential that everyone in the organization believes in one definition of quality and believes that quality relates directly to them, as individuals, and as members of a team. This is a challenge that has to be confronted head-on by management – it is no use taking the TQM implementation and calling it something else. In other words, leaving the word 'quality' out in order to avoid confusion with 'Quality Control'. I have been asked on occasion by company executives:

> 'I wish we could call this TQM something different, after all everyone thinks quality is about Quality Control, but what you are talking about affects the whole Company – it is to do with everyone.'

'It is to do with everyone' and that is precisely why it is necessary to change the perception of what quality means to the organization. What is there to be gained by keeping the old perceptions and meaning of quality? The answer is, nothing at all and the sooner that quality is re-defined to allow everyone in the organization to feel it relates to them, the better.

Quality needs can be defined simply as follows.

Quality means 'meeting agreed requirements'

Meeting agreed requirements between:

- individuals
- sections
- departments
- divisions
- companies

TQM is a tough discipline because it is not an easy matter to define requirements clearly, or to obtain agreement, much less to achieve those agreed requirements. It will take time even to get started on occasions – that is a definition of requirements, but what will be avoided is half-understood agreements, second

---

A little story

This is a story about four people named Everybody, Somebody, Anybody and Nobody.

There was an important job to be done and Everybody was sure that Somebody would do it. Anybody could have done it but Nobody did it.

Somebody got angry about that because it was Everybody's job.

Everybody thought Anybody could do it but Nobody realized that Everybody would not do it.

It ended up that Everybody blamed Somebody when Nobody did what Anybody could have done!

Figure 3.1 A little story.

guessing which lead to poor commitment and lack of achievement, as illustrated in Figure 3.1.

What happens as the TQM principles are spread throughout the organization, is that individuals begin to use a common language for 'quality'. For example, it is common to hear the words: 'My requirement is', instead of 'I think I need'. Defining quality clearly, simply and in a manner that enables everyone to understand what it means is the **first requirement** (to use the language!) of TQM implementation. The first principle of TQM is therefore:

Quality means 'meeting agreed requirements'

Concept of internal customers and suppliers

Having understood what quality means it is necessary to consider the customer/supplier relationship. It is easy to understand

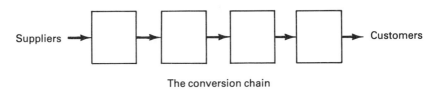

The conversion chain

Figure 3.2 Business is a chain process.

when the 'Customer' is the company buying your product or service. It is less easy to understand the concept of the 'internal customer'.

It is a fact that each person, whatever the process for which he or she is responsible, has a customer and a supplier. No one in an organization is exempt from this fact, even though some people might wish to ignore it! It follows from this straightforward fact, that each person is therefore both a customer and a supplier and has to recognize this in order to ensure the process for which he or she has responsibility is completed to the requirement. The simplest way to understand this is to ask two simple questions for every process that exists:

1. Who is my customer? (Do I have agreed requirements?)
2. Who is my supplier? (Do I have agreed requirements?)

This understanding of the chain-link interdependency of people in organizations is fundamental to achieving quality improvement. It is only as strong as its weakest link. The reason that achieving the business benefits is so difficult, is that it has to be understood and applied by everyone. Achieving this understanding is the greatest difficulty in implementing total quality successfully and within a realistic time scale.

BARRIERS TO UNDERSTANDING

What is the problem in understanding such a simple concept as the internal customer/supplier relationship? The answer to this is **attitude**! For example the attitude of a Marketing Manager when told that his customer is the Design Manager, or the attitude of a Design Engineer when told that his customer is a Production Shop Floor Operator.

Perceived status
The barriers are 'perceived status', compartmentalization, or sheer big-headedness!

'Do you mean to say that person is my customer?'
'Do you mean I have to speak to him!'
'Do you mean I have to ask him or her what he or she requires?'

The usual response is as follows:

'Not likely – I tell other people what to do!'

This status-conscious attitude is at the heart of the Western difficulties in successfully implementing the TQM Quality Improvement Process.

This conviction that management, and in many cases qualified professionals, 'know it all and have nothing to learn' is the root cause that will have the effect of destroying any TQM implementation process before it has begun. How can one person know and understand all the processes managed by all the people in the department or organization? How can one person be expert in all those processes? And most important of all: how can one person continuously improve all the processes in the organization at the same time!

The answer, of course, is that one person cannot, and that the person running the process must be the expert, whether it be a hotel receptionist running the process of booking guests in, or the secretary typing a letter, or a goods inward clerk booking in material from suppliers. Once management recognize that they have people working for them who should be experts in their job, the management role is clearly understood in terms of the customer/supplier relationship. It is to ensure that requirements are agreed and managed through communication, teamwork and management support. The realization that the manager has people working for him or her who are customers as well as suppliers is the key to good TQM management.

There is no room for the status-conscious manager who hides behind an office door and therefore breaks the line of communication to his people. How can there be a customer/supplier relationship where the customers aren't allowed to enter the shop! Each manager, each person needs to ask the question:

'What do I need to do to ensure my customer can do his or her job to the requirement agreed?'

This question does not take account of qualifications or status, only the requirements of the people in the company trying to do their jobs properly.

CONTINUOUS IMPROVEMENT ATTITUDE

The definition of quality 'Meeting Agreed Requirements', using the concept of the internal customer/supplier relationship is fundamental to the achievement of business requirements. However, business requirements never stay constant – competition is always there. Companies need to be constantly improving their service to customers, and developing new products to capture or maintain market share. It is a tough and ever-changing environment to work in and it is getting tougher and more changeable every day.

It is essential that companies recognize the importance of the process of continuous improvement in all areas and involving all people in the organization. It is hard enough to reach a situation where all people understand that quality means 'Meeting Agreed Requirements' using the internal customer/supplier concept. However, when those requirements have been met a new set of tougher requirements have to be agreed. Sometimes this is a tough fact to accept when a lot of hard work and commitment has gone into achieving a specific requirement, which may have been considered 'impossible' at one time. It is tempting to 'bask in the success' and forget that a new even more demanding set of requirements need to be agreed.

I believe that recognition of achievement and success is a key part of TQM, and will be discussed in a later chapter, but it is essential to recognize that after the celebrations, a new tougher challenge needs to be taken head on! This is the attitude of continuous improvement; not being satisfied with meeting requirements once, but improving all the time. I believe that when the continuous improvement attitude prevails in all the people in an organization, that organization is going to be, or is, world class already.

ZERO DEFECTS

When continuous improvement is the attitude in an organization, it is logical that the standard required for everyone is zero defects. However, it is important to understand that zero defects needs to be qualified by talking about:

'Continuous improvement towards zero defects'

In other words, although zero defects is the only acceptable error rate, it has to be achieved through a process of continuous improvement. It is a mistake sometimes made at the start of the TQM process to ram 'zero defects' down people's throats. This will quickly be used by the cynics to suggest that TQM is 'not real world', 'airy-fairy', 'a waste of time', or 'impossible'. They will argue that zero defects is beyond their process capability. This is an argument used very often by engineers, for example 'I can't design software with zero errors per million lines of code – you don't understand the process capability'.

The answer to this is to obtain agreement on the requirement for the product in the marketplace, which may not be zero defects! Then to ask the person 'When you have achieved this, are you going to continuously improve towards zero defects?' In other words, make sure you set and meet the requirements – and then continually improve, always changing the requirements towards zero defects. With the cynics it is useful to test their dual standards towards zero defects. For example, as a customer, they don't expect their pay-cheque ever to be wrong(!) and no one would ever allow a nurse to drop a baby. These are zero defects requirements.

Figure 3.3 TQM man.

Why don't some people apply the zero defects requirements to the work environment? It is an undeniable fact that learning and applying the TQM principles at work does lead to the very same application outside of work. When requirements are not met by hotels, restaurants, shops etc. it is sometimes clear that there is a case for TQM man!

PLANNING FOR PREVENTION

The process of continuous improvement requires an approach to situations, all situations, that can be best called Preventative. It is based on the belief that if something can go wrong then at some stage it will. The requirement is to think through fully the activity or process to be performed and ensure the necessary actions are taken to prevent things going wrong.

At this stage many people will say: 'I simply don't have the time to spend thinking things through to that extent'. This is one of the hardest principles of Total Quality Management to actually 'live' – precisely because of the huge and conflicting demands on people's time. The time pressure does not only apply to the CEO, it also applies to each individual in the organization. There is enormous pressure to 'fix' things that go wrong, the 'fix-it mentality'. It is rare that the root cause of a problem is identified and action taken to prevent the same problem occurring again. If you think about it, this is why people don't have time to apply preventative thinking and actions, it is a treadmill characterized by a 'fire-fighting', reactive management style. This approach needs to be changed in order that managers, in fact all the people not just managers, create more time to plan and prevent problems occurring in the first place. The elimination of root cause problems once and for all is a key requirement if the benefits of Total Quality Management are to be achieved.

All management meetings and all action plans should be focussed on eliminating root cause problems. A key question to ask and to keep asking is this: 'What are we going to do differently to ensure this problem never occurs again?' This question needs to be asked again and again until everyone fully understands the need to take specific actions to ensure the elimination of the root cause for ever. The challenge for management is to recognize that 'fixing' problems is not enough, and that time and training effort is needed to change from fixing to the preventative style.

Identifying and eliminating root cause problems

Western management typically have little knowledge of the tools and techniques which must be used to identify and eliminate root causes. This is in stark contrast to Japanese management who are taught tools and techniques – and, more importantly, apply them – to identify and eliminate root cause problems.

It is difficult to eliminate root cause problems; if it wasn't tough to do this it would already have been achieved. It is essential for management to realize very clearly that if they themselves do not understand the TQM tools and techniques and apply them, then there is no chance at all of fully achieving TQM business benefits. The attitude that problem solving techniques are only for the people that work for them is wrong. The use of analytical, easy-to-use problem solving tools and techniques in the board rooms of companies is a <u>fundamental</u> <u>requirement</u> of TQM.

If management are not prepared to believe this and get on with learning and applying these tools and techniques then the ability to achieve a competitive edge through TQM will be limited severely. Indeed it is almost certainly a waste of time and effort starting down the TQM route.

This book is only of value if these points are very clearly made, such that management understand what they need to do. The tools and techniques are covered in Part Three and apply to everyone in the organization through their involvement in Quality Improvement Teams (Chapter 8). The Top Team (Executive Board or Senior Management Team which, from now on, I will refer to as 'Top Team') must lead the application of tools and techniques as the first Quality Improvement Team, so the temptation for managers to skip Chapter 8 must be avoided! These techniques apply to everyone.

For example, the benefits of applying the cause and effect diagram to a major business problem is to identify clearly areas for corrective action. To show what this looks like I have included a Cause and Effect diagram (Figure 3.4) drawn up by the Board of Directors of a UK Company who very quickly learned and applied the problem solving techniques in this book to address a key business issue.

It can be seen from the diagram that there are many areas for improvement which have been clearly identified as having an impact on Top Team efficiency. One of the most important aspects of applying problem solving techniques at Board level is

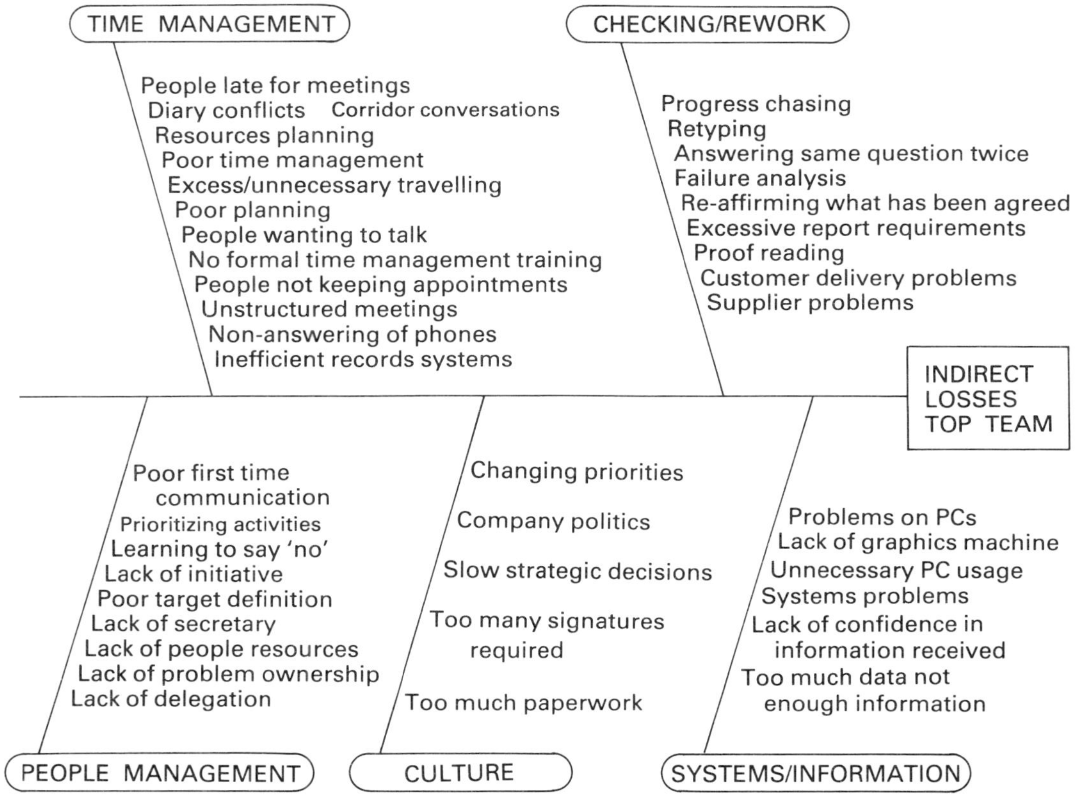

TIME MANAGEMENT

People late for meetings
Diary conflicts   Corridor conversations
Resources planning
Poor time management
Excess/unnecessary travelling
Poor planning
People wanting to talk
No formal time management training
People not keeping appointments
Unstructured meetings
Non-answering of phones
Inefficient records systems

CHECKING/REWORK

Progress chasing
Retyping
Answering same question twice
Failure analysis
Re-affirming what has been agreed
Excessive report requirements
Proof reading
Customer delivery problems
Supplier problems

INDIRECT LOSSES TOP TEAM

SYSTEMS/INFORMATION

Problems on PCs
Lack of graphics machine
Unnecessary PC usage
Systems problems
Lack of confidence in
information received
Too much data not
enough information

CULTURE

Changing priorities
Company politics
Slow strategic decisions
Too many signatures
required
Too much paperwork

PEOPLE MANAGEMENT

Poor first time
communication
Prioritizing activities
Learning to say 'no'
Lack of initiative
Poor target definition
Lack of secretary
Lack of people resources
Lack of problem ownership
Lack of delegation

Figure 3.4   Cause and Effect. Indirect lost hours – Top Team.

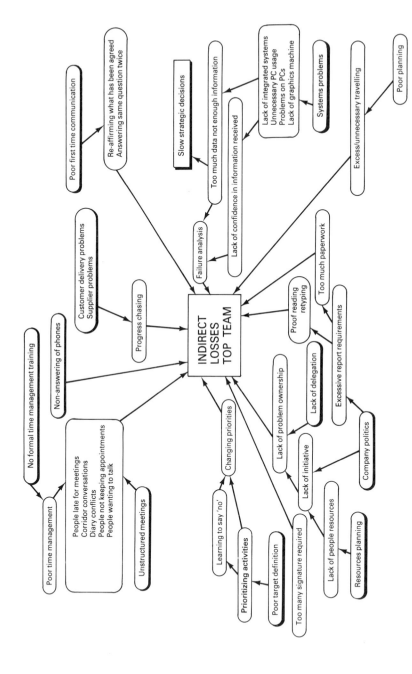

Figure 3.5 Relation diagram. Indirect lost hours – Top Team.

that all the Board members realize the total interdependency they have between each other. This approach also promotes 'consensus' management in the organization. For example, there is no problem in deciding on the need for corrective action teams combining people from different departments to be formed in order to solve a problem like poor Top Team efficiency.

Resources are more easily made available and there is no negative reaction to the request for individuals to spend time on problems which were not previously seen to be anything to do with their department. It is essential for senior management to fully understand the principle of prevention, learn to apply problem solving techniques themselves and ensure sufficient time and attention is allowed for the identification of removal of root cause problems.

If this is not understood, the company will never get off the 'fix it treadmill' – where the same problems keep recurring and the same fixes keep being applied – very often by different people. To avoid the treadmill, it is necessary to ask the same question whenever a problem is 'fixed':

'What are we going to do differently to ensure this problem never occurs again?'

COST OF TOTAL QUALITY

Cost of Total Quality is the concept of measuring, in financial terms, both the cost of failure and the cost of prevention. The cost of failure is normally termed the Cost of Non-Conformance (CONC). The cost of prevention is normally termed the Cost of Conformance (COC). Combining the Cost of Conformance and the Cost of Non-Conformance adds up to the Cost of Total Quality for a Business.

> COST OF TOTAL QUALITY
> = COST OF CONFORMANCE PLUS
> COST OF NON-CONFORMANCE

The precise definitions are:

Cost of Conformance
The cost of investing to ensure activities are achieved to the agreed requirement and problems prevented from occurring.

Cost of Non-Conformance
The cost incurred by failing to achieve activities to the agreed requirement.

The Cost of Non-Conformance in most Western manufacturing companies is typically between 15% and 25% of turnover, but in service industries the figure is closer to 40% of turnover.

It is possible to clearly identify where non-conformances are occurring and to establish an analysis of those costs in financial terms. The details of how this is done are covered in Chapter 7, but Table 3.1 indicates generic areas found in a manufacturing environment. It is essential to understand that this is total cost of

Table 3.1   Areas in a manufacturing environment

Immediate loss	Lost opportunities
Scrap	
Obsolete stock	Excess inventory
Excess test cover	Poor delivery
Direct rework	
Indirect rework	
Warranty	
Debtors	

In service activities, there are corresponding costly areas of non-conformance.

Immediate loss	Lost opportunities
Direct rework	Discounts
Indirect rework	Excess stationery
Compensation payments	
Excess checking	
Overpayment	

quality and it therefore applies to everyone in the organization – not just the shop floor.

It is necessary to establish requirements clearly across the business and to measure when those requirements are not being met. The Cost of Non-conformance is a methodology for putting a financial measure on failure by measuring wasted time or wasted material. It is important to define a standard method for measuring Cost of Quality, this will then become the method for assessing financially the effect on the business of the TQM Quality Improvement Process.

It is normal for companies investing in TQM to initially increase the total Cost of Quality before a reduction is obtained. This is because finance is required for education and training and time has to be made available as an initial investment to give momentum to the TQM process. A typical total Cost of Quality trend is shown in Figure 3.6.

It has been proved by the author and his team in client companies that a reduction of between 2% and 5% of turnover can be achieved within the first year, when the TQM implementation methods in this book are followed. This has resulted in millions of pounds being saved providing returns on investment

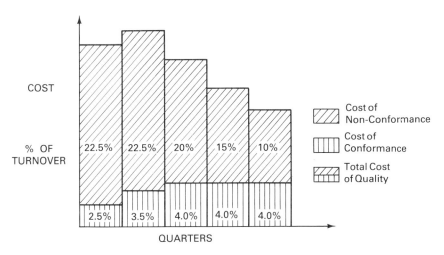

Figure 3.6   Typical cost of quality trends.

often exceeding 500% in the first year! Figures like these make
it an easy task to justify expenditure on TQM, but care must
be taken to ensure the total Cost of Quality system applied is
credible and easy to use.

It is essential to avoid 'analysis paralysis' where the thinking is
that it is better to be precisely wrong, rather than approximately
right. In other words, don't try to apply total Cost of Quality
to the last three significant figures – all the effort will go into
recording the information and there will be no effort left to solve
the problems. A set of rules must form the basis of the system
to be used at all times, thus ensuring all improvements are
calibrated against a fixed standard.

It has been more difficult for service industries or, to be more
precise, non-product areas to measure total Cost of Quality. This
is because manufacturing businesses producing a product have
usually put in measurement systems for that product. However,
even in manufacturing companies the non-product areas like
Finance, Personnel, Sales and Marketing have found difficulty
in applying total Cost of Quality methods. Again this is because
a lot of the work done in these areas involves no direct product
output.

The methods applied by the author have been proven to work
in all areas of a company because they are independent of product. They are related to the process or activity carried out by a
person. If the TQM principles are applied correctly requirements
will have been agreed between the customer/supplier, which
allows measurement of non-conformance in wasted time or
material or both to provide total Cost of Quality figures.

THE QUALITY IMPROVEMENT PROCESS CYCLE

The diagram in Figure 3.7 encompasses all the principles of TQM
outlined in this chapter and puts them into a logical order which
helps implementation:

1. Define and agree requirements
   Using the definition of quality agree the requirement between the customer and supplier by asking the questions:

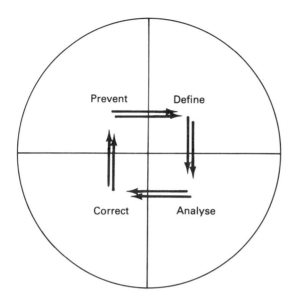

Figure 3.7 The improvement process cycle.

- Who is my customer?
- Who is my supplier?
- What requirements have I defined and agreed?

2. Measure non-conformance
   Having a measurement system to establish when the process
   is not meeting the agreed requirement and applying a
   financial measure – the Cost of Non-conformance. Ask:

   - Do I have a means of measuring non-conformance?
   - Do I have a means of measuring non-conformance
   financially?

3. Apply corrective action
   Using the non-conformance measures established to correct
   the problem by implementing a permanent cure – often
   termed a fix. Ask the questions:

   - Do I know what the problem is?
   - Do I need help to fix the problem or can I fix it myself?

4. Apply prevention system
   Ensure the problem <u>never</u> occurs again by considering

   - What process, method or system have I changed to ensure this problem never occurs again?
   - What are we going to do differently from now on?

This closes the cycle and takes us back to re-defining the requirement because requirements never stay constant; the competition is always improving and competitive requirements get tougher all the time.

This is the Process of Continuous Improvement, always tightening the agreed requirements, always eliminating error and going around the Quality Improvement Cycle again and again like a spiral until zero defects are met in the centre.

That is the Quality Improvement Cycle

PART TWO

Implementation of TQM

CHAPTER FOUR

The executive/ management role

Without the commitment of top management to TQM, there is absolutely no point in a company adopting a Quality Improvement Process. The first time a manager stops one of his people from attending a Quality Improvement meeting, or a Quality training course, all credibility will be lost. Similarly if a manager allows a product to be shipped knowing there is a problem, if typographical errors are accepted, if meetings discipline is poor, with managers arriving late or poorly prepared, then all these events will prove to the employees that management is not committed and nothing will change in the organization. Indeed, if TQM is ill-conceived and poorly managed, this will lead to an even greater divide between management and employees and do immense harm to the Quality Improvement Process. In short, management and Quality will be a 'sick joke'.

It is critically important that top management take the time out to fully understand TQM and what it can achieve for the organization, and develop an agreed (at board level) plan for implementation before attempting to implement the plan. This will require these very busy people to make time available, it cannot be delegated. Clearly before the top management in a company will commit to making time available for TQM it is necessary to answer the question 'Why?':

'Why should I spend 2 hours a week in a TQM meeting?'
'Why should I spend 2 or more days on a TQM training course?'
'Why should I attend this TQM Conference?'
'Why should I read this book?'

'I Don't Have The Time'

What this response means is that management don't have the time to improve the way the business is run. This attitude is characterized by short-term thinking and long-term extinction (or even short-term extinction).

The attitude of top management to TQM must be demonstrated whole-heartedly, every day and in every action. Especially the messages given from Top Team meetings and decisions must show the positive commitment to TQM. This must start with a clear statement of 'Quality Policy' which encapsulates the ethics and values of the company. The CEO will lead the thinking on the Quality Policy statement, as described in Chapter 6, but the Top Team must contribute and

Figure 4.1 'Just keep driving the car – don't look to see if there is a disaster ahead by reading the map!'

agree a consensus statement. This will be a vision of what the company philosophy is – and should be.

Starting from this general vision, it is possible to assess the company's current standing and to determine the necessary approach in all aspects of business. Particular aims must be expressed in a 'mission statement', to focus attention from everyone on the specific goals set by the Top Team for the organization. The approach defined by the Quality Policy statement must lead the Top Team to implement TQM from themselves and down through the organization until everyone is involved and committed.

Quality of management

The quality of management in a company is directly linked to the quality of the business. By definition it is the managers' role to

Figure 4.2   Quality of management.

manage the business – it is nobody else's responsibility. For example it is management who determine the quality of information, the quality of systems, the quality of organization and therefore the quality of products and services which determine the quality of the business.

Quality of information

Each manager should ask the following question: 'What information do I need to run my business?' If he isn't getting the information in the form required then it is his job to specify his requirement clearly. In this way it is possible to make a clear distinction between data and information. What is the use of receiving paperwork which in one week can take up most of a manager's desk? Many managers complain about the amount of paperwork but few actually do something about it. The rule is that only useful information which has been specifically defined as a requirement should be received. This will have a dramatic effect on the quality of information received by management, but of course management have to make the rules in the first place.

Quality of systems

The systems, methods and procedures that a company employs to output its products and services are critically important. However the definition, development, implementation and control of these systems is a difficult task and the ability to implement new systems successfully is important in achieving business requirements and thereby maintaining or improving a competitive edge. Management have a task to ensure that the correct methodology is used to implement systems to ensure continuity throughout the organization.

The following Total Quality Management methodology is universally applicable to all aspects of business from design through to distribution, but has to be rigidly applied.

The three-step requirements methodology
Step 1   Analyse and define existing system
Step 2   Specify completed system
Step 3   Phased implementation

This methodology is an essential element to the successful implementation of new and improved systems, methods and procedures in a company. The reason for this is that traditionally understanding of existing systems comes from either the written word which is often imprecise and requires a large amount of time to interpret, or through discussion which depends on interpretation, personal relationships etc. These difficulties in communication lead to inaccurate specifications for new systems which in turn lead to implementation and continual operational difficulties.

Integrated systems are particularly prone to communication difficulties as the areas for application are devolved into the operational parts of the company. The personnel in the operational areas need the opportunity to specify their requirements clearly. It is management's role to set the rule that through the TQM three-step requirements methodology, the operation of an existing system is clearly defined through the people who are the users. Also the new system is designed with clear understanding and involvement with the users. Finally of course, the new system needs to be implemented in a phased manner by the users, who fully understand each phase of implementation.

It is management's responsibility to set the rules – in this case the critically important use of the three-step requirement methodology to ensure successful implementation of new processes, systems and methods.

Quality of organization

Organizational change is often an area of concern for many companies, seen from the employees' point of view. Management changes can sometimes be seen as 're-arranging the deck chairs on the *Titanic*' for all the good they do. In fact, too many management changes can cause a feeling of instability and division in an organization.

In some organizations, even senior management are not made aware of the organizational changes; this breeds a feeling of resentment and instability which then fuels their employees' fears and concerns. The Total Quality approach to organizational change demands that the people are informed clearly of the changes and why they are being done.

The level of involvement in the organizational change decision-making process needs to be reviewed critically. An improved organization change without even management consultation will not provide an atmosphere where change and flexibility is welcomed – indeed it will provide totally the opposite. Certainly the Top Team in a company or division should be involved in the decision-making process and this should not be automatically decided and declared by the CEO. One of the key Japanese secrets of success is their commitment to 'consensus management'. This is common sense – if you are not involved in decisions which affect your way of working, then how are you going to show commitment? If this approach is adopted in the Boardroom, then it will also be adopted within the organization at each level. Again this approach to the Quality of the organization is a management responsibility.

Quality of products and services

'Management have a responsibility to recognise that the quality of products and services is what makes the company profitable and that everything that is done in the organization must be to support this ethic.'

This statement is simple and obvious, but it is often surprising that many companies lose sight of this fact and concentrate on internal issues which may have no impact on the customer at all. Sometimes a company will be 'Output Focussed', and 'Quality Blind'; it is management's responsibility to re-focus on customer requirements; to be specific, on the quality of products and the quality of service. Total Quality Management is about all aspects of the business, not just the products that are output; it is also about the 'Quality of Service' offered by the company.

The quality of service is determined by the quality of the people in the organization. Their attitude to the customer, and whether that customer is internal or external is critical to the achievement of a Total Quality culture in a company. For example, how many times will you wait for a telephone to ring before giving up and going elsewhere for better service? If you manage to get through and the person on the other end of the phone is unhelpful or surly, it doesn't matter how good the company product might be, the odds are you will go somewhere else.

Management need to recognize that quality is not just about products, but also about the quality of service offered by the company. This is much more difficult to achieve than product quality because it is all about people's attitude to the company and customers.

'Management leadership is the key'

This means ensuring all employees understand and are committed to what is required of them to ensure the company is successful, meets its mission statement and business requirements and therefore achieves and maintains a competitive edge.

MISSION STATEMENT AND BUSINESS REQUIREMENTS

It is essential that all employees understand the question: 'What business are we in? The answer needs to be encompassed within a clear, concise and short mission statement.

The elements of the mission statement may include:

Markets   : World, European, etc. segmentation
Technology   : High, low, product, specific
Customers   : Both internal and external
Quality of service: Meeting requirements
Profitable growth : Need to meet financial targets

"TO BE RECOGNIZED AS THE LEADING
INTERNATIONAL SUPPLIER OF . . . .
. . . .
BY CONTINUOUSLY IMPROVING OUR
PRODUCTS AND SERVICES TO MEET OR
EXCEED OUR CUSTOMERS' EXPECTATIONS"

SIGNED . . . .
MANAGING DIRECTOR

OUR ROLE IS:
" . . . .
. . . .
. . . . "

SIGNED . . . .
DEPARTMENTAL TEAM
. . . .
. . . .
. . . .
. . . .
. . . .

Figure 4.3 Typical mission statement.

A typical mission statement may read as shown in Figure 4.3.

The means of arriving at a relevant mission statement is critical, the requirement being that all members of the Executive Board or Senior Management Team – the 'Top Team' – agree and are committed to it.

The mechanism for achieving an agreed committed mission

statement is for the Top Team to brainstorm and then agree. Brainstorming allows each member of the team to put forward his or her statement in turn. In this way the key elements are agreed by the Top Team and within 2 hours or less it is possible to achieve the objective – i.e. a clear, concise and agreed mission statement which answers the question 'What business are we in?'.

The importance of all members of the Top Team agreeing the mission statement cannot be underestimated. By using the brainstorming method, each member has had to think it through and will therefore fully understand and be in a better position to communicate down the organization. Of course, a further advantage is that all members of the Top Team will be giving the same message!

Business requirements

If the Top Team is successful in achieving an answer to the question 'What business are we in?' then the next logical question is 'What do we need to be good at?'. This is what is meant by the business requirements, i.e. what does the company need to be good at in order to achieve and/or maintain a competitive edge. These may also be called Business Drivers, as shown in Figure 4.4.

The elements were discussed in Chapter 2, but it is worth reiterating that flexibility and responsiveness is determined largely by the flexibility and responsiveness of all the company employees. In communicating the mission statement and business requirements it is essential that this simple message is given.

Competitive analysis

Having established answers to the questions

1. 'What business are we in?' (Mission statement)
2. 'What do we need to be good at?' (Business requirements)

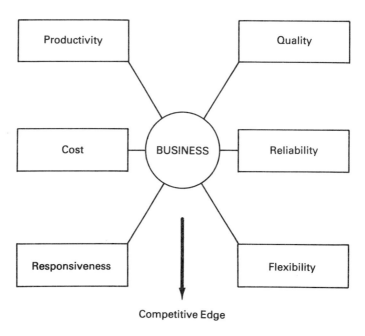

Figure 4.4   Business requirements.

the next logical question to ask is

3. 'How good do we need to be to achieve our mission statement?'

In simple terms this means being better than the competition
and being perceived by the marketplace as being the 'Market
Leader'.

The temptation is to use Total Quality to make exhortations to
people to be 'excellent' or 'the best', or worst of all 'perfect'! This
is an entirely useless approach since it does not provide specific
targets – measurable, monitorable and achievable – which
all employees can understand and be committed to. It is not
necessary to be 'Perfect' to achieve a competitive edge, it is
necessary to be better than the competition!

In order to find out how good it is necessary to be, the requirement is to complete a competitive analysis, benchmarking the

company against the competition. It is useful to use the generic business requirements to establish quantifiable performance measures. A matrix can be used to establish the measures which might include cost, product quality, reliability, flexibility, responsiveness, productivity and so on.

Competitive Benchmarking

Having established the measures, it is necessary to obtain performance figures against the competition – benchmarking the best of the competition and establishing that measure as the standard to beat. For example, a typical benchmarking table is shown in Figure 4.5.

Customer Audit

A useful method for obtaining this benchmark information is to conduct a Customer Audit which can be used to establish competitors' capability as well as your own company's capability.

Most customers are happy to give information on competitor performance – after all, this can only benefit them! A typical questionnaire is shown in Figure 4.6.

Many companies use external agencies to complete the audits which can be valuable, particularly in assessing competitor performance. The use of a questionnaire has to be considered where there are many different customers, perhaps in different countries where it is impossible to visit all customer premises.

It is important to spend some time, however, considering how to ensure a good response rate to the questionnaire. An introductory letter accompanying the questionnaire and explaining its importance to the company and the customer is essential if the questionnaire is not going to decorate the rubbish bin!

A typical letter is shown as Figure 4.7.

A further requirement is to establish, whenever possible, a named person to send the questionnaire to. Although this will take more time and money, it is most likely to be successful in establishing a two-way dialogue between the company and a real customer.

Performance measure figure	Own company	Competitor A	Competitor B	Competitor C	
Time to market	14 weeks	5 weeks	20 weeks	12 weeks	5 weeks
Delivery performance	95%	90%	96%	93%	96%
Response time to orders	5 weeks	3 weeks	4 weeks	2 weeks	2 weeks
Reliability (time to failure)	1 year	2 years	6 months	9 months	2 years
Delivered quality	95%	98%	99%	96%	99%

These figures need to be constantly reviewed by the Top Team, to ensure improvements in Competitive Performance are noted and the benchmark updated accordingly.

Performance measure	Actual	Target	Competitor A	Competitor B	Competitor C	Best practice

Figure 4.5 Typical benchmarking table.

Supplier name	Regularity of contact with Director/Sn Mngr	Delivery performance on time	Quality of service (style/courtesy)	Technical quality of product/service
A				
B				
C				
D				

Figure 4.6 Customer audit questionnaire.

Dear

CONTINUOUS IMPROVEMENT POLICY

It is our policy to continuously improve the quality of the service we provide to our customers. We are honest enough to admit that we do not offer a perfect service at all times, but we do not attempt anything less than 100%. However, we appreciate that this will take a lot of dedication, effort and commitment. We need to have increasingly close contact with our customers to enable us to improve our service to their benefit.

By working with us you will help us to improve our services continuously – this questionnaire is designed to help us help you.

Thank you for your co-operation.

Yours

Figure 4.7   Continuous improvement policy.

Having established a name or names in the company this potentially allows for the establishment of 'User Groups' reciprocal visits and so on, all of which will help to create a customer supplier relationship based on a mutual under-standing and trust. This in turn creates loyalty and is a key requirement in fending off the competition; in other words, what is often called 'Brand Loyalty'.

It is important to establish an honest and open relationship with customers where, although problems do occur between the supplier and customer, the customer understands that through his feedback, the service that is received is continually improved. There is no company in the world that is perfect. The successful companies are those that are committed to a policy of continuous improvement and it is impossible to achieve this if you don't talk to – and most importantly listen to – your customers.

OBTAINING COMMITMENT TO BUSINESS REQUIREMENTS FROM ALL EMPLOYEES

'Acceptance and understanding is a pre-requisite to obtaining the whole-hearted commitment of all employees.'

Having established the mission statement, business requirements, performance measures, competitive position, and customer feedback, there is sufficient information to begin communication to the total company. The content of the communication will follow this structure:

1. What business are we in?   : Mission statement
2. What do we need to be good at?   : Business requirements
3. How good do we need to be?   : Performance
                                        measures required
4. How do we stand against the   : Benchmark results
    competition?
5. What do our customers think   : Customer audit
    of us?   information

It is essential to specify clearly the performance measures required to beat the competition and to underline the importance to <u>all</u> the company employees (including management as employees!) – of achieving a competitive edge.

Communication methodology

This information should be given to the total workforce at least twice per year. Management should develop information, updating answers to the basic questions set out above, which is presented to their teams quarterly allowing questions and answers. Team briefs should be given using the CASCADE principle illustrated in Figure 4.8 to monthly briefs of each departmental or divisional team. Feedback through questions and answers is an essential part of this process and must be built-in to each briefing session.

FULL REVIEW OF MEASURES

Having established the performance measures required to be competitive, it is essential to complete a top-down review of measures within the company. All these measures are only of

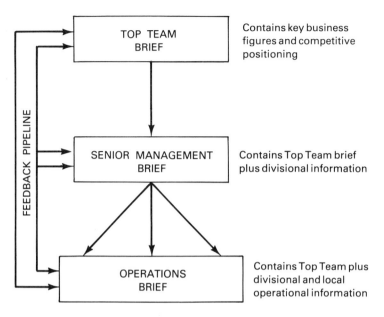

Figure 4.8 Cascade system.

value if they contribute to the competitive requirements already identified.

It may be necessary to critically examine a few assumed truths in order to achieve the right internal measures, or at least to look critically at the relevance of certain traditional values. For example, there is little point in measuring 'Standard Hours' or efficiency of manufacturing, if the delivery performance to the customer is only 50%! In many cases delivery performance line by line to the customer is not measured at all. By completing a full review of measures internally to support the competitive requirements, many bad and useless practices can be eliminated once and for all.

It is important to ensure all people recognize the key competitive measures and are then encouraged to establish their own internal measures. This can be done by management heading the brainstorm and allowing consensus on the key measures to be established. This procedure takes more time than the typical method of 'management imposed' measures, but is well worth

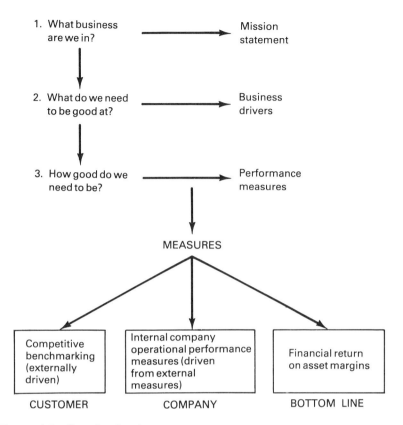

Figure 4.9 Spenley business management process.

the effort. The reason for this is two-fold. First, by involving the people who are responsible for achieving the measures, it is certain that the reason for these particular measures being chosen are understood. Second, the commitment of those people to achieving and beating the measures will be there. In this way, using this methodology for establishing measures against the competitive requirement, it is possible to ensure:

1. Commitment to business objectives from all people.
2. Everyone understands the business requirements and their own measurable contribution.

This process is shown in diagramatic form as Figure 4.9 The Spenley Business Management Process.

CHAPTER FIVE

TQM Structure and top-down requirements

TOP TEAM PLANNING AND STRUCTURE

Having reached the point where the senior management team and executives understand what TQM is, and how it can be used as the management methodology to achieve the required business benefits, there is a requirement to plan implementation. The first requirement is to form a Top Team to plan and control the implementation of TQM throughout the company. The temptation for executives is to 'appoint' a TQM 'implementation team' comprising fairly senior people in the organization, but not including the CEO and directorate. This is a mistake. If the CEO and directorate do not take full responsibility for TQM implementation by forming the Top Team themselves, then two problems will occur.

The first is that because the directorate are not 'doing' they will not fully learn the TQM principles and will not therefore practice them. This will immediately create a barrier between the directorate and the 'implementation team'. There will be a language barrier and therefore a barrier to successful implementation.

The second problem is that everyone in organizations makes judgements on what people do and not what they say. TQM is a people methodology, all people including the directorate, and if the directorate put themselves above this principle by not getting directly involved in TQM, it will fail. The respect will not be earned and it will be impossible to gain the hearts and minds of the people in the organization.

The requirement is to lead by example and the first step in achieving this is to ensure that all the directorate, including the CEO, are active members of the Top Team, planning and controlling the implementation of TQM top-down throughout the organization. The members of the Top Team should comprise the people who are responsible for leading the company.

Top Team selection

Large companies

Large companies have an Executive Board comprising the CEO Group Directorate such as Finance and Personnel, Sales, Marketing and Operational Directors. The Directors in Sales, Marketing and Operations very often have their own directorate. The structure may well look like Figure 5.1.

The group of people, in Figure 5.1, form the first Top Team in the company and have a responsibility to develop the TQM plan which is the plan across the total company. The implementation planning contained in the Chapters 5–13 relate to this group just as importantly, if not even more so, as for all other Top Teams throughout the organization.

The requirement is to develop a Total Plan for the company which can then be taken down the organization by each of the Directors responsible for Sales, Marketing, Operations, Manufacturing and so on. In this case, each of the Directors will form a Top Team of his own to plan and control the implementation locally of TQM through individual plans.

The first Top Team will then form a focal point for the total implementation plan which will ensure co-ordination of planning across the company. This requirement is of paramount importance since all the big problems in an organization are multi-disciplined and cut across functions. For this reason it is advisable to start the implementation across the company at the same time. Again, because the first Top Team is controlling the

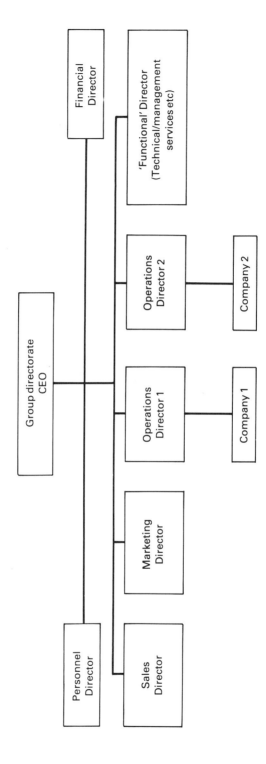

Figure 5.1 Large company structure.

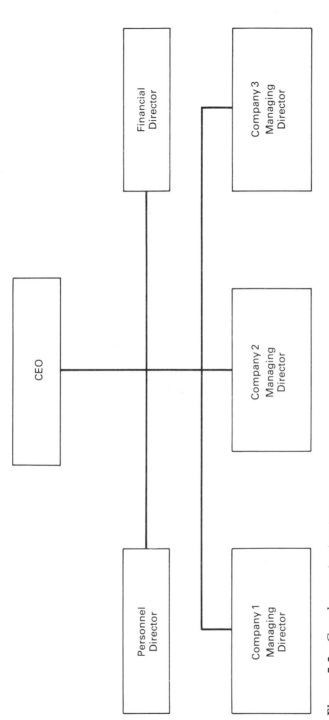

Figure 5.2 Conglomerate structure.

planning and implementation, it is possible to control and co-ordinate this work successfully.

Conglomerates

The same strategy of top-down implementation relates to the massive conglomerate-type companies. The only difference is that the structure is more likely to look like Figure 5.2.

Each of the companies will have their own structure comprising an organization similar to that described for large companies. In this case there needs to be a total plan for the conglomerates which is then top-down implemented through the companies by each 'Top Team'.

Small/medium-sized companies

The structure may look like Figure 5.3.

In this case there will be only one Top Team and one plan for the implementation of TQM in the organization.

TOP TEAM PLANNING

The above is a guideline to successful implementation. It is the first job of the CEO and his Top Team to determine the Top Team structure needed for the organization – whether it is a huge conglomerate, or a small company of 50 people. The problem is more difficult to solve the larger the organization but the principles remain the same.

TQM IS TOP-DOWN LED AND TOP-DOWN IMPLEMENTED

In every case the first Top Team has to get its act together and pull together a plan for TQM before imposing any actions on the people through the organization.

Structured planning

The Top Team need to understand that TQM implementation is a process and not a programme. It is a process of continuous improvement which requires careful planning, monitoring and

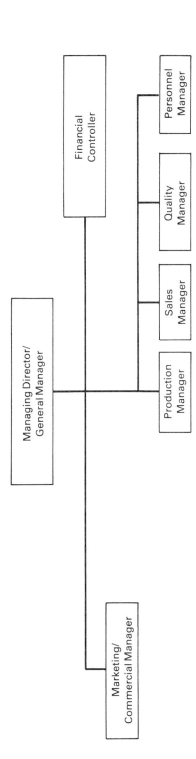

Figure 5.3 Small/medium-sized company structure.

control. It follows, therefore, that sufficient importance must be attached to TQM to warrant a specific Top Team meeting to be held regularly 'for evermore'. This is to say that just as the financial figures are reviewed, say monthly, and actions reviewed or taken to ensure requirements are met, then the TQM Continuous Improvement Process Plan is approached with the same importance. TQM or the Process of Continuous Improvement, is fundamental to the achievement of the financial requirement that the business is judged on by the shareholders.

It will not be possible to succeed with the implementation of TQM if it is seen as a 'bolt-on extra', and 'fitted in' to the monthly financial review or board meeting. This approach is indicative of an uncommitted approach to TQM implementation and will certainly ensure the failure of the continuous improvement process. The requirement is to allocate time to a TQM meeting regularly and with primary importance attached to the meeting to ensure attendance. Normally this meeting should be held monthly and should last for a minimum of 2 hours and a maximum of 3 hours.

The first commitment given to TQM implementation is to allocate the time and commit attendance to this meeting. This is not an easy task to achieve in many companies where Top Team members have crowded diaries and very little time for planning – all the time is spent 'running the business' – which is precisely why these Top Teams need to implement TQM.

The first step in improving the way the business is run is to take TQM seriously and commit to structured planning meetings. It is essential for the success of TQM that it is planned and integrated into the management requirements. The success of every activity depends on thorough planning and total commitment and the first requirement of top management is to recognize this fact and allocate the planning time accordingly.

Typically an Executive Top Team in a conglomerate responsible for many operations should meet initially monthly to develop the plan, and then quarterly to review progress and help co-ordinate the operational plans. The operational Top Teams should meet monthly, with the Directors of the operations also being members of the executive Top Team, and providing good two-way communications.

In smaller companies the Top Team need to meet monthly, although in all cases it is necessary to spend more time in the initial stages to develop the plan – typically meeting every two weeks until an agreed plan is developed. From that stage, monthly meetings are the requirement.

The elements of the plan

The planning for TQM is the responsibility of the Top Team. This team is accountable for developing, monitoring and controlling TQM implementation. The methodology is activity-based, not 'homework-marking'. It is essential for the Top Team to be seen to be leading the implementation – this means by doing not talking! When each member of the Top Team takes accountability for the successful implementation of each element of the TQM plan, there is a very good chance that the TQM implementation will be successful. Where the Top Team does not take accountability there is no chance of success.

The elements of the TQM plan are detailed in Chapters 7–12 and will act as a guide to those Top Team members who are accountable for one of the TQM implementation elements.

Top Team dynamics

Each member of the Top Team is allocated responsibility for an element and reports back to the Top Team meeting on proposed policies and activities that need to be taken into account to ensure success. The team then need to discuss the points for and against the proposal and together agree the plan. In this way all members of the Top Team are committed to the plan and will all say and do the same thing with their people in the organization.

It is important to understand that the member of the Top Team responsible for an element of the plan is there to advise the other Top Team members. It is up to the whole team to ensure the implementation of the plan, together. There are only two elements where it is necessary to fix the accountability – for all the other elements it is best policy to ask for volunteers for element accountability.

The two elements which are not voluntary are Quality Policy and Cost of Quality.

Quality Policy

The accountability for this element needs to lie with the Chief Executive or top manager in the Top Team. The Quality Policy is not just a set of words, it is a set of values by which TQM implementation will be successful. This must come from the top of the organization.

Cost of Quality

The Financial Director or the Financial Controller needs to take accountability for this element. If not, he may feel defensive where someone else in the Top Team is talking about the financial measures of the TQM implementation. It is essential for the Financial Director to fully understand the Cost of Quality principles, take responsibilities for the analysis, and for the development and implementation of the on-going Cost of Quality Monitoring Systems. This will ensure full commitment to Cost of Quality and will make financial resourcing for TQM a much simpler and shorter process.

TQM IMPLEMENTATION TEAM ORGANIZATIONAL STRUCTURE

When the Top Team in the organization is meeting to develop the TQM implementation plan, this can be termed the first continuous improvement team.

A structure for TQM implementation and continuous improvement teamwork is required for the organization, as shown in Figure 5.4.

The planning and actions required are defined in Chapters 6–13 as elements in the Top Team implementation plan. This structure must be implemented to ensure that people in the organization are allowed time formally to solve problems. It

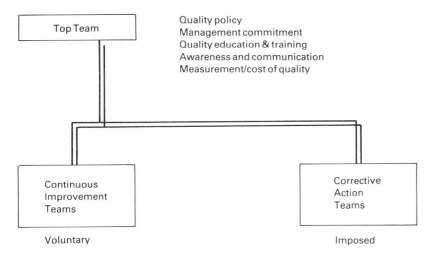

Figure 5.4   TQM structure.

means time, financial resources and training being provided – which is why these issues are an element of the Top Team planning.

The challenge is to ensure that all the people in the organization are active members of a Quality Improvement team. This is a fundamental requirement of the TQM Continuous Improvement Process and when this is achieved there will be a culture of continuous improvement in the organization. It is this structure which stops TQM implementation 'running out of steam' after the initial burst of activity and training – a problem all too common for many Western companies.

The successful Japanese companies are characterized by almost 100% involvement in Quality Improvement Teams. This is not achieved without commitment, understanding and involvement from the Top Team. It is not easy to obtain 100% involvement, but it is a requirement. Too often, Western companies will fail to recognize the importance of this Quality Improvement Team structure. A typical quote is 'we can't allow people to have an hour a week off the job!' Why not? What could be more important than meeting to continuously improve the way the business is run – and when 100% of the people in the organization, including the Top Team, are all doing this – what a competitive advantage this is!

Management commitment

This could more aptly be named 'leading by example'. It is a fundamental requirement that management lead by example in the Quality Improvement Process. This means fully understanding the Quality principles, and most important of all, practising them. Once this requirement is accepted, it is necessary to think through the actions that need to be taken to ensure success.

As already explained, the commitment to a TQM Planning meeting must be made and adhered to. It is then up to that member of the Top Team who has the responsibility for the management commitment element to advise the rest of the team on the actions they must all take. The following ideas promote a foundation to work on:

1. **Commitment to quality – first and always** – must be demonstrated. The requirement is for management to provide a focus on quality, by always putting quality first. For example, on all staff meetings, make sure quality is placed the first item on the agenda throughout the organization. A full review of measures in the organization needs to be carried out to ensure that quality is understood and is being measured correctly.
2. **Education and Training** is required for all the people in the organization to enable everyone to practise continuous improvement.
3. **Communication channels** must be improved to ensure full awareness of the company position, and the effect of the TQM Continuous Improvement Process.
4. **A Quality Improvement team** structure must be put in place starting with the Top Team and developing 100% involvement of the people in the organization through Continuous Improvement teams, and Corrective Action teams.
5. **Problem solving methods and systems** need to be estab-

lished to ensure that errors are completely removed, and never allowed to return. The tools and techniques explained in Part Three will be useful here.

6. **Recognition and reward** is a requirement to ensure 'Quality Champions' in the organization are properly recognized, and their commitment to quality re-inforced.
7. **A Cost of Quality system** has to be established to financially monitor the success of the TQM Continuous Improved Process, and to allow a priority for Corrective Action Plans to be carried out.

Along with the Quality Policy these are the elements of the Top Team TQM Implementation Plan.

It requires a continuous commitment to this TQM implementation plan by the Top Team – not in the initial stages where there is a lot of work required to develop a plan, but also a commitment when some success has been achieved and there is a tendency to settle back and think the job has been completed. In the TQM Continuous Improvement Process, there is no end, therefore there is no end to the Top Team meeting schedule.

This 'planning, monitoring and action' methodology has to be recognized as the key to success and management commitment is an absolute requirement to making it happen.

Financial support

Clearly such a major plan involving all the people in the organization cannot succeed if financial support is not forthcoming. Finance will be needed for education and training, equipment, materials and so on, to enable Quality improvements to be made. The first time a well-prepared Quality Improvement Plan is not approved by Management, because of 'lack of funds' the whole TQM Quality Improvement Process will lose credibility. Who would bother spending time to solve a problem when management doesn't provide the financial resource to implement the improvement?

All Quality Improvement plans must be reviewed formally and a positive response from Management given. There must be a commitment and involvement with the Quality Improvement plans, to ensure all Quality Improvements are to the benefit of the business.

Individual commitment

Apart from management commitment to the TQM Quality Improvement Process, there is a need for a Personal Quality Improvement Plan. This applies equally to everyone in the organization, not just management. However, it is necessary for the Top Team to begin the process by each member of the Top Team deciding on one or more activities to which he or she commits to making a continuous improvement. Some examples are included here to give an idea of the type of activities to which individuals can demonstrate a personal commitment to the TQM Continuous Improvement Process:

- Commit to a Policy of never changing the time or venue of a meeting you have called.
- Commit to starting the meeting on time and finishing on time.
- Commit to a policy of correspondence clearance within 24 hours.
- Commit to ensuring your secretary can read your writing so that she can have a commitment to zero errors and you don't then have to check her typing.
- Commit to the GOYA Policy – that is to 'get off your a***' and ensure a daily walkabout amongst your people whenever you are in the office. Also, make sure you don't always speak to the same people all the time!
- Commit to answering the telephone within three rings.

It is important that all the Top Team members start to demonstrate their individual commitment to the TQM Continuous Improvement Process at the same time – otherwise messages will be sent down the organization that only certain members of the Top Team are committed to quality. This must be avoided by Top Team planning and action! Remember that it is much easier to obtain individual commitment from the people that work for

Figure 5.5 Receptionist – three rings.

you if you are leading by example. In other words, 'I'm doing it – why can't you?' If you have any doubt that there is an activity that can be improved, it is a salutory lesson to ask those people that work for you. They will provide some ideas!

CHAPTER SIX

Quality policy

- What is the company's policy on Quality?
- What does the company mean when the word Quality is used?
- Is the company a 'Quality Company'?

These questions must all be addressed by the Top Team and clear unambiguous answers provided for all the people that work in the company. It is the role of the top person in the Top Team, that is the Chief Executive, Managing Director, or General Manager, to think through the above issues and provide a set of guidelines to the Top Team members.

The guidelines need then to be discussed at the first Top Team TQM Planning meeting and a policy and set of values agreed. It is important for the Top Person to think the Quality Policy issues through <u>alone</u> before sharing and brainstorming with the other Top Team members to obtain agreement. In this way, leadership will be coming from the top by doing. It doesn't matter if the words used are not 'slick' or 'media-style', what does matter is that they come from within. This will make communication easier and will ensure respect; everyone will know that the top person, whenever he or she speaks quality, believes in it. This is leading by example, and is absolutely critical to the success of TQM in the organization.

FRAMING A QUALITY POLICY

The Quality Policy needs to be short and succinct; it is a mistake to confuse the policy statement with a set of values which can make the 'Quality Policy' two or three pages long. This will ensure nobody can ever remember it, very few will actually read the words, and the paper will be consigned to the rubbish bin or a filing cabinet.

The Quality Policy needs to be a 'living' policy. It needs to be understood and remembered by everyone; it needs to be on the walls, desks, (and carpets!) of the business; it needs to be signed by everyone in the organization as their personal commitment to Quality. This should be done during the education and training process, not before training. The details of how this process of employee signature of the Quality Policy helps obtain commitment is included in Chapter 9 – Education and Training.

A Policy two or three pages long is not meeting the requirement! The actual words used are obviously the prerogative of the Top Team but there are certain factors that need to be included, which follow directly from the Total Quality Management Principles detailed in Chapter 3.

The Policy must underpin the following principles:

- Quality means meeting customer requirements.
- Customers are both external and internal.
- By meeting customer requirements the company will achieve and maintain a competitive edge against the competition.
- Quality means achieving a culture of continuous improvement in all areas of the company.

The Quality principles are all the information that is required to answer the three questions posed at the beginning of this Chapter.

Encompassing these principles into a short succinct form of words called the 'Quality Policy' is easier said than done! However, it is worth the mental effort and time of the top person in the Top Team, and of course the Top Team itself in the TQM planning meeting. To help things along a little, this is the Quality Policy I favour; and which also proves my own Quality Policy.

> TO ACHIEVE AND MAINTAIN A COMPETITIVE EDGE BY MEETING
> EXTERNAL AND INTERNAL REQUIREMENTS THROUGH THE
> PROCESS OF CONTINUOUS IMPROVEMENTS

Figure 6.1 The Spenley quality policy.

Quality Policy – set of values

Having established the Quality Policy, there needs to be a set of values to support the achievement of the policy. The mechanism for achieving these values is to brainstorm during the TQM Top Team planning meeting all the requirements needed to ensure that the Quality Policy can be met. It is important to go through this mechanism as it will get out, on the table, all the barriers to successful implementation. For example:

- Is Quality first against output?
- Is the company customer-orientated? Or is it being run for the employees at the expense of the customer?
- Is there a Process of Continuous Improvement?
- Is the company 'fix-it' orientated? Are root cause problems ignored?

It is an exercise in total honesty where there is a recognition that the TQM process is not going to be easy; it will take time, planning, effort and courage. It stops the process of management self-delusion setting in, while the temptation is to start plastering the walls with the newly-formed Quality Policy!

Total Quality
This is a typical shopping list of the Quality Policy values that need to be achieved in the organization:

- Achieving global competitive advantage
- Process of continuous improvement
- Eliminating waste in the organization
- Involves everyone
- Requires a cultural change; a change in attitude to continuous improvement

- Improves customer service and satisfaction
- Ensures everyone understands their role in the business and what is needed to achieve company objectives
- Everyone understands the internal customer/supplier chain
- Everyone has agreed measures between customer and supplier
- Ensures total teamwork
- Breaks down functional barriers
- Eliminate problem once and for all

The list is only a small number of elements that are brainstormed in the first Top Team planning meeting.

TQM – QUALITY OF CUSTOMER SERVICE

It is important at this stage to fully understand the total breadth across the company. In the Quality Policy the key word is 'customer'. In the set of values that are established to support the Quality Policy, it is necessary to clearly state that it is applicable right across the organization.

The diagram in Figure 6.2 is designed to clearly show the definition of Quality across all operations and functions of the company. This can be broken down into the Quality of all the

Figure 6.2 Quality of service to the customer.

functions that ultimately provide the customer service, whether this is a product, a hotel booking, a restaurant meal, an airline reservation or whatever. In other words, the Quality of service offered to the customer is dependant on <u>everyone</u> in the organization, not just those who have direct dealings with the customer.

This understanding is one of the KEY VALUES of the Quality Policy.

CHAPTER SEVEN

Measurement

INDIVIDUAL MEASUREMENT

The requirement is that every person in the organization gets used to a 'measurement culture' and finds a way of measuring his or her activities.

To demonstrate this individual commitment to continuous improvement it is necessary to draw up and maintain a 'visible' measure of progress. The best way of doing this is to use a simple measurement chart which is updated by the individual each day. It is important not to ask the Secretary to update the chart – this is defeating the object!

The chart should then be displayed in a prominent position where the individual's commitment to quality improvement can be publicly viewed. For example outside the manager's office, not inside. Not only does this show commitment but it also has the effect of ensuring the manager really does make efforts to improve, since his or her failures are publicly on view.

Experience of this approach has shown that people respect the manager for firstly accepting that he or she isn't perfect, and are then prepared to follow the example set, whereby failure is not hidden, and there is a determination to improve. This is strong and positive leadership, and provides the atmosphere which everyone else in the organization will follow suit and agree to a Personal Quality Improvement Measure, again which is fully visible.

The process of adopting an individual measure and charting

progress, leads to the establishment of a 'measurement and improvement culture' in the organization.

AGREED BUSINESS MEASURES

This measurement culture is understood and practised by everyone in the organization, and allows the use of business measures in all areas of the company.

Business measures are not the individual measures discussed in the last section of this Chapter – these are the hundreds, even thousands of measures which are taken day-in, day-out by the organization to ensure customer requirements are met every time.

These measures, as detailed in Chapter 4, are the result of a top-down review, ensuring the company is focussing on external customer requirements which provide a competitive edge to the company. For example, the requirement to deliver 100% on time, the product or service that the customer expects. These external customer measures then drive a whole series of internal customer measures throughout the organization. The TQM methodology for defining the correct measures is based on communication and involvement.

Communication

As detailed in Chapter 4, it is necessary to ensure everyone in the organization is aware of the key external customer measures the company is measuring, and why they are important. In other words 'if we do this we will achieve and maintain a competitive edge in the marketplace'. These measures then need to be fully visible to everyone in the organization as everyone should know how the company is doing – they are all part of the company after all!

There are methods for achieving this:

- Key external customer measures should be displayed throughout the company, on simple measurement charts, showing monthly, weekly or even daily results, dependent on the type of business.

- If there is a Network Information System, the key measures should be available on computer terminals available to everyone.
- All staff meetings must include an update on company performance.

There is sometimes concern that the total visibility of failure which measurement charts obviously show can be detrimental to customers or potential customers visiting the company. This concern needs to be discussed in the Top Team meeting and the individual circumstances of the company and its customer base taken into account. However, I have never known any customer, or potential customer, be anything but impressed with the total commitment to quality improvement which full visibility of measures demonstrates.

Involvement

The ability to ensure that the internal customer measures in the organization fully support and contribute to the external customer measures is dependent on the involvement of all people. This begins, as discussed, with the understanding and full visibility of the external measures required.

The next stage is to define the Divisional, Sectional or Departmental measures needed. This should be done by the Top Team who have the responsibility to cascade down the external measures and then involve the people below them in the organization in the definition of the internal measures required. This, in time, should be cascaded down lower into the organization until a full set of Agreed Measures is obtained.

The Measurement Top Team member has the responsibility for planning this process on behalf of the organization, and co-ordinating the measures.

The key to success is to obtain agreement between the internal customer and supplier in all cases. This is the application of the TQM principles detailed in Chapter 3, using the internal

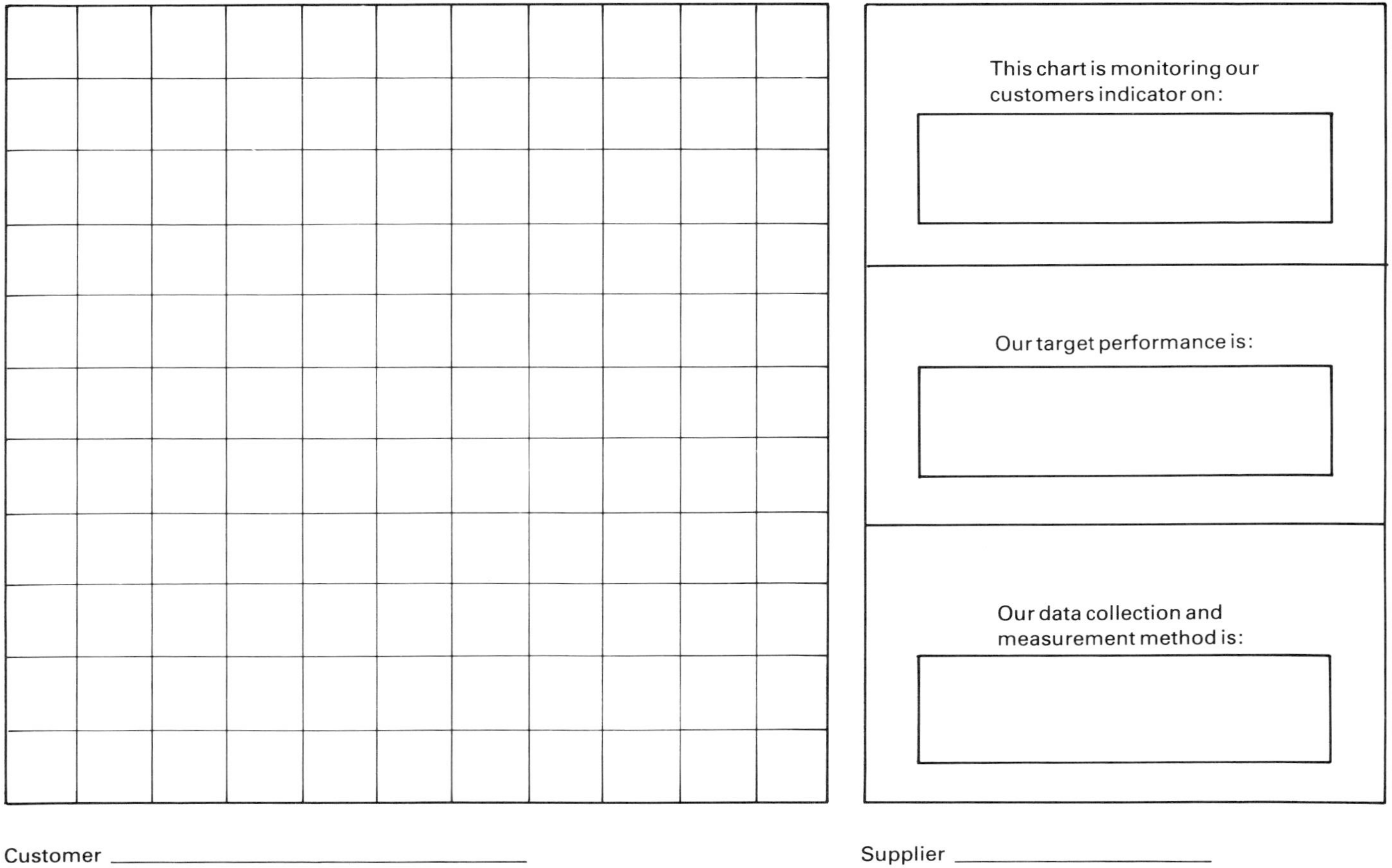

This chart is monitoring our customers indicator on:

Our target performance is:

Our data collection and measurement method is:

Customer _____

Supplier _____

Figure 7.1 Team indicator chart.

customer/supplier principle, and defining agreed requirements at all times. The customer/supplier relationship will be between division at one level, between departments at another level, between the sections at another level, and ultimately of course between individuals.

At all times requirements need to be agreed between the customer and supplier, and measurement charts should be established. It is a good idea to have a section on the measurement chart which identifies who the customer is, who is the supplier, and to have a signature from each to demonstrate agreement to the measure. A typical chart layout is shown in Figure 7.1. This can be done for divisions, sections, departments, and of course individuals and shows that the TQM principles have been correctly applied.

The total involvement of everyone in the organization in the measurement cascade, ensures that the people doing the job can measure their own work, and because of the involvement and commitment are able to correct problems when they occur, rather than wait for some 'specialist' to correct the problem. Or even worse 'throw the problem up to management' to solve. This measurement culture will allow up to 90% of problems to be solved when they occur between the internal customer and supplier.

However, 10% of problems will be out of the scope and influence of the people doing the job; these problems will require some management support and effort to resolve, possibly involving skilled problem solving techniques, like Taguchi, DOE (Design of Experiments), or SPC (Statistical Process Control).

It is important to remember that simple measurement methods applied with commitment, intelligence, and involvement of all people will solve 90% of the problems in an organization, continuously.

Cost of Total Quality – measurement

It is necessary to measure the effect of the TQM Quality Improvement Process in the organization in financial terms.

Applying the Cost of Total Quality System enables this, by providing a financial standard.

As detailed in Chapter 3

Cost of Total Quality = Cost of Conformance +

Cost of Non-conformance

Cost of Conformance is the cost of investing to ensure activities are achieved to the agreed requirement and problems prevented from occurring.

Cost of Non-conformance is the cost incurred by failing to achieve activities to the agreed requirement.

The Cost of Conformance should be measured initially to determine the total cost of investment in the TQM Quality Improvement Process. There will be an investment required in terms of people's time, the facilities required, and systems and equipment to enable people to improve the way they run the business.

TQM has to be budgeted for and the following items identified and established as investment costs. In other words, the Cost of Conformance Costs should be viewed as 'investment capital', not as a 'consumable cost'.

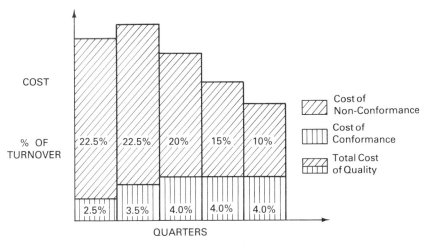

Figure 7.2 Typical cost of quality trends.

COC – people's time (100% of employees)
Education and training time : 10 days/annum
Formal problem solving time: 1 hour/week

This can easily be converted into a financial figure based on this hourly rate for employees, and so give a message of the financial commitment in people's time that is required. Remember it may take up to two years or more to get 100% of people into improvement teams – this doesn't happen overnight!

When this commitment to people's time is measured financially it may cause some concern; remember this is an investment that will be returned hundreds of times over.

COC – materials costs
> Specialist support costs
> Books
> Conferences

These costs are necessary to ensure State-of-the-Art knowledge in TQM, and may include specialist consultancy and training skills, videos and so on.

COC – facilities
The training facilities to enable formal education, and to accommodate improvement team meetings need to be established as a permanent requirement. The exact requirements are detailed in Chapter 9 on Education and Training, but may incur extra costs if there is not a suitable training facility in existence. Again, these costs may be significant and a budget is required.

SYSTEMS AND EQUIPMENT

Improved methods of collecting data and displaying information, such as Shop Floor Data Collection Systems, Retail Point of Sale Terminals, Computing Booking Systems for Hotel Reservations, Airline Reservation Systems and so on, must be considered.

It is not recommended that the cost of equipment/systems is included in the Cost of Conformance, as this expenditure is always viewed individually with a financial business case. However, it is important to understand that as people become more aware of what can be done to improve efficiency and productivity, more requests for systems and equipment improvements will be made than before, and management need to be aware, be able to respond and control this expectation.

It is not possible to successfully obtain the benefits of TQM, without being prepared to invest because

Investment in COC (Cost of Conformance) is a pre-requisite to Reduction in CONC (Cost of Non-Conformance).

Figure 7.2 shows this relationship. There should be no surprises!

The Cost of Non-Conformance is the cost incurred by failing to achieve activities to the agreed requirements. The implementation plan for ensuring education of CONC must contain the following elements:

- A Cost of Quality Analysis (CONC)
- A Company Cost of Quality Model (CONC)
- A Full Cause and Effect Analysis

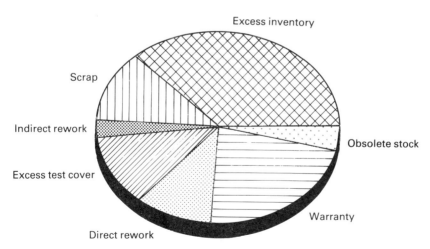

Figure 7.3 Quality costs in manufacturing activities.

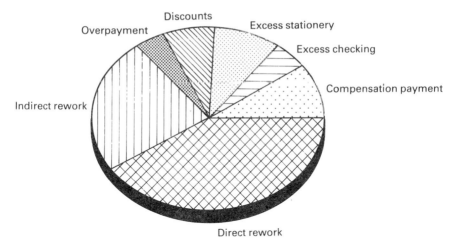

Figure 7.4   Quality costs in service activities.

- A Cost-Prioritized Corrective Action Plan
- Cost of Quality and Tools and Techniques Education
- Formula of Corrective Action Teams to reduce the non-conformance costs.

Cost of quality analysis

Typical cost of quality analyses for manufacturing and service activities are shown in Figures 7.3 and 7.4.

CHAPTER EIGHT

Quality improvement teams

Implementing a Quality improvement team culture into the organization is a key factor in ensuring the TQM Quality Improvement Process does not tail off after the initial enthusiasm. This was discussed in Chapter 5, where the improvement team structure was outlined. The structure is simple to understand but difficult to implement successfully.

One of the biggest problems in the TQM implementation process in the West is keeping enthusiasm and commitment going after the initial Cost of Quality work has been completed. This is because the Quality improvement team requirements are not fully understood at Top Team level. Too often, Quality improvement teams and Quality circles are seen as 'nice to have' but not essential.

It is important to understand that the successful implementation of Quality improvement teams is an absolute essential to the achievement of a continuous improvement culture. The requirement is to obtain 100% employee involvement in improvement teams. When this is completed, 100% of the people are actively working on Quality improvement.

This is the key competitive edge in any organization, and is the secret of success for Japanese companies. Although the Japanese methods for achieving TQM have been studied in detail for many years, this 100% Quality improvement team involvement is always admired but often put down to the 'Japanese culture'. In other words, it is 'impossible to achieve in a Western culture'. This type of ignorance is what will

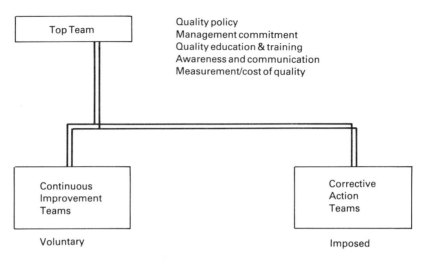

Figure 8.1   Quality Improvement Team structure.

keep Western companies lagging behind the Japanese. Why shouldn't it be possible to achieve 100% employee involvement in the Quality improvement process? There is no good reason. The implementation of the structure detailed in this book will provide the foundation, whereby, over a period of time, 100% employee involvement can be achieved and maintained.

PUTTING THE STRUCTURE IN PLACE

The Top Team need to have a member who is responsible for Quality improvement teams. It is his or her job to define the policies, plans and actions which need to be taken to obtain 100% involvement. These plans then need to be agreed at Top Team level, and of course implemented by all members of the Top Team.

Policy

1. To obtain 100% employee involvement in Quality improvement teams.

2. To allow improvement teams the time, during working hours, to meet formally. This should be for one hour maximum per week, typically.
3. To ensure 100% of people are educated in problem solving techniques.
4. To ensure 100% of people understand and practise good meetings discipline such that all improvement team meetings are productive, and not just 'whingeing sessions'.

Planning

The Top Team who is planning and maintaining the Quality improvement process is the first Quality improvement team to be formed. This is an important structure to make, and an important point of understanding for all members of the Top Team. They need to feel part of the TQM team culture and provide a role model for the rest of the organization.

Figure 8.2 Management commitment.

Structure

There are two types of improvement team:

- Imposed : Corrective action teams
- Voluntary: Continuous improvement teams

The first teams to be established in the TQM improvement process are the corrective action teams. As detailed in the previous Chapter, it is necessary to identify areas for improvement, prioritized financially, and obtain profitable benefit quickly. By following the Cost of Quality implementation planning, the corrective action team structure is achieved, in the early stages of TQM implementation planning.

Cost of Quality, therefore, is the vehicle for driving corrective action teams. The nature of corrective action teams is transitory, they are formed in order to solve a particular problem and when that is done they disband. It is the task or project style of team working, often under pressure. They are a necessary part of the Quality improvement team structure, and will provide major benefits to the organization.

Continuous improvement teams, on the other hand, are groups of people who meet together voluntarily to improve Quality. They may come from the same work area, or the same work function; for example a group of Secretaries. There are no set rules as to who should be part of a continuous improvement team. It may include people from Design, Marketing, Sales, Manufacturing and Finance, who may be meeting to continuously improve the process of product introduction, sales order processing, customer service etc. As already stated, the Top Team are meeting to ensure the process of continuous improvement across the whole organization is successfully established and maintained.

It must be understood that because of this, it follows that everyone in the organization can be a member of a continuous improvement team. This includes Managers, Project Leaders, Clerks, Sales Executives, Marketing Managers, Accountants, Engineers, Directors, and Secretaries. The teams may be Departmental, Inter-departmental, Inter-factory or Inter-organization etc. In many successful companies continuous improvement teams are established between the company and its customers, which ensures the rapid formation of a business process culture between customer and supplier, and a continuous improvement in customer satisfaction.

MANAGEMENT ROLE IN CONTINUOUS IMPROVEMENT TEAMS

Continuous improvement teams cannot be successful if management don't think it applies to them. This has traditionally been the problem with Quality circles which is another name for continuous improvement teams. In many cases management saw Quality circles as something for the workforce only, 'it doesn't apply to me'. This led to a lack of understanding of what the Quality circles were there for, what they did, and consequently a cynical view of their contribution to the business at work. There would be many attempts by middle management to stop Quality circles meeting, and at best a resigned tolerance of their existence.

This attitude is basically ignorant, not to mince words! The management must understand they need to improve as well as the people working for them, and therefore provide a role model, an example for their people. This is best done by being involved in a continuous improvement team themselves. The Top Team can claim to be a continuous improvement team. One of the tasks of the Top Team is to ensure that their management understand the improvement team policy, and learn how to operate a successful continuous improvement team. This will include the learning and application of problem solving techniques and of good meetings discipline.

When management are aware of how continuous improvement teams work by being involved, they are then in a position to encourage their people to follow suit. It follows that continuous improvement teams take longer to establish than corrective action teams, in the TQM improvement process. As long as this is understood by the Top Team, there is an excellent chance that continuous improvement teams will become a part of the company culture.

The manager's role in a continuous improvement team formed by members of his staff, has to be that of a 'respected helper'. In other words, the manager needs to be there to help guide the improvement team forward and to unblock problems that they come up against. It is not necessary to attend every meeting, but it is necessary to show interest and commitment to the team. It is also important to be fully aware of the project or projects that the continuous improvement team work on. This is to ensure that the project is going to provide benefits and not be a 'waste of time and effort'. In other words be careful to avoid projects that are irrelevant, unwieldy, or too far out of the scope of the improvement team. If this happens, the team will not be successful and there will be a reluctance for those people to continue.

Choosing projects

When a continuous improvement team meet for the first time, the requirement is to 'brainstorm' problems. This is the formal method of each person in turn thinking up of problems that affect he or she doing his or her job to requirements. It is not unusual to obtain as many as 50 problem areas in a ten-minute brainstorm.

These problems are then analysed to see how they fall into three catagories, as shown in Figure 8.3

T – 'Totally' under the group control, that is to say problems which can be solved by the group themselves with no assistance.

P – 'Partially' under group control, but which need specialist help to resolve, either from the manager, or other departments.

N – 'Not' under control at all, problems which are entirely out of the scope of the group and which should be referred to the Top Team.

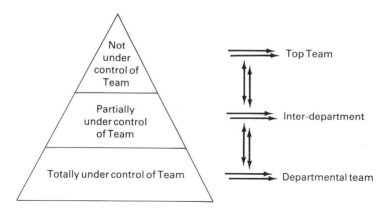

Figure 8.3 Problem solving structure for improvement teams.

The 'T' problems are usually solved by the group within a short time, provide quick benefits, and a feeling that the team is working.

The 'P' problems need guidance from management to ensure that the basis on which the problems should be chosen to solve first is right. These type of problems are tougher to solve than the 'T' problems, and need to be discussed with the manager to ensure the project chosen is valid and supported. These type of projects may take up to 6 months to solve. It is usual for continuous improvement teams to successfully complete two projects every year.

The 'N' problems need to be reviewed by the group with managers to ascertain whether a corrective action team should be formed which for example, would include people from Marketing, Design, Sales, or even from the supplier or customer.

Continuous Improvement Teams have great value in not only improving their own work methods, but also identifying problems which need to be addressed by the company on a larger scale. This is a good example of how continuous improvement teams and corrective action teams can work together.

Review of projects

It is important for the Top Team to establish a structure whereby all the continuous improvement team projects are formally received. This is necessary to ensure projects are valued, good work is recognized, and the necessary resources are planned, budgeted for and implemented.

The first request is for all members of the Top Team to take responsibilities for helping teams get started, and keep going, in their department – in other words to feel ownership. It is the Management's responsibility to educate their people so that everyone knows what a continuous improvement team is, how it works and what the benefits are to the individual and to the company. This is part of the education and training process, and it is vital that it is the manager who gets these messages across, and provides the route by which people volunteer to become members of a continuous improvement team.

It follows that this step should not be taken until the Top Team in a company is fully competent as a continuous improvement team itself. The culture of the continuous improvement team is then generated top-down throughout the organization. This approach obviously takes time, but is essential for the successful achievement of 100% involvement in the organization, and to on-going continuous improvement.

CHAPTER NINE

Education and training

The education requirement is to ensure that everyone in the organization knows what is required of them, and why. The training requirement is to ensure that everyone is capable of solving the problems that inhibit the achievement of their objectives. It is not sufficient to send people on Problem Solving training courses alone, and think this will cover the TQM requirements. It is necessary to tailor the Total Education and Training Plans to the achievement of company objectives.

By adopting this policy, the TQM education and training will become part of the company culture – a focal point for TQM which is always being updated and improved as new and better problem solving methods become available, or are developed internally. This will help the company achieve and maintain its competitive edge, through people.

STRUCTURE

The education requirement is to ensure everyone understands their role, and what is required of them. The measures established top-down in the organization should be included in the education and training material, to ensure full understanding of company objectives.

The training structure must be top-down, starting with the Top Team and cascading down the organization, as shown in

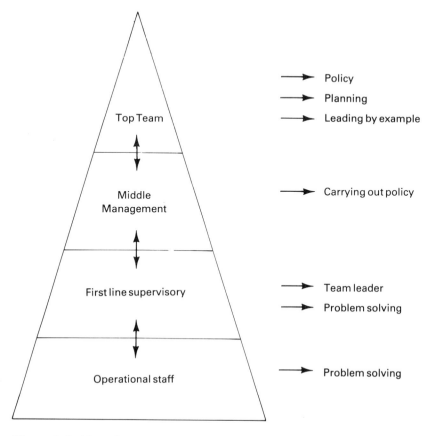

Figure 9.1 Top-down training structure.

Figure 9.1. The golden rule to successful implementation is to ensure managers train their own people. This is necessary to show management commitment, and to ensure managers actually understand the TQM principles and methods. After all, if you don't understand, you can't train. It also stops managers 'talking a good fight', and not actually fighting! In other words how can a manager continue with non-Quality methods when he's just trained and preached at people to adopt TQM principles.

PLANNING

The Top Team need to be trained before anyone else; in many cases this will require some external consultancy and training organization. Choosing the right people to do the job is of critical importance. The key selection criteria should be that the people understand the business the company is in and that the consultants chosen have a proven track record in TQM implementation in their own right. There is no substitute for experience when it comes to implementing a successful TQM process!

Clearly, the education and training planning is a key element of the overall TQM Quality improvement process. It is up to the Top Team member responsible for this element to ensure that his colleagues understand the 'top-down' policy, and take the opportunity to integrate the other clients of the Top Team plan with the education and training planning. For example:

1. **Management commitment**
   One of the best ways to demonstrate management commitment is for the managers to train their people.
2. **Measures**
   Using the education and training process to underline the importance of the measures used.
4. **Cost of Quality**
   Managers taking the opportunity to demonstrate to people during the training course, what has been achieved on Cost of Quality, what the corrective action teams are doing and so on.
4. **Quality improvement teams**
   Managers explaining the improvement team structure (Chapter 8), and taking the opportunity during the training course to encourage people to form or join continuous improvement teams. Again this shows management commitment.

Top Team
The need is to understand clearly the principles of TQM and plan the TQM implementation before launching the plan.

Team	Role	Course elements	Time
Top team	Policy planning	TQ principles Business strategy Performance measures	3 days
Middle management	Carrying out policy plans	TQ principles Business strategy Performance measures Team leadership Problem solving	5 days
First line	Problem solving team leader	TQ principles Team leadership Problem solving	5 days
Operations staff	Problem solving	TQ principles Problem solving	3 days

Figure 9.2 Total quality course structure.

Middle Management

To understand the principles of TQM, be aware of and contribute to the Top Team implementation plan. The Top Team need to take input from middle management and alter or modify the overall plan if necessary. This will help middle management commit to the whole process. This is a critical requirement as it is the middle management who will be mainly responsible for the training of the majority of people in the organization.

Therefore, the middle management training should include a heavy input from members of the Top Team. Courses need to be structured to meet three key requirements for middle management:

1. To understand TQM principles.
2. To renew the Top Team plan and agree implementation.
3. To develop a training course which will be suitable for the people who work for the middle management.

There is a lot of work to be done in any organization to meet these three requirements. The planning should be on iterative processes, whereby piloting of courses at all levels should be attempted and feedback obtained before fully committing the training plan.

One of the key contributors to success is the attitude of some of the middle management, when asked to do the training of their people; the response is normally:

'What me? I can't stand up in front of people and train them'.

This is a barrier that needs to be dismantled in two ways. The first is to explain quite clearly that this is a requirement in order to show management commitment, and that there can be no exceptions to this request. The second is to accept that there will be fears and concerns which need to be listened to and acted upon. For example, many people will need some help on presentation style and technique before 'going live'; this training will have to be provided for some of the middle management trainees.

It follows that the Education and Training Planning needs to be meticulous, detailed, and patient.

FACILITIES

It is no use starting the training off in a cramped Conference Room, or hastily organized training facility of some sort. This is Quality training, people are totally intolerant of anything which is not 'Quality'. To use the language – to meet their requirements. This means the provision of a training facility which looks and feels right, with decent furniture, full audio and visual equipment, and syndicate rooms for team working.

The facility should form a focus for Quality training and be established and maintained as such as a permanent requirement. It may be desirable to provide rooms in the same facility for the Quality improvement team to meet.

Administration support for the training is a key requirement – double booking of rooms is not allowable! This means the presence of full-time education and training facilitator and administration staff, ideally located in the Quality training facility.

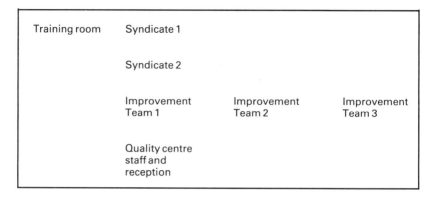

Figure 9.3 Typical quality training centre.

There is a need for a focal point for Quality, not only to ensure the training is carried out correctly, but also to provide a 'helpline' for individuals. For example, a trainee may want some 'quiet time' to produce a presentation, someone will want a measurement chart, and somebody else will want to see how a continuous improvement team works, before deciding to go ahead and form a team.

A typical layout for a Quality centre is shown in Figure 9.3.

PROBLEM SOLVING

The ability to solve problems is a key requirement of the continuous improvement process. The challenge is to ensure 100% of people are able to meet the requirements, throughout the organization.

There are three categories of problem solving:

1. Problem solving for everyone
2. Problem solving for teams
3. Problem solving for specialists

Taking each of these categories in turn:

Figure 9.4   'What do I do now?'

1. Problem solving for everyone

Training is required for 100% of people in the organization to learn the right approach to problem solving. This needs to be simple and effective so that it can easily be applied to everyday problems. It is not sensible to bombard people with '75 tools and techniques' of ranging complexity, which is an approach some-times adopted by companies attempting to establish a problem solving capability in their people. The problem with this approach is that so much time is spent in learning the individual techniques that no time is left for understanding how to apply them!

The majority of problems can be solved with the technique described in this Chapter – simple, easy-to-use, and successful. Before describing the appropriate technique, however, there is an absolute requirement to understand the 'problem solving cycle'. The approach to problem solving which is required from 100% of people. It is essential that this problem solving cycle is fully understood before training people in tools and techniques, otherwise nobody will know when to use which technique. The problem with many tools and techniques courses is that, because the problem solving cycle is not fully explained or understood, people have great difficulty in understanding their application.

The problem solving cycle in Figure 9.5, and has four steps:

STEP 1   The first step is to clearly define the problem – to use the Japanese terminology 'What is the fact'. The temptation is to jump to conclusions without ever really studying the problem in the first place.

STEP 2   The second step is to analyse the information and establish the root cause problem.

STEP 3   The third step is to solve the problem by applying a corrective action, which meets the immediate requirement.

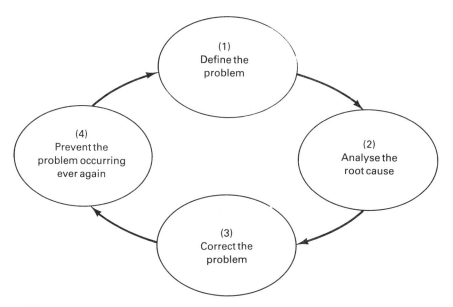

Figure 9.5   Four-step problem solving cycle.

STEP 4 The fourth step is to take the actions to ensure the problem can never occur again. This is very often different to Step 3 as it may mean a change to a process method, or system. It may be the promise of new or additional training, and better communication between people. This is the key prevention step; this problem should never be allowed to happen again.

When 100% of people think in this way there is an attitude of continuous improvement through problem solving. However, it is extremely frustrating for people to try to adopt this way of thinking and attacking problems if they are not given the tools and techniques to actually define the problem, or analyse the root cause. Part Three explains clearly the basic tools and techniques which can be used in the problem solving cycle.

2. Problem solving for teams

The problem solving cycle is applicable to teams of course, but the dynamics of problem solving are important to understand and continue. It is well known that the pooling of ideas and energy of like-minded people is a powerful method for resolving issues, and is more effective than a single shot by one person. However, it is important for the 'team' to be trained to act like a team! This is in addition to the tools and techniques training that all people will receive, and it should not be underestimated in importance. There is no value in a corrective action team, or continuous improvement team arguing about what is the most likely root cause, or 'whingeing' on about how poor Marketing are! Things cannot be done if some members of the team turn up late for the meetings, or don't turn up at all, if the meeting overruns or never starts on time. In short, there can be problems when you bring groups of individuals together.

What is needed is simple, basic training in team problem solving principles and techniques.

Principles of team problem solving

The first requirement is to observe good meetings discipline. This is applicable to all teams in the company, and especially the

Figure 9.6   Working together at board level.

Top Team, whose job it is to lead by example (see Figure 9.6). Sometimes it is not easy to remember, let alone with all the things that are necessary to be a successful team member!

The second requirement is to appoint a team leader for the CITs and CATs. It is the team leader's job to ensure everyone adheres to the meeting discipline, books the room, ensures everyone knows and keeps to time, keeps a record of actions and notes etc. It is also the team leader's job to facilitate the meeting. The facilitation job is to ensure the smooth running of the meeting, making sure everyone has their say, using a flip chart to record ideas. This is a leadership role and should be recognized as such. Training needs to be given to team leaders to enable them to facilitate team problem solving in the most efficient and practical way.

In the case of CITs and CATs the team leader will also provide the means of communication for the team upwards, across, or down the organization. The team leader in a corrective action team is often an imposed duty falling to the person recognized as the 'owner' of the problem. In a voluntary continuous improvement team, however, the leader is elected by the members, and then assumes the responsibilities of leader. This is often a fertile breeding ground for the emergence of potential supervisors or managers.

3. Problem solving for specialists

Up to 90% of all problems can be solved with simple, easy-to-use problem solving methods which everyone should learn and apply. However, there are always times when it will be difficult to define the problem clearly, or get to the root cause, or root causes. This is where specialist help is needed, and there is a requirement to train people who can offer this expertise when required.

From a management viewpoint in implementing Total Quality it is important to differentiate problem solving techniques, which everyone can learn and apply easily, from the specialist methods. There is no reason why a Top Team member should not become a specialist in one or more of the techniques. Indeed the ability to use the Relationship Diagram, for example, would be of immense use to the Top Team.

It is not possible or even advisable for me to state catagorically which techniques should be used by whom, or even at which stage of the problem solving cycle. The reality is that once capability and experience is established in the organization, it will become clear when to use the relevant techniques. Indeed as people get used to the use of the problem solving cycle, they will begin to look for new and improved tools and techniques, or those tools that specifically meet their requirement. A mature Quality organization will be aware of tools and techniques worldwide, will know when and how to apply them, and will also develop some tools and techniques of their own. This state of achievement is called:

'World class problem solving'

PROBLEM SOLVING SYSTEM

Even though everyone may be trained in problem solving techniques and understands the problem solving cycle it is a considerable help to have a system. This system is a simple, but formal method for the logging of a problem that the individual cannot solve on their own. The system must be available to everyone in the organization, who might otherwise be ignored.

The requirements of a problem solving system are:

Simplicity   – the procedure should be easy to understand and follow.

Formality   – there must be a written log of the problem.

Accountability – the problem needs to be 'given' to a person or team who agrees to solve the problem within an agreed timescale and to agreed results.

Co-ordination – problems and their solutions should be logged and made available to anyone in the organization. This ensures that if the same problem occurs again, there is a known solution which can be applied.

This requirement of known solutions can be tremendously effective in ensuring quick solutions of problems, and of course as information which allows prevention systems to be applied across the whole organization.

A typical problem solving form is shown in Figure 9.7. It is important to note that the individual must first talk to his or her immediate manager, and agree that the problem cannot be solved between them. This stops the system being abused by people who see it as a way of 'posting problems upwards!' Having agreed that the problem cannot be resolved at that level, a plan is drawn up identifying the person or persons who can solve the problem. This could mean the formation of a Corrective Action Team, or even a Continuous Improvement Team for example, or sometimes just a single person.

Agreement is needed between the originator and the problem solving group, or individual, who will need the originator's help in agreeing completion times and critical success factors.

```
┌─────────────────────────────────────────────────────┐
│ ORIGINATOR:     ..........    EXTN: ..........        │
│ REF NO:         ..........    DATE: ..........        │
│ DIVISION/DEPT:  ..........                            │
│ SECTION:        ..........                            │
├─────────────────────────────────────────────────────┤
│ WHAT IS THE PROBLEM?:                                 │
│                                                       │
│                                                       │
│                                                       │
│                                                       │
│ CLASSIFICATION: T/P/N                                 │
├─────────────────────────────────────────────────────┤
│ ACTIONEE ...................................          │
│ AGREED FORECAST COMPLETION DATE ..............        │
│ ACTION TAKEN:                                         │
│                                                       │
│                                                       │
│                                                       │
│                                                       │
│                                                       │
│                                                       │
│ SIGNED OFF BY ORIGINATOR ..........  DATE ........    │
└─────────────────────────────────────────────────────┘
```

Figure 9.7   Problem solving log.

Prevention of problems

Once a formula for logging problems and their solutions is in place, there is a tremendous amount of information available to the organization on better ways of doing things. For example, a method for ensuring the telephone is always answered within three rings in a sales office might be developed in one location as a result of a problem logged. The problem might be a lost order! Once this improved system has been implemented in that office, there must be a mechanism and clearly the same system is applied to all the sales offices across the organization. This can be achieved if the problem and solution is logged and available to the organization at all levels. It is up to the problem solving Top Team member to devise a system to enable this to happen across the organization.

CHAPTER TEN

Involvement and commitment

'Acceptance and understanding is a pre-requisite to obtaining the whole-hearted commitment of people.'

TIMING

The timing of communication to the organization regarding TQM progress is critical. It is tempting but wrong to hold a major launch explaining what is going to happen on TQM, before the Top Team is actually educated and into the planning. There are two reasons for holding off until a little later.

The first reason is that an expectation of change and improvement will be given to the people in the organization without the capability to meet this expectation. This will lead to disappointment and cynicism and reflect badly on the integrity and capability of the Top Team.

The second reason is that there will be no 'common language' amongst the Top Team members, which will lead to the conclusion that 'they are not working together and just don't know what they are talking about'.

As explained in Chapter 9 – Education and Training, the top-down nature of the education and training process allows an excellent opportunity to fully explain what the TQM process is about, what it is expected to achieve for the organization, and the individual's role in the Continuous Improvement Process. It follows, therefore, that the Top Team should work closely within the team education and training to ensure successful implementation. In this respect it is important for the Top Team to be fully educated in TQM, and be into the planning of its implementation, before considering a TQM launch. This will ensure all the Top Team members are seen to understand what they are talking about. It will also 'feel real' to the people in the organization when the Top Team talk in detail about the planning, the structure, the approach to training, and so on. There will be facts, and plans including timescales etc., and a clear indication of how everyone will be involved in the TQM continuous improvement process.

COMMUNICATION METHODS

As the TQM planning starts, and the Cost of Quality corrective action teams begin to make an impact, there will be a requirement to formally communicate the TQM plans.

There are two actions that lead to a successful launch of these plans to the organization.

The first is to prepare a TQM Presentation which should be given by the appropriate Top Team member to their people. This presentation needs to be prepared by the Top Team and fully agreed and understood by all Top Team members. It is important that the same messages are given by all the Top Team to ensure accuracy, credibility and commitment.

The second action is to prepare a quality newsletter which is the written record of the launch presentation. It is a good idea to maintain production of the quality newsletter, as a means of written communication on the TQM plan progress.

TQM launch presentation

The planning of the presentation should be meticulous in terms of time, location and Top Team participation. It is essential for one or more of the Top Team members to actually give the presentation, but for all of the Top Team to be able to understand and answer the questions which will follow. This launch should only take place with the total Top Team agreement.

Management style

All the TQM launches and quality newsletters will be useless, of course, if the management style is not open, and leadership is not given to the people. It follows that, as I have stated before, all managers must be trained in the TQM principles and problem solving methods, so that they can actually help their people continuously improve. Again, even if the managers are experts on problem solving this is not likely to be of much use if his or her management style is not conducive to two-way communication. The shortest way I can describe the requirement is to ask all managers to follow the GOYA principle.

GOYA principle

GET OFF YOUR A***!!!!!!!!

'It's amazing what you learn by talking to people!'
'It's also frightening and humbling to realize how much you don't know.'

RECOGNITION AND REWARD

As the TQM Quality improvement process is implemented 'Quality Champions' will emerge. These are people who are outstanding in their attitudes, dedication, and commitment to Quality. They fight the cynics, even when they may be at management level! It is important to recognize who these people are, and to ensure some means of reward to them. This will help to give these 'Quality Champions' more confidence and provide a culture of recognition for the right people.

Identifying who these people are is not as easy as it might seem. Traditionally, the people who have been rewarded are the best 'fire-fighters', even though in some cases they are the same people who 'started the fires' in the first place! The requirement is to look closely at the Quality Policy and set of values which comprise the Quality culture, and calibrate people's performance and attitude against these criteria. For example, how much time is spent in successfully preventing problems occurring? Compare this with the amount of time spent in correcting problems, i.e. 'fire-fighting'. What is the rate of uptake of continuous improvement teams in a department or section? How many problems are being noted and solved in a department or section?

It is all about personal commitment; some individuals will become determined to succeed whilst others will adopt a 'wait and see' attitude. Those individuals who are determinedly committed to the successful implementation of the Quality improvement process are worth their weight in gold! They will appear at every level of the organization and need to be encouraged and supported by management. It is management's role to ensure the right people are recognized, the people who are walking demonstrations of the Quality Policy.

It is particularly important to provide encouragement and support in the early stages of TQM implementation, in order to make it absolutely clear that management are serious about TQM. Recognizing and rewarding the 'Quality Champions' sends the right signals down the organization, and will help to ensure the rest of the people understand the new set of values which the organization has adopted through TQM. The main reason for recognizing and rewarding people is to ensure the correct values are understood in the organization.

Methods of reward for individuals

'Quality Champions' can be rewarded in a number of ways. Basically the question is whether to reward financially or otherwise! This depends on the organization and the decision must be made by the Top Team only after considerable time and discussions have taken place. The dangers of financial reward are that it could be dangerously divisive, yet correcting it would have the effect of ensuring people 'take seriously' the management initiative on TQM. There is no simple answer to this question, it depends on the type of business, organization, whether suggestion schemes exist or not, and so on. If financial incentives are given it is sensible to keep them to reasonable levels, major financial rewards will certainly cause divisions and inhibit teamwork. Perhaps non-financial incentives could also lead to discussion – for example it is not a good idea to reward a 'Quality Champion' with a Rolls-Royce! How do you follow that? Do lesser 'Quality Champions' get a smaller car, or even a bicycle!

I don't believe it is necessary to adopt a policy of giving high-value rewards in order to ensure that 'Quality Champions' are recognized. The fact that they are recognized at all is the key factor; the tangible reward can be something relatively low value but useful. For example, calculators, pens, watches, bags, etc. are very well received and appreciated by people who have been recognized as 'Quality Champions'. These types of rewards, which are visible, useful, and practical, are not likely to cause divisions, but will be appreciated by the recipients. It is a fundamental aspect of the individual's commitment to the Quality improvement process, that the person will want to do the job right even without a reward. This is the culture that the organization is fighting to establish – the key requirement if individual recognition and reward is that the right people are recognized – not the value of the reward.

Day to day management role

There can be a temptation at Top Team level to consider that once a recognition and reward policy and system has been established then the work is complete. It is easy to forget that the primary purpose of the recognition and reward system is to ensure that the individuals who demonstrate commitment to the Quality Policy are recognized, and given encouragement and support. This helps underpin the TQM implementation process.

Ensuring the right people are recognized is probably the toughest task facing the Top Team. Each manager must ensure that he or she knows the people in his department/section. This can only be achieved by adopting the GOYA Principle described in the previous Chapter! In other words taking time out every day to walk the office, or the shop floor, asking questions, judging attitudes and commitment. It will not be difficult to make a judgement on who the quality champions are as well! The method for nominating quality champions needs to be discussed and agreed by the Top Team, but only when each Manager has formed a value judgement on the people and attitudes prevailing in his department, section, or organization. It is essential to have this 'gut feel' before deciding on the method of nomination. For example, is it going to be a peer group nomination, or maybe nominations by each manager? How do you know the selecting manager is using the correct criteria? Is there a 'blue-eyed boy syndrome'? All of these factors and many more need to be discussed before agreeing to the method of nomination. Whatever method is chosen, the key requirement is that it is fair, and <u>seen</u> <u>to</u> <u>be</u> <u>fair</u>.

Recognition and reward for teams

It is possible to extend the individual recognition and reward systems to successful teams. For example, Continuous Improvement Teams or Corrective Action Teams who have successfully completed a project may qualify for a reward. This could be on the successful completion of every project – say two per year, or on the first successful project the team completes. Rewards could be the same tokens given to individuals, where each member of the team receives a pen, or watch, for example. Alternatively there may be a case for rewarding the team by giving the members and their partners theatre tickets, or dinner, for example. This idea helps to mature the team spirit of the members.

There may be the opportunity for all the Continuous Improvement Teams, or Corrective Action Teams to enter their project for an annual award given by the organization for the 'Top Quality Team'. This event would take the format of the teams presenting their work to a 'panel of judges' who would decide the top team based on an agreed set of requirements. The reward for this team could be to represent the organization at National or even International Conferences. It could be an overseas study and exchange tour of organizations in other countries, Europe, Japan, USA, etc. The reward criteria here is status, and recognition that the Top Quality Team has an ambassadorial role on behalf of all the people in the organization. This type of approach is a powerful motivation to the 'Quality Champions'.

Building on this recognition and reward method for teams, it is beneficial to organize exchange visits with other TQM organizations. In these visits team members get the opportunity to talk to other 'Quality Champions' from different organizations. The process is interesting, educational and lifts the spirits of team members, who may be solving difficult issues and problems. Opportunities should be taken to send as many quality teams as possible to external events, such as quality conferences and courses. It is essential in these cases to ask each team to write a short report on their views of the conference, with suggestions for actions that could be taken by the organization to improve the implementation of TQM. This type of approach keeps the whole process going – it keeps people's interest and is a vehicle for continuous improvement.

Recognition and reward as part of education and training

Every single person in the organization will be trained in the TQM Quality Improvement Process. As people complete the course, the signing of the Quality Policy and the presentation of the Policy as a reward for completing the course is a powerful method of recognition and reward. It may be advantageous to include the Quality Policy with a 'Certificate of Achievement' on completion of the course.

A typical certificate would look like that one shown in Fig. 10.1. This type of reward certificate approach incorporated with the Quality Policy is a powerful reinforcement of the Quality message, particularly if the certificate is framed. This allows the framed certificate to be put in the individual's work area, either on the desk or the wall. It can be seen that in this way the TQM Quality Improvement Process is becoming part of the culture – literally in or on the walls of the organization! Having the signed

```
┌─────────────────────────────────────────────┐
│                                             │
│          RECOGNITION  CERTIFICATE           │
│                                             │
│  THIS IS TO CERTIFY THAT ................   │
│  HAS ATTENDED A TRAINING COURSE IN          │
│  TOTAL QUALITY CONTINUOUS                    │
│  IMPROVEMENT.                                │
│             SIGNED ..................        │
│                                             │
│  I AM TOTALLY COMMITTED TO CONTINUOUS       │
│  IMPROVEMENT.                                │
│             SIGNED ..................        │
│                                             │
└─────────────────────────────────────────────┘
```

Figure 10.1 Recognition/Reward certificate.

Quality Policy/certificate of achievement is a constant reminder of the individual's commitment to Quality, and a visible commitment throughout the organization.

Profit sharing

The TQM Quality Improvement Process implemented successfully will generate increased profit for the organization. Who should share in these profits? Surely there should be a method for ensuring everyone in the organization shares in the financial successes in an equitable manner. This is probably one of the hardest issues to tackle for a successful company. There are many methods, including a bonus based on salary, across the board bonus applied equally to everyone in the organization, or share ownership.

Of all the methods, probably the one which fits the ethics and long-term requirements, of the TQM Quality Improvement Process is the Share Ownership Scheme.

The idea of everyone in the organization owning shares and therefore working for the organization as a shareholder is not new. However, the opportunity to either give or offer shares at reduced rates, is worthy of serious consideration as a means of rewarding success.

CHAPTER ELEVEN

Supplier strategy

There are few businesses where there is no reliance on an external supplier, or suppliers. This applies to industrial companies who purchase material, add value to it and sell to their customers. It also applies to the service industries who rely on sub-contract staff, or third party suppliers for food, laundry, cleaning, catering, etc.

Take the example of a hotel which is offering conference facilities, and is relying on an audio-visual company to supply the projector. It is no use blaming that company if the equipment arrives late, or it is not the equipment asked for by the customer. The customer's contact is with the hotel, not the audio-visual company. It is this realization that there is a critical dependency on suppliers which forces the need for application of TQM into the supplier base.

DEFINITION OF SUPPLIER

In this context it is any external supplier – that is to say a person, or organization supplying a service or product to the company. This includes companies who supply material, components, products etc., to which the company adds value before selling on to the customer. It is almost impossible to find a company or business that does not depend on this type of supplier. It also includes sub-contractors and suppliers who provide a service to the company, which is then sold on to the customer.

Then, of course, there is the area of facilities management – the provision of support services to the company. This includes cleaning, catering, mailing distribution and transport, and so on. Facilities management has become very big business where many companies have been formed to provide a complete port-folio of services. It is becoming increasingly critical for com-panies to develop and apply a clear TQM supplier strategy.

TQM SUPPLIER STRATEGY

The strategy is simple for the suppliers – 'To adopt exactly the same TQM policy, attitudes, and actions required of the com-pany'. This means that every supplier to the company must adopt the same TQM principles and Quality culture. If this isn't the case, the company can never achieve the business objectives targeted through continuous improvement. It follows that every supplier must be assessed, and their ability to meet the TQM policies and requirements clearly qualified.

What is required is a joint company/supplier commitment to TQM. This joint approach can only work when the company and supplier personnel work together to meet agreed requirements. This approach requires time and effort on both sides. Existing supplier relationships must be examined, for example, is it the company purchasing policy to keep a large number of suppliers for a particular product or service, and 'play one off against the other'. This type of approach may succeed in knocking down the incoming costs, but who is to say that a long-term Purchasing Agreement with, say two suppliers, would not achieve the same cost reductions. It is a strong negotiating point to offer maybe yearly or even longer contracts to suppliers and it is normal to achieve good cost reductions with this type of approach. How-ever, the other major benefit, of course, is the ability to develop a joint TQM understanding with suppliers, which results in a long-term business partnership. It isn't possible to develop a long-term business partnership with suppliers if they are being 'played off against each other', and if there is therefore little prospect of long-term contracts. Clearly the TQM approach means that the purchasing policy in the company must be reviewed, and in many cases changed from a multi-supplier base for the same product/service to a single or double supplier only.

In fact it is impossible to achieve world class performance without developing the same type of continuous improvement policy with suppliers as in the organization. The same principles apply which are outlined in this book, but practically of course, and it is necessary to reduce the supplier base to manageable levels.

This is first achieved through the supplier assessment procedure; the reduction of the supplier base is a key activity in TQM implementation and must be very carefully executed. It will take time and effort, involving the careful qualification of every supplier to the company. The suppliers will need to be categorized after assessment into the following levels:

Supplier status

Approved	:	Supplier meets all requirements
Conditionally approved	:	Supplier agrees to correct deficiencies found
Failed	:	Unacceptable supplier

This simple categorization will have the effect of reducing the supplier base into manageable types. The approved supplier will be to the desired Total Quality standard requiring continuous improvement actions. The conditionally approved will require education and training, whilst the failed should be taken off the supplier base.

Supplier assessment process

This process is a well-defined set of requirements which need to be thoroughly understood within the company, before specify-

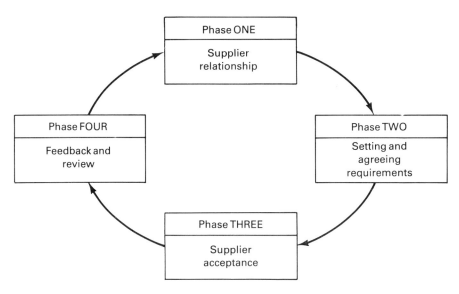

Figure 11.1   Supplier assessment cycle.

ing them to the suppliers. It can best be described as a four-phase cycle as shown in Figure 11.1.

Justifying TQM supplier strategy

The development and implementation of the TQM supplier strategy takes time and effort. It is an investment in the prevention of error and a true Cost of Conformance. It should not be seen as an added cost, but as a means of reducing the Cost of Non-conformance. The Cost of Quality work within the company will identify clearly the importance of the TQM supplier strategy.

CHAPTER TWELVE

Time to market

There is a major difference between the Japanese approach to design, and traditional Western methods – TQM principles, have been applied to the Japanese process, whereas typically there has been a total lack of TQM application in the West. The failure to apply TQM principles results in the serial approach to design, which forces the design process through the functional departments in the organization. For example, in basic terms:

Marketing specification

↓

Design and development

↓

Manufacture

↓

Sales

In this type of approach it is left to each department to complete their individual part of the process, largely in isolation, before handing on to the next department. Typically there is little communication between the departments, except where handing over from one department to another. At this stage there is usually plenty of communication but unfortunately it can often follow the lines of the following:

'Between Design and Manufacture'.

Manufacturing: 'How do you expect me to put this product through my production line with this new design. I haven't got the right equipment.'

Design: 'Well, I didn't know that, nobody told me!'

The blame for this all too common situation lies firmly and squarely on both Design and Manufacturing. It is no use Design complaining that Manufacturing people are 'greasy oily characters who screw up my design'. Equally it is no use Manufacturing claiming that Design people are 'smart-a.. characters who wouldn't know one end of the production line from the other'. It is ludicrous to think that Marketing, Design, Manufacture, or Sales could be completed in the serial manner just described, but that's exactly what happens typically in the West.

Of course it is not as simple as this – in most cases there is a complete lack of understanding of what actually goes on in a company at each interface level, whereby management monitors the success of new product introduction, and the ability to complete each phase within the targeted time. In other words, the Product Introduction Meeting concentrates on the time targets, much more than the product and customer requirement. This leads to an attitude in each department to 'get rid' of their part of the product introduction process as soon as possible. Marketing will want to 'get rid' to design as soon as they can. Design will want to hand over to Manufacturing, again as soon as possible – particularly if the design is not technically challenging any more – and has become boring! Manufacturing, of course, will want to output the product, no matter how, to meet the pressure from sales.

Unfortunately, when the customer, who has largely been forgotten throughout this process, gets the product it doesn't actually do what he expected it to do! The result of this is obvious; the customer is not satisfied, and goes elsewhere the next time.

The scenario I have just described has been enacted hundreds, if not thousands of times throughout the Western world during the last 30 years or so. The main beneficiaries of this situation have been, of course, the Japanese who have managed to get their products to the market and meeting or exceeding the customer's requirements. In the case of television sets in the 1970s, they set a whole new standard for reliability which far exceeded the customer's expectations. No wonder they have been successful.

THE SIMPLE ANSWERS

There is a simple answer to the problem of getting products to the market and meeting the requirement of customers, and also, of course, meeting gross margin targets necessary to be successful as a company. The answer is to totally change the management view of the product introduction methods away from departmental responsibilities to total responsibilities of the people involved throughout the whole process.

The business of getting products to the marketplace must be viewed as a 'total process', completely independent of the functional departments existing in the company. It is disastrous to 'shoe-horn' new product process requirements into the existing departmental structure of the organization. It is also disastrous for management to consider that there could possibly be anything as simple as the design process completed by the Design department, or the manufacturing process completed by the Manufacturing department. Getting products to market is not a simple, serial process, whose individual and very specific knowledge and experience exist solely within departmental barriers. How can the people in Manufacturing not have an input at the Design and Development stage? How can the Sales teams have no contribution to make at the marketing specification stage? After all they do talk to the customers!

This compartmentalized thinking by management totally fails to realize that everyone involved at each stage of the process must be involved from the beginning right through to the end. This is the simple answer to the success of competing with the Japanese. It is not a new idea, so why hasn't it happened in the West? The answer to this question is very much what the book is all about – only through the application of TQM can Western companies hope to compete with the Far Eastern machines.

TQM applied to the product to market process

It is essential to use the problem solving cycle at top level to provide a common understanding within the Top Team of the product introduction process. The problem solving cycle is the core process that is used throughout the product introduction procedure. This strategy is based on the understanding that it is not possible to ever achieve a situation where there are no problems to address throughout the product introduction process. A sentiment I am sure anyone reading this book who has been directly involved in product introduction will whole-heartedly agree with! It follows, therefore, that there must be a common approach to the elimination of problems by everyone involved in the product introduction process.

Through TQM everyone will understand and be able to apply the problem solving cycle, which provides a common language and common understanding totally independent of department or functions. At Top Team level it is necessary to use the cycle to determine how the product introduction procedure should be defined, maintained and controlled. This could affect the way the company is organized, whether to 'make or buy', to set up a new factory, to organize new distribution capabilities, to acquire new business to support the product in a new market or new country, and so on. Whatever decisions are made during the defining of requirements stage, there will be the need to apply the problem solving cycle for as long as the product is being marketed and sold.

At each stage in the development of the product introduction process using the problem solving cycle the following questions should be asked:

1. What is the requirement/problem?
2. Who must be involved in defining the requirements or solving the problems?

3. Who is responsible for ensuring requirements are met or executed?

If this procedure is followed it is possible to define the product introduction requirement at each stage, who is involved in defining and agreeing them, and who is responsible for meeting them.

This approach will avoid the pitfall of designing a product introduction procedure around functional barriers. It will ensure everyone understands their role in the process, and provide the foundation for a 'team approach'. The problem solving cycle must be applied to each stage in product introduction.

Stage 1: Define market requirement

This is typically the first phase in the product introduction process. It is not possible to provide a clear market requirement at this stage in isolation within the Marketing department. Inputs must be sought from representatives at each stage of the product introduction process that is to say, from Design, Manufacturing,

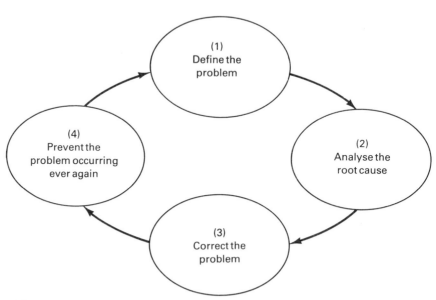

Figure 12.1 Problem solving cycle.

Sales, Finance, etc. It is up to the Top Team to define clearly the need for Marketing to follow this procedure.

This is an iterative process where the broad requirements specified by Marketing will be subjected to the cycle of:

Analyse   : Analysing requirement
Correction : Correcting errors
Prevention : Preventing problems reaching the later stages of design, manufacturing, sales, customer service, etc.

When the Team has obtained an agreed market specification, it is possible to decide whether to proceed to the next stage. This should be agreed at a formal Phase Review where representatives for each area of the company propose the recommended course of action to the Top Team. There is no reason why it should be only the Marketing department who make this recommendation – the TQM principles demand that it is a team approach, and therefore 'team commitment'.

The involvement of design, manufacturing and sales production people at this stage will obtain their commitment to the success of the product throughout the product introduction process. It will teach them that it is an iterative process, and impossible to define clearly a market requirement that will never change. Market requirements change constantly; it is the company that understands this and is organized and committed to the management of change that will be successful.

Stage 2: Product definition requirement
The requirement is to complete detailed planning, including technical specification project plans, etc. Again the problem solving cycle must be used by the team to ensure that the product definition is understood and agreed to by all people concerned.

Stage 3: Design and development
This stage is to demonstrate the ability to meet the requirements specified in the previous two stages. The problem solving cycle will be used to analyse problems, correct them, and then ensure

that they don't happen again. For example, correcting problems found in a power supply design, should be carried out on the product which is the third stage in the problem solving cycle. However, it is necessary to go one stage further to stage 4, and prevent the problem occurring again by, for example, committing the change to engineering standards. Therefore, this knowledge is captured for ever, and will become the company standard to be used in future.

There is a heavy involvement with suppliers at this stage of the product introduction process, and they must be seen as integral members of the 'product introduction team'. Again the suppliers will be committed to the problem solving cycle, to ensure the ability to continuously improve the product. The team approach to Design and Development, and the 100% application of the problem solving cycle will ensure maximum efficiency in progressing through this critical stage; and to the successful progression to stage 4.

Stage 4: Field trial and full-scale manufacture

This is the most critical of stages in one respect. That is because there is nobody between the product and the customer! Again the problem solving cycle will be used before the product is considered to be capable of meeting customers requirements in the marketplace.

Stage 5: Mature product requirement

This is the process of reviewing continuously the performance of the product in the marketplace. It will give the opportunity to consider whether to sell into different countries, different markets, modify the product to provide a further revenue stream, etc.

It is beneficial to use the problem solving cycle to define the requirement of the product in meeting company business targets. Then, to analyse the problems and opportunities, with the object of reducing cost, increasing marketplace, etc. Then, to correct the problems, or take advantage of the opportunities, the final stage of prevention is to use all the knowledge and information gained to prevent problems occurring again. This is the process of continuous improvement applied to the product introduction process in the company. It must be reviewed, and improved upon in the company at regular intervals and the problem solving cycle must be applied throughout the total process, ensuring the involvement of the people in the organization at every stage. The old traditional and failed ideas must be thrown out, to be replaced by the TQM approach to product introduction. The ideas in this chapter are specifically aimed at getting this message across, and are absolutely essential to achieve success in the world marketplace. It will provide the capability to continuously improve through commitment, involvement and determination of all the people in the organization.

CHAPTER THIRTEEN

Organizational design

CULTURE

After many years' experience of implementing Total Quality into organizations large and small, and across different businesses, one key issue has become increasingly obvious and constant. The organizational culture is the main reason why Total Quality Management is required for companies to meet the competitive challenge by focussing on customers' requirements. The previous chapters in this book give a straightforward approach for the heads of companies to adopt which will provide a customer focus in their organization.

It is worth asking the question 'Why is this book of any value to the Chief Executive Officer of any company?' – or if you prefer 'What is the value of Total Quality to any company and why is it required?' The answer to these questions lies in the nature of the organizational design companies adopt. It is an organizational design which is hierarchical and top-down typically in information flows with many functional groups and 'managers' at many levels.

This organizational design is adopted because it is necessary to create management control and accountability top-down throughout the company. Without it nobody can see who they work for, there would be no effective review of performance, and no clear lines of communication. It is an organizational style adopted where many companies have demonstrated excellent management control at all levels of the hierarchy. Training at all levels has been dissected, leadership skills enhanced and management information systems implemented to give top management the information needed to control the company. So how could so many companies with an excellent management organization and control of information have such a difficult time competing in world markets? What is wrong with this traditional hierarchical approach? The answer, strangely enough, is nothing at all!

It is essential for all companies to adopt a structure which will give good management control and clear lines of communication and accountability. The problem does not lie in the fundamental organizational structure that companies adopt but in the mistaken belief that somehow this 'internally' focussed organization will automatically be satisfactory for meeting 'external' requirements.

These external requirements get in the way of the internally focussed organization because information flow and material flow go horizontally across the organization and not vertically as is the case with internal management information and control. Look at the focus companies have internally.

1. All CEOs can easily reel off their organization structure.
2. Most Directors' time is spent in internal organization of resources.
3. Most 'management' time is spent preparing information for senior management.
4. Most meetings are concerned with meeting internally focussed measures.
5. The most important measures in the organization are financial by a long way.

Approximately only 10% of time is spent on external focus.

1. How many CEOs have a mission statement?
2. How many Boards have clear 'business drivers'?
3. How many Boards understand the key performance measures required of their company to ensure customer satisfaction?
4. How much time do top management spend talking to their customers?

5. How much time do senior management spend doing competitive benchmarking – finding out about their competition and emulating best practice?
6. How much time is spent in defining, measuring and monitoring the performance measures which are critical to meeting customer requirements?
7. How much time is spent ensuring everyone in the organization has a customer focus and clear performance measures?

The list of questions is long and depressing for it is a fact that most companies do not spend any more than 10% of their management time focussing on customer requirements. It is little wonder that companies demonstrating this internal view of life sooner or later meet severe competition problems. Many companies in the manufacturing business have clearly found this out too late and some companies in the service sector are beginning to realize that there is a better way of spending management time. For those who do not realize these cold, hard facts of life, there is only one way to go – OUT OF BUSINESS.

Sooner or later another company will begin to meet customers' requirements better and will force the less externally focussed to go out of business.

ARE YOU AN INTERNALLY OR EXTERNALLY FOCUSSED COMPANY?

Internally focussed organizational cultures

- Unclear who the customers are.
- No performance measures reflecting customer requirements.
- No good personal relationship built up with the customer.
- No understanding of the customer's business.
- Complete lack of understanding of external customers within the workforce.
- Meetings cultures where senior management spend up to 90% of their time in meetings, mainly on internal measures, or on dissatisfied customers!

- Poorly run and ineffective meetings, where no actions are agreed, decisions are made on very little information in case the facts get in the way!
- Poor morale and commitment at all levels.
- Enormous amount of senior management time deciding on the 'structure' of the organization – with external customers' requirements <u>never</u> coming into the discussions.

Externally focussed organizational cultures

- Pro-active attempts to define customers' requirements through understanding of the customers' business.
- Good problem-solving skills particularly at the customer interface, involving education of the customers' staff where necessary.
- Exactly the same approach as above for suppliers, seeing them as 'part of the business'.
- Clear mission statement and business drivers.
- Clearly defined performance measures reflecting customers' requirements.
- Everyone in the organization understands the internal customer concept and has performance measures agreed reflecting the external customer needs.
- There is a positive approach to problem solving and open discussion on how to resolve problems.
- High morale due to the customer focus and positive attempts at solving problems at all levels throughout the organization.

MAKING THE TRANSFORMATION TO A TQM ORGANIZATION

Nothing will change unless the CEO realizes that there is a transformation needed. Very often, particularly when companies are demonstrating good financial results, there is a tendency to 'leave things alone'. This approach would work well if nothing else changed as well! Unfortunately there is nothing so certain as change. This means that companies must always be looking for ways of improving their products/service, constantly re-evaluating their markets and competitors and prepared for unforeseen worldwide events which can spark a recession. Providing the company is geared to external change factors, then it is possible for the organization to respond faster, and more

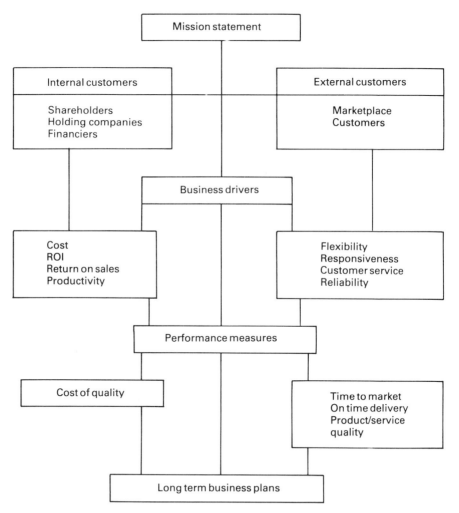

Figure 13.1   Spenley business process.

successfully than the competition. History has shown that those companies which are externally focussed always provide a more perceptive, flexible and competitive response to change than the internally focussed, rather complacent companies.

This understanding of the unpredictability of some external factors should be enough to convince all CEOs of the need for change, quite apart from the obvious sense of keeping close to the customers' requirements. When the CEO is convinced that an externally focussed company is sharper, faster and more competitive, then the transformation process from internal to external can begin. The Spenley Business Strategy Model in Figure 13.1 shows how the organization should act to link the elements of strategy.

THE ROLES OF THE QUALITY MANAGER
AND THE TOTAL QUALITY MANAGER

One of the problems of using the words Total Quality management is the expectation from Quality professionals that this is in their area of responsibility. After all, it must be the Quality manager's job to put in Total Quality – who else is responsible? It is essential to understand that Total Quality has no more or less to do with the Quality manager than the sales manager, production manager, commercial manager, or any other manager!

It follows, therefore, that the existing Quality manager should basically get on with implementing Total Quality along with all his or her colleagues on the Top Team. In other words, the role of the Total Quality manager is totally different to the role of the traditional Quality manager in the organization. The reasons for this should be clear after reading the contents of this book; Total Quality involves everyone in the organization, in everything that they do at all times, forever! It is not a technical specialism, nor is it narrowly defined within product quality terms of system accreditation. It is about the total organization, involving everyone at all levels. For this reason, and because achieving Total Quality means meeting requirements which involve people in a chain-link process across functional and departmental boundaries, it is necessary to have a co-ordinating function. This co-ordinating function can be achieved by the Top Team with the help of a Total Quality manager.

The difficulties of co ordinating departments and functions in an organization in such a way that the company meets the requirement agreed with the customer 100% of the time should not be underestimated. There is no chance of achieving success when the Top Team doesn't understand that the organizational design encourages compartmentalization between departments, to the detriment of meeting customer requirements. Even when they do there is so much work required to encourage and maintain good links between departments, that many Top Teams give up in desperation and frustration.

There is a strong case for providing a focus on co-ordination in the organization, by appointing a Total Quality manager. The role of the TQ manager needs to be very carefully defined. It may be seen by some members of the Top Team to be an opportunity to 'off-load' responsibility, or possibly even find a 'scapegoat' for failure. The Chief Executive must not allow this kind of thinking in his Top Team – it is clearly the responsibility of the whole Top Team to ensure the success of Total Quality in the organization. However, the use of a dedicated resource to provide planning, co-ordination and the necessary day-to-day support across the company is worth serious consideration.

Requirements for the Total Quality manager

The ideal would be a respected line manager with experience of the organization who is aware of the practical difficulties of implementing Total Quality. The person needs to have good interpersonal skills, and the ability to 'sell' the principles to people at every level.

Because of the need to look across the total organization, it is probable that familiarization with all parts of the organization is achieved before attempting to do the job. There is nothing worse than someone coming into a part of the organization which is unfamiliar to them and then attempting to tell everyone how to

Figure 13.2 'I wish they'd get out and help me!'

improve their jobs! It is both courteous and sensible to find out about the functions before getting involved. It will probably also be necessary for the TQ manager to become well versed in business and financial matters. This will ensure a good understanding of the need for a mission statement, business drivers and performance measures. A sound understanding of competitive benchmarking is essential, as is the ability to talk to both customers and suppliers.

Tools and techniques are the key to achieving successful problem solving and it follows, therefore, that the TQ manager must become an expert. It is no good knowing as much as everyone else on the TQ training courses, this is not enough. The requirement is to be capable of using complex problem solving tools such as multivari analysis, Taguchi, and SPC, Design of Experiment, relationship diagram etc. A particular requirement is the ability to flowchart the key processes across the organization – business process analysis.

As can be seen from the above it is not difficult to justify the appointment of a full-time Total Quality manager in most companies. It is very often used as a career move, albeit sideways many times, to help develop company and business knowledge in a key person, which will allow that person to take over a key Top Team role. This can be the Chief Executive or Managing Director's position, or a member of the Top Team dependent on the company requirements. However, it is an excellent career development opportunity as well as providing more resilience in the difficult process of implementing Total Quality successfully.

Providing the right person is appointed, the role is fully understood by the Top Team and the necessary plans are established and monitored, the TQ manager will be seen as a valuable and necessary addition to the Top Management team.

CHAPTER FOURTEEN

Summary

TQM requires careful planning and patient implementation. There can be no short cuts, and each step should be securely established before attempting to move on. The Top Team must lead and must be committed. Their adoption of the CEO's Quality Policy statement is a crucial foundation for the planning and implementation to rest upon.

The first step is to define the business strategy over a five-year period. As described earlier in the book, it is essential to determine a 'mission statement' for the business and the key 'business drivers' needed to achieve the mission. It is possible to integrate both the internal and external requirements for the business by recognizing the different customers the company has:

Internal : Shareholders, holding companies, financiers
External: Customers, marketplace

The mission statement should clearly define the products and services offered and the markets operated in, whilst ensuring that the company meet these external requirements at a profit.

The preceding Spenley Business Model shown in Figure 13.1 is useful for reminding the company CEO and Board of Directors that there are internal and external customer requirements to be met. It is essential to use the model to provide the understanding that the external requirements can only be met by taking different actions than is the case to begin with, and by making the necessary management time available to implement the transformation process into the company.

KEY BUSINESS PROCESSES

When the key business drivers have been agreed it is necessary to define the business processes associated with the drivers. The business processes always go across the organization which is the reason an internally-oriented organization has difficulty in control, since the organizational structure is vertical, as shown in Figure 14.1.

The business processes could be:

- On-time delivery performance
- On-time development of products/services
- Time to market
- Product Quality

These would be relatively easily defined by the company, following the establishment of its mission statement and business drivers, but it is a complex matter to define the processes across the organization.

BUSINESS PROCESS ANALYSIS

The analysis of key processes defines the departments and people involved, what their input and output requirements are

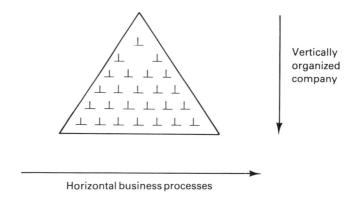

Figure 14.1 Horizontal processes – vertical organization.

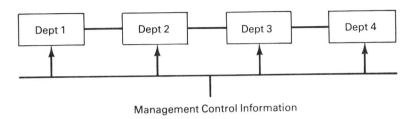

Management Control Information

Figure 14.2 The business process.

and the control mechanism which is required to ensure the process is effective.

From the diagram in Figure 14.2 it is clear that once the business process is defined it is possible to use the vertical organization hierarchy to control the total. With the implementation of the Total Quality process defined in earlier chapters of this book, everyone will clearly understand their requirements, have their own performance measures and be able to implement continuous improvement throughout the organization.

The structure of CATs and CITs ensure all problems can be addressed across the process whether they are multidisciplinary and therefore across departments, or whether applicable to one department.

This understanding of the key processes is why the Total Quality principles really work in an organization and is the beginning of the transformation from 'internal' to 'external' oriented focus.

PART THREE

Tools and techniques for TQM

Contents

1. BRAINSTORMING

What is brainstorming?

Brainstorming is an idea-generating technique. A group of people throw out their ideas as they think of them, so that each has the opportunity to build on the ideas of others.

How to brainstorm

The group leader presents the situation for which ideas are sought. The wording should encourage specific, tangible ideas, not abstract ideas or opinions. The leader makes sure that the members understand the situation under consideration, the objective of the brainstorming session, and the process to be followed.

There are two methods of brainstorming. The most familiar is **free wheeling**, where:

- Group members call out their ideas spontaneously.
- The scribe records the ideas as they are suggested.

The discipline of brainstorming is maintained by four basic rules. However, the informality of the process generates an atmosphere of freedom. These rules are:

- No evaluation.
- Encourage wild ideas.
- Build on the ideas of others.
- Strive for quality.

In **round-robin** brainstorming,

- The leader or scribe asks each member, in turn, for an idea.
- Members may pass on any round.
- The session continues until all members have passed during the round.
- Ideas are recorded as in free wheeling.

Each approach has its advantages and disadvantages, but up to 80 ideas may be brainstormed. A way of reducing the number of items generated and evaluating them is called 'List Reduction'. This will help the team to concentrate on the most important items.

When to use brainstorming

To generate as many potential ideas as possible often in the context of cause and effect analysis.

Tips on improving the team's use of brainstorming

There are several recommended 'idea-spurring' questions to

Reasons why electric light doesn't turn on	
Power failure	Storm
Bulb loose	Power plant failure
Not plugged in	Old bulb
Lamp corroded	Broken bulb
No current to house	No contact
Bill not paid	Wall switch turned off
Bulb holder missing	Circuit breaker operated
Switch broken	Burnt out bulb
Cord cut	Missing bulb
Cord chewed by dog	Switch missing
Slot meter empty	

Figure A.1   An example of a brainstorm.

help group members build on each others' proposals. These questions could include:

1. What else is like this?
2. What other ideas does this suggest?
3. Greater frequency?

2. LIST REDUCTION

What is list reduction?

Before a list of ideas or factors can be shortened, everyone in the group must have a clear understanding of all items on the list. The first activity, therefore, is for the leader to go through the items asking if there is need for clarification. If yes, the suggester should be asked to briefly explain what he or she meant by the comment. The discussion should not go beyond simple clarification at this point.

How to list reduce

The group identifies some filters, criteria that should be satisfied for an item to remain in consideration, some of which could be:

- Is this item likely to improve the situation?
- Is it feasible?
- Can we afford it?

Keeping the agreed upon criteria in mind, group members review, or in appropriate cases vote on, each item. If there is any doubt items are bracketed, rather than crossed out, so that the group can go back to them later if necessary. In general the group focusses on and continues to evaluate only the non-bracketed items on the list.

The process may be repeated, with different or more stringent criteria, until the list is reduced to about half a dozen options. This represents a manageable number of options for applying some of the other evaluative tools.

When to use list reduction

List reduction is a filter technique. When used after brainstorming it is useful to combine it with a clarification process.

3. CAUSE AND EFFECT ANALYSIS (FISHBONE DIAGRAMS)

What is Cause and Effect analysis?

Cause and Effect diagrams are also known as 'fishbones' (because of their shape) or Ishikawa diagrams (after their inventor, Dr Kaoru Ishikawa, the Japanese Quality Control statistician).

Cause and Effect analysis is a systematic way of looking at effects and the causes that create or contribute to specified effects. The effect being analysed can be expressed as a problem or as 'desired state' and the things that have to be in place for us to get to where we want to be.

A fishbone is an organizing technique for processing lists of ideas into groups to make understanding clearer.

How to draw a Cause and Effect diagram

In order to provide a full analysis for any given effect, the causes can be represented on a cause and effect or fishbone diagram such as the one shown (Figure A.2) to illustrate the statement 'lamp doesn't turn on' and the major possible causes which might explain why the lamp doesn't light. Related causes are grouped together on bones of the fish which have been labelled with the common factor.

- Identify the area or 'effect' to be analysed or the desired state to be reached.
- Hold a brainstorming session with your team to establish all the major possible causes.
- Write the effect/desired state in a box at the end of the main spine of the fishbone. Add several bones, drawn at an angle.
- From the results of the brainstorming session form groups of causes under a number of headings comprising the main factors contributing to the effect being analysed.
- On each of the major bones, write the contributory factors which the group consider to be part of each cause.
- Then decide whether you need to collect additional data to further understand the relationships of cause to effect.

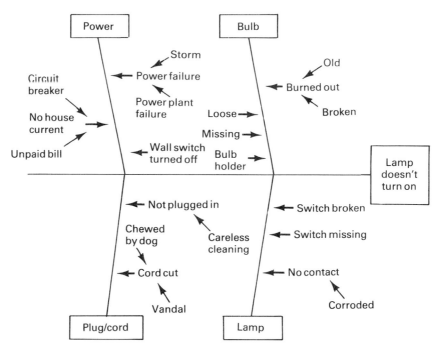

Figure A.2   An example of a cause and effect diagram.

ADDITIONAL TIPS FOR CONSTRUCTING THE CAUSE AND EFFECT DIAGRAMS

It is often the case that the following general headings apply:

Cause and Effect rules

1. Participation by everyone concerned is necessary to ensure that all causes are considered. Everyone involved, must be free to voice their ideas. The more ideas mentioned, the more accurate will be the diagram. One person's idea will trigger someone else's.
2. Do not criticize any ideas. To encourage a free exchange, write them all down. A brainstorming approach is often appropriate for these early steps.

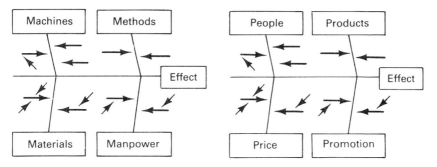

Figure A.3   Cause and Effect – additional tips.

3. Visibility is a major factor of participation. Everyone in the team must be able to see the diagram. Use large charts, large printing, and conduct the diagram sessions in a well-lit area.
4. Group together various causes which have a common theme or link and create a 'bone' for each theme.
5. Understand each cause as it is mentioned to ensure its proper placement on the diagram. Use the technique: Why, what, where, when, who and how.
6. Do not overload any one diagram. As a group of causes begins to dominate the diagram, that group should become a diagram itself.
7. Construct a separate diagram for each separate effect.
8. Circle the most likely causes. This is usually done after all possible ideas have been written up on the Cause and Effect diagram. Only then is each idea critically evaluated. The most likely ones should be circled for special attention.
9. Create an improvement-orientated atmosphere in each session. Focus on how to improve a situation rather than analysing how it arose.

When to use Cause and Effect diagrams

The Cause and Effect diagram has nearly unlimited application. One of its strongest attributes is the participation and contribution of everyone involved in the subject under discussion.

These diagrams are useful whenever a situation needs to be understood fully and the relationship between the various factors involved explored. This might be in the context of solving a problem or understanding all the areas which need to be addressed to make a desirable change take place.

4. PARETO ANALYSIS

What is Pareto analysis?

Pareto analysis is a technique for recording and analysing information which easily enables the most significant aspects to be identified. A pattern usually becomes apparent when we look at the relationship between the numbers of items/occurrences of any situation and their relation to the 'cause' under consideration. The pattern has been referred to as the '80/20 rule' and shows itself in many ways.

Pareto analysis shows at a glance which areas can be regarded as the 'vital few' needing priority measures to tackle them and which are the 'trivial many'.

The accomplishments of the Pareto analysis are:

- Some areas, previously not considered significant, are identified as belonging to the 'vital few'.

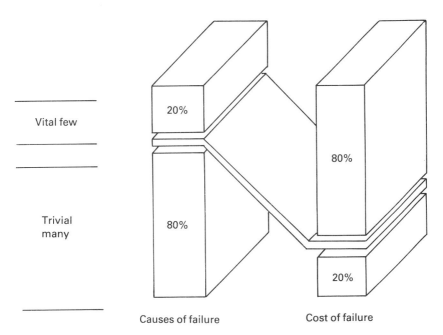

Figure A.4 Diagram showing the 80/20 rule.

- The 'trivial many' are identified: this is not new but the extent is usually surprising.
- Priorities are established.

How to construct a Pareto

Calculate totals
Taking information from a data or check sheet, list the items in rank order and calculate cumulative percentages. An analysis done in this manner relating to causes of mis-sorted mail is shown in Figure A.5.

Draw the Pareto diagram
Draw a bar chart which plots the cumulative percentage against the activities. It may be useful to group minor activities as 'others'. This is illustrated in Figure A.6.

Interpret the results
The candidates for priority action – the 'vital few' – will appear on the left of the Pareto diagram where the shape of the cumulative diagram will be steepest. The 'trivial many' should not be ignored, however, because sometimes what is apparently minor at first can become much more significant at a later date if it is left untreated.

Activity (failure)	Frequency	% of Total	Cumulative (%)
A. Poorly addressed	11	38	38
B. Wrongly addressed	9	31	69
C. Postroom error	4	14	83
D. Divisional error	2	7	90
E. No address	1	3.4	93.4
F. Item unreadable	1	3.3	96.7
G. Royal Mail error	1	3.3	100
TOTAL	29	100	100

Figure A.5 Pareto construction.

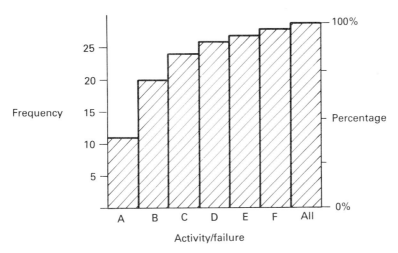

Figure A.6 Pareto diagram.

It is important when choosing the data to be charted to have
a clear view of the ultimate purpose of the diagram. In the
example given above if the purpose was to tackle those areas
which most frequently caused failure then the correct data was
charted. If the aim was to identify those activities which caused
the greatest number of items to be mis-sorted the diagram could
be quite different. Figure A.8 illustrates the revised ranking of
the categories when this criterion is used.

Activity (failure)	Frequency	% of Total	Cumulative (%)
C. Postroom error	240	42	42
B. Wrongly addressed	109	19	61
D. Divisional error	106	18.5	79.5
A. Poorly addressed	76	13	92.5
G. Royal Mail error	41	7	99.5
F. Item unreadable	2	0.3	99.8
E. No address	1	0.2	100
TOTAL	575	100	100

Figure A.7 Pareto example.

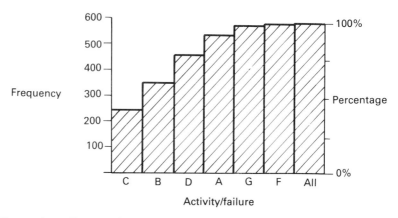

Figure A.8   Pareto chart.

When to use Pareto

Pareto can be used to great advantage in many situations where volumes of data exist. It assists with clarifying and prioritizing those aspects which warrant the commitment of resources in order to gain maximum advantage. Its major uses are in frequency based data and tracking that priorities remain the same even when volumes of data available varies widely.

5. DATA COLLECTION TECHNIQUES

In this section we are going to describe three data collection systems. Data sheets, frequency tables, and check sheets.

What are data sheets?
Data sheets are used to determine how often an event occurs over a designated period of time. Information is usually collected for events as they happen.

What are frequency tables?
Frequency tables are used to record the distribution of events within chosen boundaries.

What are check sheets?
Check sheets are used to record how often an event occurs.

Although the purpose of these techniques is to collect – not analyse – information, they can often help to indicate an area for action.

When to use data collection techniques

- To collect the information needed to analyse the present situation.
- To collect information needed to evaluate suggested courses of action.

Complaint	Jan	Feb	Mar	Apr	May	Jun	Jul	Aug	Sep	Oct	Nov	Dec	Total
Damaged Mail		11							1	111	11	卌	13

Figure A.9 An example of a data sheet.

Class Boundaries (lbs)	Frequencies
109.5–119.4	1
119.5–129.4	4
129.5–139.4	17
139.5–149.4	28
149.5–159.4	25
159.5–169.4	18
169.5–179.4	13
179.5–189.4	6
189.5–199.4	5
199.5–209.4	2
209.5–219.4	1
TOTAL	120

Figure A.10 Example of a frequency table. Distribution of the weight of 120 students.

TYPES OF TELEPHONE CALL	DEPARTMENT		
	Mails Branch	Personnel	Finance
Customer query	卌卌	卌	卌卌
Wrong numbers	卌1	1111	卌卌卌
Headquarters		11	1

Figure A.11 Example of a check sheet.

6. HISTOGRAMS

What is a histogram?

A histogram shows the distribution of some characteristic. Because of its immediate visual impact, a histogram is more effective than a table for displaying information.

How to Construct a histogram

- If the data is not already arranged by frequency make a frequency distribution table.
- Label the axis 'frequency' and mark values and units on it.
- Using the information in the frequency distribution table, construct vertical bars for each of the classes, with height corresponding to frequency.

An Example of a histogram

Data has been taken from the frequency distribution table in Figure A.10.

When to use histograms

Whenever appropriate to increase the visual impact of numerical data.

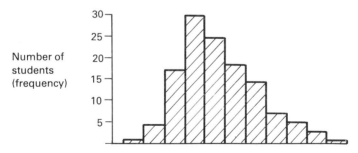

Weight range in pounds from 109.5 to 219.5 in 10 pound steps

Figure A.12   An example of a histogram.

7. FLOW CHARTS

What are flowcharts?

Flowcharts show the inputs, activities, decision points, and outputs for a given process. There are many variations that have been adapted for specific purposes (e.g. to show flow of paperwork through an administrative system; to show movement of materials through an operational system).

How to construct a flowchart

Flowcharts use standard symbols connected by arrows to show how the system or work process operates. To construct a flow chart, identify the major activites to be completed and decisions to be made as the work process is implemented. Then check the logic of the plan by following all possible routes through the chart to ensure that you have planned for contingencies.

Use the symbols shown in Figure A.13 when drawing a flow chart.

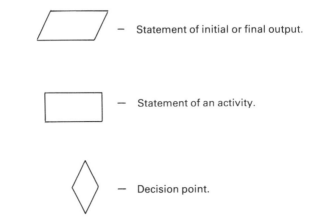

Figure A.13   Symbols used in a flowchart.

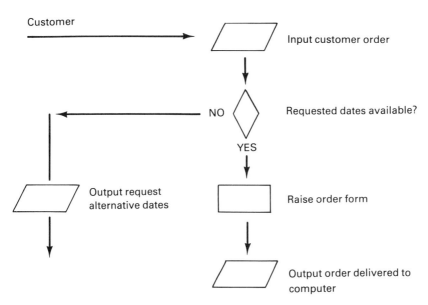

Figure A.14 An example of a flowchart. Responding to an HDS Order Enquiry.

When to use flowcharts

Flowcharts are particularly useful for documenting the steps of a work process either to analyse the current situation or to provide a plan to follow.

8. GANTT CHARTS

What are Gantt charts?

A Gantt chart is a diagram that documents the schedule, events, activities, and responsibilities necessary to complete a project.

How to construct a Gantt chart

Although there are many variations, all Gantt charts document what is to be accomplished, by whom, and when. The steps required to construct a Gantt chart are:

- Break the implementation plan into achievable steps.
- Assign responsibility for each step to a team member.
- Decide how long each task will take, and set a realistic completion date.
- Document the assumptions on which the plan is based, and the contingency plans to implement if those assumptions are not valid.

When to use Gantt charts

Gantt charts are particularly useful when managing a complex multi-phased task or where the aim is to optimize the use of resources or manpower.

SCHEDULE

Task	Assigned to	Week ending							
		1/6	8/6	15/6	22/6	29/6	5/7	12/7	19/7
Liaise with districts	Andrew								
Process bids	Helen								
Discuss bids with MT	Helen								
Discuss van movement	Peter								
Deploys vans	Peter and Helen								

Figure A.15 An example of the use of a Gantt chart, using a transport project.

9. FAILURE MODE EFFECT ANALYSIS – GUIDELINES

1. List part/process under consideration, e.g. gear.
2. For each part/process list all possible failure modes, e.g. fracture, excess vibration.
3. List possible effects of failure, e.g. gearbox failure, increased maintenance etc.
4. List possible causes of failure, e.g. material, heat treatment, incorrect gear form etc.
5. Probability factor – assess how likely failure is. Base on reliability data if possible, if not use best judgement.
   1 = Failures extremely infrequent.
   10 = Failures almost certain to occur.
6. Severity factor – assume failure has occurred. Will this have impact on customer? Assume also the customer will get the defect.
   1 = Customer will not notice.
   10 = Safety of product affected.
7. Detection factor – what is the probability the customer will subsequently receive the product?
   1 = Will not reach the customer.
   10 = Customer will receive product.
8. Multiply together to obtain risk factor (improvement weighing).

10. IDEAS EVALUATION

Purpose

To identify ideas that the team can work on.

Method

Take the brainstorm lists and evaluate and categorize each idea into one of the following groups; mark up the lists with the appropriate capital letter indicated below:

T = Totally within the team's control to work on, and to be able to produce a solution to the problem which is likely to be implemented.

P = Partially controllable within the group, i.e. the team may be able to come up with some solution, but the total problem would probably need the involvement of other departments.

N = Not team controllable as are ideas over which the group has no direct control at all, e.g. redesign the building.

- During this process it may be appropriate to cross out any ideas which are totally superfluous.
- Take all the 'T' type items and decide which one the team members would like to tackle (note in many cases it will be appropriate to do a data gathering exercise first, to measure which is the most significant problem).

11. PAIRED COMPARISON

Purpose

- To get group consensus on the selection of an item from a list (e.g. which problem shall we tackle?).
- To avoid problems with voting systems.

Rules

- Each member does his or her own chart.

Method

- List all contending items (in any order) on the left.
- Compare item 1 with item 2 – decide which is the most important and ring the appropriate number in column 1 row 1.
- Repeat, comparing item 1 with item 3 etc. and ring the appropriate number in each succeeding column.
- Then after item 1 has been compared with all the others, go on to item 2 and repeat the cycle of events until all items have had a paired comparison.
- Count up all the ringed '1's on the chart and put the total against item 1. Do this for all the other numbers.
- Use the Vote Matrix to record the votes for each item from each member's chart. Add the votes across each row to find out the circle's total score for each item.
- The maximum score will identify the major item to look at first.

No.	ITEM							
1		1 2	1 3	1 4	1 5	1 6	1 7	1 8
2		2 3	2 4	2 5	2 6	2 7	2 8	
3		3 4	3 5	3 6	3 7	3 8		
4		4 5	4 6	4 7	4 8			
5		5 6	5 7	5 8				
6		6 7	6 8					
7		7 8						
8								

VOTE MATRIX FOR PAIRED COMPARISONS

No.	Member votes																	Totals	Ranking
1																			
2																			
3																			
4																			
5																			
6																			
7																			
8																			

Figure A.16   Paired comparison chart.

12. WHY–WHY DIAGRAM

Purpose

- To provide an alternative method of identifying root causes to a problem.
- To practice divergent thinking technique.

Rules

- Brainstorm the causes.
- Identify the major cause.

Method

- Take a selected cause and use a WHY–WHY diagram to explore the underlying causes of the problem.
- Each divergent step of the WHY–WHY analysis is produced asking 'why?', as shown in Figure A.17.
- The answers to the question 'why?' are causes of the problem.

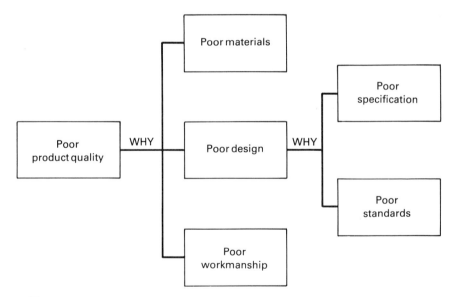

Figure A.17   Example of Why–Why diagram.

13. HOW–HOW DIAGRAM

Purpose

- To creatively explore and consider numerous solution alternatives instead of jumping to the 'obvious solution'.
- Helps members determine the specific steps that should be taken to implement a solution and hence formulate a specific action plan.
- It helps practice a divergent technique.

Method

- Begin with a solution statement and explore possible ways of accomplishing the action at each stage by asking 'how?' (Figure A.18).
- At each stage of the chain a convergent process can be used to narrow the list of alternatives before the next divergent step is taken.
- Advantages and disadvantages, change of success, and relative cost of each alternative can be established to get a more objective selection process.

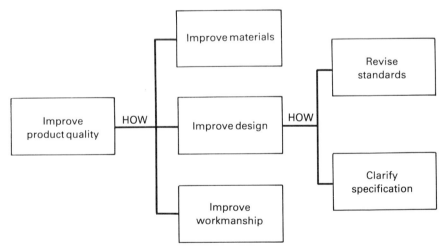

Figure A.18 Example of How–How diagram.

PART FOUR

Case studies

CONTENTS

These case studies are taken from the CBI/Pera International National Conference Tour of the UK, 'Achieving World Class Performance'.

1. Pitney Bowes
2. Boots The Chemists
3. King & Fowler Limited
4. Texas Instruments
5. Dowty Aerospace

ONE

Benchmarking: measuring the processes

Phillip Jackson, European Operations Director,
Pitney Bowes Plc

Pitney Bowes Inc, USA, is a $3 billion business, its prime market being postage meters and paper handling machines. Listed in the Fortune 500, the company has a continued 10% growth; it is against this background that expectations for Pitney Bowes UK were set.

Prior to TQM implementation, the UK company had a factory turnover of £11m, declining market share and lack of performance indicators. The parent company believed that the UK company's manufacturing standards were poor and needed significant improvements in order to compete in a global market and to be a worldwide supplier of product. TQM was seen as a practical vehicle for change. Since this time, the UK has successfully developed and marketed product for consumption both in Europe and the North American markets.

'If you can't measure it, you can't improve it.'

Having made the decision to implement TQM within their manufacturing division, Pitney Bowes' senior management team analysed their business and pinpointed two main areas which demanded investment – technology and people. Indeed, improvements through effective investment in people became the company's ultimate vision. Having created the vision, this had to encompass a set of strategic goals – increased market share, becoming a least cost provider, reducing time to market and, above all, a focus on customer satisfaction.

Using the key executive technique of competitive benchmarking, the company's senior executives compared their procedures with those of their international competitors, so identifying the areas in which they had to succeed. Further benchmarking, initially against their US mother company and secondly against best practice companies worldwide, enabled the Manufacturing division to create standards and key measures. Using this information, they also set real targets in inventory, product quality and lead time to market.

Corrective Action Teams (CATs) were introduced to address the company's key target areas. Trained in problem solving techniques, the teams identified processes and problems and introduced new procedures, with appropriate measures in all areas. These highly visible measures, based on the teams' own solutions, encouraged ownership of the processes.

Phillip Jackson maintains that 'if you can't measure it, you can't improve it'. However, before TQM implementation he became aware that measures are useless in themselves; it is ownership of the measures that matters. 'The best illustration I can give of this', he says, 'is when I went to the assembly floors and saw massive wall charts at each end of the production line – with no data on them. When I asked why, I was told: 'People don't like bad news!'. The reason for this attitude is that measures were used by management as a stick, not as a carrot. They were not owned by the people who ran the production line.' Now there are measures on every area of Pitney Bowes' shop floor; staff are committed to their drive towards zero defects and proud of their achievements.

These achievements are impressive. The company is now a £100m business, work in progress is 50% lower whilst throughput is three times higher. Lead times have been reduced from six months to one month over the space of two years, with a two-day lead time for special orders. On one of the production processes, stock turns have increased from two to 11 in the space of three months. There have been space savings of 60% and labour reduction of 30% – with the workforce themselves actually requesting labour reductions on the production line. As Phillip Jackson says: 'That is the power that you can get through a team.'

The original vision of Pitney Bowes has been achieved and its people are demanding a different type of leadership, which provides training and support, but which grants them ownership of their processes. Staff are becoming results–oriented and demanding growth in their own personal aspirations.

Phillip Jackson's message is clear: 'You have to create measures within all aspects of your business, ultimately leading to customer satisfaction. These will drive your business.'

Response time to customer orders

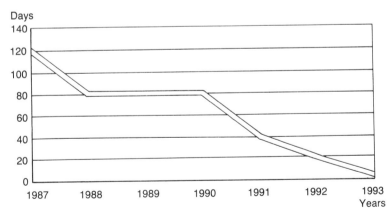

Responding to customer orders – one of Pitney Bowes' key measures

TWO

Step change improvements through TQM

John Campbell, Store Planning,
Boots The Chemists

Unique among UK multiple retailers, Boots The Chemists has maintained a substantial inhouse facility to provide and maintain the company's infrastructure. This store planning facility has a staff of 350, responsible for £135m of company expenditure. Its activities include creative design, planning, project management and implementation of a substantial capital development programme, store cleaning and a facilities management service for a property portfolio in excess of 2000 sites.

Before TQM implementation, the Store Planning department faced a major problem – a reputation for being 'big, slow, expensive and inscrutable', according to John Campbell.

BUSINESS PROCESS ANALYSIS: BUILDING A BUSINESS CASE FOR CHANGE

The Store Planning group's senior management team saw TQM as a vehicle for change. Analysing their business in great depth, they built up, not a series of 'nice to have' changes that TQM could effect, but a business case for change which when implemented gave immediate benefits – a step change improvement.

The balance of the evidence came from the application of an essential technique – Business Process Analysis – which identifies and traces the key processes across the business. This analysis highlighted the need for simplification in store planning processes. Prime goals were improved customer focus, strengthened project management, the creation of performance measures and regular benchmarking – all to improve the bottom line. As John Campbell explains: 'clarifying processes and procedures has been our most time consuming – and most valuable – work.'

Further contributions to the case for change were made by an analysis of the Cost of Quality – the Cost of Quality Conformance weighed against the Cost of Non-Conformance, such as abortive work, errors and rework. This amounted to a staggering £2.5m – or 25% of Store Planning's cost base – and 17% of this cost base was due to the Cost of Non-Conformance.

Having defined these goals and identified the key value adding processes needed to reach their targets, Store Planning has restructured its entire operation. A Store Design Concept for clients has been defined and standard 'models' applied in place of expensive, bespoke technical solutions. Project management processes have been established, a post-scheme 'after-care' system set in place and cost control re-evaluated. The result – a transformed, customer-oriented organization, whose services are now 'indispensable' and 'value adding', according to its customers.

The relocated department, reduced in establishment by 13%, now has fewer management layers and its staff are empowered through Continuous Improvement Teams. Performance drivers and measures are in place and a purpose analysis has been undertaken for each area of Store Planning; each member of staff has a performance contract. Following this swift step change – which gives staff the conviction to 'buy in' to the TQM process – the infrastructure is now in place to ensure continuous improvement.

The process of change

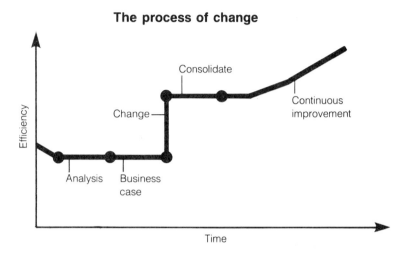

Step change improvements through Total Quality

THREE

Customer partnerships

Allan Arthur, Chairman,
King & Fowler Limited

King & Fowler Limited is a leading UK metal finishing company which has supplied high quality surface coatings to the aerospace and defence industries since 1955. Approved by the Civil Aviation Authority, more than 60% of the company's £2.2m turnover in 1991 was generated from the aerospace markets.

The company has maintained an excellent reputation for process quality, but, prior to the implementation of TQM, customer perception of King & Fowler was one of poor responsiveness. In 1990, with the decline of the defence sector, customer focus became a critical issue; it was deemed vital to meet customer needs more completely, both in the aerospace sector and in the wider commercial market.

PARTNERS IN QUALITY

The first crucial step was the development by all directors of the 'Company Objective' – a drive for excellence whilst seeking to meet customers' needs in total service and strong relationships, as well as in terms of process finishing.

In 1990, King & Fowler's core business was segregated into three product groups, allowing improved customer focus within each group. Simultaneously, a series of customer conferences was held to develop more proactive relationships with customers. These had specific themes and audiences; for example, product designers were invited to discuss the cost savings and performance benefits associated with the use of different finishes.

Different themes notwithstanding, the key message of these conferences remained the same: King & Fowler and its customer partners, by agreeing their key requirements and the processes for measuring delivery of those requirements, could benefit from regular orders and consistent performance respectively.

The conferences resulted in two major partnership opportunities, with organizations committed to the principles of TQM. The first partnership was established with a leading manufacturer of escalators and autowalks, which was seeking a Quality-conscious company to provide surface coatings of a consistently high standard. The second partner, manufacturers of switchgear equipment, demanded an improved finishing service for their recently rationalized manufacturing sections.

The key to success in customer partnerships is top level commitment – of time, effort and finance. At the outset, the objectives of all partners were clarified – to minimize total costs, maximize product development and service development, and gain competitive advantage. Once key requirements were established and the crucial business processes identified, intra-company project teams were allocated to each process, setting targets and monitoring performance regularly. Driven by senior management, the partnerships encouraged employee involvement and ownership at all levels, with appropriate training provided. In addition, computerized quality systems were set in place.

Allan Arthur stresses the long-term nature of these customer partnerships. 'We and our partners will apply TQM principles throughout; reducing costs by improved design and waste elimination are constant processes, and we have Continuous Improvement Teams in both partnerships which meet regularly to address these issues.

Both partnerships are flourishing and contribute some 30% improvement to the annual revenue of King & Fowler. Moreover, the development of King & Fowler's own suppliers as Quality companies has been a natural progression.

All in all, the two partnerships have had a dramatic effect on the company, as Allan Arthur explains: 'success in our partnerships has given us a competitive advantage to develop similar relationships and has been a platform for improving management and technology skills in the company, enabling us to meet the challenges of winning new customers in new market sectors'.

FOUR

Company-wide commitment

Ken Sanders, Managing Director, Texas Instruments

Texas Instruments Incorporated, with headquarters in Dallas, Texas, is a high-technology company with sales or manufacturing operations in more than 30 countries. Texas Instruments products and services include semiconductors, defence electronics systems, software productivity tools, computers and peripheral products, custom engineering and manufacturing services, electrical controls, metallurgical materials and consumer electronics products.

GAINING COMPANY-WIDE COMMITMENT

Texas Instruments, like many other successful companies, until recently adopted what Ken Sanders calls 'the traditional approach to business' – working hard to meet product or service specifications. However, it was discovered that, although their products met these specifications, the company still had a significant number of dissatisfied customers on its hands.

In order to rectify this problem, the company adopted a Total Quality Culture – a commitment by all employees at all levels to achieve customer satisfaction through continuous improvement. A technology-driven company, Texas Instruments has 'turned itself inside out in order to satisfy the customer'.

Quality steering teams were set up, one at board level and several at middle management level, to identify the company's key processes using the key executive technique of Business Process Analysis, and the company reorganized itself according to these processes instead of traditional hierarchical blocks. This broke down traditional barriers, enabling a specific process such as product delivery to be tracked across the organization, and non-value-added activities winnowed out.

As Ken Sanders points out, alongside the customer objective and business strategies was another need – to look at the company's people and understand their role in the TQM process. 'People satisfaction in the TQ process is just as key an objective as customer satisfaction. TQ is about everybody, about the whole organization; the priority is to understand that process and who is going to make a difference. It is about releasing our employees' energies by communicating to them clearly, openly and objectively what we need.'

Texas Instruments has instigated a training and education plan for every employee, covering key skills, safety and specific business information. Within this plan is a core TQC curriculum with eight separate training courses; TQC awareness training is mandatory for every employee, with new recruits receiving their training within three months of joining the firm.

Training in key TQ techniques – benchmarking, Business Process Analysis and Cost of Quality at board level, and problem solving techniques further down the organization – armed all employees with the skills to execute their particular jobs. As a result each member of staff is committed to the TQ process, because they understand why the company has adopted it, the associated benefits and the essential role they play within it.

The benefits of this approach have been numerous; cycle time has been reduced from 55 to 25 days and inventory halved. In addition, error rate has been reduced with a subsequent increase in customer satisfaction – over 60% of customers buying semiconductors have cited Texas Instruments as their preferred supplier.

The company's focus on its people is an example from which UK industry can benefit, as Ken Sanders points out. He quotes Patrick Haggerty, a former chairman and chief executive officer of Texas Instruments Incorporated, who made this statement as long ago as 1965. 'There's probably no greater waste in industry today than that of willing employees, prevented by insensitive leadership from applying their energies and ambitions in the interests of the companies for which they work.' As Ken Sanders maintains, a concerted TQ approach can help companies to harness this wasted talent.

Total Quality Culture

**Training and educational planning
for all employees**

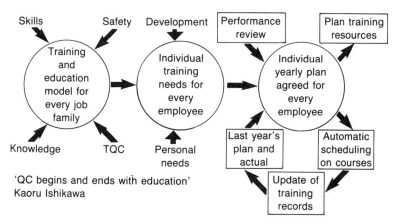

Total Quality Culture staff development plan for Texas instruments

FIVE

The Cost of Quality: why TQM makes financial sense

Tony Belisario, Managing Director, Dowty Aerospace

Dowty is the aerospace 'arm' of TI Group plc. Tony Belisario, now managing director of Dowty Aerospace, initially implemented TQM into Dowty Fuel Systems; this case study is based on his experiences there.

Dowty Fuel Systems' core products are mechanical fuel metering systems, pumps and actuating systems, as well as the gas turbine engines that power commercial and military aircraft. A £50m business in 1989, prior to TQM implementation, 95% of its turnover was then military; its management was complacent but its customers dissatisfied. Because the company did not listen to its customers it failed to win significant business on the European Fighter; but as Tony Belisario points out: 'although a major blow, that was the best thing that ever happened to our company in terms of changing our attitude to our customers.' The TQM process was subsequently set in place to improve customer performance and company culture.

THE COST OF QUALITY: BOTTOM LINE
BENEFITS THROUGH TQM

A critical mass of Dowty Fuel Systems' senior executives 'bought in' to the TQM process from the outset, following an off-site awareness day for the company's entire senior team, which outlined the bottom line benefits of the process. From this group of convinced executives, a steering committee was set up, which defined quality policy and the values and culture necessary to achieve it. It was recognized that early successes were vital to ensure that all staff 'bought in' to the practical benefits of TQM process.

Analysis of the Cost Of Quality (COQ) was one of the first TQM executive techniques utilized by Dowty Fuel Systems' steering committee. This is a measurement of the Cost of Conformance, which is the deliberate investment made to ensure good quality, weighed against the Cost of Non-Conformance – the price of getting it wrong. A £50m business, the company discovered that £6m was being lost through non-conformance – and this was a conservative estimate.

Tony Belisario stresses that Cost of Quality analysis, which pinpoints where a company can improve its performance, provides overwhelming financial benefits: 'every pound you save from the Cost of Non-Conformance – in our case over £6m – can go straight on the bottom line. The alternative is to go out, sell more product and make a profit on it, and of course that is a much more difficult task.'

COQ was broken down into several key areas – scrap and rectification, excess and obsolete inventory, indirect rework, non-productive engineering, receivables and others, and delivery performance. Just four weeks after analysing COQ, Corrective Action Teams (CATs) were put in place by the committee for each of these areas, determining key processes and methods for improvement, and implementing performance measures. This swift action was a vital part of the plan to gain quick results.

The CATs were each set a major objective. The machining CAT, for example, was required to halve errors in six months

– no mean feat for the most error-prone part of the business. Trained in problem-solving techniques and statistical process control, the team was able to meet its target in the required six months; after ten months they had achieved an 82% improvement. As Tony Belisario explains, this team proved to be a valuable marketing tool: 'clearly, you are going to get TQ sceptics. Every time I had a problem these guys got on their feet and explained their achievements – and the non-believers were convinced! They also gave presentations to our end customers, which convinced them that we were serious about changing.'

Other statistics are equally impressive. In three years, Dowty Fuel Systems has improved already healthy margins by 50% and trebled its return on capital in the same time span. Service to customers has also improved significantly.

Tony Belisario has helped to facilitate the implementation of TQM in another organizaiton and other parts of Dowty. When asked to explain the benefits of the process he is disarmingly straightforward: 'TQM eliminates waste and improves profitability. It also improves customer satisfaction both internally and externally, which gives competitive advantage, which in turn leads to more business.'

Achievements to date

Cost of Quality

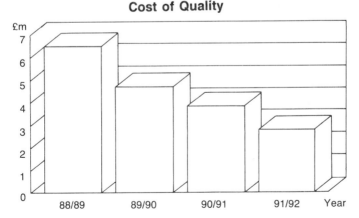

Declining Cost of Quality at Dowty Fuel Systems

Pera International contact addresses

Pera International
Pembroke House
Lydiard Millicent
Swindon
Wiltshire SN5 9LS
UK

Tel. 01793 772555
Fax. 01793 770183

Pera International also has offices in:

Oxford, UK:	Tel. 01993 702233
	Fax. 01993 702625
Melton Mowbray, UK:	Tel. 01664 501501
	Fax. 01664 501264
London, UK:	Tel. 0171 629 2860
	Fax. 0171 409 2557
Paisley, UK:	Tel. 0141 887 7828
	Fax. 0141 887 8105
Kuala Lumpur, Malaysia:	Tel. 010 603 202 1525
	Fax. 010 603 202 1249
Singapore:	Tel. 010 65 323 0633
	Fax. 010 65 323 0933
Barcelona, Spain:	Tel. 010 34 3 419 73 16
	Fax. 010 34 3 419 16 79

Index